HONEST
JOHN

HONEST JOHN

A LIFE OF JOHN MATTHAI

BAKHTIAR K. DADABHOY

PENGUIN

VIKING

An imprint of Penguin Random House

VIKING

Viking is an imprint of the Penguin Random House group of companies
whose addresses can be found at global.penguinrandomhouse.com

Published by Penguin Random House India Pvt. Ltd
4th Floor, Capital Tower 1, MG Road,
Gurugram 122 002, Haryana, India

First published in Viking by Penguin Random House India 2025

Copyright © Bakhtiar K. Dadabhoy 2025

10 9 8 7 6 5 4 3 2 1

ISBN 9780143468493

Typeset in Adobe Caslon Pro by MAP Systems, Bengaluru, India
Printed at Thomson Press India Ltd, New Delhi

www.penguin.co.in

For

Ajoy, Alok, Ananda, Anil, Ashish, Badrinarayan, Bhupal, Chandralekha,
Devendra, Devinder, Dilip, Dipak, Gunasekharam, Jaya, John Prasad,
Kayala, Krishnamurthi, Madho, Madhukumar, Mahendra, Muralimohan,
Nand Kishore, Neeraj, Niraj, Nishat, Priyamvada, Sarjana, Sirra,
Sivaprasad, Seema (D), Seema (K), Smita, Sunil, Virender and Vishnu

In memory of
A.K. Samanta and M. Ravi Babu

It matters not how strait the gate,
How charged with punishments the scroll,
I am the master of my fate,
I am the captain of my soul.

—'Invictus' by William Ernest Henley

Contents

Foreword

I turned ninety-four last November, and I am perhaps not exaggerating when I say that I am the last person alive who knew John Matthai, or at least the last person who can claim to have known him well. He was my father-in-law. Daddy, as I called him, had a long innings with the Tatas and that was when the Matthais, and my family, the Powvalas, first met.

My father, Manek Kavashaw Powvala, was invited to join Tatas by Sir Dorab Tata in 1927. He had read economics and law at Gonville and Caius College, Cambridge, the same college that the famous physicist Homi J. Bhabha joined in 1927. But Father was seven years his senior in age and the two never met at Cambridge.

While in England, Father also joined the Inner Temple in London and was called to the Bar in 1925. After a year's practice as a junior barrister, he joined the Tatas in 1927. Father was transferred from Tata Sons to Tata Iron and Steel Company (TISCO) in its sales department in Calcutta, where he rose to be sales manager. After a variety of assignments, all with the steel industry, save for a short stint of six months with Tata Aircraft during the war, he became a director of Tata Industries in 1954. He continued his association with TISCO, becoming resident director at Jamshedpur and Calcutta.

Daddy had been with the Tatas since 1940 and had held a variety of posts at Tata Sons, Tata Chemicals and TISCO. He left the Tatas to join government as a cabinet minister, first as the finance member in Lord Wavell's executive council, and later minister of Industry and Supply, before taking over the railways and transport portfolio. As is well known, he was independent India's first railways and transport minister and later became independent India's second finance minister. He resigned in 1950 after a disagreement with Pandit Nehru and rejoined the Tatas.

Our families met frequently, and a romance blossomed between me and Ravi, Daddy's younger son. We first met at a dinner hosted by a friend of my parents in Calcutta, especially in honour of the Matthais' visit to Calcutta. Ravi and I soon started dating and corresponded regularly when I went to Newnham College, Cambridge, to read English and social anthropology. We were married in November 1954, and it was only after I became part of the Matthai family that I got to know Daddy and Achamma, my mother-in-law, well. What really struck me was the warmth with which I was welcomed into the family. I felt as though I really belonged. An interfaith marriage in the mid-1950s could well have resulted in much friction, but I think that it was the very high level of education of both our families that made things so smooth.

As we spent more time together, I started to understand why Daddy and Ammachi, as I called her, were so universally respected. Daddy was seen as being a formidable person, a man with a serious demeanour and an eminence which many thought precluded intimacy or even small liberties. But at home, he was an entirely different person. In the company of his family, Daddy was affectionate and relaxed. It was our custom to spend the evenings together and this was when he would speak about the significant events in his life. Whenever Daddy recounted certain events he found amusing, he would chuckle at the memory.

Daddy lived a very disciplined life: everything worked like clockwork thanks to Ammachi. He never missed his evening walks: three rounds of the Oval Maidan in Mumbai, even at the most stressful of times. This discipline and regularity extended to his smoking a cigar and enjoying a beer during lunch and whiskey at dinner time!

He was known for his unimpeachable integrity and one example of that was his use of the official car when he was vice chancellor of Kerala University. When he travelled to Trivandrum for meetings, he would use the official car but would not allow my mother-in-law to travel with him. Ammachi would follow in a separate car. Perhaps he carried it to extremes, but that was the kind of man he was.

In 1957, he was vice chancellor of Bombay University in its centenary year and organized a torchlight procession that ended at the university as part of the celebrations. Daddy was never afraid to boldly speak out against what he thought was wrong even if it meant opposing powerful people. I recall he had a serious difference of opinion over the tenure of the rector with the Governor of Bombay who was the chancellor of Bombay University. He zealously guarded the autonomy of the university, preventing what he thought was interference by politicians in the working of an educational institution.

Sadly, Daddy passed away at the relatively early age of seventy-three in November 1959 after he was diagnosed with cancer of the liver. He was chairman of the board of directors of Tata Memorial Hospital in Mumbai at the time, and I remember that when the doctors were conferring among themselves about his illness, he used the time to hold a board meeting! Our families suffered twin blows when my father succumbed to lung cancer in April 1960 in New York.

The world has changed enormously in the four-score and ten years that have passed since I was born (to say nothing of my father-in-law's time). Today's generation has little knowledge of the physical, material, moral, political and social environment prevailing in our country at that time. Bakhtiar K. Dadabhoy's excellent biography of John Matthai therefore serves two objectives: It not only introduces this generation to an eminent man who I was fortunate to know very well but is also an important account of a nation in the making.

Mumbai   **Syloo Matthai**
9 February 2025

Introduction

John Matthai's name has little resonance for today's generation, but he was one of the brightest stars in the firmament in his time. Matthai, in his life, was many things to many people. For his students in Madras (now Chennai), he was the shy, introverted professor who was one of the most lucid exponents of economics. For Tata Chairman J.R.D. Tata, he was the director the Tatas could always turn to for sagacious advice. For Jawaharlal Nehru, who greatly respected his ability and integrity, Matthai filled two cabinet posts even though the parting was somewhat unpleasant when Matthai resigned from the cabinet in a huff. For his successor, C.D. Deshmukh, he was the former finance minister who thought nothing of accepting posts below his status when he agreed to lend his knowledge and stature, first, as chairman of the Taxation Enquiry Commission and later as chairman of the State Bank of India (SBI). In the last part of his life, he lent his gravitas to the post of vice chancellor of Bombay and Kerala universities. He was also the founder-president of the National Council of Applied Economic Research (NCAER) and the first chairman of the Court of Governors of the Administrative Staff College of India (ASCI) in Hyderabad.

A lawyer and an economist by training, Matthai was invited to join the interim government under the viceroy, Lord Wavell, in September 1946, and later became the first railways and transport minister of independent India. He led the railways during the horrors of Partition—perhaps the most difficult phase in its history. Later, he became finance minister, a post from which he resigned in May 1950 after differences with Nehru over the role and function of the Planning Commission.

A man of unimpeachable and uncompromising honesty, he could not tolerate dishonesty or hypocrisy in others. Nehru called him 'Honest John',[1] a sobriquet that provides the title of the book. The viceroy, Lord Wavell, whose interim government Matthai joined, described him as the most level-headed and probably the most capable and intelligent of his ministers. Lord Mountbatten found him an 'absolutely first-class man, balanced, reasonable and with a sense of humour'.[2]

Matthai studied history at Madras Christian College and later joined its staff as a tutor in history in April 1906 and continued in that position till 1908. It was at this time that he appeared for the Mysore Civil Service examination but failed to qualify, one of only two failures in what was otherwise a glittering academic career. The second was his failure to get a Tata scholarship. Many years later, J.R.D. Tata jokingly said that he would recommend him with retrospective effect!

In 1908, Matthai joined the Madras Law College for studying law and completed his BL degree in 1910. In July 1911, he set up practice in the Madras High Court. Matthai's legal practice was on the criminal side and the remuneration he received for his first case was a bunch of bananas! He started out as a lawyer but gave it up since he had too many scruples about twisting the truth to his advantage given that the lines between a 'lawyer' and a 'liar' are often blurred.

In 1913, Matthai sailed to England to study at the London School of Economics and Political Science (LSE). He was the first Indian to get his DSc from LSE (in 1916). He came under the influence of the famous Prof. Sidney Webb and worked for his DSc degree under Webb, who at the time was at the height of his powers and fame. A Fabian socialist, economist and reformer, Webb co-founded the LSE in 1895 with a bequest left to the Fabian Society. Later, Matthai did a BLitt from Balliol College, University of Oxford, generally regarded as the intellectual powerhouse of the Oxford elite.

On his return to India, he worked as assistant registrar of co-operative societies in Madras. He left to join the Indian Educational Service combining the chair of economics in Presidency College, Madras, with the corresponding chair in the university. He lectured both at the university and at the college. Matthai served on the Indian Tariff Board (1925–34) and was its president during the last three years of his tenure. He wrote a pamphlet which remains one of the most lucid expositions on the subject. Matthai made valuable contributions while serving on the Tariff Board, developing industries such as steel, textiles, paper and glass. He also served as Director General of Commercial Intelligence and Statistics under the government.

Later, he headed the Taxation Enquiry Commission (1953–55), the first such commission to be set up since 1925, where his thorough and careful study of public finance in India provided a framework for the future tax policies of the central and state governments. His report and recommendations were groundbreaking since he wanted to use taxation as an instrument of economic development and distributive justice. He felt that one could not leave the problem of inequality to market forces. His report recommended that the government should not hesitate to use taxation as a means of redistributing incomes.

Matthai, however, did not belong to the set of leftist economists who were enamoured by the Soviet model and who believed that it was the most suitable way to industrialize a vast underdeveloped country like India. Thanks to Nehru's infatuation with Fabian socialism (or his own version of it), it was this trend of thought that dominated every discussion on development and commanded the attention of politicians, intellectuals and the media.

Matthai was one of the most lucid exponents of economics, but he was never doctrinaire. Even though Prof. Webb was his guide, Matthai was at no time a leftist or socialist professor of economics. He was a pragmatic economist who had a thorough understanding of what free enterprise could do. He was not opposed to planning; he was, after all, one of the principal authors of the Bombay Plan, a memorandum submitted by a group of industrialists to the government in 1944 led by J.R.D. Tata, G.D. Birla and Sir Purshotamdas Thakurdas. It was a plan intended to double per capita income in fifteen years. It was in the nature of a perspective plan giving primacy to the state in economic matters. But it would be too much to say that the leading practitioners of private enterprise in India at the time had authored a plan that handed over total control of the economy to the state. What they had in mind was a mixed economy, in which the state and private enterprise would be partners. Matthai was well aware of the role of the state in promoting industry, but he did not want it to become an entrepreneur.

Matthai eventually resigned as finance minister after failing to reconcile his differences with Nehru over, ironically, planning. When confronted with the economic chaos that accompanied a bloody Partition, his first concern was that of a practical economist who wanted to get the wheels of production moving. He believed that the task before the government was not to recast the economic structure but to piece together the fragments into which it had broken, before reshaping it. He wanted the government to determine the priority of the plans that were already under execution. For him, current problems such as food shortages, housing and mass illiteracy were all pressing problems that were to be dealt with immediately if the cooperation of the people on whose behalf planning was to be undertaken was to be enlisted.

Nehru, who had been greatly impressed with his tour of the USSR in the 1930s, was a dreamer and a visionary who wanted a grand overall plan. He had contempt for the capitalist class, whom he dismissed as having no vision, grit or capacity to do anything big.[3] Matthai was neither against planning nor a planning commission but thought that the time was not yet ripe. He wanted to set the economy right first and thought that immediate and pressing problems should not be ignored for the sake of a grandiose plan for the future. So, when Nehru set up the Planning Commission in 1950, Matthai thought it untimely, calling it a 'parallel cabinet'[4]. He believed it was not merely ill-timed but in its working and general set-up ill-conceived.[5] Matthai resigned and the parting of ways with Nehru led to some hurt feelings on both sides.

Matthai considered his long association with the Tatas to be the happiest period of his life. He joined the Tatas in 1940 and served as adviser to J.R.D. Tata and also director-in-charge of Tata Chemicals for two years. J.R.D. was a friend and relied greatly on his advice in sensitive areas that required wisdom and sound judgement. It was as Tata director that he helped in drafting the Bombay Plan, as noted above, in 1944. After he left the government, Matthai served as director of TISCO (now Tata Steel) and TELCO (now Tata Motors). He was also chairman of the Sir Dorabji Tata Trust, the first non-Parsi to hold the post. In this role, he helped establish the Demographic Research Institute in 1956, which is today the International Institute for Population Studies.

Matthai was a man with a very dignified demeanour and Sir Homi Mody, a Tata luminary who later became Governor of Uttar Pradesh and who was known for his wit, said that Matthai had all the advantages of face, figure, manner and voice and invested everything he said with an air of profundity. The two were colleagues and there were many humorous exchanges between them. Mody once said that even if Matthai said 'Good morning', it sounded like a papal benediction.[6] Matthai was not, however, lacking in a sense of humour and his wit gave a sharp edge to his sense of repartee.

Matthai had a number of firsts to his credit. In 1955, he became the first chairman of the newly formed SBI. He was also the founder-president of the NCAER in New Delhi, the first chairman of the Court of Governors of the Administrative Staff College of India, Hyderabad, and the first chairman of the National Book Trust. Towards the end of his life, he was successively vice chancellor of Bombay and Kerala universities.

Matthai was married to Achamma, who was also an achiever in her own right, having been awarded the Padma Shri for her work in the social sphere. Matthai himself was honoured with the Padma Vibhushan in 1959 for his contributions to the nation, making them one of the very few couples to have both received a Padma award. The couple also had two famous sons: Ravi Matthai, who was the first full-time director of the Indian Institute of Management Ahmedabad (IIMA) and was responsible for the high reputation it still enjoys. Ravi died early, aged only fifty-seven, but left a lasting legacy. His name is still taken with great respect even to this day.

Another son, Duleep Matthai, was a highly influential figure in India's nascent environmental movement in the 1970s that first flagged the long-term environmental risks arising from the loss of forest cover, a result of unfettered industrial and agricultural development. He was a founding trustee of the World Wildlife Fund in India and played an active role in promoting the organization within the country. Matthai also had a daughter, Valsa, his first-born, who died tragically in New York in 1944.

* * *

I first heard of John Matthai from my father when I was a young boy. The reference to him was an indirect one. After attending a function in Ahmedabad (perhaps a convocation of IIMA, I am not sure) he referred to Ravi Matthai, the first full-time director of IIMA, as the son of the famous John Matthai. The name meant nothing to me at the time nor did it pique my curiosity. I was happy to retain my ignorance and there the matter stood for many years. It was only later in high school, while reading up for a school quiz, that I discovered John Matthai's claim to fame.

I encountered John Matthai again, or rather his memory, when I was first introduced to Vivek Matthai, Ravi Matthai's son, and John's grandson, at a lunch in Mumbai. This introduction took place quite appropriately (though I had no knowledge of the connection at the time), at the residence of Silloo Billimoria, the daughter of Sir Ardeshir Dalal, a colleague of Matthai's at the Tatas and a co-author of the famous Bombay Plan. Vivek and I became friends and often bumped into each other at the Cricket Club of India. The seed of this book was, I think, sown at around this time. Vivek had read my biography of J.R.D. Tata and perhaps saw some merit in me as a future biographer of his grandfather. If memory serves me right, it was when I wrote the authorized biography of music conductor Zubin Mehta in 2016 that Vivek said to me, 'You must write on my grandfather. He deserves a detailed biography.' That thought stayed with me, and more importantly with Vivek, who nudged me over the next six years to take his suggestion seriously.

I remained non-committal for a long time, but at Vivek's prodding, continued to periodically read up about a forgotten personality whose name, strangely, means very little even to persons who are considered well informed. John Matthai, a distinguished son of India, was one of the founders of modern India but is largely forgotten today. Other Malayalee personalities such as Sir C. Sankaran Nair, V.K. Krishna Menon and K.P.S. Menon have received more attention. It is strange and unfortunate that Matthai, who had such a varied and distinguished career, has been so easily forgotten; lesser personalities have had their biographies written during their lifetimes. We have a penchant for forgetting the noble and the dead.

It took more than thirty years after his death for someone to think of honouring his memory by writing about his life. V. Haridasan's concise biography on the occasion of Matthai's birth centenary in 1986 has merit but does not presume to be a definitive biography, a fact the author himself readily acknowledges. He wanted it to provide source material for a future biography, as indeed it has. I have drawn from it liberally but not promiscuously (and hopefully with no lapses in citation), in writing this biography. As always, all such endeavours owe much to those who have gone before.

It is unfortunate that a man with Matthai's brilliance and integrity has had little written about him, and almost nothing done to remember him. Matthai himself did not make life easy for a future biographer. He was not a particularly social person, so even in his time, there were not many who could say that they knew him well. He had few friends; perhaps his inherent reserve and eminence kept people away. Nor did he leave much behind that could be used by a future biographer. Like Rudyard Kipling, who destroyed his correspondence with a view to frustrate future biographers, Matthai (who once quoted Kipling in Parliament in connection with the late running of the Grand Trunk Express) also seems to have destroyed many of his private and official papers. While Matthai's actions may not have been intentional, they reveal a lack of concern about his posthumous reputation. Matthai may never have considered himself worthy of a biography. This is in complete contrast to the present day, when mediocre civil servants try to assume a larger-than-life persona by writing their memoirs, or worse still, have hagiographic accounts written about them.

While Vivek Matthai does have some personal papers of Matthai in his possession, they are at best a scanty resource. However, any document or information is grist to the mill for a biographer starved of archival material. Vivek produced letters, invitations, telegrams, written material, photographs and other relevant material at regular intervals over the last few years to supplement my own efforts at digging out material on his grandfather. I owe him my grateful thanks.

The Tata Central Archives, Pune, apart from some photographs, has limited material on Matthai. Whatever there was, came to me via Vivek. Perhaps the single largest collection of papers on John Matthai is available at the Prime Minister's Memorial Library (PMML), New Delhi. These documents were donated by his wife Achamma after Matthai passed away in 1959. While almost all the correspondence with Nehru and Sardar Vallabhbhai Patel is available in the respective volumes devoted to the correspondence of these leaders, of particular value is the long manuscript Matthai wrote towards the end of his life, and which was later serialized by the *Times of India*.

The manuscript gives his views on many subjects and people and is an invaluable window into the mind of an otherwise reserved and secretive man. I have drawn liberally from it in my account of his life: Matthai's words embellish my own modest prose on numerous occasions. Apart from the John Matthai papers in the PMML, I have also drawn extensively from the selected works of Nehru, and the collected volumes of Sardar Patel's correspondence. These have proved to be an invaluable resource. The private papers of C.D. Deshmukh and Sir Purshotamdas Thakurdas at the PMML have also proved useful.

* * *

The book is divided into four parts. Part I deals with Matthai's early life and education, his brief flirtation with the law and his service in the Indian Tariff Board. His entry into the Tatas and the famous Bombay Plan round off the first part. Part II deals with his entry into the interim government of Lord Wavell and subsequent appointment as independent India's first minister for railways and transport. I have covered his tenure in some depth, including what some readers may consider an overly detailed account of the railway budgets he presented. I believe this detail to be essential since they are connected to the criticism, debates and deliberations in the assembly on not only the budget but also his handling of the portfolio in general. The budgets also provide a picture of the state of the Railways at the time and the many challenges Matthai faced.

Part III deals with his tenure as finance minister and my treatment of the general budgets and debates is similar to the one adopted for the railway budgets. Like the railway budgets, these too throw light on the state of the economy and Matthai's handling of the economic situation in those days. The devaluation of the rupee is also dealt with in some detail. There is a detailed narrative on Matthai's resignation, which created a stir at the time, and reveals the slowly deteriorating relationship between him and Nehru.

Part IV deals with his career after his resignation from the cabinet, his continuing association with Tatas, and his helming of the Taxation Enquiry Commission, the SBI and his tenures as vice chancellor of Bombay and Kerala universities. I have devoted an entire chapter to the Taxation Enquiry Commission because it was the first systematic inquiry into taxation and the recommendations it made guided the budgets of the future. This may be of limited interest to the general reader but will hopefully be read with interest by students and practitioners of the dismal science. His chairmanship of the Court of Governors of the Administrative

Staff College of India, Hyderabad, and of the National Book Trust also find mention. The last chapter deals with his demise.

Before I conclude, a word about the names of places in the book: Calcutta is now Kolkata, Madras is now Chennai, Bombay is now Mumbai and Poona is now Pune. These and other older names have been retained since these were used in the period covered in the book.

The aim of this biography is to introduce Matthai to a new generation, even as it rekindles the memory of a man whose name today only seems to merit a furrowed brow and blank expression. It also provides a window to that period in history—Matthai's life and work provide a picture of those tumultuous times as well as describe the thinking that went into the making of modern India. It is hoped that this account of his life will return Matthai's voice to current discussion and fill an important gap by throwing light on one of the more substantial, but almost forgotten men, in the public life of those times.

PART I

1

The Matthais of Kottayam

The Syrian Christians owe their presence in Kerala to the proselytizing zeal of missionaries during the colonial period, particularly after the early 1800s. In a more restricted sense, however, Syrian Christians trace their origins to the first century CE, when St Thomas the Apostle is believed to have landed in Kerala. As a result of this, they are also known as Christians of St Thomas. The community derives its designation as Syrian Christians from its early association with the East Syrian Church of Christianity and its traditional use of the Syriac language in church services.

According to local tradition, St Thomas landed on the coast of Kerala in 52 CE near Cranganore (present-day Kodungallur), some 30 km north of Cochin. He began to preach the gospel and is said to have established seven churches in the region. St Thomas found a receptive audience among the local Hindu and Jewish populations, and many of his converts were high-caste Nambudiri Brahmans, the dominant landowning caste of Kerala. Many Christians in the region claim descent from these early converts among the local peoples.

One group, however, traces its ancestry to Thomas of Cana, a merchant who led a party of Syrian Christians to Kerala in the middle of the fourth century CE. Some authorities, however, question the historical accuracy of these accounts. They suggest that Christianity was introduced to Kerala by Nestorian missionaries (a sect named after a heretical fifth-century bishop) during the sixth century. Further migrations from Syria during the ninth century revitalized the Christian Church in Kerala. The Christian community in Kerala maintained its ties with the Christian homeland by continuing to get its bishops from Antioch, an ancient centre of the Eastern Orthodox Church.

The Portuguese arrived in India in 1498, and as their numbers grew, so did the power of the Church of Rome. Condemning the Syrian rites and practices, the Portuguese set out to Latinize the church in Kerala, and by the early seventeenth century, the Roman Catholic Church was dominant in the region. In 1653, however, some Syrian Christians reasserted their traditional beliefs, swearing before an open-air cross that they would never accept the supremacy of the Pope and Western Christianity. As a consequence of this, and due to later splits within the community, the Syrian Christians of Kerala are now divided between the Syrian Orthodox, Catholic and Protestant Churches.

Challiyal John Matthai, who later courted national and international fame as Dr John Matthai, was born into a Syrian Christian family on 10 January 1886, the fifth son and seventh child of Challiyal Thomas Matthai and his wife Hanna (Anna in Malayalam) in Calicut (now Kozhikode). The Matthais were a Syrian Christian family from Kottayam who changed their allegiance to the Church of England represented by the Church Mission Society (CMS).

The Church Mission Society

The CMS was founded in England in 1799 with the avowed purpose of carrying out missionary and educational activities around the globe. The pater familias, Challiyal Thomas Matthai, was educated in an institution in Kottayam that was set up with the help of CMS missionaries. When Colonel John Munro became the Dewan of Travancore, he initiated the process for starting a college in Kottayam. He also wrote to the CMS, requesting it to depute highly qualified missionaries who could work as teachers in the proposed college. In the meantime, the British Parliament ratified a charter empowering the East India Company to start missionary and educational work. In 1813, Maharani Gouri Lakshmi Bai of the Travancore royal family granted land and donated other resources for the construction of a college building in Kottayam.

The British administrators, the royal family of Travancore and the CMS missionaries were all convinced that education alone could lift the people from ignorance and poverty and saw the college as a first step in this direction. In 1817, Benjamin Bailey, a CMS missionary, took charge as the first principal of the college in Kottayam. He laid the foundations of a modern secular education by implementing a curriculum with a strong concentration of subjects such as Syriac, Sanskrit, Latin, English, Greek, history, mathematics and geography. The college continued to get generous funding from the Travancore royal family and the East India Company. It was called Kottayam College to distinguish it from a similar institution in Serampore. In later years, it came to be known as CMS College.

Joseph Fenn, who succeeded Bailey as principal of CMS College in 1818, realized that the students were lagging behind in English, mathematics and physics, and therefore initiated a feeder programme in the form of a grammar school. The idea was that those who attended the grammar school would be able to meet the challenges of the college. This grammar school later evolved into a separate entity called CMS High School.

Bailey continued his association with the college, setting up Kerala's first printing press there in 1820. He designed the modern Malayalam script and adapted it for printing in his own printing machine. When the Maharaja of Travancore visited the college, he was so impressed by Bailey's invention that he invited him to Trivandrum (now Thiruvananthapuram) to set up a printing press there. Bailey is also credited with compiling a Malayalam dictionary and translating the Bible into Malayalam.

Richard Collins, principal of the college from 1855 to 1866, established the department of Malayalam with a view to streamlining the teaching and learning of the language. The contribution of the missionary teachers of the college to the development of Malayalam went beyond the application of printing technology. The facility of a printing press resulted in the department publishing the first-ever college magazine in south India in 1864. The college inaugurated the era of scholarly publishing in Kerala, and it is no surprise, that Kerala in general, and Kottayam in particular, boasts of a very high concentration of newspaper and magazine publishers.

The CMS missionaries were originally sent to assist the Syrian Christians of Kerala. This association continued till 1836, when the partnership between the two came to an end over a dispute concerning land and funds jointly owned by the Syrian Jacobite Bishop and the missionaries. However, the establishment of the universities of Bombay Calcutta and Madras boded well for the college. Its students were allowed to sit for the matriculation examination of the Madras University and Thomas Matthai, John's father, became the first student from his school to pass the examination.

Cherian Matthai, Thomas Matthai's second son, in a letter he wrote to C.K. Thomas, principal of CMS College, in 1937, said that his father was the first to pass the matriculation from Kottayam, and probably Travancore as well. While it may not represent any kind of achievement in today's world, it was undoubtedly considered a major accomplishment in those days. Cherian said that he had heard stories of people travelling long distances to see the boy who had passed the Madras examination.[1]

Thomas Matthai started teaching in the same institution and later become headmaster of the school, a position he held till 1880. A gifted and dedicated teacher, he was highly respected in Kottayam and was popularly known as Matthai *asan*.[2] Many years later, in 1960, a portrait was unveiled at the college in his memory. He was a good musician and sang in the choir of the Kottayam Cathedral, even translating hymns from English into Malayalam. Thomas Matthai's wife, Hanna, belonged to the Thayyil family, a highly respected family of Syrian Christians in Kottayam. Her family was said to be one of the earliest converts to Christianity.

A Failed Coffee Planter

Thomas Matthai also tried his hand at growing coffee. Around 1875, he and a few friends started a coffee plantation in the high ranges of Travancore.[3] Given his English education and the fact that there was a boom in coffee prices from 1860 to 1880, Thomas thought that he could make a success of the business. He put his hard-earned savings in the venture, and since his was the most respected name in the group, money was raised in his name through promissory notes.

But unfortunately, the venture failed. Apart from the pecuniary loss, what perhaps hurt Thomas more was the humiliation and loss of face he had to suffer. The business failed due to depressed coffee prices during 1878–88, a result of cheap coffee from Brazil that had captured the world coffee market. The havoc caused by the borer and leaf disease added to their woes. Gloomy prospects for coffee resulted in many coffee plantations switching to the cultivation of tea. When Thomas's creditors wanted their money back, he found that he was unable to pay them immediately. His pride was deeply hurt, and a humiliated Thomas decided to leave Kottayam for good. Not only that, he also decided to never set foot in Kottayam again, a promise he kept till his death. He resigned his position from the school and left for Palakkad (now Palghat) to join the education department of the Madras Presidency as a deputy inspector of schools. Even when he visited his family, he would stay in a nearby place and invite his family to meet him there. He saved money by living frugally and insisted on paying all his outstanding loans, including those that had become time-barred.

A Large Family

The Matthai family was a large one. Thomas had six sons and four daughters. His eldest son, Thomas Matthai Jr, graduated from Madras Christian College (MCC) and joined the secretariat of the Madras government. The second son, Cherian, after graduating from MCC, obtained a teaching qualification and joined the education department of Cochin State rising to become the director of public instruction. He remained a bachelor. After retirement, he was appointed protector of the depressed classes in the state and did much for the uplift of the weaker sections. In recognition of his many contributions, he was honoured with the title 'Rao Bahadur'.[4] He lived on a large estate in Trichur (now Thrissur). Verghese Kurien, who later became famous as the father of India's milk revolution, was his grand-nephew and he visited him there during vacations. John was very devoted to Cherian and stayed with him for long periods when the latter was ailing with cancer, a disease to which he finally succumbed.

In 1892, tragedy struck the family. The third son, Matthai Matthai, who stayed with his elder brother Thomas Matthai Jr in Madras, was studying at the MCC. A cholera epidemic was raging at the time and tragically both Thomas Matthai Jr and Matthai Matthai succumbed to the disease. Thomas Matthai rushed to Madras to see his sons, but it was too late. The fourth son, Jacob, studied engineering in Madras and went to England for higher studies. On his return, he joined the Madras government as a superintending engineer. He too remained a bachelor.[5]

Thomas Matthai was transferred to Calicut and it was here, on 10 January 1886, that John Matthai, the fifth son and seventh child, was born. He was baptized as Johannan at the Church of South India Cathedral by a German pastor. It was later shortened to John, the name by which he became famous. It was not uncommon for Syrian Christian families to draw up the horoscope of a newborn child—John's horoscope was cast by a famous astrologer in Calicut. Unlike the nugatory vaticinations of most members of his profession, two of the astrologer's predictions proved to be remarkably prescient. He had said that the child would have a close connection with trade and industry and would also become a *mantri* (minister). Later in life, John jokingly referred to these predictions, saying that his association with the Tata group and his holding cabinet posts had proved the astrologer right. But he himself was never known to believe much in astrology.[6]

Thomas Matthai was a loving but strict father, as one incident of John's childhood shows. John had lent a book to a friend, who never returned it. Aware of this fact, Thomas asked John about the book. Fearing punishment, the latter said that it had been lost. As a result of this lie, it is said that the senior Matthai did not believe anything John said for nearly a year. It was an early lesson in truthfulness, which John never forgot.[7] Later in his life, John would earn a reputation for unimpeachable and uncompromising integrity, a trait that prompted Nehru to give him the nickname 'Honest John'. Even M.O. Mathai, Nehru's personal secretary, who rarely had a good word for anybody (and who disliked John), grudgingly admitted that John was a 'man of personal financial integrity'.[8]

The sixth son and eighth child of Thomas Matthai was George, who became a famous zoologist. In academic attainment, he was his elder brother John's equal, if not superior. He was educated at Emmanuel College, Cambridge, from where he received his MA degree. Famous for his work on corals, he was recruited to the Indian Educational Service while still in England. On his return, he became professor of zoology at Government College, Lahore. He was awarded the ScD (Doctor of Science) by Cambridge in recognition of his brilliant research work. ScD is the highest degree awarded by Cambridge for distinguished research in science and only those who show proof of distinction by some original contribution to the advancement of science or learning, are so honoured. With a substantial body of work accumulated over a number of years, George could not have been a more deserving recipient.

In 1925, George married Mary, the second daughter of C. Chandy of the Mysore Civil Service, who later became vice chancellor of the University of Mysore. A son, Ariel, was born to the couple, but in 1931, tragedy struck when Mary died prematurely. George needed someone to look after his young son and hired a Swiss nurse, who he ultimately married. In 1938, George took leave for a year to carry out further research at Cambridge. When the Second World War broke out in September

1939, he was forced to leave his family behind. The separation lasted for six long years. George retired in 1942, but the long separation took its toll. He died suddenly in June 1947 when he returned to Cambridge to continue his research on corals.[9]

There were four daughters: Mariamma, who was the eldest sister and the second child; Rachel, the second daughter and fifth child; Elizabeth, the third daughter and ninth child; and Kunjamma, the fourth daughter and last/tenth child. Mariamma married W.T. Jacob and they had four children: two sons and two daughters. Their second child and first daughter, Annamma, married Kurien Kurien and they had four children: three sons and a daughter. Their youngest child was Verghese Kurien, who as we have noted, became famous as the 'Milkman of India'. Verghese was thus John's grand-nephew. Rachel married E.I. Joseph and Kunjamma married K.C. Varughese. Elizabeth studied medicine in India and England and was employed with the government in Madurai. She died early, succumbing to influenza in 1925.[10]

Their mother, Anna Matthai, lived to a ripe old age. After her husband passed away, she stayed with her second son, Cherian, in Trichur.

* * *

John grew up in a religious atmosphere. His parents were devout Christians, and it was natural for him to be influenced by their religious outlook. But he was very tolerant of other religions throughout his life. While he was a Syrian Christian, he considered himself a Christian in the larger sense of the term. There was nothing sectarian about the adherence to his faith. Many years later, he wrote that he did not merely belong to the Christian community but by experience had found use for his faith.

John said that he had no denominational predilections or commitments having found enough solace and inspiration in the various forms of the Christian faith and worship in which he had participated. He believed that the deepest things in Christianity were too fundamental to be sectarian. His people had for centuries been members of the ancient Syrian Church in south India, but by virtue of his father's employment, and his own wanderings, he found himself for the most part in places where no provision existed for worship according to Syrian rites. He therefore, had to form temporary attachments to whatever forms of worship he had access to. 'I was baptized in the German Lutheran Church, I was confirmed in the Church of England, as a student in Madras I was closely connected with the Free Church of Scotland and as an undergraduate in London I frequently attended Mass at the Brompton Oratory.'[11]

As we shall see later, John would marry his wife, Achamma, in the Syrian Jacobite Church. Having 'sampled the faith', as he put it, at so many different points, he developed a firm conviction that there was a fundamental unity underlying all sections of the church and that the essence of Christianity lay 'in the teachings of Christ as embodied in the Sermon on the Mount, his personality as it emerges from the Gospels, and the working of His spirit through the fellowship of those who share the faith'.[12]

As a Christian, Matthai did not regard with any apprehension the movement for the revival of Hindu religion and culture. He believed that if this led to a better acknowledgement of spiritual values in the country, Christianity would in the end gain rather than lose. The greatest danger to Christianity, Matthai felt, was the spirit of materialism, which was rampant and the indifference and scepticism that went with it. The recognition of religion as a vital force in individual and national life provided a common ground on which free and friendly examination of different approaches to the truth could be based.[13]

He said that he found much more in common with a true-believing Hindu than with a nominal Christian.[14] He believed that an honest exchange of religious experiences and ideas would be a valuable means of both testing and enriching the Christian faith. One often heard stories of mass conversion of Christians to Hinduism. John said that this did not worry him because 'the church in India today carries on its decks a large number of passengers who make a convenience of it but make no contribution to it'.[15] The bane of the church in all ages, John said, had been its passive membership. A smaller, but more active membership, would in the end be of more service to the church and also to the country.[16]

2

Clever John

John Matthai matriculated from the Basel Evangelical Mission High School in Calicut. The Basel Evangelical Missionary Society (more commonly known as Basel Mission), a non-denominational Protestant missionary organization, was established in Basel, Switzerland, in 1816. Basel missionaries first landed on the Malabar Coast in 1834, and the Society, inspired by Pietism and Calvinism, combined its religious activities with industrial activities. The Malabar district was known for its caste rigidity and the Basel Mission used industrial activities to challenge not only the caste system but also the existing belief systems and the religious practices that supported it.[1]

The praxis of Christianity introduced by the Basel Mission resulted in the creation of a class of converts who disowned their previous caste affiliations, acquired new industrial skills, and developed a new way of looking at life and work. The Mission started the first modern industries in Malabar and the district of South Canara (present Dakshina Kannada) of Karnataka State. Through its industrial activities and efforts to spread basic education, and establish orphanages and hospitals, it challenged the belief systems that existed in not only Malabar district but in Kerala as a whole.

Early Education

Matthai's school was established in 1834 and later developed into a college of the second grade. Since Basel was in the German-speaking part of Switzerland, there were a number of German missionaries at the Mission. The activities of the Basel Mission ended abruptly with the outbreak of the First World War, when German missionaries became suspect in the eyes of the colonial rulers.[2] After the war broke out, they were interned, and the management of the college was handed over to MCC.

Matthai was a brilliant student who stood second in the matriculation examination in Madras Presidency. For his F.A. (First Examination in Arts), he joined the Zamorin's College in Calicut. Zamorin's College was founded as an English-medium school in 1877 by the Zamorin of Eranad to educate members of the royal family. The Zamorin was the hereditary ruler of the kingdom of Calicut. The college acquired its present name The Zamorin's Guruvayurappan College in 1981.

Matthai passed his intermediate examination from Zamorin's College with flying colours, securing a high first class. (Another famous alumnus was V.K. Krishna Menon, who also studied at Zamorin's College but nearly a decade later.) Matthai then joined MCC, which had also been the alma mater of his brothers, with history as his major.

MCC traces its origin to the General Assembly School founded on 3 April 1837 by the Reverend (Rev.) John Anderson, a missionary from the Church of Scotland. Anderson was a pioneer in introducing English-medium education in south India. However, the real progress of the school started with the arrival of the Rev. William Miller, a Scottish educationist and Free Church of Scotland missionary to Madras. Miller who was only twenty-four years old when he arrived in 1862, was in fact the real founder of the college. Within two years of his arrival, Miller upgraded the school into a college adding F.A. in 1865 and later B.A. (1867) courses. With the support of a few other Protestant missions in Madras, he transformed the institution into an ecumenical enterprise, and named it Madras Christian College on 1 January 1877. Miller's catholic vision, personal touch, advocacy of social causes, combined with his contributions to education, endeared him to generations of students and MCC became a household name in South India. He built the buildings for the college and hostels with contributions from his family, the government and donations from philanthropic old students.

The syllabus included Indian, British and European history and also political science, political economy, industrial history and English literature. Matthai studied selections from Geoffrey Chaucer, William Shakespeare, Lord Tennyson, Leslie Stephen and George Eliot. Unlike his elder brother Cherian, who opted for Sanskrit as his second language, John took Malayalam. Unsurprisingly, John Matthai shone in college as well. He won the Miller Gold Medal in 1903–04 and shared the Gunn Gold Medal for his academic achievements. He was awarded the Jubilee Medal from the university in 1905 and was one of two students who graduated in the first class in the BA history examination. His classmate, N.S. Subba Rao, who later became principal of Maharaja's College, Mysore, stood first.[3]

Matthai joined the staff of MCC as a tutor in history in April 1906 and continued in that position till 1908. It was at this time that he appeared for the Mysore Civil Service but failed to qualify, one of only two failures in what was otherwise a glittering academic career. The other was his failure to get a Tata scholarship. His father had been saving money to send him to England to appear for the Indian Civil Service (ICS). Unfortunately, the Arbuthnot Bank of Madras failed and Thomas Matthai lost almost all his savings. The bank's failure shattered any hopes John may have entertained of appearing for the ICS.[4]

Briefly a Lawyer

In 1908, John Matthai joined the Madras Law College and completed his Bachelor of Law degree in 1910. He started work in the chambers of T. Richmond, a leading English lawyer from Madras, in July the same year. Sir A. Ramaswami Mudaliar, who later went on to have a distinguished career in public life, was also a junior with Richmond at the same time. Matthai needed two character certificates to enrol as a *vakil* (lawyer). One was supplied by William Skinner, the principal of MCC, and the other by C. Madhavan Nair, a leading lawyer from Kerala.

Having failed to go to England, Matthai set up practice in the Madras High Court in July 1911. The Madras High Court had original jurisdiction in criminal cases and Matthai practised on the criminal side. His first case was a criminal appeal in the Madras High Court against the judgment of a district court that had sentenced seven persons to transportation for life. Ramaswami Mudaliar acted jointly with Matthai in this case. They won the case, and all the accused were acquitted. But since the fee for the case had already been paid to their senior, neither Mudaliar nor Matthai got anything for it, either from the clients or from their senior. Matthai noted with wry humour, 'The seven accused came to see me later and presented me with a bunch of bananas which was all the remuneration I received for the case. I don't believe Mudaliar got even this.'[5]

When he was in Madras, Matthai took a keen interest in Christian missionary activities. He participated in a Christian Students' Camp and heard G.S. Eddy, an evangelist of world renown, deliver lectures on ethics, honesty and Christian morality. He soon realized that the actions expected from him as a lawyer were at variance with what he had heard at those lectures. It is said that he was defending a murder accused at the time and had to 'coach' the witness. Matthai realized that if he continued as a lawyer, he would have to go against his conscience.

Matthai's forensic abilities were undisputed, and briefs came to him with respectable speed, but in October 1912, he decided to abandon the legal profession. 'Then he gave up wig and gown as though they were the symbols of double dose of original sin.'[6] All his life, Matthai was known for his unimpeachable integrity, both intellectual and financial, with perhaps only one blot, which filial duty demanded, something that is discussed later in the book.

His decision came as a surprise to many, including his senior, T. Richmond. Sir C. Sankaran Nair, who went on to become a member of the viceroy's executive council was a judge of the Madras High Court at the time. He knew the Matthai family well and conveyed his unhappiness at Matthai's decision. They all felt that a bright future awaited Matthai in the legal profession and that he would one day be elevated to the bench. But Matthai held firm, despite all the pressure on him to change his decision. There was also another reason. As he recalled many years later, even after five years of successful practice, he had not conquered the urge to go to England.

In Madras, Matthai stayed at the hostel of the Young Men's Christian Association (YMCA) and took an interest in their activities as a young lawyer. The YMCA was founded in 1844 by George Williams in London, with the aim of putting Christian values into practice by developing a healthy body, mind and spirit. It was popular from the start and grew rapidly to become a worldwide movement founded on the principles of muscular Christianity.[7] The Madras branch was founded in 1890 and was located near the high court. Matthai's sudden exit from the legal profession was followed by an equally precipitous entry into the YMCA when he joined as assistant secretary general and, in that capacity, edited a journal titled *Young Men of Madras*.

At a YMCA students' camp held at Pallavaram, near Madras, in 1912, Matthai was chosen to make the closing missionary appeal to students. It was usual for zealous Christians to make impassioned appeals to Christian students to play their part in the proselytization in India. Matthai, who was never a bigoted Christian, in his address reminded them of some elementary truths: 'Under the changing and developing conditions of this country, what India needs is not new methods or new organisations, but a little more elementary virtues of love and truth, and for producing this I know of no more potent means than the revelation which God vouchsafed to men in Christ Jesus.'[10] Matthai was all for creating a sympathetic understanding of all religions, and was both a Christian by birth and in spirit.

Matthai had joined the YMCA in the spirit of service, but disillusionment soon set in when he realized that he was not making much of a difference. After his spell with the YMCA, Matthai decided to go abroad for higher studies. He applied for a Tata scholarship but was turned down. There was only one scholarship offered by the Tatas in those days and it went to someone else. Many years later, when he became a Tata director, he told this to Tata chairman, J.R.D. Tata. 'I mentioned this some time ago to my friend, J.R.D. Tata and he told me that if I cared, he was prepared to recommend me now for a Tata scholarship with retrospective effect!'[9] But help came from his elder brother Cherian, who held a responsible job as headmaster and earned a princely Rs 200 per month. He agreed to fund Matthai's education abroad and it was on the strength of this offer that Matthai proceeded to England in 1913.

The London School of Economics and Political Science

Matthai applied to the London School of Economics and Political Science (LSE) and was admitted to the Michaelmas Term.[10] His address in the application form read: Arkbrook, Home Park Road, Wimbledon S.W. His subjects included economic history, elements of economics, population, currency history and local government. He also studied geography, the modern state and the British Constitution. The terms in the second year were largely devoted to research. In early October 1915, he applied to do research under Prof. Sidney Webb for a period of six weeks on 'Some Economic Aspects of the War'.

He worked for his DSc[11] degree under Webb, who was at that time at the height of his powers and fame. A Fabian socialist, economist and reformer, Webb co-founded the London School of Economics in 1895 with a bequest left to the Fabian Society.[12] In 1912, he was appointed its Professor of Public Administration, a post he held for fifteen years. His wife, Beatrice Potter, who he married in 1892, shared his interests and the couple were both members of the Labour Party. They took an active interest in politics, and in 1922, Webb was elected as a member of Parliament (MP) from the Seaham parliamentary constituency.

Matthai's Thesis

In 1916, Matthai became the first Indian to be awarded a DSc from LSE. The title of his thesis was 'Village Government in British India', which was published by T. Fisher Unwin in London in 1915, with a preface by Webb, who was his thesis guide. It was a descriptive study whose aim was 'to bring together the chief facts about village local government which have been noticed in Indian official publications especially during the last fifty years'.[13]

Webb, in the preface to the thesis, exploded the myth that a panchayat should only be a caste panchayat.

> One suggestion . . . is that we sometimes tend to exaggerate the extent to which the cleavages of caste have prevailed over the community of neighbourhood. How often is one informed, 'with authority' that the *panchayat* of which we catch glimpses must be only a caste panchayat! It is plain, on the evidence, that . . . there have been and still are *panchayats* of men of different castes, exercising the function of a Village Council over villagers of different castes.[14]

Matthai wrote, 'The object of this essay is to present a connected picture of the methods adopted by the village community to meet . . . simple administrative needs, so far as they may be gathered from the relics which have survived and have been recorded. It also aims at showing how far these simple expedients have been retained or refashioned under British rule.'[15]

He made it clear that the question he sought to answer was not 'how a village in British India is administered, but rather in what parts of this administration and to what extent are the local officers and institutions of the village community utilized'.[16] The study was confined to British India and excluded the native states. There were chapters on education, poor relief, sanitation, public works, administration of justice, and watch and ward. We will briefly touch upon all of them.

As regards education, Matthai said that the outstanding feature of schools was their secular character and the earliest instrument was the village priest. In the Malabar area of Kerala, the village astrologer (*panikkar*) was also the schoolteacher and 'the dignity of his position has ever been upheld by a judicious combination of fortune-telling and pedagogy'.[17]

Commenting on the subject of poor relief, Matthai wrote that in ordinary times, there was no state-organized system of poor relief. A great deal was left either to individual charity or to certain informal organizations. Individual charity had perhaps had more to do with the relief of the poor in ordinary circumstances than any organized agency. He said that apart from individual charity, the work of poor relief in an Indian village under normal conditions could be said to be distributed between the family, the caste and the village community.[18]

Matthai said that so far as the idea of sanitation was present in any form in the village, it was carried out by, among others, the physician, the midwife, the scavenger, the priest and the astrologer.[19] He observed that the arrangements made by the village community for the erection and maintenance of its public works, such as wells, tanks, channels, roads and buildings, constituted a notable feature of village local government. The most important of these works, as was to be expected in a predominantly agricultural country, was the maintenance of a sufficient water supply for agricultural as well as domestic purposes.[20]

According to Matthai, the headman was in charge of the arrangements for watch and ward in the ancient village community. His chief assistant was the village watchman, who was practically like a personal servant.[21] The usual method of settling disputes in the village community, Matthai observed, was by referring them for arbitration to the headman. He settled small disputes himself but was assisted by a council of elders in more important matters. The headman also possessed powers of criminal justice, which he exercised with some degree of oppression at times but was generally restrained by the influence of village opinion.[22]

Matthai's thesis, basically an enumeration of facts, was largely descriptive in nature. The first book to be published on India by LSE, it received a favourable review in *The Times*. The reviewer said that but for the preface by Webb it would have been a better book! Webb, as noted before, was a socialist while the conservative *Times* championed the cause of the aristocracy.[23]

* * *

Matthai, as we shall see later, had a long and happy association with the Tatas. What is perhaps not so well known is the fact that his mentor, Webb, also had a Tata connection. Once Jamshedpur came up, Sir Dorab Tata invited Sidney and Beatrice Webb, with a team from London University, to give their recommendations on the establishment of social, medical and co-operative services in Jamshedpur.[24] Since labour welfare was a priority area Sir Dorab called upon the Webbs in 1917 to write a memorandum on 'Medical Services in the Welfare Work at Sakchi'.[25] Webb headed a committee of academics from London to plan the welfare services whose execution was taken up by dedicated social workers such as A.V. Thakkar, popularly known as Thakkar Bapa.[26]

* * *

Since the allowance Matthai received from his brother was only Rs 150 a month, he had to supplement his income by seeking part-time employment. He worked as a research assistant for the India Office, which was planning constitutional reforms in India and was collecting material for the proposed reform. Matthai was employed in collecting this material and he received £400 per annum for the job. This welcome addition to his meagre income helped him lead a modest existence in London. It also helped him gain a new insight into the problems India faced.

One of Matthai's interests in London was teaching in a Sunday school. The children were mainly working-class boys, between ten and twelve years of age. In one of his first classes, the boys found it difficult to follow him. When he asked them, 'Am I speaking English or am I speaking my own Indian Language?' quick came the reply, 'Alf and Alf Guvnor' ('half and half Governor'). When he was leaving London, the brightest boy in the class thought it was up to him to say something that would especially please Matthai. He said, 'You know, sir, when you first came here, you were very black. Now, you are getting a little white.'[27]

University of Oxford

After completing his thesis from LSE, Matthai went to Balliol College, University of Oxford, for his BLitt degree. Balliol owes its name and existence to one of the rough, tough barons of the thirteenth century. John de Balliol kidnapped the Bishop of Durham, and as a penance he was forced to finance the studies of sixteen needy scholars in Oxford. Matthai's aim in going to Oxford seems to have been to imbibe the atmosphere of this storied university since he was already a DSc (though snooty Oxbridge thought very little of degrees from the fledgling LSE at the time).

Balliol is generally regarded as the intellectual powerhouse of the Oxford elite. After he became prime minister in 1908, Herbert Asquith who was from Balliol, said that its trademark was the 'tranquil consciousness of an effortless superiority.'[28] It is the Oxford variation of the Renaissance ideal of the *sprezzatura*, the art of doing the most difficult things with the aristocratic composure of the perfect gentleman. It is said that even obscene examples of lavatory graffiti were translated into faultless Latin and Greek.[29]

Balliol was in many ways the natural choice for Matthai. The college boasted a connection with India that dated back to the 1850s. The period when the classical philologist Benjamin Jowett was Master (1870–93) is considered the starting point of Balliol's golden period. Apart from academic brilliance, the college also fostered character, qualities of leadership and the desire to excel. Jowett wanted to train an elite that would go forth and govern the Empire.[30] Balliol men had toiled for the Eastern Empire from the 1850s, and in Jowett's time, the college became virtually a finishing school for those wanting to join the Indian Civil Service (ICS). Between 1853 and 1947, as many as 345 Balliol alumni had worked in India—the majority of them in the ICS. Jowett had made the college a welcoming destination for Indian students. From 1853 to 1947, the college had eighty-eight Indians, and 1870 onwards, it had at least one Indian in residence every year.

At the end of the nineteenth century, there were more than forty Balliol men in the House of Commons. As already noted, many Balliol alumni had served as colonial administrators in India. One of these, Lord Curzon, rose to be viceroy of India. In more recent times Chris Patten, the last Governor of Hong Kong and chancellor of Oxford University from 2003 to 2024, studied at Balliol, as did his predecessor as chancellor, the labour minister and historian, Roy Jenkins. It was the latter who said that Balliol had produced more politically influential figures than all the other colleges put together: 'Life is just one damn Balliol man after another,' he observed.[31]

Balliol stars include prime ministers Herbert Asquith, Harold Macmillan, Edward Heath and Boris Johnson. Other famous alumni include King Olav V of Norway, and the writers Robert Southey, Matthew Arnold, Aldous Huxley and Graham Greene, among many others. Historian Arnold Toynbee, who was a tutor when Matthai attended the college, was also from Balliol. Many years later, Matthai revealed how he had read all twelve volumes of Toynbee's magnum opus *A Study of History* rather than D.C. Somervell's abridged version in three volumes. Matthai's own achievements make him eminently suited for inclusion in this list of illustrious alumni.

The distinguished historian, A.L. Smith, served as Master from 1916 to 1924. When Matthai met him in the process of seeking admission, he told him about his DSc work in London. Smith was less than impressed and asked him if he had any other educational qualifications to buttress his claim for admission. In the end, Matthai was admitted to Balliol in June 1917 on the strength of his degrees from Madras University! Matthai was anxious to get admission to Balliol and told Smith, 'Sir, I have been a rolling stone all along.' Smith replied, 'That is good, a rolling stone gathers no moss and so is not spoiled.'[32] There were around sixty Indians in Oxford at the time, including the statesman and diplomat K.M. Panikkar and the politician Dewan Chaman Lall.

Matthai must also have met C.D. Deshmukh, who was at Jesus College, Cambridge, at the time. Deshmukh would go on to top the ICS in 1918 and later became the Reserve Bank of India's first Indian Governor. They would have a lot to do with each other later in life. Little did the two know at the time that Deshmukh would succeed Matthai as finance minister in 1950. In his memoirs, Deshmukh mentions Matthai's name in connection with the Indian students at Oxbridge. He observes,

'I must not forget . . . Mukundilal, R.P. Patwardhan and John Matthai from Oxford.'[33]

Matthai joined the Oxford Union Society, better known as the Oxford Union. The Oxford Union is the world's most prestigious debating society. Established in 1823 to uphold the principle of free speech, it is a forum for the exchange and debate of a wide range of ideas and opinions. Its members have the unique opportunity to challenge, question and interact with a broad range of speakers, both inspiring, erudite and controversial. It was in this famous debating forum that Matthai honed his debating skills. His wit and sense of repartee were sharpened at Oxford, something that stood him in good stead when he was in the legislature and later when he was a member of the cabinet.

* * *

In 1915, the Oxford University Press published a short paper titled 'India and the War', which was written by Matthai. In it, he opined that the effect of the First World War must be sought among the educated class, which wielded an influence immeasurably beyond what its small numbers signified. He said it was safe to say that it would have no effect on the great masses of the people—at any rate no direct effect. Matthai believed that the war would greatly strengthen the spirit of nationalism that had been growing in India in recent years. This spirit would not be restricted to a small minority but 'sooner or later, in whatever form, will be carried forward to the masses'.[34]

He said that while various aspects such as language, traditions and culture were helpful in preparing the ground for such a sentiment, 'it does look as if some kind of a revolt against a common system of government is the thing that primarily brought it to conscious life in many of the European countries which have been the great homes of nationality.'[35] Matthai argued that while the war had shown the educated class as a loyal body willing to cooperate with the government, it would in all likelihood also strengthen the spirit of nationalism among them. He observed, 'The primary cause of the hostile element in Indian nationalism is the extent to which Indians are shut out of the higher offices; to remedy this is the immediate necessity.'[36]

Matthai believed that on the positive side, nationalism would be prompted by the war to devote itself more than ever to the condition of the masses. This added sense of social needs, Matthai said, would strengthen the desire for security and peace and 'also lead to a deeper cultivation of the ancient spirit of the race'.[37] Matthai in his conclusion wrote with much feeling about the tragedy of the war that was unfolding before the world.

> There was no black or brown and white in the blood which flowed from Calvary. Nor is there in the warm, precious, human blood which flows over the battle-fields of Europe. All of it is red alike, and every drop of it, without distinction of race betokens the sob of a broken mother-heart. Therefore, while this great elemental struggle is driving us back to a sense of eternal values, let us put back – all of us, both those who won and those who lost, those who laughed and those who wept – let us put back the things that divide and hold fast to the things that bind.[38]

* * *

After he left Oxford, Matthai spent a year in Ireland studying the co-operative movement under Sir Horace Plunkett. Sir Horace was an Anglo–Irish agricultural reformer, pioneer of agricultural co-operatives, Unionist MP, supporter of Home Rule, Irish senator and author. He believed that the industrial revolution needed to be redressed by an agricultural revolution through cooperation and proclaimed his ideals under the slogan 'Better farming, better business, better living'. He made a lasting impression on Matthai, whose first appointment after he returned to India was with the co-operative department of the Government of Madras. It was rumoured at the time that Matthai was being considered as private secretary to the Secretary of State for India. This was not to be, but Matthai would, in the fullness of time, go on to fulfil a greater destiny when he returned to India in 1918.

3

Back Home

Matthai and the Cooperative Movement

On his return to India, Matthai, who had worked for a year under Sir Horace, joined the co-operative department of the Madras government as officer on special duty in early October 1918. A great deal of Matthai's work in London and Oxford had to do with agricultural economics. The Madras government was then thinking of appointing an officer in the co-operative department for developing special types of societies. They sent an ICS officer from Madras, a Britisher who was then working at the India Office to interview Matthai, who went to London from Oxford one afternoon to meet him. Matthai said that the interview lasted nearly an hour during which the ICS officer did practically all the talking and he hardly got a word in. Matthai recounts:

> I remember going back to Oxford feeling I must have made a poor impression on him having had so little to say for myself. I however got the appointment and later while I was Madras, in some context the file regarding my appointment happened to pass through my hand and I saw the letter which was sent to the Madras Government by the officer who interviewed me in London. What he said was this 'Matthai is an intelligent young fellow, but like most Indians who have been in England, he is inclined to talk a great deal'.[1]

Later, Matthai became personal assistant to F.R. Hemingway, an ICS officer who was the registrar of co-operative societies, continuing in that post till May 1919. He was posted as assistant registrar of co-operative societies at Calicut but returned as personal assistant a month later. In Matthai's own words:

> I worked as assistant registrar under a senior British member of the I.C.S. who was then registrar of co-operative societies in Madras. A week or so after I joined the Department, he and I had to go on tour for inspection and were travelling in the same railway compartment. In conversation, he called me 'Matthai' and I called him 'Mr.____'. He suddenly stopped for a while and said: Now with regard to vocatives, I call you 'Matthai', and you call me 'Sir'.[2]

Cooperative Movement in India: A Brief Background

In 1876, an intense famine devastated the Madras Presidency, killing an estimated 10 million people and plunging the entire farming community into large debts. The government took a number of steps, including setting up a Famine Commission. In 1892, the Governor of Madras, Lord Wenlock, directed Sir Frederic Nicholson, then collector of Madras, to study the problems and challenges the farmers were facing. Nicholson, an ICS officer, had earlier served as the collector of Tirunelveli, Madras and Coimbatore. The author of the *District Manual of Coimbatore*, he was considered an expert on the agrarian economy in the Madras Presidency.

His report, which paved the way for the co-operative movement, took five years of research and writing, and was finally published in 1895. By 1904, the first legislation on cooperation was passed and co-operative agricultural credit societies and co-operative banks were to be established on the lines of those that existed in Germany and Italy. Nicholson was hailed as the pioneer of the co-operative movement in India. (He was also the 'Father of Fisheries' in the Madras Presidency. Nicholson sent proposals to the government for the initiation of a small bureau of fisheries for Madras with the aim of increasing fish production, promoting fish-based industries and improving the conditions of fishermen.)

Nicholson summed up his report in just two words: 'Find Raiffeisen'. Nicholson was referring to Friedrich Raiffeisen, who along with compatriot Franz Hermann Schulze-Delitzsch and the Italian Luigi Luzzatti pioneered co-operatives in Europe. Raiffeisen based his co-operatives on the principles of self-help, self-governance and self-responsibility. Known for their trustworthiness against financial crises, most were called

Raiffeisenbanks. They spread to other parts of Europe and America. Rabobank, the Dutch co-operative whose first two letters come from Raiffeisen, was the last triple A-rated co-operative bank.[3]

Sir Denzil Ibbetson, an ICS officer who became a member of the council of the governor general of India, while moving the Cooperative Societies Bill in October 1903 had said that the bill sought to create 'small and simple credit societies for small and simple folk with simple needs and requiring small sums only'. He added that cooperation must be built up from the bottom, and not from the top.[4] As Sir Horace Plunkett pointed out in his foreword to Eleanor Hough's *The Cooperative Movement in India* (1932), what India had was a policy, and not a movement. Unlike in Europe, it was created by resolutions of the government and was not a grassroots movement.

Matthai's Treatise on Cooperation

In 1925, Matthai wrote a book on the co-operative movement in India, and it marked the culmination of his formal association with the subject. His treatise, *Agricultural Co-Operation in India: A Handbook for Students and Social Workers*, was published by the Christian Literature Society for India, Madras, in 1925, and was the first book in a series that aimed at placing before the readers scholarly studies of the important questions of the day.[5]

In the introduction to the treatise, Matthai distinguished cooperation from other forms of business undertakings and traced its development in England. He said that the term 'cooperation' was difficult to define partly because those forms of cooperation that had survived the test of time were 'not the result of any carefully thought-out theory of life or business but were primarily expedients devised to meet certain specific situations and difficulties'.[6] He said that the movement in its more successful form was represented by societies that grew up almost unconsciously as practical solutions 'rather than as an embodiment of a distinct theory of economic organization'.[7]

Matthai traced the history of the movement and found that it was largely a result of the Industrial Revolution. It was an association where workers controlled the instruments and results of production. Matthai quoted the philosopher John Stuart Mill, who observed that the form of association of the future was 'an association of labourers themselves on terms of equality collectively owning the capital . . . and working under managers elected and removable by themselves'.[8]

The main purpose of agricultural cooperation, Matthai said, was to eliminate the middleman.[9] The aim of such cooperation was to make the small farmers their own middlemen and to help them organize themselves on a co-operative basis so that they could undertake various processes connected with their business. Matthai analysed cooperation in various European countries, such as France, Belgium, Germany, Italy, Ireland and Denmark. In most European countries, agricultural cooperation originated in mutual credit societies and therefore it was generally thought that the first step in agricultural organization was to start a co-operative credit society.

Comparing the co-operatives of Denmark and Ireland, he said that in Denmark, the primary motivation was the business motive. There was no intention to regard agricultural cooperation as part of a scheme for building up a rural civilization and as a first step in the fight against the evils of an over-industrialized society. But this, Matthai said, was distinctly the leading idea in the mind of Sir Horace, who founded the Irish Agricultural Organization Society in 1894. Matthai, as we have seen, had spent a year in Ireland and been in direct contact with Sir Horace. He said that Sir Horace's work in keeping alive the 'higher aims' of the co-operative movement was of great interest to a student of cooperation. There was a conscious desire to not only improve business but also secure 'the production of fine human beings'.[10]

One great contribution of Ireland, according to Matthai, was the idea that agricultural cooperation could be used as the means of creating 'a new social organism in rural areas based on common effort and interest'. 'The interest of the Irish movement lies chiefly in the fact that Sir Horace Plunkett is the greatest living example of an apostle of cooperation considered both as a mode of business and as a spiritual message.'[11] Matthai was still very much an idealist and the 'spiritual side' of cooperation had much appeal to him at the time. Later, however, his attitude to cooperation became more pragmatic.

Matthai also touched upon the two main types of societies in Europe and the applicability of these models to India. As noted, there were two main types of co-operatives in Europe, known respectively as the Raiffeisen and the Schulze-Delitzsch types, from the names of their founders.

Both originated in Germany, and both were concerned in the main with the problem of raising capital on the combined security of those who joined. The former were started for the benefit of rural communities, while the latter were intended for those in urban areas. Matthai said that the Raiffeisen was taken as the chief model in India, but the Indian co-operative also had features of the Schulze-Delitzsch type.

He said that in Indian reports, there was a tendency to draw too rigid a line between the two. They did not represent 'competing ideals' but were simply 'concrete specimens of an organization shaped almost wholly by local circumstances'. Matthai believed that the primary consideration everywhere should be the prevailing circumstances.[12]

Matthai covered a lot of ground in his book and dealt with various issues, such as the summary of legislation on co-operatives, types of co-operatives and lending by them, rural indebtedness, deposits and loans, local management, the role of the state in the co-operative movement and cooperation for purposes other than credit. Towards the end of the book, Matthai made some general observations about cooperation which are of interest. He said that the primary purpose of co-operatives was economic; a lack of data meant that no accurate estimate of the economic benefits could be made. One certain fact was that co-operative societies throughout India possessed a total working capital of over Rs 35 crore and the difference between the interest levied on this sum by societies and the interest that would have been levied by local moneylenders 'represents a not inconsiderable saving to the rural population'.[13]

* * *

The co-operative movement made good progress in the Madras Presidency during the period 1918–20, with the number of registered societies nearly doubling from 2600 to 5000.[14] It was Matthai's idealism and his intention to contribute to the economic uplift of the people that had prompted him to join the department. However, he soon found himself at odds with his superior and so he decided to leave the department. He joined Presidency College as a professor of economics on 1 June 1920. The post was initially a temporary one but was made permanent a month later.

Matthai wrote in 1925 that the challenge was to loosen the government's grip on cooperation over the years. Unfortunately, it only increased. 'Cooperation has failed, but cooperation must succeed,' wrote the All-India Rural Credit Survey Committee in 1954. These were the words of B. Venkatappaiah, a member of the committee who went on to become deputy governor of the Reserve Bank of India, chairman of the SBI and later chaired the Agricultural Credit Review Committee in 1969.

Professor of Economics

Matthai's post was made permanent on 5 July 1920, and he was absorbed into the Indian Education Service. He became the acting professor of economics, filling in for H.J. Allen, the professor of economics and principal of the college. But strangely, it appears that Presidency College had no post of professor of economics at the time and Allen was the professor of history during the year. This makes Matthai the first professor of economics at the college. In fact, there was no separate department of economics at the college and Matthai was attached to the history department. Later, after the retirement of the first professor, Gilbert Slater, he was appointed part-time professor of economics in the University of Madras, along with his work at Presidency College.

Some background about Madras University and Slater's contribution is in order here. The Madras University, along with the universities of Bombay and Calcutta, was established in 1857 on the model of the University of London of the time. However, it functioned only as an examining and affiliating institution in the field of higher education. The university expanded its scope and functions after the enactment of the Government of India Act 1904 and it ceased to be merely an examining body, adding teaching and research to its activities. Though specific grants to establish three departments—namely, Indian economics, Indian history and archaeology, and comparative philology—were received in 1912 itself, suitable personnel could not be appointed immediately due to a paucity of qualified scholars.[15]

The department of economics was able to get its first professor—Gilbert Slater, the principal of Ruskin College, Oxford—only after three years of searching, in December 1915. He started the economics department the following year. Thus, 1916 marks the beginning of the teaching and research of Indian economics in Madras University.[16]

Slater is famous for the earliest village survey in India. Soon after taking charge, he initiated his village studies by first visiting a village 140 km south-west of Madras, in February 1916. His village surveys were the first of their kind in India in which he attempted to understand the Indian economy by examining the dynamics of village society through the means of obtaining a composite understanding of both the social as well the economic forces that shaped them. Slater also went looking for 'the Raiffeisen' that Nicholson's province had. At the office of the registrar of co-operative societies, he found the clerks sleeping, with no clue as to the whereabouts of their boss, whose expertise apparently was in the Tamil almanac.[17]

Given Slater's breadth of view on various socio-economic problems, he was invited by the Government of Madras to be their publicity officer on the completion of his five-year tenure in the department of economics. He resigned from his post in April 1921 to take up his new position, which was for one year. Even before that, he was nominated as a member of the newly constituted Madras Legislative Council. After two years of distinguished service, he resigned and returned to England in April 1922. He resumed his lectures on Indian economics at Oxford University to Indian students, and to the ICS probationers at the LSE. When Slater relinquished his position in October 1921, the university, on the suggestion of the government, appointed Matthai as a part-time professor in 1922. He served in the department of economics until 1925, when T.K. Duraisamy Iyer took charge as acting professor.[18]

One of those in the department of economics in Matthai's time was P.S. Lokanathan, who was Slater's research student and had done his master's in economics from Madras University. Apart from Slater, he was also influenced by Matthai, then recently returned from England, and Duraisamy Iyer who specialized in indigenous banking. He was appointed reader at Madras University in 1927 and, given his initiation under Slater and Matthai, it was no surprise that he chose to pursue his doctorate from LSE. On his return, he became acting professor in 1935 and was elevated to professor of economics in 1941–42. His basic area of interest was industrial problems, but he also worked on many areas of immediate policy concern and social significance.

Lokanathan was one of India's earliest financial journalists and was editor of the G.D. Birla-owned *Eastern Economist*. Later he also became editor of the *Hindustan Times*. He assisted Matthai in the drafting of the Bombay Plan but was not a signatory to it. Lokanathan was the founding Director General of the NCAER, in which capacity he was a junior colleague of Matthai, who went on to become the institution's first president. He was the first executive secretary of the United Nations Economic Commission for Asia and the Far East (ECAFE). A highly respected figure, he also enjoyed the confidence of Prime Minister Jawaharlal Nehru.

As professor of economics, Matthai took classes in economics and economic history for BA (Hons) students in history. He also went to Mysore to deliver lectures at the University of Mysore. Matthai stayed in the Wesleyan College hostel. In an article he wrote many years later for a newspaper, Matthai recalled that as a professor in the university, he visited Mysore often to deliver special lectures at the university and for examining in economics. In the course of one of his visits to Mysore, he was introduced to a barber who used to shave Winston Churchill when he was a young subaltern in the army at Bangalore. Matthai said that the barber was fond of telling a story about the future prime minister of Britain. He said that when his regiment was transferred from Bangalore, Churchill gave him a sovereign as a present and said, 'Sahib going now, but Sahib coming back *burra* sahib.'[19]

Matthai was essentially an introvert and so it is hardly surprising that he kept to himself. It appears that the only person he confided in was his friend, M.A. Candeth, who was professor of history at Presidency College. Candeth, a friend of Nehru's from Cambridge, was recruited directly to the Indian Educational Service. He also became a close friend of Sarvepalli Radhakrishnan, but later the friendship came under strain and was reduced to fragmentary contacts. Candeth was the son-in-law of Sir C. Sankaran Nair, the famous lawyer and politician who served as president of the Indian National Congress in 1897. Candeth's son, Lieutenant General K.P. Candeth, was in charge of the Indian Army's Western Command during the Indo-Pak War of 1971 and had also played an active role in the liberation of Goa from Portuguese rule in 1961. Candeth died, tragically young, in 1934.

Students who studied under Matthai in Madras Presidency College remembered him as silent, shy and cloistered. They came to know him as one of the most lucid exponents of economics. They also knew that he could not be approached for any undue favour, and was in fact, even incapable of being persuaded to attend the usual run of social functions. Besides his classroom lectures, he buried himself in his books in the library or his house.[20] Matthai continued to read voraciously throughout his life.

Matthai may have been an introvert, but he was a powerful public speaker from his student days. He also had a wry sense of humour, something that was not immediately obvious to someone who was making his acquaintance for the first time. During his stay in Madras, he had started taking active interest in the Anglican Church of Madras, preaching sermons in the church and delivering popular lectures at the YMCA. It was at this time that his eloquence came to the notice of the Governor of Madras, Lord Willingdon, who impressed by his articulation nominated him to the Madras Legislative Council. From his student days, Matthai was famous as an orator, and he continued to be in demand as a public speaker even later in his life.[21]

Marriage

It appeared for a long time that John Matthai would not marry. His eldest brother, Thomas Matthai Jr, lost his wife prematurely and this seemed to act as a psychological barrier to marriage. In fact, John and his younger brother George, were the only two who ultimately did marry, albeit belatedly. Matthai was thirty-five when he got married to Achamma John on 28 August 1921, the marriage being solemnized at the Jacobite Church, Trivandrum. Achamma's father, Elanjikal Jacob John, was an eminent lawyer in Trivandrum. He too was an alumnus of MCC and for a while was also a tutor in that institution. He did his law from Madras Law College in 1894 and had a flourishing practice in Trivandrum. Jacob John and Cherian Matthai, John Matthai's brother, were fast friends and when the latter visited Trivandrum on official work, he resided with Jacob John.[22]

Jacob John belonged to the Elanjikal family, which was an influential family of Syrian Christians in Central Kerala. They were large landowners, and later two of Achamma's brothers became ministers, one in the erstwhile Travancore-Cochin State and the other in the newly formed Kerala State. It was at Cherian's suggestion that John Matthai went to meet Achamma. It seemed but natural to recommend for marriage the daughter of his fast friend. John Matthai was then teaching at Presidency College, Madras, and had to travel to Trivandrum for the meeting. Having no place to stay, he stayed at the retiring room at Trivandrum railway station. Little would he have guessed at the time that he would be independent India's first railways and transport minister. John Matthai and Achamma liked each other and were soon married.

After the church wedding, the marriage party drove to Matthai's residence, where a large party had assembled. In the evening, Matthai held a reception, where his non-Christian friends were also invited. Among the attendees were Chief Justice R. Viraraghava Iyengar and many judges of the high court. Matthai's colleagues and acquaintances from the university were also in attendance.[23]

Achamma, who was born on 21 February 1898, was twenty-three when she got married. It proved to be a happy marriage. Achamma was both intelligent and educated. She had done her schooling in Trivandrum and her BA(Hons) in 1920 from the St John's Diocesan College in Calcutta. She was one of the first women from Kerala to obtain a college degree and that too from another state. Syloo Matthai says that Achamma's father was a very forward-looking man and this explains his educating his daughter at a time when women graduates were few and far between.[24]

She proved to be the perfect foil for the serious-minded Matthai, and was in fact, an achiever in her own right. A dedicated social worker throughout her life, she worked tirelessly in refugee camps during Partition. She served as the honorary director of the women's section of the ministry of rehabilitation from 1947 to 1950 and was chairman of the Central Social Welfare Board from 1962 to 1966. She was also actively associated with handicrafts and served on the export committee for handicrafts set up by the central government. She was also chairman of the Kerala Emporium in Delhi. Achamma was on the governing board of Lady Irwin College and was vice chairman of the Delhi School of Social Work.

Later, in Bombay, she worked with the Bharat Sevak Samaj and set up Anand Kendra, a home for street children. She was the actively involved with the Young Women's Christian Association and also served as its president for many years. She was vice president and a life member of the Indian Council for Child Welfare. She collected funds for a working women's hostel in Bombay which was named Achamma Bhavan in her honour. During her career, Achamma was associated with many committees and organizations either as president or vice president. She knew Nehru well in her own right, and not just as the wife of a cabinet minister. Fittingly, she was honoured with the Padma Shri in 1954 for her many contributions in the sphere of social work. (In fact, she received her Padma award four years before her husband, who got his Padma Vibhushan in 1959. They are among the very few couples to be so honoured. C.D. Deshmukh and his wife Durgabai were both recipients of the Padma Vibhushan, a record which is unlikely to be equalled for a very long time.)

In the Legislature

The Madras Legislative Council was set up in 1921 under the Government of India Act, 1919. On Lord Willingdon's request, it was inaugurated by the Duke of Connaught on 12 January 1921. The term of the council was for three years. It consisted of 132 members, of which thirty-four were nominated by the governor, with the rest being elected. The second and third councils under this Act were constituted after the elections held in 1923 and 1926, respectively. The fourth council met on 6 November 1930 and its life was extended periodically till the provincial autonomy under the Government of India Act, 1935, came into operation.

In many ways, the Madras Legislative Council sowed the seeds of a fully representative democratic form of governance, which was realized after Independence. It was responsible for many progressive legislations, which were subsequently replicated across the country to empower the weaker sections of society. Matthai was sworn in as one of the thirty-four nominated members of the council on 13 November 1922 by the president of the council, Sir P. Rajagopala Achariyar. A few leading personalities from Madras Presidency who later courted national fame were also members of the council. They included C.P. Ramaswami Aiyar, R.K. Shanmukham Chetty, P. Subbarayan and A. Ramaswami Mudaliar.[25]

In his first term, which lasted for a year, Matthai chose to observe more and participate less, though he did take part in debates that interested him and in which he thought he could make a useful contribution. During a discussion on a bill to regulate state aid to industries, he told the house about the situation that obtained in England: ' . . . as far as England is concerned in all aids given under the Development Commission, the distinction that is made is between profit making concerns and non-profit making concerns, and not between individuals and joint stock companies.'[26] His intervention earned him a place in the Select Committee on the bill.

Matthai was nominated to the council for a second term and took office on 26 November 1923. His speech on the budget in March 1924 was much appreciated by the members. He marshalled his facts with his usual thoroughness and spoke persuasively and knowledgeably about the subject. He started his speech by saying that the budget dealt with matters which it was his business to teach as an economics professor, and that was his only excuse for occupying the attention of the house. Calling it a development budget, he said that 'the foundations of public finance in this Presidency have been laid in such a way that it is possible for us hereafter to undertake large schemes of development'.[27]

He said that little had been done to stimulate investment, and the government could do a great deal by undertaking public borrowing. He believed that since future generations would benefit from the schemes undertaken, they should also share the cost of those schemes. He thought that even education and sanitation could be financed through this method. As far as the farmers were concerned, he thought that the government should help them to produce more. He believed that the co-operative movement had the potential to achieve much more.[28]

On 26 March, Matthai was involved in an interesting, if somewhat unusual, discussion. During the discussion on the demand for education. S. Satyamurti, one of Matthai's pupils, who was the leader of the Congress in the legislature, raised the question of the conduct of Prof. Smith of Presidency College, who it was alleged had spent more time in setting up his laboratory than in delivering lectures. Matthai observed: 'If we are going to lay down a quantitative standard of work in respect of people who are engaged in University teaching you would be laying down a principle which is likely to carry you to a somewhat dangerous situation.'[29]

When Matthai was asked how many lectures he himself had delivered, he replied with self-deprecating humour: 'As for the number of lectures I have delivered, I must say that I have delivered hundreds of lectures. And may I say this, that I have carried it to such an extent that there is nothing now that I detest more than the sound of my own voice.' Matthai continued with his spirited defence of Prof. Smith.

> If you are going to lay down standards . . . we would be impairing the sense of values in education. I am prepared to submit to any test which this council may impose upon me. But I do say that if the House is going to lay down tests of this kind, I would be compelled in spite of my best intentions to permit the business of education to degenerate into a routine, soulless and mechanical thing.[30]

Writing about this incident many years later in a newspaper article, Matthai said that Satyamurti saw the humour in what his old teacher had said and withdrew his motion.[31] The matter was dropped after other members also testified to Prof. Smith's efficiency and conduct. There was also another occasion on which teacher and pupil had an amusing interaction. Matthai, on one occasion, had pleaded for the poor man's toddy. Satyamurti reacted by saying that he was surprised to see his old teacher encouraging toddy drinking. Matthai said in jest that he would not risk being seen in a toddy shop in Satyamurti's company![32]

Matthai took an active role in the discussions on the Malabar Tenancy Bill. He thought that there was a strong case for the reform of the system of land tenure in Malabar. At the time, there was a monopoly in regard to land in Malabar and Matthai believed that wherever one found something like a monopoly, there was a need for reform.[33] He wanted the ordinary tenant to be treated not only with fairness but also with generosity, stressing that he had a right which must be safeguarded at all costs.

Participating in the discussions on the budget for 1925–26, Matthai noted that more money would be required for agriculture, forest preservation and cooperation. His observation with regard to the industrial policy of the government was less than flattering.

> I find it difficult to convince myself that there is anything like a strong case for continuing the industrial policy of Government . . . There is first the question of industrial education and there is secondly the question of industrial experimentation . . . if we are going to have a really effective system of industrial education, we have to relate that education in a very real and organic way with the general educational work in the country.[34]

Matthai said that one could not allow the educational work on the industrial side to run in one channel and the general educational work of the country in another. Given Nehru's socialism a few decades later, and the idea that the public sector should occupy the commanding heights of the economy, Matthai's views on the role of government in promoting pioneer industries are worth reproducing. ' . . . unless it is absolutely certain that Government in point of technical organization, in point of ability to take risks and to face them is in a position of immeasurable superiority to private industrialists, Government have no business to carry on pioneer industries.'[35] Matthai was not denying the need for industrialization; he merely was against the government playing the role of an entrepreneur when it was not required.

Some of the views and ideas Matthai formed at this time stayed with him for the rest of his life. He was a proponent of vocational education, and in this, he came close to Gandhi's basic education. While Matthai was against total prohibition of all sale of alcohol because he knew it would be impossible to enforce, he advocated temperance and the role of the state in checking the evils of alcohol consumption. He even wrote a book on the subject. In *Excise and Liquor Control* (written in 1924), he studied the excise duty on alcohol with special reference to the Madras Presidency. While noting that excise revenue formed a considerable part of the finances of the provinces, the levy of excise on alcohol gave rise to the social and moral aspect as distinct from the purely financial aspect of the excise problem.

As regards prohibition, he said that two conditions must be satisfied before the state undertakes restriction of the consumption of a commodity. First, there must be a powerful appetite to consume the commodity to excess, and second, such excessive consumption must result in great social harm.[36] A government monopoly of the production and sale of alcohol and taxation, were according to Matthai, the two principal regulative methods for the control of alcohol.

Matthai's study, which was largely with reference to toddy and arrack, concluded that the average individual expenditure on alcohol in the Presidency continued to form a large proportion of the average individual income. But he said that since production of liquor in India was essentially a domestic industry, prohibition would be very difficult to enforce. He did not think that prohibition was the answer to the drinking problem in the Presidency at the time.[37] He felt that 'local option', a form of local referendum against drinking, could perhaps, provide a more suitable remedy.[38] We don't know if his views changed somewhat, when later in his life, he was known to enjoy his beer during lunch and whiskey in the evening.

Matthai's experience in the assembly proved to be invaluable for his future and prepared him for the bigger challenges he would face in his career. Even though he called himself a 'backbencher', his speeches and in-depth analyses commanded the respect of all those who heard them. In many ways, the Madras Legislative Council was an indispensable training ground for Matthai providing him with first-hand knowledge of the policymaking process.

4

From the Tariff Board to the Tatas

It is generally thought that Jawaharlal Nehru was the initiator of protectionism in India since he was instrumental in setting up, what many consider a highly damaging socialist model where centralized planning held centre stage. This is fallacious. As far back as 1921, the first Indian Fiscal Commission had recommended protection for select industries. Later, between 1923 and 1939, in an era of administratively determined exchange rates, the Indian Tariff Board recommended higher import duties for a variety of items, including iron and steel, cotton textiles, sugar, paper and gold thread. For some of these imports, cheap raw material was first sourced from India.[1] Matthai served on the Tariff Board from 1925 to 1934 and was its president from 1931 to 1934. He wrote a pamphlet[2] on the subject, which remains one of the most lucid expositions on the subject.

Protectionism: A Brief Background

Britain followed a policy of free trade with India from the mid-nineteenth century until the outbreak of the First World War. Although import duties were levied by the government, these were merely for revenue purposes and not for protecting Indian industries. In case the same goods were manufactured in India, the protective effect of any such duties was nullified by imposing a countervailing excise duty.

The first stage in the policy of protectionism in Indian was the Parliamentary Resolution of August 1917, which initiated the constitutional reforms based on the Montagu-Chelmsford Report. The policy was now to increase the role of Indians in every branch of administration and encourage the 'development of self-governing institutions with a view to the progressive realization of [a] responsible government in India as an integral part of the British empire'.[3] As a necessary corollary, this meant a greater role in deciding commercial and financial policies. Public opinion was in favour of a policy of protection; and once the policy of the principle of responsible government was accepted, it was only a matter of time before the policy of protection was adopted.

Since there was a widespread view that India's fiscal policies were dictated by Whitehall in the interests of British trade, the Joint Select Committee of Parliament, which examined the Government of India Bill of 1919, believed that a satisfactory solution could only be achieved by granting the government of India liberty 'to devise those tariff arrangements which seem best fitted to India's needs as an integral portion of the British Empire'.[4] Since this could not be guaranteed by a statute without limiting the power of Parliament to control the administration of India, this was sought to be achieved through the famous Fiscal Autonomy Convention, which was finally adopted in 1921. The Convention stated that the Secretary of State for India was to avoid interfering in tariff arrangements when the Government of India and its legislature were in agreement.

The final stage in the evolution of a policy of protectionism was the appointment of the Indian Fiscal Commission in October 1921, with Ibrahim Rahimtoola as its president. The famous Cambridge economist John Maynard Keynes was its vice president. Of the other ten members, six were Indians, and four were Englishmen. Rahimtoola, along with others such as Gopal Krishna Gokhale and Madan Mohan Malaviya, had fought a hard battle over the previous decade to get the colonial government to support Indian industrialization as well as fiscal autonomy.

The Indian Fiscal Commission began its work in November 1921 and submitted its report the following year. While the majority of the members recommended a policy of discriminating protection, five of the seven Indian members added a long dissent note to the main report, arguing that its arguments for protection were too tentative. The overall recommendations were in tune with the nationalist view that late entrants, such as India, would need some government intervention to provide an initial push to the industrialization process.

The committee wanted the protection of select industries to be based on three criteria. First, India should have a natural advantage in the industry that was to be protected. Second, protection was needed to ensure its development. Third, it should eventually be ready to face global competition once protection was removed. There were some other guidelines as well. Protection should not impose a heavy burden on domestic consumers through higher prices and raw materials, and capital goods were to be imported free of any protective duties. Intermediate goods used in Indian industry were to be taxed as lightly as possible and there should be no tax on exports.

The Commission looked at the issue of import tariffs from two angles: protecting infant industries and diversifying the Indian industrial structure. However, despite its overall support for protection, the Commission also took a detailed look at related issues, such as its impact on productivity, wages, inflation, monopoly profits, government revenues, foreign capital and imperial preferences (such as free trade agreements within the British Empire). Protection was to be temporary since it would impose economic costs over the long term.

There were two major reasons why the British gave in to these demands. First, they were trying to neutralize the growing opposition to their rule by accepting the nationalist argument that industrialization led by the state was needed for India to break the shackles of a colonial economy. Second, the recent world war had shown that the Indian economy did not have the resilience to deal with economic disruptions.

The Tariff Board

The policy of discriminating protection was accepted by the government and approved by the legislature in the form of the famous Resolution of 16 February 1923. The Resolution recommended the creation of a permanent Tariff Board to advise the legislature on the claims of various industries for protection. It was constituted in July 1923, with Matthai joining as a member in June 1925.

Reminiscing about his time at the Tariff Board many years later, Matthai wrote that of his first inquiries was an inquiry into coal. Sir Alexander Murray, who was then head of Jardine, Skinner and Co., was one of the people they examined. 'Something that he said in his evidence has stuck in my mind ever since. The trouble with Indian coal', he said, is that it is not nearly as black as it is painted.' Later, Matthai says that one of his first reports after becoming president of the board was very critically reviewed in the press. Arthur Moore, who was then editor of the *Statesman*, said in a leading article that the Indian Tariff Board was fast becoming a serious rival to the Danish author Hans Andersen in the compounding of fairy tales. Matthai does not reveal which industry this pertained to.[5]

The case of the steel industry was the first to be referred to the board. Although the Commission had recommended that the board be constituted on a permanent basis, the government appointed an ad hoc board for steel. The practice of constituting a new tariff board in each fresh case became the norm though part of the personnel of the board was on occasion continued for other inquiries. The status of the board was that of a fact-finding and advisory body. It consisted of a senior civil servant, an economist and a businessman. In most cases, written and oral evidence was obtained and there were also inspections of factories of industries under inquiry. Cases were referred to the board by the department of commerce, who screened applications for protection.

The board would make an exhaustive study of production costs, imports and possible effects of protection on consumers and other industries. It then sent a detailed report to the government along with its recommendations. The report would be studied in detail by the commerce department and if accepted, the recommendations would be put before the central legislature in the form of a bill or an amendment to an earlier bill. The recommendations were generally accepted in toto and acted upon by the government. In rare cases, the recommendations were implemented by executive orders.

Protection to the Steel Industry

The first tariff board was appointed in July 1923, mainly to inquire into the claims of the iron and steel industry for protection. This basically meant protection for TISCO. The war years (1914–18) had been good for business and the Tatas had made ambitious expansion plans. But this optimism was belied. Metal smelted out of scrap from French and Belgian battlefields flooded the Indian market, and the change in the rupee–sterling ratio further weakened India's position on account of exchange fluctuations in Europe.

The position of the company deteriorated, and by 1921, it was forced to ask for protection. Rumours were rife that TISCO was on the verge of liquidation. The tariff board inquiry granted protection to the steel industry in 1924, but the next few years were hardly any better. The flow of cheap foreign steel into the country hit the industry hard. By April 1927, international prices collapsed and output shrank to below pre-war levels. Countries were forced to adopt various measures to protect their industries—tariff barriers were raised and the British steel manufacturers even gave a rebate to their customers. The Steel Industry (Protection) Act, 1927, introduced a system of protection for seven years and was intended to establish TISCO on a firm footing. But the measures proved to be inadequate and once again TISCO was faced with the spectre of liquidation or a government takeover.

Matthai was president of the board from 1931 to 1934, and it was in this capacity that he received the memorandum submitted by TISCO in 1933. The Steel Industry (Protection) Act, 1927, required the government to inquire into the necessity of continuing protection to the steel industry. The terms of reference of the inquiry were contained in a resolution dated 26 August 1933 of the Department of Commerce, and the 1933 inquiry presided over by Matthai came to be known as the Statutory Inquiry. Its terms of reference included a report on the further continuance of protection, and if so, in what form. The board was given the liberty of also examining the claims of industries making iron and steel products. It issued a questionnaire, visited factories, and took oral evidence in Calcutta and Bombay.

The Tatas said that while they were grateful that protection had kept the industry in active existence, it was by no means adequate to establish the industry permanently on a sound footing.[6] The memorandum pointed out that the protection should be adequate not only to enable TISCO to become profitable but also serve as an encouragement for setting up other steel works in the country. Given the confused state of world trade, and the great changes affecting production, consumption and costs, even the protection granted from 1924 onwards had failed to provide the desired measure of assistance to the industry as it existed.[7]

Matthai did not agree with the Tatas' contention that the protection that was granted was inadequate. He contended that the supposedly low level of protection was not to blame for TISCO's woes. If the board's proposals failed to yield the intended 8 per cent return on invested capital, it was because of the company's eagerness to establish a monopolistic position and its lavish expenditure on high salaries being paid to covenanted employees. The pampering of dealers by giving discounts and the money spent on providing municipal and other services to Jamshedpur which even non-Tata persons were enjoying also came in for criticism.

The points were argued over six days during the oral testimony of the Tata team lead by Sir Ardeshir Dalal, a former ICS officer who had joined the Tatas. Matthai would hardly have guessed that seven years later, he and Dalal would be colleagues in the Tatas. The Tatas, led by Dalal, refuted each of the allegations made by Matthai. Dalal pointed out that while steps had been taken to reduce expensive foreign personnel, indiscriminate Indianization was not desirable. Dalal observed, 'Nor must it be imagined that a progressive institution like the steel company can wage a racial vendetta against foreign skill.'[8] He said that experts would be imported whenever the needs of industry demanded not only in the interests of the company but also in the larger interest of the country itself.

He agreed to apply the pruning-knife and to reduce overheads wherever possible but said that 'such efforts cannot reasonably be made at a speed not commensurate with the maintenance of technical efficiency'.[9] Dalal also said that no Indian employee of Tatas had been paid more than was necessary. The point about the company's rebates was answered by arguing that such rebates were common elsewhere, and that the company needed such discounts to break into new markets where other manufacturers had established themselves.

Dalal pointed out that the losses suffered by the company were a result of the prolonged strike of 1928. The company, in an attempt to downsize, resorted to not filling up vacancies. It also worked out a scheme of standardized wages in 1927 which was calculated to raise the average rates while avoiding individual reductions. Despite the considerate nature of the measures adopted, strikes occurred throughout 1928, and even when work resumed, unrest continued. It was not until 1931 that normalcy was restored. Dalal estimated the loss to the company to be to the tune of Rs 2.22 crore, a figure Matthai refused to accept because he considered the reasoning to be too vague. He was, at least initially, not in favour of extending the protection for a further period of seven years. He also refused to accept the stand taken by the earlier boards that the intention of protection was to build up existing industries and create a favourable climate for new units.[10]

Dalal stood firm on the demand for protection from 1933 for a further seven years and was non-committal about its continuance beyond that period. The report that was signed in April 1934 is one of the most comprehensive studies on the subject. It noted that in spite of the fall in the demand for steel products, the industry made substantial progress, maintained its output and greatly reduced its costs of production. TISCO's share rose from 30 per cent of the market in 1927–28 to 72 per cent in 1932–33. The report noted that the return on capital was only a meagre 2.25 per cent, which was far short of expectations. The board also noted with satisfaction that the protection had been responsible for the growth of a re-rolling industry.[11] The report also covered other industries that made railway wagons, underframes, and equipment for track and rolling stock. In the end, even though the duties suggested by TISCO were reduced, protection was granted till March 1941. During the Second World War, the duties were continued by legislation with steel prices frozen at October 1939 levels, adjustable to meet actual increase in costs.

The board also examined the claims of industries making iron and steel products. An examination of the tin plate industry revealed that no industry had made better use of its opportunities than this industry and the board recommended an enhanced duty. For wire and the wire-nails industry, the board recommended that the duties should be confined to those classes that were already protected. Wire used for fencing was exempted from protective duty. The industry manufacturing screws also received no protection. Steel pipes and asbestos pipes were similarly exempted from protective duty.

Protection to the Paper Industry

In 1924, the board was asked to consider the case of the paper industry. It found that most mills were dependent on Sabai grass and had little chance eventually of becoming independent of protection. The board noted that bamboo was plentiful and of good quality, but a good deal of exploratory work had to be undertaken for making bamboo pulp. It recommended that the government advance finance to companies which were in this business.

When Matthai was president in 1931, the matter of protection to the paper industry was examined once again. The government asked the board to examine how far the Bamboo Paper Industry (Protection) Act, 1925, had achieved its objective and what kind of protection, if any, should be continued after March 1932. The board called upon interested parties to submit written representations through a press communique issued on 30 March 1931.

The board found that Indian mills had supplied a large part of the market for printing and writing papers and the figures indicated a rapid increase in the consumption of paper in India. There had been a considerable increase in the use of indigenous materials even though the use of imported wood pulp had also increased. The price of both pulp and paper had fallen. The board estimated the market for paper at about 25,000 tonnes a year.[12]

The supply of bamboo, the board noted, was plentiful and the quality of paper produced from bamboo proved to be satisfactory for most purposes. Improved practices resulted in a substantial reduction in the cost of production. The board observed that bamboo was the future of the paper industry, and that paper made from bamboo would eventually be able to dispense with protection. While all future expansion would be mainly based on bamboo, the board also recognized the role of Sabai grass in the paper industry. While recommending the continuation of protection, the board declared that the withdrawal of protection would lead to the disappearance of bamboo as a paper-making material. It also emphasized Indianization, and research and training. The recommendation on Indianization, one of the earliest, was far ahead of the times.[13]

Matthai, in fact, wanted the adoption of the principle relating to Indianization to be made a condition for granting concessions for the exploitation of forests. He wanted the paper pulp section of the Forest Research Institute, Dehradun, to be developed so that it could coordinate the experimental work done by the mills. The Bamboo Paper Industry (Protection) Act, 1932, was passed to give effect to the board's recommendations.

Protection to the Glass Industry

In October 1931, the board was asked to examine the question of extending protection to the glass industry. Its report on this subject was one of the most comprehensive reports prepared by Matthai on any subject during his tenure. The board found that it was in 1892 that the first glass factory on modern lines was started. By 1900, five modern factories were established, two of which did not survive very long. At the time of the inquiry, there were fifty-nine factories, twenty-six of which were engaged entirely in the manufacturing of bangles. The bangle-manufacturing factories were concentrated in the United Provinces.

The board noted that the principal constituent of glass was silica, which was obtained from sand and sandstone. Borax was imported from Tibet and therefore easily available. Soda ash, which constituted about 25 per cent of the total raw materials, was imported. The oxidizing agents used were potassium nitrate or saltpetre, which was available in Bihar and refractory material manufactured from Indian clays were almost as good as English clays. Sand and limestone were plentiful.

The board concluded that the glass industry substantially satisfied the condition of natural advantages postulated by the Fiscal Commission as a precondition for protection. Though deficient in soda ash, this handicap, in the opinion of the board, was compensated by the other advantages possessed by the industry. The disadvantages ascribed to Indian labour had by now disappeared and the expanding market was thought to be another advantage.[14] The board recommended that the protective duties should remain in force for a period of ten years so as to instil confidence among the investors about the future of the glass industry.

The board also recommended setting up an institute for research and training in glass technology which it wanted located at the Harcourt Butler Technological Institute in Kanpur. It noted that an incidental advantage of protection was that it encouraged the establishment of factories in the country by foreign manufacturers who previously had supplied the market with goods manufactured in their own countries. The increased use of indigenous labour and materials and the stimulus to competition were generally accepted as beneficial results of a policy of protection. This was also an idea that was ahead of its time, but it was only after Independence that it was widely accepted in the form of technology transfer from abroad.[15]

The board submitted its report in March 1932, but the government took more than three years to announce its decision. In the end, it decided to reject the application of the glass industry for protection. The main reason for this was the fact that in the United Provinces where the glass industry was concentrated, soda ash constituted 70–75 per cent of the cost of raw materials. The government had become more rigid in insisting that the principal raw materials required for the industry should be available in India before protection was granted. Matthai believed that the industry possessed sufficient advantages to compensate it for the absence of soda ash, but the government was not persuaded by his argument. He observed,

'In the earlier years the Government of India had adopted a more liberal interpretation of this condition.'[16]

Protection to the Textile Industry

Between 1927 and 1931, the textile industry increased its production, but it was adversely impacted by Japanese competition. Matthai thought that the textile industry required some protection, and he favoured specific duties based on the different weights of cotton. The handloom industry had benefitted from the duty on piece goods but not from the duty on yarn which had enabled the mills to raise its price. Hosiery was an important subsidiary industry and also had a claim to protection. As far as silk yarn was concerned, Matthai found that most of the imported artificial yarn was used by the handloom industry, and both mills and the handloom industry were affected by the competition from imported artificial silk piece goods.

Matthai decided to continue the duty on raw cotton in the interest of the cotton cultivators. However, he seems to have displeased the government when his report refused an extension of preference for the finer count of British textiles as it was now possible to manufacture them in the country itself. This is perhaps why his term as president was not renewed.

According to the economist H.L. Dey, protection would have shown more effective results if the execution had been better. He believed that the scope of the policy adopted was extremely restricted and the procedure followed in its execution was 'unduly rigid and dilatory'. Unsurprisingly, results fell short of what might have been achieved with a more 'generous outlook' and a higher tempo of execution.[17] Dey, however, attributed the expansion of industries such as steel, sugar, paper and cotton textiles industries, at a time when similar industries abroad were in a depressed state, to protection.[18]

* * *

In *Tariffs and Industry*, a pamphlet written a decade later, in 1944, Matthai discussed the effects of the tariff protection and its need in the future. He said that it was remarkable that while most countries had shown a heavy decline in industrial production during the period of the Depression, the principal industries in India had showed an increase in output. The steel, cotton piece goods, sugar, match and paper industries had all registered remarkable progress. This he attributed to the policy of protection, whose effects had begun to show during these years. Matthai observed, 'Whatever criticism may be made regarding the protective policy adopted in India, the immediate success of that policy, as disclosed by these facts, deserves recognition as an achievement which testifies in some measure to its soundness and efficacy.'[19]

Matthai argued that after the war, tariff protection for Indian industries would be unnecessary for many years to come. Since the object of protection was to help local industries against foreign competition, the extent of protection required would depend on how far the Indian industries would be exposed to competition. The abnormal demand for articles of all kinds for war purposes, the restriction of imports, and the difficulties of shipping and of foreign remittance would largely eliminate foreign competition in manufactured goods. He said that even after the termination of hostilities, these conditions would prevail. Matthai believed that it would be reasonable to assume that for a period of approximately five to ten years, the demand for consumable as well as capital goods would outstrip supply, and existing industries would be kept more or less fully occupied. 'The problem during this period will be how to meet a reviving demand from countries which have been starved of goods with the limited supply available rather than to restrict supplies so as to avoid overproduction and uneconomic competition.'[20]

He went on to add that while tariff assistance had its uses under certain conditions, it served no purpose if the conditions required for efficient and successful operation of industries were lacking. 'The chief abuse to which a protective policy is liable is that the immediate relief which it affords is apt to make both the government and industrialists oblivious to the fundamental factors which determine the growth of viral and healthy industries.'[21] He added, 'The protection by tariffs is a matter which even the stalest bureaucracy can handle with apparent success. But the internal reconstruction necessary for a vigorous forward-looking policy of industrial development will call for energy and vision such as only a national government responsible to the people and sensitive to their aspirations can possess.'[22]

Matthai said that while protective tariffs would not play an important role in the period immediately after the war, the question still remained as to what the national policy would be towards protective measures in the long run. He said that India's big drive towards industrialization would require the large-scale imports of capital goods and would place her in the position of a net importing country. It would be necessary for her to restrict imports of consumable goods so as to conserve foreign exchange for the purchase of plant and machinery.

After the transition to a normal peace economy had been completed, problems of trade competition not dissimilar to those that had arisen in the war years could well arise again. Arguing for free international trade, he said that a world economy that is based on an 'expansionist rather than a contractionist outlook on trade' was in the best interest of all. 'To this plea a free India cannot return a blank negative without damaging her position in the eyes of the rest of the world and without ultimately stultifying herself.'[23] Making a plea for freer international trade, Matthai observed, 'Although during this period India will be preoccupied with measures needed for her economic salvation, she cannot forget that she also has duties to other nations. Indeed, her own interests require that she should develop an international outlook in economic matters.'[24]

The Matthai Family

By the time Matthai joined the Tariff Board he was the father of two children: Valsa, a daughter, was born on 15 July 1922 and Duleep, a son, was born on 18 October 1924. Ravi, the youngest child was born on 6 August 1927 when he was with the board. Soon after Ravi was born, the children were sent to England, where they lived with an English family for three years. On their return, they were sent to Nazareth Convent, a boarding school in Ooty (now Udhagamandalam). Since Matthai, as chairman of the Tariff Board, had to tour frequently, it was perhaps thought that the interest of the children would be better served by sending them to a boarding school. Sending children to boarding school has always been an elitist affair. However, sending children to boarding school at an early age, not uncommon in England, was still rare in India. Nazareth Convent has now long been overshadowed by the other two more famous institutions in Ooty—Lawrence School and Good Shepherd, but it appears that at that time, it was an exclusive institution that catered to the children of the royalty and the upper class.

After spending about three years in Ooty, the two boys—Duleep and Ravi—were taken to Trichur, where they were tutored at home.

Valsa continued in Ooty, from where she completed her Senior Cambridge examination in 1938. A bright student, she attended Elphinstone College in Bombay. Musically inclined, she played the violin. Later, she went to Colombia University, New York, to study journalism but met with a tragic end, details of which are covered in the next chapter. After being tutored at home, Duleep and Ravi were sent to the newly created Doon School in Dehradun which started in 1935.

The school's founder was S.R. Das, brother of the famous freedom fighter, C.R. Das. S.R. Das had been educated at the Manchester Grammar School, a prestigious boys' school founded in England as far back as 1515. He went on to have a distinguished career, becoming advocate general of Bengal and a member of the viceroy's executive council. Das wanted to establish a school based on the British private boarding model for Indian boys in India. Envisioned as a secular institution open to all, Doon School was to specialize in the broad-based education of boys who would later serve free India. Its first headmaster, Arthur Foot, wanted it to be an 'aristocracy of service' inspired by ideas of unselfishness, not one of privilege wealth and position.[25] In theory, it may have been open to all, but there was no hiding its elitist character, then, as now. Later, Matthai was the chairman of the board of governors of the school and Ravi himself was a member of the governing board in the late 1970s.

Ravi's interests included swimming, hiking and mountaineering, painting, sculpture, dramatics and music. He had fond memories of his headmaster, John Martyn, who at first was deputy to Foot, and later became the second headmaster of the school. We shall return to Ravi Matthai and his contribution to management education in India in the Epilogue.

Director General of Commercial Intelligence and Statistics

Matthai had performed his duties on the tariff board with diligence, impartiality and sympathy. His recommendations for Indianization and his emphasis on research and development showed him to be farsighted at a time when both were comparatively new concepts. In 1934, the British government recognized his work on the tariff board by making him a Companion of the Order of the Indian Empire (CIE).

Never afraid to take a stand, the outspoken Matthai had serious differences of opinion with Sir James Grigg, the finance member. Matthai was relieved of his charge as president of the board and there was an attempt to transfer him to the education department of the Madras Presidency as a principal of a college. Matthai resisted and in the end, he was appointed Director General of Commercial Intelligence and Statistics in 1935 in Calcutta, where he served for five years. His deputy was J.V. Joshi, a Cambridge-trained economist, who later became economic adviser to the RBI.

Matthai rejected an offer from Sarvepalli Radhakrishnan, then vice chancellor of Andhra University, to join as professor of economics. Radhakrishnan was on the lookout for the best talent in the country and the list of recruits to the faculty of the Andhra University in the 1930s was a roll call of distinguished Indians in the 1960s and 1970s. Humayun Kabir, who later became a cabinet minister, and the communist Hiren Mukherjee, who later became an MP, were among the first to join. Radhakrishnan also invited V.K. Krishna Menon on the recommendation of political theorist and economist Harold Laski, but like Matthai, Menon too didn't want to make the move to Waltair (Visakhapatnam). Others who joined included the economist V.K.R.V. Rao, the mathematician Sarvadaman Chowla and the German chemist Ludwig Wolf, who was forced into exile by Adolf Hitler.[26]

As Director General of Commercial Intelligence and Statistics, Matthai was nominated as an official member of the Indian Legislative Assembly and in that capacity took part in the debate on the Ottawa Agreements in 1936. The Ottawa Agreements were twelve bilateral trade agreements providing for mutual tariff concessions and certain other commitments, negotiated in July–August 1932 by Britain, Canada and other commonwealth dominions and territories. The agreements succeeded in giving the dominions a larger share of the British market, but they did not arrest the decline in Britain's share of the imperial market. The agreements were modified in 1937, 1938 and many times since 1945.

Matthai had to make a speech from the official benches supporting the extension of the agreement, which he says he did with many mental reservations. Muhammed Ali Jinnah, who was in the Opposition, was strongly against the agreement. He had several discussions with Matthai during the session and this helped him build up a powerful brief against its renewal. Sir Muhammad Zafrulla Khan was then commerce member and Matthai's boss, but Matthai says he found himself in far greater sympathy with Jinnah, whose speech at the end of the debate practically led to the rejection of the agreement by an assembly packed with nominated members. Matthai thought that Jinnah would have been a tower of strength to independent India if circumstances had not created so impossible a gulf between him and the Congress. In Matthai's words:

> S. Satyamurti was the Deputy Leader of the Opposition under Bhulabhai Desai on the Congress benches. Satyamurti as an old pupil of mine said in his speech something to the effect – of course very politely – that he was distressed to hear his old tutor talk such unqualified nonsense. He was followed by Avinashilingam Chettiar, whom also I had taught in Madras and who expressed much the same sentiments about the speech. Sir James Grigg, the Finance Member at the time, was sitting in front of me in the house. He turned round to me and said: 'I say Matthai, it is about time that you got up and apologized to the House for your old pupils.'[27]

Joining the Tatas

In 1940, Matthai resigned and joined the Tatas. As we have seen, he had interacted closely with the Tatas when he was president of the tariff board. The request for protection by the steel industry was spearheaded by the Tatas, who had a very big stake in steel. He acquired an in-depth knowledge of a wide variety of industries (many of which were run by the Tata group) thanks to the numerous studies conducted by the tariff board. This, coupled with his reputation for fairness and impartiality, made him an ideal candidate for employment by the Tatas. This was also all of a piece with J.R.D. Tata's belief that rather than utilizing the services of experts as and when required, it would be better to have the best talent working full time for the Tatas. It was in keeping with this policy that solicitor J.D. Choksi and economist and stockbroker, A.D. Shroff, were inducted into the Tatas.

There was also a precedent of distinguished ICS officers joining the group. John Peterson, an ICS officer who was director of munitions during the First World War, was appointed director-in-charge of Tata Steel and it was he who put the young J.R.D. Tata through his paces when he first joined the Tatas. In 1931, Sir Ardeshir Dalal, another ICS officer, joined as a director. Thus, senior government officers were hardly a rarity in Tatas. Little surprise then that when Matthai retired as Director General of Commercial Intelligence and Statistics, Calcutta, in 1940, he was welcomed into the Tata fold with open arms to reinforce the elite corps the Tatas were building. As R.M. Lala, J.R.D.'s biographer, observed, 'For the next couple of decades these men were to steer the Tata enterprises.'[28] J.R.D. and Matthai shared an affectionate bond based on mutual trust and respect.

Tata Chemicals

The company Matthai joined was Tata Chemicals, which was set up at Mithapur, on the coast of Saurashtra in Gujarat on 1 January 1939. It was a challenging task since Tata Chemicals suffered many setbacks in its early years. A foreign expert even told J.R.D. that they were 'in the wrong place doing the wrong job'. J.R.D. is said to have replied that this was not the first time they were faced with such a situation and that the hopes of the people that they had aroused could not be dashed.[29]

Tata Chemicals was born beside the Arabian Sea in the arid area of Okhamandal in Gujarat. But there was a salt works there even before the Tatas came on the scene. A Manchester-trained chemical engineer, Kapilram Vakil, had seen the promise of recovering salt and marine minerals from seawater with the aim of ultimately developing an integrated heavy inorganic chemical complex. At the heart of this enterprise would be the manufacture of soda ash. It must be remembered that at the time, salt and salt-based products were the monopoly of foreign companies. Even ordinary salt was imported from Aden, a city in Yemen, for India's consumption. Not for nothing did Gandhi undertake his famous Salt March.

After a survey, Vakil decided on a point almost 11 km from Okha, the westernmost tip where the Gulf of Kutch begins. But the Okha Salt Works, as it was called, proved to be an ill-starred venture. Faced with the apathy of an alien government, it collapsed and Vakil reached out to J.R.D. to rescue his dream. Mithapur was in the territory of Sayajirao Gaekwad III, the Maharaja of Baroda, and that enlightened ruler asked the Tatas to assist with what he believed to be a project of national importance.[30] The Tatas were persuaded by the argument since there was no denying that India's self-reliance in the manufacture of glass, ceramic, textiles and a host of other industries depended on the production of soda ash.

J.R.D. may have been Vakil's knight in shining armour, but he hardly knew what was in store. The Tatas had to create a new township and that too in a barren area. The ship carrying the boiler and generator ordered for the new factory was torpedoed when the Second World War broke out. As the second consignment ordered from neutral Sweden left for its journey via the Soviet Union, that country too joined the war. Thinking that this shipment was also lost, J.R.D. ordered another from the USA. One day, a message was received that the second shipment had arrived overland to the Gulf, and to everyone's surprise, it finally turned up in Bombay harbour. But the travails of Tata Chemicals had just begun. The manufacturing process of soda ash was a closely guarded secret and was the monopoly of only a handful of countries. It involved fifteen process and power units, all of which needed to work perfectly, individually and in unison. Vakil laboured unsuccessfully to perfect his own design and ultimately died a broken-hearted man in January 1946.[31]

On 10 June 1940, Matthai joined Tata Chemicals as an executive to look after its work at a difficult time. Few records survive to show what he did there, but it is certain that he must have brought his usual sagacity and organizational ability to bear on the management of the company. On 1 January 1941, he was appointed director-in-charge of Tata Chemicals. As Matthai observed many years later:

> After leaving government service, I served off and on for fifteen years in the House of Tata which I look back on as the period of my life that I enjoyed most. The first job I did in Tatas was to look after Tata Chemicals which I did for three years. It was struggling hard in my time but has since recovered splendidly – I have no doubt on the foundations I laid so well and so truly.[32]

Matthai is right when he says it was struggling hard. But perhaps his tenure was not as happy as he made it out to be if what J.R.D. told his biographer Lala is any indication: 'John Matthai was chairman of Tata Chemicals and he got a bit fed up. And then I made him vice-chairman of Tata Steel. Then he was all right.'[33] As for Tata Chemicals, it turned the corner only when J.R.D. placed his trust in a young America-trained chemical engineer, Darbari Seth, who had joined the company in 1943, a tale that is beyond the scope of this narrative. As J.R.D. observed, 'Of all the companies with which I have been concerned, none has had to overcome so many difficulties compounded with bad luck, as has been the lot of Tata Chemicals.'[34]

What is not in doubt, however, is the fact that Matthai spent the happiest years of his life with the Tatas. In a letter he wrote to J.R.D. in April 1944, he says as much.

> I have valued my association with the firms ever since I joined them and I am very happy to think that I have earned their confidence to this extent. Bombay House has not merely provided me with work which it is worthwhile doing but, in many ways, it has been a haven of refuge to me and I feel very lucky.[35]

On 6 June 1944, Matthai was appointed director of Tata Sons Ltd. He resigned from Tata Chemicals on 1 August 1944 on being appointed special director and director-in-charge of TISCO, continuing in that position till 24 April 1946. He succeeded Sir Ardeshir Dalal, who had left the Tatas to join the viceroy's executive council as member of the new planning and development department.

As noted earlier, J.R.D. was convinced that the best talent had to be available to Tatas in-house. The first step was spotting talent. Attracting it came next, and perhaps the most difficult of the three, holding on to it. J.R.D. had considerable success in all three. He was also concerned by the lack of statistical information and data on which new initiatives could be based. He set up a statistics department in 1940 under Y.S. Pandit, who left his job with the Bombay government to join the Tatas. In those days, statistics were compiled only by the government; industrial houses did not care much for such activity.

The Tatas started compiling statistics on a variety of subjects and these were appreciated not only in India but also abroad.[36] J.R.D. was a pioneer in realizing that staff functions should have a knowledge base. He also established the Department of Public Relations in 1943, another first in India's corporate world, which was headed by Minoo R. Masani. A few years later, Matthai took charge of the expanded Department of Economics and Statistics. Initially, the statistics gathered were available only to Tata directors, but in time, *The Statistical Outline of India*, compiled by the Tatas, became a vital resource for both industry and government.

The Director's Grand-Nephew

There is an amusing story involving Matthai and his grand-nephew Verghese Kurien when the former was the director-in-charge of TISCO.

As noted, Verghese Kurien was the son of Achamma Kurien, who was Matthai's niece (his sister Mariamma Jacob's daughter). Verghese was only twenty-two when his father Kurien Kurien died prematurely. On hearing of his death, his maternal grand-uncle Cherian Matthai, John Matthai's elder brother, took Kurien and his family to Trichur, where he lived in a large house. Cherian Matthai, the patriarch of the family, was director of public instruction of the Cochin State. A bachelor, he was fondly referred to as 'Master Matthai' and he lived in a sprawling house on a huge estate with a boat club and golf course. Verghese remembers spending his summer vacations there even before his father's demise.[37]

Verghese received a bachelor's degree in mechanical engineering from the College of Engineering, Guindy, in 1943. He wanted to join the army as an engineer, but his mother talked him out of it. She persuaded him to join the Tata Steel Technical Institute, Jamshedpur, on a recommendation by John Matthai. Matthai put in a word to the managing director, Sir Jehangir J. Ghandy, asking him to consider his nephew's application if found 'competent'. Kurien joined as a graduate apprentice in 1944—a prestigious selection considering that the company took only ten 'A' class apprentices every year.[38]

All went well till Matthai visited Verghese at the apprentices' hostel. The apprentices were the lowest in the officer category and no senior officer ever visited the hostel. Matthai's visit attracted much attention and soon Kurien's colleagues knew who he was. They were convinced that Kurien, given his connections, would rapidly move through the Tata ranks. Kurien says that they were very nice to him and also very careful around him. He found this unbearably oppressive and on Matthai's next visit to Jamshedpur, Kurien told him that he no longer wanted to stay in Jamshedpur because he was merely the boss's grand-nephew.

Matthai appreciated his sentiments but told Kurien that he was being extremely silly because he was considered the best apprentice and would reach the very top in the Tatas. Unconvinced, Kurien left Jamshedpur, much to Matthai's displeasure. The government had announced a scheme of sending some 500 young Indians abroad for specialized training and Kurien applied for a scholarship. He was selected for a scholarship in dairy engineering. He was sent to the Imperial Institute for Animal Husbandry and Dairying (later the National Dairy Research Institute), in Bangalore, where he spent eight months before being sent to America to study at the Michigan State University, on a government scholarship.[39] He returned in

1948 with a master's degree in mechanical engineering (metallurgy) with a minor in nuclear physics. Since he had ostensibly been sent to study dairy engineering, he took a few courses on the side on the subject.

On his return, Kurien contacted the government, who had sent him on a scholarship, and he was asked to get in touch with the Ministry of Education. By this time, Matthai had become India's finance minister and Kurien stayed with him in Delhi. He met the undersecretary in the education ministry, who told him that he would have to report to Anand in Gujarat. Kurien didn't know where Anand was and expressed his reluctance to go there. The agitated official told him that he would be sued by the government for Rs 30,000, the amount it had spent on his education. Kurien angered the official even further when he said he could not wait for the letter of appointment because he had to go home for lunch. After prophesying (rather inaccurately to put it mildly), that Kurien would not go far in life, the official asked him for his address. Kurien gave Matthai's address and left.

When Matthai asked him if he had got his release, Kurien replied in the negative and asked his grand-uncle if he could help him. Matthai emphatically refused and took great pleasure in pointing out that since Kurien had rejected his advice on earlier occasions and wanted to build his own future, he would receive no help from him. 'You have made your bed my boy. Now go lie in it.'[40] Meanwhile, when the undersecretary realized that Kurien was Matthai's grand-nephew, he recommended a higher salary of Rs 600 a month for him. This required the approval of the finance ministry, which the undersecretary believed would be easily procured. But he had not reckoned with the opposition from what he believed was the least likely source: Matthai himself. The principled finance minister would not allow any favour to be shown to his grand-nephew. Verghese observed, 'Such were the principles and standards of the Government of India those days.'[41]

* * *

Matthai's greatest contribution while he was with the Tatas was his role in what came to be known as the Bombay Plan. J.R.D. Tata always maintained that his real achievement was to get Matthai into the Bombay Plan. It was Matthai who actually wrote the report or at least a large part of it. It is to this landmark document in the history of Indian planning that we now turn.

5

The Bombay Plan and After

In January 1944, a comprehensive document titled *A Brief Memorandum Outlining a Plan for the Economic Development of India* was published under the signatures of five eminent industrialist and three technocrats. Apart from John Matthai, the list included Sir Purshotamdas Thakurdas; G.D. Birla; J.R.D. Tata; Kasturbhai Lalbhai, the textile millowner from Ahmedabad; Lala Shri Ram, an industrialist from Delhi; stockbroker and economist A.D. Shroff; Sir Ardeshir Dalal and P.S. Lokanathan, who however was not a signatory to the Plan.

Purshotamdas Thakurdas, the seniormost of the group, was the doyen of the business community and enjoyed unrivalled prestige as a front-ranking leader of big business in India. Though his name carries little resonance for today's generation, his outstanding and manifold contributions to public life, industry, insurance and banking made him one of the brightest stars in the Indian firmament in the first half of the twentieth century. At his peak, he was on the board of seventy companies, many of them from the Tata group.

This ninety-page document, published in two parts in January and December 1944, and famous as the Bombay Plan, generated widespread interest in India at the time of its publication. This was hardly surprising since it was authored by leading personalities from the world of Indian business and commerce. It was also important because it was a unique document in the history of post-colonial development. Nowhere in the developing world had a group of business leaders come together to articulate such a comprehensive vision for national development, outlining as they did a bold economic blueprint for India's economic transformation, with ambitious targets for a post-War independent nation. Before we discuss the Bombay Plan, it would be interesting to take a brief look at the history of planning in India.

Planning in India: A Background

In the decades leading up to Independence, planning emerged as the language through which Indian aspirations were expressed. Japan's development after the Meiji Restoration of 1868 showed what a central authority could accomplish. Later, the Soviet Union's rapid advance through its first five-year plan raised the hopes of many in India who thought that planning was the way forward.

By the mid-1930s, the necessity of some form of planning and state intervention in the economy had come to be accepted in Indian academic circles. The idea of planning is supposed to have been first articulated by the engineer–statesman Sir M. Visvesvaraya, in his book *Planned Economy for India*, published in 1934, where he pioneered an economic and social plan. The knighted, white-and-gold turbaned former Dewan of Mysore, who was then on the board of TISCO, advocated centralized planning for India. What is generally not known is that his efforts were preceded by a bureaucratic initiative by Sir George Schuster, finance member of the viceroy's executive council, who in 1930 mooted the idea of planning in official circles when he circulated a paper titled 'Notes on Economic Policy'. In the paper, Schuster spoke of the need for an Economic Advisory Council for India on the lines of the one that had been set up in England recently.[1]

By 1934, the Federation of Indian Chambers of Commerce and Industry (FICCI) was also taking an interest in planning. Two of its prominent members, G.D. Birla and Nalini Ranjan Sarkar, who presided over the annual general meeting in 1934, sketched their own plans. For Birla and other businessman, 'such arguments for planning expressed an aspiration for a modern economy in which domestic enterprises could prosper while being protected from foreign competition'.[2] In a sense, the idea of planning itself evolved from the realization that private enterprise in the colonial regime was incapable of carrying forward the task of industrialization. It was only through a planned effort that the question of production and distribution could be solved in the interest of a proper capitalist development.[3]

In October 1938, the Congress's National Planning Committee (NPC) was set up for a complete survey of the Indian economy. Eight months earlier, in February 1938, Subhas Chandra Bose, the newly elected Congress president, had addressed a meeting in Haripura, Gujarat, where he spoke of the need for a 'socialistic solution' to India's problems through a 'planning commission' that would begin a comprehensive scheme of industrial development under state ownership and control.[4]

The NPC was formed at a meeting that included politicians and other prominent men of India in October 1938. Initially, Visvesvaraya became the chairman of the committee for a very brief period. Later, Bose wrote to Nehru offering him the job over telegram. Nehru, who was in London at the time, accepted the offer when he returned in November 1938. Led by Nehru and managed by the economist K.T. Shah, the fifteen-member committee included industrialists, scientists, economists and a sceptical Gandhian, J.C. Kumarappa. The NPC's office was housed in a number of places in Bombay, including the Bombay University building. After the Second World War, J.R.D Tata provided room for it in the New India Assurance Building.[5]

The principal task accomplished by the second session of the NPC in June 1939 was the setting up of twenty-seven subcommittees to consider different aspects of planning. A subcommittee was also formed which was to draft letters to the government of India and the provincial governments. The idea was to suggest to them the desirability of utilizing the forthcoming census operations in 1941 to collect additional information of various kinds which would help in drawing up a plan. The subcommittee, after preparing a note on census and statistics, was to consult the statistician P.C. Mahalanobis at Calcutta and Matthai in Bombay and suggest what data should be collected in future by the government at the Centre and those of the different states.[6]

The Second World War broke out in September 1939 and the next meeting of the NPC could only be held in May 1940. Two more sessions were held in quick succession in June and August the same year. Nineteen subcommittees submitted their reports before the fifth session was over in September 1940. Planning had now become part of India's preparation for Independence, but although the basic concept of planning was borrowed from Russia, the plan of the NPC was far from a socialist one. The Indian elites were trying to replace the colonial state by one of their own—one that would have a comprehensive role to play in transforming Indian society.

The NPC was revived again in 1945, after the war was over, but before that the government set up a Post-War Reconstruction Committee in 1941. Soon after the formation of the Reconstruction Committee of Council, the government created a new department of Planning and Development, which was headed by Sir Ardeshir Dalal, who was closely associated with FICCI. During the war, the role of the government expanded as did that of wartime controls. Observers recognized in these developments the germ of economic planning. Realizing that decolonization was imminent, the colonial government was keen to mirror nationalist thinking wherever possible: Colonial policies would be more likely to gain traction if dressed in nationalist colours, and if they accepted socialism. The Planning and Development Department produced two reports that echoed the NPC in its emphasis on industrialization, interventionism and protectionism.[7] However, before the publication of the government reports, the Bombay Plan was published in 1944, in whose preparation Dalal played a role in his capacity as a Tata director. The pre-eminent role, however, was that of Matthai, who according to J.R.D., drafted the document after discussions with his colleagues.

As the war drew to a close, planning seemed to be the flavour of the season. Almost everyone across the ideological spectrum seemed to have their own solution to the problems faced by the economy. In 1944, in particular, plans abounded. Apart from the government's own report on planning, and the Bombay Plan, there was the communist M.N. Roy's People's Plan, the Muslim League's own Planning Committee and even a Gandhian Plan, written by Shriman Narayan Agarwal, with a foreword written by Gandhi himself. Of these, by far the most influential was the Bombay Plan. There was a close resemblance between what the authors of the Bombay Plan aspired for and the programmes the government proposed in its plans. This was hardly surprising since all the people who authored the Bombay Plan were in the policy committees of the government, and as noted before, Dalal, who was a member of the council, was one its authors.

The Bombay Plan

The Bombay Plan was published at a time when India was on the threshold of momentous changes. By 1942, wartime production had made it the eighth-most industrialized country in the world and the Indian Army's deployment in the Allied military campaign had led to the accretion of substantial sterling balances, with India emerging as a creditor. There was also the feeling that Independence was not too far away. It was in this atmosphere of general optimism that these very influential individuals from the business world came together to prepare an economic blueprint for an independent India.[8]

The initiative for the Bombay Plan came from the Tatas. In November 1942, J.R.D. wrote to Purshotamdas informing him that the first meeting of the informal Post-War Economic Development Committee would be held in the board room of Bombay House in December. The leading capitalists it appears had been thinking about this for some time though the matter was kept secret. That the major initiative came from the Tatas is evident from a letter Matthai wrote to Purshotamdas on 5 December 1942, in which he also enclosed relevant papers, notes and the agenda. Later, when the committee started functioning, clerical and other support came from the Statistical Department of Tata Sons. The Tatas bore half the costs, while the other members financed the rest.[9]

The first meeting, a hush-hush affair, was held at Bombay House on 11 February 1943 and was attended by Purshotamdas Thakurdas, G.D. Birla, Lala Shri Ram, Kasturbhai Lalbhai, A.D. Shroff, Matthai and J.R.D. Ardeshir Dalal, the only other 'author' of the plan, does not seem to have been associated with the venture at this time. The Bombay planners assumed that if a national government came into existence, it would embrace the whole of India and would be federal in nature. They also assumed full freedom in economic matters. The aim was not to vindicate capitalism but to analyse it, with a view to modifying it to enable it to render the best possible service to the country. The role of the state and state control were considered vital. It was agreed that the state would lay down a general plan for the development of industries, and such control should carry with it an obligation to assist industries if required. However, care was to be taken to avoid over-centralization and not curb individual freedom.[10] Licensing was considered to be a suitable means of exercising state control.

The committee decided that the problems of agriculture should be examined not merely in relation to their bearing on industry but also because it was the most vital economic activity of the country. The planners, no doubt influenced by Keynesian economics, wanted due consideration to be given to the question of providing public works as a means of countering cyclical fluctuations. However, they wanted the focus to be on public works that were directly productive.

The initial 'Note' on planning, prepared by Matthai in June 1943, was deliberated upon by the committee in August. By December of that year, an outline was drafted by Matthai with the help of, among others, Lokanathan. The draft envisaged an increase of only 60 per cent in agriculture. Both Birla and Purshotamdas thought that this would expose them to the charge of being biased in favour of industry and wanted the increase in agriculture to be 100 per cent or more during the fifteen years of planning. Matthai revised the outline accordingly.

The Plan was presented at a press conference held at Bombay House on 19 January 1944 and was widely publicized: Press conferences were held, advertisements placed, and free copies distributed to libraries and influential people. The authors met with government officials, made efforts to enlist the support of political leaders and spoke at public events. A joint meeting was held for members of important commercial bodies.

Ideology

The Plan was originally intended for private circulation only—the decision to publish it in pamphlet form came at a later date. While it did not represent the opinion of the whole business community, it claimed immediate attention because it set forth the considered views of some of India's most prominent and influential businessman, all of whom were 'inspired by more than a fair measure of public spirit and responsibility'.[11] Given the fact that it broke new ground and was bold in its vision, it is hardly surprising that it was invested with exceptional significance. The framers of the document thought that a national government was essential for safeguarding India's economic interest and took upon themselves the task of planning for India's post-war economy. The Bombay Plan represented a search for a new style of capitalism that would chart a middle path between state-led planning and private enterprise. The planners envisaged a mixed economy, in which the state and the private sector would play a complementary role, 'thus proposing an almost visionary compromise between the two systems of free market operations and state control in independent India'.[12]

The Plan advocated centralized planning and encouraged a strong partnership between the state and private enterprise. The Bombay Plan can also be seen, as part of the belief of the importance the industrialists thought would be due them, and the role they expected to play. They believed that as patriots and business leaders, they would play a historic role in bringing about a major transformation, where all sections of society would share in the prosperity that would follow. It is surprising that the authors of the Plan, all of whom had a strong commitment to free enterprise, recommended a number of restrictive measures, such as graduated income tax, price control, ceiling on dividends and appointment of government directors on management boards of private sector companies.

The meeting at Bombay House, in December 1942, was convened against the backdrop of a fierce intellectual debate among economists about post-war reconstruction. Was it socialism or capitalism that offered a more efficient system? It soon became clear that the main ideological battle was being fought in Britain. Ranged against each other were the Austrian economist Friedrich August von Hayek, who was at LSE, and the famous Cambridge economist, John Maynard Keynes. While Keynes advocated active state intervention and the desirability of state-funded programmes, Hayek favoured non-interventionism and free trade. Keynes advocated state intervention in demand management and the use of public expenditure to avoid cyclical unemployment. He wanted governments to increase their expenditure, an injection of funds that would increase the aggregate purchasing power of consumers by a multiple of the original amount, i.e., the multiplier effect.

Hayek, on the other hand, favoured the market economy to efficiently perform the task of allocation of resources through the decentralized decisions of buyers and sellers. He condemned central planning according to a single plan. He believed that large-scale spending by the government would lead to runaway inflation, and worse still, political turmoil. He feared planning with centralized control since it would subvert individual freedom. Liberty was an end in itself and 'could not be bartered away to add to the sum total of economic satisfaction'.[13]

Hayek, however, was not advocating complete laissez-faire. He was in favour of a minimum income for all, a comprehensive social security organization, and actively combating general fluctuations in the economy as well as large-scale unemployment. He was not against planning per se but against planning that was a substitute for competition. Nor was competition incompatible with systems of social security. Both were against authoritarian regimes, and they recognized that capitalism could not be allowed without moral constraints.[14]

Keynes had said that the Great Depression was due to a failure of aggregate demand. This diagnosis appeared to be validated when during the Second World War war-induced demand finally ended the Depression. Deliberate state intervention was now accepted as a way to boost the economy. Nations increasingly based their macroeconomic management policies on Keynes's ideas, which held much appeal for Matthai, Shroff and Lokanathan. His prescription of demand management and public spending resonated with them, and this found a place in the Bombay Plan.

It was unusual for a group of businessmen to think of planning. J.R.D. said that initially it was a desire to do something to develop the country that had brought the group together. According to his biographer, R.M. Lala, J.R.D. gave the credit for shifting the focus of the committee from a deliberative body to an articulate one, to G.D. Birla. When the committee was searching for a structure, it was Birla who suggested that they decide what kind of standard of living was being aimed at and then ascertain in quantitative terms what was needed to achieve it. J.R.D. observed, 'What is needed? So many calories of food requiring so many million tons of grain, so many meters of cloth, housing – how many cubic feet of housing, so many schools etc.'[15] The concept of quantifying made things easy, and it was on this basis that Matthai wrote the Plan. It also helped that the Tatas had an Economics and Statistics Department since 1940. Figures on food consumption, cloth consumption and the like were available, and these enabled the committee to fix targets, quantify the items required and calculate the kind of investment needed.

Objectives

The principal objective of the Plan was to double India's per capita income within fifteen years, and in so doing, ensure that all citizens attain 'a general standard of living which would leave a reasonable margin over the minimum requirements for human life'.[16] These were defined in terms of essential needs. Food was quantified at a daily 2800 calories per person, the minimum per capita requirement of cloth was calculated at 30 yards and the minimum accommodation was pegged at 100 sq. feet per person. Expectedly, there were serious shortfalls in the production of all the metrics. India was barely producing five-sevenths of the food required. Its cloth production would also have to be doubled, and 55 million dwelling units built at a cost of Rs 1400 crore. The Plan also projected a need for 7,00,000 doctors and 14 million nurses. It set the ambitious target of eradicating illiteracy in fifteen years and proposed that both education and medical services should be free. With population growing at 5 million per year, this required a trebling of India's aggregate national income over the fifteen-year period. The fifteen-year blueprint for India's post-war economic development envisaged capital investment of Rs 10,000 crore.

Based on the calculations regarding the basic needs, the planners arrived at a per capita poverty line of Rs 74 at pre-war prices. They envisaged a 130 per cent increase in agricultural output, a 500 per cent increase in industry and a 200 per cent increase in services. The Plan spoke of three leaps, with the first leap concentrating on basic industry and the consumer goods industry and a focus on importing technology to economize on limited foreign exchange. The second leap would continue to focus on basic industries; in the third leap, social services were to be allocated the largest amount, with a special focus on communications.

The authors of the Plan believed that India's primary economic need was rapid industrialization and it was this big push that was envisaged as the centrepiece of development. In the first phase, the focus was on basic industries, such as power, mining, metallurgy, iron and steel, engineering, chemicals, armaments, transport and cement. They placed special emphasis on power, which they felt would open the door to economic development. The importance the planners gave to these basic industries can be gauged from the fact that a third of the Plan's outlay was allocated to basic industry.

While the emphasis was to be on power and capital goods backed by serious investments in railways and roads, consumer goods such as textiles, glass, leather goods, paper and oil, would also be supported. Cottage industries were also given due importance since they would provide employment and counter the tendency of highly mechanized large-scale industry to create unemployment. Using a capital output ratio of 2:4, the Plan arrived at a working capital need of Rs 4480 crore to bring about aggregate industrial output in the fifteenth year to Rs 2240 crore.

Notwithstanding the emphasis on industrialization, the planners realized that agriculture would remain the predominant occupation. The initial emphasis was on growing crops for feeding the population— the overall acreage for cereals, pulses, fruits and vegetables was to be determined keeping in mind the per capita requirements of a nutritive diet. The production of commercial crops, such as tea, jute and cotton, was to be adjusted according to trends in international trade. The planners were of the view that agriculture faced three main challenges: small and fragmented holdings, large-scale rural indebtedness and soil erosion. Consolidation of holdings was considered the best solution. A radical suggestion was the introduction of model farms: one farm for every ten villages, making for a total of 65,000 farms.

A sum of Rs 845 crore was allocated for measures to increase agricultural production. Of this, Rs 200 was earmarked for soil conservation, Rs 400 for canal irrigation works, Rs 50 crore for wells and Rs 195 for the development of model farms. As far as rural indebtedness was concerned, the planners felt that the rise in agricultural prices after the war had benefitted the population and that the rural indebtedness had come down and was not more than Rs 200 crore at most. They felt that rural debt could be addressed through co-operative societies once they were provided with long-term finance.

Part II of the Plan dealt with the issues of land revenue and land revenue systems. The planners advocated a gradual replacement of the zamindari with the ryotwari system. Along with the change in land tenure that was meant to create a new class of peasant proprietors, the Plan called for a uniform basis of assessment across India. Fixing an exemption limit for agricultural income and taxing the surplus were also suggested.

It was thought that once agriculture and industry were on the path to growth, a 200 per cent increase in trade and services would follow. The planners recommended measures to integrate internal markets by removing all bottlenecks to trade. They also set ambitious targets in the transportation sector: Expanding railway mileage from 21,000 miles to 62,000 miles; doubling the surface transport from 3,00,000 miles to 6,00,000 miles, and boosting coastal shipping and port facilities. Foreign trade was not given much importance since the key aim was self-sufficiency in food and meeting internal demand.

The planners did not simply put forth the necessary capital allocations: Resource mobilization was an important part of the Plan, and it carefully examined various sources of financing. Hoarded wealth could fetch at best Rs 300 crore, sterling balances with the RBI about Rs 1000 crore and India's positive balance of trade was estimated at Rs 600 crore. Savings—domestic as well as corporate—were pegged at Rs 4000 crore. The gap of

Rs 4100 crore was to be met through foreign borrowing (Rs 700 crore) and deficit financing. That five noted capitalists should have come up with this idea was in itself remarkable. Conservative concerns were sought to be assuaged. The Plan stated that, 'There is nothing unsound in creating this money, because it is meant to increase the productive capacity of the nation and in the long run is of a self-liquidating character.'[17]

An important issue that the planners discussed in Part II of the Plan, was the distributive aspect of the increased production and the role of the state inherent in planning. 'Levelling up' was to raise the general income of the lower-income groups, while 'levelling down' implied a reduction in the over-consumption by the higher-income groups. 'Levelling up' was more difficult and entailed measures to boost full employment, increase wages and implement land reforms, among other things. Drawing their inspiration from Keynesian economics, they backed state spending on public works to tackle seasonal unemployment. As far as 'levelling down' was concerned, the principal instrument was to be taxation and it is remarkable that a group of capitalists should have proposed a steeply graduated income tax, which would keep personal incomes within limits.

Developmental leaps of the kind envisioned by the planners required the concerted exercise of state power, if not outright authoritarianism. The Soviet example weighed heavily on the planners' minds. Purshotamdas sent Matthai clippings from M.N. Roy's weekly, *Independent India*, on economic data from Soviet republics, which 'makes a telling support for the Plan which you have drafted'.[18] The planners saw an important role for the state both in increasing production and in ensuring its equitable distribution.

The planners believed that neither socialism nor capitalism existed in its pure form anywhere: All economic forms would be a combination of both. But they were careful to point out that interventions by the state had to be democratic and that if a planned economy involved a restriction of individual freedom, it would be of limited duration and for specific purposes. The mixed economy would be based on both planning and free enterprise. Thus, the operational framework of the Plan was capitalism but a modified capitalism that gave the state a greater role in the market. The planners wanted the work of planning to be entrusted to technocrats, a group of personnel who would be specially trained to work under a centralized body that would have sufficient powers of coordination.

The planners visualized a significantly larger role for the state in the initial phase both in terms of ownership and control. Even more than state ownership, it was state control that was emphasized by the planners. There was a lingering fear of excessive state control which was voiced in the later edition of the Bombay Plan in 1945. When they were working on the Plan, von Hayek's libertarian classic, *The Road to Serfdom*, had not been published. In the 1945 edition of the Plan, the authors sounded a word of warning by invoking his ideas. They cited the examples of Germany and the Soviet Union, where a planned economy functioned under a dictatorship and the state exerted a degree of authority over the activities of its citizens which provided little scope for individual freedom.

In 'normal times', the planners argued for a smaller role for the state which was to be limited to management of currency and finance and coordination of general economic activity. State ownership was recommended for sectors important for public welfare or security. They also proposed that industries owned by the state need not necessarily be managed by the state. They could be run by public corporations or private enterprises.

The initial copies of the Plan proved to be a bestseller and there were many reprints. In June 1944, Part I of the Plan was published as a Penguin special and the second part in December 1944. Later, both parts were published together by Penguin UK. As noted before, the Tata Sons statistical department was responsible for research and data collection. The public relations department was headed by Minoo Masani, a former general secretary of the Congress Socialist Party, who had joined Tata Chemicals in 1941 and from 1943 headed the public relations department. He supervised the translation of the plan into vernacular languages. In London, Beram Saklatvala of Tata Limited took the lead in countering criticism in the British press. Enthused by the initial sales, J.R.D. wanted an illustrated popular edition to be published on the lines of Masani's *Our India*, with illustrations by C.H.G. Moorhouse, which had become a runaway bestseller. It was decided that it would be published by Oxford University Press. This illustrated edition titled *Picture of a Plan* (published in late 1945) had numerous illustrations and explored the ideas of the Plan in five chapters.

Reception

Thanks to all the publicity, the Plan attracted widespread attention. Long and detailed reviews by Bombay-based economists P.A.Wadia and

K.T. Merchant appeared in the *Bombay Chronicle* and *Hindustan Weekly*, respectively. Apart from the national press, the international press in the US and Britain also took heed of the Plan, with the reports generally being enthusiastic and positive.

The Plan was debated by all shades of Indian political opinion and by the colonial bureaucracy in New Delhi and London. In London, it came up for debate in the House of Commons. The Secretary of State for India, Leopold Amery, was asked if the government intended to use the proposals outlined in the Plan in its own scheme for post-war reconstruction. In India, Wavell said that even if there were different ideas about economic development, both the planners and the government had the same objective, namely to ensure a substantial increase in the standard of living in the country. He asked Sir Theodore Gregory, his economic adviser, to draft a suitable official response to the Plan. In his budget speech in 1944, the finance member, Sir Jeremy Raisman, called the Plan a useful document but questioned its financial assumptions. A month later, he met the planners with the member for supply , Ramaswami Mudaliar.

All the relevant departments of the Government of India prepared detailed analyses of the Plan. While all were in agreement with the general objective of the Plan, criticism was directed mainly at its financial aspects. Gregory noted the difficulty in implementing the Plan given the prevalent constitution based on provincial autonomy and the fact that such planning had been undertaken only in authoritarian regimes such as Russia, Germany and to a smaller degree in Italy. Gregory dismissed the Plan's profligate financing scheme and centralizing tendencies in a lengthy note. After reading it, Amery wrote to Wavell saying that while the government should not encourage a purely destructive attitude to the Plan, it seemed desirable that comments like those of Gregory's should be ventilated in order to avoid the Plan from being regarded as sacrosanct. He suggested confidentially supplying copies of the note to the editor of *The Economist*. The editor duly obliged with an article that criticized the plan for its neglect of agriculture and its recourse to autarky which would prevent the Indian economy from enjoying the benefits of foreign capital and the international division of labour.[19]

Notwithstanding, the reservations of the government, the RBI was given the task of analysing the financial aspects of the Plan. J.V. Joshi, senior economist at the RBI, warned against relying too much on the sterling balances given the fact that the UK would not be in a position to release this reserve immediately. He also cautioned against the inflationary impact of the use of this balance. As noted before, Joshi, a Cambridge-trained economist, had served as deputy to Matthai when the latter was Director General of Commercial Intelligence and Statistics in the 1930s.

Further proof of how seriously the government was taking the Plan came when it decided to ask the planners to clarify some of the criticisms raised by government officials. A meeting was held in the house of Sir J.P. Srivastava, member of council for food and the deputy president of the Reconstruction Committee of the Council, in April 1944. Apart from Srivastava, the finance member, the supply member, Gregory and secretaries of the concerned departments attended. Amongst the authors Purshotamdas, J.R.D., Shri Ram Shroff and Matthai were present at the four-hour meeting, where they explained their ideas.

The immediate fallout of the meeting was that Wavell offered Dalal charge of the planning portfolio in his executive council. When Wavell established a new department of planning and post-war reconstruction in June 1944, Dalal was appointed as its head and a member of the viceroy's economic council. His appointment showed that the ideas of the Bombay Plan and those of the colonial government were not irreconcilable. However, J.R.D. and Birla were less than pleased. The former was annoyed enough to refuse to spare Dalal when Wavell asked the Tatas to relieve him so that he could join government. Birla thought that Dalal had no business to accept the job and fumed that he had not had the courtesy of even consulting the other planners when he was offered the job.[20] Dalal assumed charge in August 1944. This is why he was a signatory only to Part I of the Plan and not Part II, which was published in December 1944.

The Plan had its share of detractors. Sir Ziauddin Ahmad of the Muslim League moved a resolution against it in the central legislative assembly on the grounds that it proposed a national government whose jurisdiction in economic matters extended to the whole of India. Calling it an unholy alliance between Indian and foreign capitalists, he said that it was the easiest way to destroy cottage industries, a criticism that N.G. Ranga of the Congress echoed. When asked by assembly members if the government had accepted the Plan, Dalal said that while the objective was the same, the government was making its own plan. In April 1945, the government issued its *Statement of Government's Industrial Policy*.[21]

K.T. Shah, an economist, who was secretary of the Congress's national planning committee, was scathing in his criticism. Left-leaning economists also denounced it, with M.N. Roy calling it 'the programme of Indian Fascism'.[22] He was against its emphasis on industry and for its inflationary financial proposals. Bombay economists, Wadia and Merchant, criticized it for its emphasis on industry and its dismissive attitude towards agriculture. They also raised the issue of inequality, arguing that individual gain remained the driving force of the Plan. The Plan was also critiqued for its unrealistic targets though most of the criticism centred on deficit financing and its inflationary risk. Birla, upset at the widespread criticism, wrote to J.R.D. in August 1944: 'The main target of attack is the businessman and the critics treat yourself and myself as a symbol of the business community.'[23]

Perhaps what worried the planners the most was how Gandhi would react to the Plan. There were reports that Shriman Narayan Agarwal, a professed Gandhian, who was also Jamnalal Bajaj's son-in-law, was writing his own Gandhian plan. There were rumours that K.T. Shah, who vehemently opposed the Plan, had discussed the Plan with Gandhi. Gandhi had just been released from jail and J.R.D., Birla and Purshotamdas met him in Juhu in Bombay. A copy had been sent to him when he was imprisoned at the Aga Khan Palace in Poona. Since Birla was the closest to Gandhi, J.R.D. and the others wanted him to get Gandhi's opinion on the Plan. J.R.D. was worried that Gandhi may express a view, which would then be used to discredit them. Their fears were not entirely unfounded. When Agarwal's *The Gandhian Plan of Economic Development for India* was published, it had a foreword written by Gandhi, who praised it as one which was 'in full sympathy for the way of life for which I stand'.[24]

The choice of Dalal as member was influenced by the government's attitude towards Indian industrialists. Amery wrote to Wavell that whoever was appointed would have to show that he was as bold in his conceptions as the Bombay planners but more practical. Wavell wrote back to Amery that Gregory had exposed the hollowness of the Plan and concluded that it was 'not really a plan at all, but only a statement of aims supported by a number of arguments none of which would hold water'.[25] The idea was to show the planners that government was both more capable and willing to help the industrialists than the Congress, with its idée fixe about immediate and unqualified power. Thus, apart from its administrative uses, Dalal's appointment was also a way of weaning the industrialist away from the Congress. It was the government's animosity towards the Congress and its efforts to dissociate the powerful industrialists that determined its response to the Plan. Dalal's appointment was a significant victory in this regard. With one of the authors of the Plan heading the planning department, and with the others included in one or the other policy committees under that department, the government could claim to have rallied the entire group of industrialists to the cause of planning.[26]

Matthai, Homi Mody and the Sapru Committee

Even though the Bombay Plan did not mention the partition of the country, the planners laid down the essentials of what they wished independent India to be in economic terms. They clearly implied that a divided India was preferable to big business rather than a united India weakened by divisive forces.

The Non-Party Leaders' Conference was held in Delhi on 7 February 1944. Towards the end of the year, its standing committee set up a committee, the Sapru Committee on Constitutional Reforms to look into the communal and minorities question from a constitutional and political angle and submit its recommendations within two months. One of the members of this committee was Sir Homi Mody, who in turn nominated a subcommittee consisting of himself, Matthai and Nalini Ranjan Sarkar, a former finance minister of West Bengal, to look into the financial implications of Pakistan. Sarkar could not attend the meetings of the subcommittee and it was left to Mody and Matthai to submit their memorandum on the subject. The study was later also published independently in 1945 as *A Memorandum on the Economic and Financial Aspects of Pakistan.*

While the main committee, headed by Tej Bahadur Sapru, recommended a united India, Matthai and Mody disagreed and signed a note of dissent. They believed that if a scheme that presupposed the political unity of India was unacceptable to the Muslim community, and if the forthcoming elections vindicated the Muslim League position, then Partition should not be ruled out. In their note, they said that the political problems admitted of no delay and that the direction of political affairs should be placed in the hand of leaders who enjoyed the confidence of the people. Mody wrote another note, in which he bluntly declared that he was not in favour of ignoring the Pakistan demand and that the events of the last few years should not be forgotten.[27]

Matthai and Mody analysed in detail the economic consequences of Partition. They assumed that Pakistan would consist of two economic zones and visualized two possible scenarios. In the first, Partition would be carried out according to the then existing boundaries of provinces, and the Muslim-majority provinces would form the new state. In the second, the boundaries would be redrawn according to the contiguous Muslim-majority districts of Punjab and Bengal. They believed that Pakistan would be a viable economic unit if Partition was carried out province-wise. If, however, the boundaries were drawn on the basis of Muslim-majority districts, Pakistan would not find itself in a good position. In both cases, they stressed the need for co-operation between the two states in economic and defence matters, emphasizing that a large free-trade zone would be essential for the future development of both economies. They advocated the concept of the 'optimum economic unit', under which the two nations would have minimum customs barriers and large-scale trade. They also spoke of a common policy on defence.[28]

Matthai and Mody concluded that if the objective was to maintain existing standards of living and budgetary requirements on a pre-war basis (excluding defence), Partition was feasible on economic grounds. However, if the goal was to raise the general standard of living, then this could only be achieved with effective co-operation between the nations in the areas of defence and the economy. Without such cooperation, Partition would prove to be an economic disaster for the newly formed states. They believed that so long as political separation did not prevent a free exchange of raw materials and finished products, Partition appeared to be quite feasible.

Their study emphasized the dominant position of Calcutta in the future division of the country and without it, eastern Pakistan would be little more than a rural slum. They succeeded in establishing the importance of Calcutta in the minds of the business leaders and the importance of retaining it in India.[29] The third member, Sarkar, even though he had taken limited part in the deliberations of the subcommittee, disagreed with Mody and Matthai. He believed that the division, both province-wise and district-wise, as proposed by them would be highly prejudicial to Pakistan and he concluded that Pakistan was not a practical proposition either economically or financially.[30]

Long before Matthai and Mody made their study, Dalal had, in February 1943, looked at the consequences of Partition in his *An*

Alternative to Pakistan, in which he stressed how difficult it would be for Pakistan's economy to function efficiently after its separation from India. He urged Hindus to make concessions to the Muslims so that the country could remain united. Birla's *Eastern Economist* too had in a series of studies focused on the economic implications of Pakistan. It predicted that Pakistan would become an economically viable entity only after a decade. Birla himself explored this issue in his *Basic Facts Relating to Hindustan and Pakistan*, published in June 1947.

However, any hopes of economic cooperation between the two new states were dashed with the bloodshed that accompanied Partition. A few days before India became independent, Matthai, then serving as member for industry and supply in the interim government, noted that he had not anticipated the horrible consequences that Partition would have for the economy.

A Modern Plan

When Matthai, who wrote both parts of the Plan, solicited the opinion of H.V.R Iengar, an ICS officer who later became governor of the RBI, Iengar told him that he was very impressed by the broad sweep of the document and the manner in which various parts had been worked out in detail and integrated into the whole. Three decades later, while delivering the John Matthai Memorial Lecture at Kerala University, Iengar said that he was amazed as to how modern the Bombay Plan was conceptually. Further, he observed that while the Five-Year Plans initiated by India had focused only on growth, the Bombay Plan had also considered the distributive aspect when it was published many years ago. [31] The Bombay planners were perhaps the only capitalists in the world to draft an economic plan with a strong social concern. In many ways, it was the inspiration for India's first Five-Year Plan.

More than four decades later, in 1986, when R. Venkataraman, then vice president of India, spoke at the launch of J.R.D.'s book of speeches, *Keynote*, he recalled that the Bombay Plan was one of J.R.D.'s contributions to India. Modest and self-deprecating as always, J.R.D. said: 'My only contribution to it was to arrange for the Bombay Plan to be written. It was done mainly by Dr John Matthai, but after considerable discussion.'[32]

Unfortunately, the hopes of the planners were belied when controls and industrial licensing—the measures they had proposed to ensure more equitable economic progress—turned into a maze of controls and red tape, which mushroomed at an alarming pace. After Independence, a series of inquiries were instituted against big business houses to probe war profiteering. Nehru's leftist pronouncements added to the uncertainty. The adoption of a socialistic pattern only added to their insecurity. When the Second Five-Year Plan showed below par results, they became a bitter critic of planning the way it was being implemented by the government. They realized that government itself had become a bottleneck.

The public sector was expected to grow not only in absolute terms but also relative to the private sector. The Industrial Policy Resolution adopted in 1956 increased the number of industries reserved for the public sector. By the mid-1950s, there existed a wide gulf between the business leaders and the government. Ironically, as we shall see later, Matthai resigned from the cabinet over differences with Nehru on the role of the Planning Commission. By the mid-1960s, the license-permit-raj was in full bloom.

In this connection, it would be illuminating to take a look at Matthai's views on nationalization. In a talk to the Rotary Club, Bombay, in June 1956, Matthai said that there were conditions in which state enterprises were required but believed that free enterprise should be the normal practice. If an industry was to be nationalized, the case for it should be established beyond doubt.[33] He also said that the impression that nationalization was an essential element in socialism was not supported by socialist thinking or practice. He wanted the government to proceed with caution in the matter of nationalization and wanted it to be limited in scope and applied selectively to specific industries and not categories of industries.[34] When an industry was to be nationalized, Matthai said, two things were important: Firstly, there should be a good case for it in the national interest and secondly, the public and interested parties should be educated as to the grounds on which the decision was taken.[35] Matthai voiced his concern at the loose talk of nationalization going on in high places at the time.

> I do so not merely because the country needs all the free enterprise now available for its development but because I see no justification, either practical or ideological, for the decline resulting from government policy in freedom of enterprise, which in reality is one of the greatest freedoms in a democratic community.[36]

Even though each one of the authors of the Plan were terribly disillusioned, and did not play the role they had expected to play in independent India's economic policymaking, at a personal level, they continued to serve on government committees when called upon to do so. Individually, they may have been marginalized, but their influence as a body was evident in India's Five-Year Plans. The Bombay Plan served as a reference point for all these plans, and it is perhaps no exaggeration to say that even the Planning Commission was inspired by it. Iengar asserted that it was all there in the Bombay Plan: the concept of massive state intervention in the economy, a mixed economy with the coexistence of private- and public-sector enterprises, the emphasis on heavy industry, and the need for foreign capital and deficit financing. Notwithstanding the influence on India's Five-Year Plans, it is thought that perhaps the most significant legacy of the Plan was in legitimizing the idea of planning.

The National Planning Committee's Subcommittee

When Nehru was released from jail in June 1945, he decided to revive the NPC, which was in a dormant state since 1940. In September, an informal meeting was held in Bombay. The members of the NPC who attended included K.T. Shah, Ambalal Sarabhai, Nazir Ahmed and J.K. Mehta. J.R.D. and Matthai also attended as special invitees. This meeting resulted in the formation of a subcommittee consisting of C.V. Mehta, A.D. Shroff, Manu Subedar and Matthai with K.T. Shah as the convenor. The purpose of the subcommittee was to prepare a list of priorities for the NPC to consider after taking into account all the developments that had taken place during the period when it had been largely inactive. [37]

The priorities subcommittee met in October and reiterated the stand of the NPC on the priority of industrialization in planning. The state was to have a monopoly in heavy and defence industries, and exercise control over all industries through fiscal policy and price fixation of important industrial and agricultural products. The subcommittee also placed emphasis on technological and industrial research initiated by the state. The state, it was assumed would be a federal democracy in which the claims of the federating units would be taken into consideration. At the first full and formal meeting of the NPC held in November 1945, the recommendations of the subcommittee were accepted and instructions issued to incorporate them in the main report.[38]

The Tragedy in New York

In March 1944, two months after the announcement of the Bombay Plan, tragedy struck the Matthai family. Matthai and Achamma's first-born child and only daughter, Valsa, was reported missing in New York. Valsa, who was pursuing a course in journalism at Colombia University, was last seen alive when she left International House, the massive thirteen-storey lodging place built by John D. Rockefeller Jr for foreign students, at 4.50 a.m. on 20 March. It had snowed heavily through the night and before dawn it lay eight inches deep on the streets of sleeping Manhattan.[39] Another report held that Valsa had returned after a dance recital she had given for the benefit of Indian relief and that she had disappeared into the building and not outside it. This theory was later disproved by subsequent events.

Valsa never returned, and the reason why she left her room early in the morning remains a mystery. She was not missed for more than twenty-hour hours. Then Pritha Kumarappa, an Indian student, and Salma Bishlawy, an Egyptian, two of Valsa's closest friends, went to her room to check on her. The key was in the outside lock and the bed had not been slept on. Her room and her clothes were in order; even her purse was there, with lipstick, identity cards and $17 in cash.

At first, it seemed like a routine disappearance to detectives of the West 100th Street police station. But after a few days, the search had spread across the US, with the Federal Bureau of Investigation, the state department and even British diplomatic circles joining the extensive search. Suspecting foul play, the detectives of West 100th Street police station made a thorough search of International House. Apart from thoroughly searching the 550 rooms of the building, they drained the water tanks and shovelled their way through 150 tons of pea coal. They found no clues as to what had become of her, or to the inevitable questions that followed her disappearance. Where was she going in the snow before dawn? If she was dead, then where was her body? In case she was still alive, had anyone seen her?[40]

The police questioned taxi drivers, residents of the area and ticket sellers at the Hudson River ferry terminals. The Hudson was dragged but all efforts proved futile. It did not appear to be a planned disappearance. Usually, people who attempt to vanish are in search of love or money. Valsa had $1400 in her bank account, a large sum in those days, so money was obviously not a concern. She was known to be on friendly terms with a young officer, Lieutenant Elmer Rigby of the Army Medical Corps and the two had met on the afternoon before her disappearance. However, the casual and friendly tone of the letter that Valsa had written to the young officer, and which he showed to the police, did not point to a romantic attachment.

Valsa's friends told the police that she was brilliant and interested in her studies. She smoked and also visited nightclubs occasionally in groups. But a different picture emerged as the police dug deeper. She was an habitue of nightclubs and sat at nightspot tables with American girls and American and British officers night after night. Her friends reluctantly admitted that she had hangovers, missed classes and was repeating first-semester subjects. Pregnancy and amnesia were both ruled out. At the end of it all, the police still knew nothing about what had happened to Valsa. There was also still no answer as to why she had left her room at 4.50 a.m. that fateful morning.

J.J. Singh, president of the India League of America and the 'One Man Lobby' for India in America, thought he had the answer: Valsa had never seen snow, and was so fascinated that she could not resist walking out into it. Captain John J. Cronin, who was in charge of the investigation, and a student of abnormal psychology, pondered this idea seriously because he knew that sensitive people depressed by rain, snow or bleak landscapes are sometimes driven to suicide. When all investigations drew a blank, Cronin saw only one real possibility: Valsa had drowned in the Hudson River. There had been numerous cases of bodies turning up months later, and especially after thunderstorms.

Cronin's hunch proved to be right. On 18 May, three days after a thunderstorm, and nearly two months after she disappeared, Valsa's body was found floating near Yonkers, a city on the Hudson River in Westchester County, New York. The discovery brought to an end a mystery that had puzzled everyone and caused untold sadness to Matthai and Achamma. It is said that the first-ever habeas corpus in India was the one filed by Matthai for Valsa. The delay in the discovery of her body had raised everyone's hopes in Bombay, including that of J.R.D., who wrote about it in his letter of condolence to Achamma.

J.R.D. seems to have made a brief acquaintance with Valsa before she left for the US. 'I had not known Valsa very long before she left for the States but that she was an unusually intelligent and attractive girl with a bright future was self-evident as were also the bonds of love and understanding between her and her parents.'[41] In another letter written at the end of December 1943, J.R.D. thanked Matthai for sending him Valsa's letter, which he had read with 'much interest and amusement'. He noted, 'I bet you are pretty proud of your daughter and, rightly too!'[42]

In the same letter, he told Matthai why he approved of Valsa going to the US:

I am very glad you sent her to the States as it is young Indians like her who in contact with American youth can best help to remove the silly ideas and misconceptions about India which bogus yogis and our dear rulers have planted there. For this reason and also because I believe that American ideas and American drive and zest for doing big things will be badly wanted here to carry out the great development which we all look forward to, I wish more Indian students going abroad would go to America instead of England whose conservatism and traditionalism is the last thing we shall want.[43]

According to Syloo Matthai, it had been decided to send Valsa to Sommerville College, Oxford, but it was J.R.D. who thought that she should go to the United States for further studies. Since Valsa had shown a talent for writing she enrolled at Columbia University to study journalism.[44]

When news was received of the discovery of Valsa's body, J.R.D. wrote a touching letter to Achamma on 18 May 1944. He said that the lack of news all these weeks 'had led many of us to feel with increasing confidence that the solution of the mystery might lie elsewhere'. He offered his, and his wife Thelma's deepest condolences, saying that he realized how little use words were at such dark moments in one's life. 'Nevertheless, I hope you may derive some measure of consolation from the knowledge that your friends feel deeply for you and share your sorrow, none more than Thelly and myself.'[45]

He ended with a postscript: 'Please do not take the trouble of answering the letter.' Enclosed with J.R.D.'s letter was Thelma Tata's own brief note to supplement what her husband had written. 'We all had such hopes that there would be some good news – but God willed otherwise – may he grant you the strength to bear this terrible loss.'[46]

Jamshed J. Bhabha, scientist Homi J. Bhabha's younger brother, who was in Tatas, also wrote to Achamma. He said that it was with hesitation that he was writing to express sympathy on behalf of his mother and on his own behalf at the tragic loss the Matthai's had suffered. 'Knowing how closely knit (like our own) your family was, we realise how profound must be your grief after the long period of terrible and fruitless suspense, and how futile must appear the attempts of friends to console'.[47]

It is said Matthai had a habit of saying, 'Life is grim business'. Valsa's tragic death was undoubtedly the saddest incident of his life. Syloo Matthai narrated how her in-laws maintained a studied silence about Valsa. Her husband Ravi, however, did not hesitate to speak about her when required.

PART II

6

The Interim Government

Though the seeds of the interim government were sown before the end of the Second World War, the idea of Indianization of the viceroy's executive council could only be made public with the shift in mood following the war. The failure of the Cripps Mission (1942), the subsequent Quit India Movement and imprisonment of Congress leaders led to Britain's 'Indian problem' worsening. The growth of the Muslim League only made the matter more complex. Thus, the Simla Conference in 1945 and the Cabinet Mission sent by Prime Minister Clement Attlee in 1946, were both responses to deteriorating conditions.

When the Cabinet Mission's talks in the summer of 1946 failed to produce a settlement, the viceroy, Lord Wavell, decided to form an interim government composed of representatives of the Congress, the Muslim League and smaller minority communities. On 22 July 1946, he wrote to both Nehru and Jinnah inviting them to join an interim coalition government. He thought that there should be fourteen members in the cabinet: six of them from the Congress, five from the Muslim League and the other three representing minority interests. The important portfolios would be divided equally between the Congress and the League. He made it clear that neither the Congress nor the Muslim League would be entitled to object to the names submitted by the other party, if they were acceptable to the viceroy. Both Nehru and Jinnah rejected the proposal creating a complete deadlock. In all probability, Gandhi, who was a ruthlessly sharp political negotiator, also played a role. As Matthai said in 1947, the final failure to reach a satisfactory settlement with the Muslim League stemmed in part from the 'Gujarati mentality' of the Congress leadership—'i.e., that of a trader driving a hard bargain'.[1]

To break the deadlock, the Secretary of State for India asked the viceroy to request Nehru to form the government. On 6 August 1946, Wavell invited Nehru to form the government. On 17 August, Nehru asked the viceroy to allow him to form a full-strength ministry by filling the five Muslim seats with non-League Muslims. Wavell demurred and asked Nehru to leave the Muslim seats vacant. On 24 August, a communiqué was issued from Delhi, declaring that the new executive council would take charge on 2 September.

The Congress formed the interim government. Nehru, Patel, Rajendra Prasad, Sarat Chandra Bose, Chakravarti Rajagopalachari and Jagjivan Ram were nominated to the cabinet. The three minority positions were filled by Sardar Baldev Singh (Sikh), C.H. Bhabha (Parsi), and John Matthai (Indian Christian). Three Muslims—Asaf Ali, Sir Shafaat Ahmad Khan and Syed Ali Zaheer—were also included in the government, while two Muslim seats were left vacant. Nehru wrote to Wavell that some of the members, including Matthai, would join later, after a week or so, due to ill health or other reasons and said that some temporary arrangements would have to be made till then. (Matthai joined on 13 September.) The Muslim League rejected the idea of a one-party government and Jinnah declared that Wavell had gone back on his earlier commitments. The Muslim League observed a protest day on 2 September, flying black flags on their houses and shops throughout India.

The Muslim League Joins

However, Jinnah soon realized that Muslim interests could be better served if the League joined the government. On 13 October, he wrote to Wavell that he had come to the conclusion that it would be 'fatal to leave the entire field of administration of the Central Government in the hands of the Congress'[2] and moreover the interim government might include Muslims who would not command the 'respect and confidence of Muslim India'.[3] A series of meetings took place between Jinnah and Wavell and ultimately the League joined the government on 25 October. Sarat Chandra Bose, Shafaat Ahmad Khan and Syed Ali Zaheer resigned to make way for the Muslim League ministers.

But it was an uneasy modus vivendi from the start. The Congress was unhappy with the way the League was included in the government. In a letter Nehru wrote to Wavell on 26 October, he complained that the choice of ministers itself indicated a desire to have conflict rather than to work in co-operation. At a speech given at the Meerut Congress on 21 November, after handing over the Congress presidentship to J.B. Kripalani, Nehru said, 'It was clear from Mr. Jinnah's statements that the League entered the government not to work it but because they feared they would be weakened if they kept out.'[4]

From the beginning, the League considered itself a separate bloc and acted accordingly. Every effort was made by them to take the help of the British government and oppose the national struggle. The Congress also resented the fact that Jinnah had decided to join the government on Wavell's and not Nehru's request. Jinnah had also made it clear that the Muslim League members of the cabinet would not be answerable to Nehru. To make matters worse, the Muslim League had nominated a scheduled-caste Hindu, Jogendra Nath Mandal, as a cabinet member. This, it was thought could challenge the Congress's claim of being the sole representative of the deprived classes.

Matthai was invited to join the government in July, presumably as a representative of the Christian community. He was then on leave from Tatas and was holidaying at Kodaikanal. It was not something he was expecting. Till then, he had taken no part in the political life of the country, nor had he held any position in an organization representing the Christian community. Politics had little attraction for him—his time and energy were occupied by his work in Tatas. An undecided Matthai did not immediately reply to the viceroy's invitation, preferring instead for a clearer picture to emerge. He also wanted time to consult his colleagues in Tatas whose advice he valued. Meanwhile, there were reports in the newspapers about a possible disagreement between the viceroy and the Congress regarding the formation of the interim government. Since Matthai's opinions on public matters had brought him nearer the Congress than any other political body, he sent a non-committal reply to Lord Wavell asking for more time. Events showed that Matthai had judged the situation well. In the end, Wavell's proposal to form an interim government did not materialize and Matthai resumed his duties with Tatas when his leave ended in July.

In August, Wavell invited the Congress to form a government by themselves, leaving it open to the Muslim League to join later. The Congress accepted the offer, Matthai's name once again found a place among those invited to join the government. Matthai observed:

Ostensibly the invitation came to me in my capacity as a member of
the Christian community, although I gather later that my previous
experience in administration, business and academic economics was the
real reason for my choice, and the fact that I was a member of a minority
community only provided a political justification for my appointment.[5]

Matthai's being a Christian was a political justification for what was
essentially a meritocratic appointment. Matthai heard of the proposal to
appoint him from Nehru, who was passing through Bombay on his way
back from Wardha, where the Congress Working Committee had met to
discuss Wavell's offer.

Matthai may have been chosen for his technical acumen, but the fact
remains that he was a member of a minority community as well. He says that
his previous contacts with the different sections of the Church helped him
in facing the responsibilities that fell to him as a Christian member of the
first cabinet of free India.[6] In the wide variety of Christian denominations
that prevailed in India, he found his varied experience a useful basis for
emphasizing the essential unity of the Church and the need, particularly in
the new situation in India, for a common organization and policy.

He said that in the Constituent Assembly formed for drawing up
the Constitution, the chief responsibility for looking after the interests
of the Christian community was handled with ability and success by two
eminent Indian Christian leaders, Dr H.C. Mookerji, a Protestant lay
leader and Father J. D'Souza of the Society of Jesus, who between them
represented the two important wings of the Church. They worked in such
close unison with each other that it was a pleasure to co-operate with them.
Matthai observed,

> Their labours in the Constituent Assembly have resulted in the inclusion
> of suitable provisions in the Constitution for effectively safeguarding the
> interests of the Christian Community ... As a member of the government,
> I did not take a direct part in these negotiations but confined myself to
> informal meetings and consultations with these two leaders.[7]

Matthai Joins the Interim Government

Matthai resigned from Tata Sons on 31 August 1946. Writing to him on
3 September, J.R.D. Tata said that his resignation had been placed before

the directors and that he was enclosing a copy of the resolution the board had passed. J.R.D. wrote feelingly about Matthai's departure. It is obvious that Matthai's many sterling qualities, not least his unimpeachable honesty and sagacious advice, had greatly endeared him to the chairman of Tatas.

> Parting with you is a great wrench to me and to all of us here, but it is some consolation to know that you are leaving us to fill a role of such national importance, and that we are indirectly contributing to this great purpose. I know that you are not going to have an easy time, and that your burden will be a heavy one, but I know also that no one is better fitted for the task then you are, and that in the sphere with which you will be concerned, the destinies of the country will be in safe hands.[8]

J.R.D. went on to say that it had been a privilege to have Matthai as a colleague and a friend and hoped that the Tatas and his own loss would not be a permanent one and they would have the pleasure of welcoming him back in the not too distant future.[9] The board of Tata Sons in its resolution accepted his resignation with 'great regret' and placed on record their appreciation of his services. They wished him all success in his new assignment and looked forward to welcoming him back soon.

Maulana Abul Kalam Azad, who did not know Matthai personally, wrote a very warm letter to him in February 1947, when he became Matthai's cabinet colleague, remembering that 'Jawaharlal and I were both of the opinion that there could be no better choice for the Finance portfolio...'[10] Matthai says that he was less hesitant to join the government this time given that the invitation had been conveyed to him personally by Nehru. In the early part of their association, at least, Matthai was a great admirer of Nehru.

> He made an enormous impression on me. I can hardly think of any person with whom my first contact has been quite so thrilling an experience. His wonderfully expressive face, his romantic past, his conversation and whole personality so unselfconscious, his complete oneness with all that was good in India—all these made the prospect of working under his leadership something altogether irresistible. I have always disliked physical discomfort. But I remember vividly my feelings after my first meeting with Pandit Nehru, that if he ever asked me to go to prison with him, I should find it difficult to refuse.[11]

Matthai's relationship with Nehru would change due to differences that arose between them due to their divergent views on the role of the Planning Commission a few years later, but in his recollections, Matthai said that he still regarded Nehru as one of the most inspiring men he had ever met. At the time of the formation of the interim government, Tatas had been considering various schemes of expansion and needed all their experienced personnel, particularly in the top management. Knowing this, Matthai was reluctant to ask for permission to leave them and join the interim government. This difficult choice was taken out of his hands and settled for him by J.R.D., whom Matthai called 'a man of rare understanding and public spirit'[12]. J.R.D. decided to fly to Delhi to personally discuss the question with Nehru and his colleagues, who were then engaged in discussing the details of the new government with Wavell. It was decided that Tatas would release Matthai for the period of the interim government, which was then not expected to last more than a couple of years, and that in the meantime, if Tatas was short of senior personnel, the government would agree to Matthai rejoining Tatas. It was on these terms that Matthai joined the government as finance member in September 1946.[13]

Matthai's personal finances also took a sizeable hit when he agreed to join the government. But money meant little to a man like him. His views on money are best conveyed in what he told Parliament in March 1949 when he was finance minister. He said that life was just as interesting and enjoyable as it had been when he was earning a multiple of his present salary. The things that mattered most in life were interesting work, wholesome food, the pleasures of family life and the enjoyment of nature and art and reading a few good books. '. . . it does not seem to me the difference between a high level of income and a moderate level of income makes any difference whatsoever'.[14]

It appears that Wavell's first choice for the finance portfolio was not Matthai but C.D. Deshmukh, who was RBI governor at the time. The latter gives us some details in his memoirs. On 23 May 1946, Wavell wrote to Deshmukh asking him to consider becoming finance member. He said the final decision would depend on the reaction of the political parties concerned, but he wanted to know if Deshmukh himself was open to the idea. Deshmukh politely declined saying that by temperament and training, he was unsuited to the exigencies of a political post and what was more, could render better service in his technical position and with possibly greater continuity.[15] Deshmukh recommended Matthai's name for the post to his friends V.P. Menon and Shavax Lal. Deshmukh recalled, 'As it happened, Matthai was offered the post and accepted it; but he did not retain it long (and the same thing would have happened to me had I accepted earlier.)'[16]

It was expected that C. Rajagopalachari and Matthai would divide the Finance and Industry and Supply portfolios between themselves. Rajagopalachari ultimately chose Industry and Supply leaving Matthai with Finance, unwilling to shoulder the heavy responsibility the portfolio brought with it. Nehru and Azad then proposed Matthai's name, well aware of his aptitude for and knowledge of economic affairs. Azad wrote to him saying that Matthai's 'attitude of moderation and compromise on all communal questions as well as relations between the Congress and the League, practical attitude, constructive and cautious attitude on political questions, dispassionate judgement and constructive statesmanship'[17] would be very valuable in the coalition.

Writing about the formation of the interim government many years later, the non-Congress, non-League Matthai recalled that in forming it, the Congress

> [T]ook a wise step when it invited some men having no party affiliations to join. It gave the country a feeling of confidence ... that the somewhat rigid orthodoxies by which the Congress had bound itself as a movement would be relaxed with the responsibilities of government. Moreover, it was a clear recognition on the part of the Congress that the main problems facing the country were not political in character but were concerned with daily needs.[18]

Matthai's first feeling on entering the room of the finance member in the secretariat was a revival of unpleasant memories of the encounters he used to have in his official days with a former finance member, Sir James Grigg. Matthai's assessment of one of his predecessors is rather uncomplimentary. Matthai called him an 'odd character, a clever man but totally lacking in appreciation of the better side of Indian life'. As a man of finance, his abilities were mediocre, but he made up for it by 'assertiveness in argument' and by 'pungent phrasing' which he employed in his discussions with officials and also in his file notings. Matthai observed, 'He left behind him as Finance Member little by which he might be remembered. Among the many Britishers who held the Finance portfolio, there is none whose budget speeches provided less guidance for those who followed him, and showed less vision and understanding of the broader aspects of Indian finance.'[19]

One of the important matters facing Matthai when he took over charge had to do with the problem arising out of the disparity between the controlled prices of Indian cotton and the higher prices ruling in foreign markets. On 4 October 1946, Matthai, Rajagopalachari and C.H. Bhabha discussed the issue in the presence of Purshotamdas Thakurdas and Haridas Madhavdas, president and vice president, respectively, of the East India Cotton Association. In view of the disparity, it was decided to impose an export duty of Rs 20 per bale on all cotton leaving the country. The cabinet accepted the proposal and promulgated an ordinance to that effect at the end of October. It was also decided to discontinue control over prices of jute and jute goods and to levy an enhanced duty on raw and manufactured jute goods. The jute growers could now enjoy the benefits of world prices.

Matthai Makes Way for Liaquat Ali Khan

However, Matthai was destined to hold the finance portfolio for only a very short period. When the Muslim League decided to join the government two months later, the Finance Membership was given to the Muslim League, who nominated Liaquat Ali Khan to the office. Rajagopalachari, considering Matthai's close connection with Indian industries for many years, volunteered to transfer Industry and Supply to him and accept Education in its place. Matthai held this portfolio from 26 October 1946 to 13 January 1947.

Matthai says that he was not privy to the negotiations that preceded the formation of the coalition government in October 1946. It had been assumed at the beginning that there would be no change in the finance portfolio and therefore Matthai thought his position was safe. But he had not reckoned with the demands of the Muslim League. The League was very keen on getting the home department and this demand led at one stage to what appeared to be a complete deadlock. It was at this stage that Matthai was summoned to a meeting of the Congress Working Committee with Gandhi in New Delhi.

Matthai discovered that the committee was prepared to transfer Finance in lieu of Home to the Muslim League. This was partly because of the inherent importance of the home department and partly because its holder, Sardar Patel, was such an outstanding figure in the Congress that its surrender would have been a blow to Congress prestige and difficult to explain to the party. By all accounts, Patel himself was unwilling to relinquish charge of the home portfolio and when Wavell tried to convince him to do so, Patel said that he was willing to give up home but, with that, to leave the government altogether.[20] When Wavell was informed about the decision to transfer Matthai, the viceroy told Nehru that he was reluctant to move Matthai from the finance portfolio in view of the latter's special knowledge of economic and financial matters. It was also because as Wavell put it 'Dr Matthai has the confidence of Mr. Jinnah'. Lord Wavell's letter was read to the Working Committee in Matthai's presence and, given the existing relations between the Congress and the Muslim League, caused him much embarrassment.[21]

From 12 October, the negotiations on portfolios for the entry of the Muslim League in the interim government dominated the scene. Jinnah told Wavell that he wanted either External Affairs or Defence. He was prepared to leave Finance with Matthai and suggested a redistribution of portfolios, with the Muslim League taking Defence, Commerce, Transport, Posts and Air, and Law. Over the next two days Wavell, Jinnah and Nehru exchanged letters to decide on portfolios for the League. Matthai was the consensus choice for Finance, and it was felt that Baldev too should continue in Defence. Nehru wanted to retain External Affairs. But that meant that Patel would have to surrender Home if the League was to get one of the big four departments.

The list of ministers Jinnah sent to Wavell also held some surprises: Liaquat Ali Khan, I.I. Chundrigar, Abdur Rab Nishtar, Ghazanfar Ali Khan and J.N. Mandal. Chundrigar from Bombay and Khan from Punjab were complete unknowns. Azad wrote, 'They were dark horses about whom even members of the League had little information.'[22] Jinnah deliberately bypassed moderate leaders such as Khwaja Nazimuddin and Ismail Khan, who had a national reputation and were widely expected to be nominated, selecting his henchmen instead. The inclusion of a scheduled caste member, J.N. Mandal, was an obvious counter to the right claimed by the Congress to nominate a Muslim.

Nehru confirmed to Wavell that Home would remain with Patel and also made it clear that he deeply regretted the choice the League had made saying that it indicated a desire to have conflicts.[23] Nevertheless, Wavell, who was disappointed with the names Jinnah had suggested, continued to be sanguine about the future interim government believing that it would do a lot of good and produce a more accommodating spirit after a few weeks of joint administration.

While acknowledging that it was not the cabinet he would have chosen, Wavell tried to persuade Jinnah and Liaquat not to insist on Home or Defence. The next few days were full of tension and Wavell feared that the interim government would not outlive the cradle. Meanwhile, the Congress had agreed to part with Finance and Commerce. Eventually the tug-of-war ended when Jinnah agreed to accept the portfolios offered. The three other portfolios Jinnah accepted were Posts and Air, Health and Legislative. He nominated Liaquat to Finance, Chundrigar to Commerce, Nishtar to Posts and Air, Ghazanfar to Health and Mandal to Legislative. Nehru would continue as leader of the House and Nishtar would be leader of the Council of State.[24] Wavell's thoughts on the eve of the swearing-in of the League ministers summed up the challenges he faced. He felt that the distribution of portfolios showed the difficulty of settling matters between the two parties and considered that the agreement reached itself represented an achievement.[25]

The assembly reconvened on 26 October 1946 and the new cabinet took its place there. Matthai was given the Industries and Supplies portfolio, one that he held till 13 January 1947, when he took over as Railways and Transport Minister from Asaf Ali. The atmosphere was cordial with Nehru and Liaquat sitting next to each other. Patel, Asaf Ali and Chundrigar shared the bench next to them. On the first afternoon, Matthai backed up a speech by Liaquat on a resolution on Bretton Woods. At his press conference, Liaquat said that nowhere in the world did a government like the present one exist and it was a novel experiment. He said that they had entered government 'with the intention of working with our other colleagues – but you cannot clap with one hand'.[26] According to Jinnah's biographer, Hector Bolitho, 'The two hands did not clap together, and the Interim Government achieved nothing of enduring value.'[27] (Subsequent research has shown that such a sweeping statement requires qualification. Such an analysis, however, is beyond the scope of this book.)

Matthai in his all too brief tenure as minister of industry and supplies was responsible for introducing the Rubber (Production and Marketing) Bill, 1946, which laid a strong foundation for the development of the rubber industry in India. On the termination of the Rubber Control and

Production Order, which expired on 30 September 1946, it was thought necessary to establish a statutory body to look after the interest of rubber producers in India.

Matthai, Wavell and Mountbatten

During his tenure of office, Matthai came in touch with the last two British viceroys of India, Wavell and Mountbatten. He says that they formed an extraordinary contrast to each other and since they were both Englishmen 'the English national character must be presumed to be a strange amalgam of irreconcilable traits'[28]. Wavell was the strong silent type who communicated his thoughts by his behaviour and by the changing expression of his face. Matthai recalled that he talked so little that even a half an hour conversation with him became 'a somewhat difficult ordeal'.[29] The conversation invariably began with the usual question, 'Anything important in your department?' Matthai, who did his homework well, would pause at the end of each subject for some response but seldom got any.[30]

There were times when silence extended into discomfort. During these awkward intervals, Wavell kept 'fingering and moving' a large variety of pencils of many colours that he always kept on his table. Matthai was put off at first, but as he got to know him better, he discovered that although Wavell did not follow the technical details of the subjects, he had a firm grasp of essentials and was a shrewd judge of men. He read the character of each individual in his new cabinet quite accurately—and when occasionally he allowed himself to talk about them, he did so with a sense of humour, which coming from a man of such few words was irresistible. Matthai called him a man of deep human sympathies, which he showed by kindly deeds rather than by words. But he lacked political judgement and the instinct for subtle compromise. Matthai observes, 'It was a serious lack in the school which faced him in India and in the end led to his premature retirement.'[31]

J.R.D. had a somewhat similar experience to narrate when he first met Wavell, only this time the pencils were replaced by four rows of paperweights. A silent Wavell lifted the paperweights and moved them from one place to another as J.R.D. watched. J.R.D. said that he had the bright idea of stretching out his hand, lifting a paperweight and surprising Wavell by saying, 'Checkmate! General.' He recalled that a smile broke out on his face at the thought and that was when Wavell lifted his single eye (one of his eyes had been replaced with a glass eye) and found his guest grinning at him for no apparent reason.[32]

It appears that things didn't go very well at that first meeting. Wavell in a diary entry written in late January 1944 called J.R.D. 'conceited and unhelpful' and after meeting him for lunch in April of the same year, called him 'a supercilious and tiresome young man' in another diary entry.[33] It was obvious that the two didn't share the same chemistry. The genial J.R.D. had been unable to find a personal equation with the viceroy. It was at that lunch meeting that Wavell broached the subject of sparing Sir Ardeshir Dalal to join the viceroy's executive council. Wavell thought that J.R.D. was pleased that the offer had been made but was not so sure the Tatas could spare him. Many of the top Tata men had received knighthoods (Homi Mody, Ardeshir Dalal, Sorabji Saklatvala and Jehangir Ghandy) and feelers were also sent to J.R.D. to gauge his interest in a knighthood. J.R.D. conveyed his lack of interest, and the matter was dropped.[34] Wavell might have had a personality that found it difficult to reach out to others, but he was a sensitive man who read and wrote poetry in the midst of the war. His book *Other Men's Flowers*, an anthology of English poetry— enhanced by his own introduction and annotations—was to become one of J.R.D.'s favourite books. First published in 1944, during the darkest days of the Second World War, it has remained in print ever since.

It appears that Wavell was a complex character who behaved differently with different people at different times. Sir Henry Channon, a British Member of Parliament, was Wavell's loyal friend in British political circles. Two days after his friend's death on 24 May 1950, he wrote:

> What a curious man Lord Wavell was…great in his way, full of humour, a touch deaf, with the power of shutting his mind, or almost all of it, to the assembled company…He often gave the impression of being dull… But if he liked somebody or was amused…the problem was not how to make him talk, but how to stop him…He was not a politician or a statesman…as a writer, a friend and a general he was supreme…His one eye had an uncanny way of seeing through one's weaknesses…he remained in some ways a simple soldier…[35]

Matthai encouraged Wavell by telling him that if the coalition 'could keep together for the next month or two it might turn out all right'.[36]

Nehru and Liaquat spoke sensibly on most matters, while Nishtar and Rajagopalachari were more loquacious., The others generally kept silent unless it was their subject.[37] Wavell remarked that the cabinet meetings continued to pass in a sensible atmosphere and wanted the leaders to be as reasonable outside the cabinet as inside it.[38] The League continued to oppose the Congress in the press but decided to refrain from embarrassing the government in the assembly. Consequently, a good amount of business was transacted. However, both sides made it clear that their fundamental opposition remained unchanged.[39]

Lord Mountbatten left a different impression on Matthai. His recollection of him at the first interview he had with him as a member of his executive council 'was that of a man who was terribly anxious to leave his mark behind him, who although he spoke with ability and knowledge seemed to speak primarily for effect, and who came determined not merely to fulfill but, if possible, to outdo the target set for him by the British Cabinet'.[40] He had amazing energy and an uncanny sense for spotting the people who could be of use to him. Matthai lost direct touch with him after their first few official meetings. Matthai says that Mountbatten was concerned almost entirely with the constitutional mission for which he had been sent and day-to-day administration held little interest for him. 'If I had any opportunities after my early official meetings with him of estimating his work and personality, it was largely through the reactions on my departmental duties of the constitutional changes he initiated as Viceroy and later guided in his capacity as the first Governor-General of free India.'[41]

And what did Matthai think of Jinnah, one of the main actors on the political stage at the time? Matthai had a high opinion of Jinnah, who he had first met in 1934, when the two had travelled to India by the same ship. Jinnah was returning from London at the end of his brief period of practice at the Privy Council. There were very few passengers on board and the two were thrown together a great deal and spent much of their time discussing Indian problems. Matthai observes:

> I was greatly attracted by the blunt straightforward way in which his mind worked, his instinct for getting to the root of a problem, his impatience at crookedness and hairsplitting, his amazing confidence in himself and his robust patriotism. His chief drawback was his personal vanity, but I have found by experience that vain persons are easy to

handle in negotiations because vanity presents a weak spot which can be pierced by the soft word and the delicate touch. He was then an out and out Indian nationalist, as good a nationalist as any in the country.[42]

Later, as noted before, Matthai came in touch with Jinnah again in the Legislative Assembly at the time of the debate on the Ottawa Agreements in 1936.

* * *

It was during Matthai's brief tenure as the finance member that the government took the decision to abolish the salt tax. When the Congress assumed office, Gandhi was staying in Delhi. The salt tax was to him a crying symbol of India's servitude and when the time came to fight British imperialism by openly breaking its laws, he made the demand for the abolition of the salt tax, the principal war cry for his followers. When freedom came, it was only natural that the removal of the salt duty should be uppermost in his mind.

Matthai says that almost the next day after he had assumed charge, Gandhi sent for him and asked him to take immediate steps to abolish the tax. Matthai observes that he met Gandhi several times to discuss the subject. He said that he would have preferred to postpone a final decision until he had had time to examine it in the light of the general budgetary situation. This however did not satisfy Gandhi.

> In the end we reached a settlement on the basis that while individual small-scale production would be free from duty, government would undertake large scale manufacture of salt on up-to-date lines, which at a price not higher then privately produced salt, would yield a profit to government and at the same time enable the consumer to obtain salt of good quality.[43]

This decision was finalized a few days before the Muslim League joined the government. After Liaquat Ali Khan became finance member, he decided to reopen the question and asked the cabinet to go back on the decision already arrived at. This led to much tension between the two sections of the cabinet. Since the Congress had a majority and Lord Wavell was generally opposed to any attempt by the coalition cabinet to revise the decisions of its predecessor, the original decision was allowed to stand. But Liaquat Ali Khan implemented it in a half-hearted manner. While abolishing the duty in his budget, he took no steps whatever for the large-scale expansion of the salt industry under government auspices which was an essential part of Matthai's scheme. Moreover, since the tax was removed, the finance department had little interest in the administration of salt. The subject remained a neglected one until it was transferred to the Industry and Supply Department after Partition.

In mid-February, Wavell and Liaquat met to discuss budget proposals. Since it was a coalition government, the normal practice of putting these up to the executive council one day before the budget speech could not be followed. It was decided that after Liaquat and Wavell had discussed them, Nehru and Matthai would be invited to study them. The rest of the cabinet would be taken into confidence just before the budget speech.

Liaquat Ali Khan's Budget

The coalition government's budget that Liaquat Ali Khan presented in February 1947 was a controversial one and the subject of much adverse comment. Some background is in order here. The Congress offered the finance portfolio to the League hoping that because of the technical nature of the subject, the latter would either decline the offer or soon make a fool of themselves in case they accepted it. This proved to be a serious error of judgement. The League called the Congress's bluff; they not only accepted the offer, but Liaquat Ali Khan proved that he was well-equipped to do his job.

The removal of economic inequalities and transition to a socialist pattern of society had been the two major objectives of the Congress since at least 1929 and its election manifesto of 1946 also reflected this emphasis. After the war, leaders such as Nehru and Azad publicly denounced what they called 'war profiteering' by the industrialists asking the government to take strong action against businessman who had not only earned excess profits during the war but had also indulged in large-scale tax evasion.[44] Liaquat Ali Khan took the protestations of Nehru and others seriously. He declared that his proposals were based on the declarations of responsible Congress leaders and admitted that but for Nehru's statements on the subject, he might have never thought about the matter.

Liaquat Ali Khan proposed a business profits tax (of 25 per cent on profits exceeding Rs 1 lakh per annum), which was estimated to produce Rs 30 crore, an increase of one anna in corporation tax which would generate Rs 4 crore, a changed super-tax which would yield Rs 2 crore, a dividend tax and a capital gains tax which would generate more than Rs 3 crore. He also proposed a high-powered tribunal to deal with tax evasion. This was a follow-up to the Prevention of Corruption Bill, 1946, which had been piloted by Patel in October 1946. The bill had been considered in January 1947 after consulting the provincial governments.[45] These proposals were discussed by Nehru and Matthai with Wavell and Liaquat at a meeting on 17 February. The meeting was amicable and Liaquat had no difficulty in getting Nehru and Matthai to agree with his recommendations.

Matthai vividly recalled the scene of the meeting. It was held in Wavell's study late in the evening after the Legislature had risen. The viceroy came to the meeting straight from a game of golf still wearing his golf jacket and tweeds. The four of them sat round a little table and Liaquat Ali Khan read out the main proposals. The underlying idea behind the proposals was that the excess profits tax had been removed too early and that it was necessary to find fresh taxes to take its place in view of the large, estimated deficit. Matthai says that he was in agreement with this view.[46]

In fact, during his brief tenure, Matthai himself had asked the Central Board of Revenue to examine possible sources of revenue to replace the excess profits tax. Liaquat Ali Khan's main proposals were to increase the rate and scope of the super tax and to introduce two new taxes viz. the capital gains and business profits taxes. Industrial profits were still high and large-scale evasion of taxes was rampant. Conditions in this respect had in fact not materially changed since the war ended. The belief that deflation was round the corner, the principal assumption on which Sir Archibald Rowlands, the previous finance member, had based his budget reliefs in the previous year was entirely falsified. No budget of recent years was based on such completely mistaken hypotheses as the budget presented by the last British finance member.[47] Matthai agreed with Liaquat that the 1947 budget should proceed on the assumption that war conditions still persisted. But he insisted that the new taxes should be regarded as modified as soon as conditions changed and that this should be clearly stated in the finance member's budget speech. Nehru concurred with Matthai on this.

The full cabinet heard the proposals on 28 February and were in agreement with them. Azad wrote in his memoirs that they were not against the proposals in principle but having secured their assent Liaquat proceeded to frame extreme specific measures. But later Patel and Rajagopalachari were violently opposed to his budget.[48] Before framing his budget, Liaquat Ali Khan had discussed its underlying principles with the cabinet, and at least at that time, the Congress leaders found nothing objectionable in his proposals. But once the budget was published and the reaction of big business was known, the Congress leadership did a volte face denouncing the budget as giving a most unpractical turn to Congress demands. They said that the taxes proposed would impoverish all rich men and permanently damage commerce and industry.

Patel and Rajagopalachari, who made no secret of being pro-capitalist, felt that the budget was a way of harassing businessman. They even charged that the budget was based on communal considerations since the majority of big businessman were Hindus. Other Congressmen argued in a similar vein. In a surprise move, Nehru joined Patel and C.H. Bhabha, the commerce member, in writing to Wavell on 5 February dissenting from the record of the cabinet meeting of 28 February that had earlier endorsed the budget. By then, Matthai had become Railways and Transport minister. Wavell was incensed with Nehru, who was in full sympathy with the proposals. It appeared to him that the Congress was trying to backtrack in the face of the budget's unpopularity with its big business supporters. This lack of veracity on Nehru's part also seems to have rubbed off on his biographer, S. Gopal, who wrote that Liaquat had introduced a wide-ranging budget without full discussions with his colleagues or even Nehru on at least the general nature of his proposals.[49]

Before the letter to Wavell, C.H. Bhabha had written to the cabinet secretary, Sir Eric Coates, on 3 March objecting to the way the minutes of the cabinet meeting had been worded. He objected to the words 'which the Cabinet approved'[50] saying that Liaquat had merely read out his proposals and had answered some questions. Such a matter could hardly be approved at the eleventh hour and a short meeting. Since Liaquat did not choose to take the other cabinet ministers into confidence while framing his proposals, it was therefore not proper to say that the cabinet had approved them.[51]

An angry and embarrassed Wavell noted in his diary on 5 March 1947:

Nehru, Patel and Bhabha have sent in minutes, dissenting from the record of the Cabinet meeting at which Liaquat explained his taxation proposals. The record says that the proposals were 'approved'. These minutes now say that their writers do not agree that they were approved. Poltroons, especially Nehru! They now find that the Budget is not popular with their big business supporters and are trying to rat or hedge.[52]

H.M. Patel of the ICS, who was then serving as the secretary to the interim cabinet, had something similar to say. He recalled that all the proposals had been explained to everybody in the cabinet and nobody had had any major objection at the time. He said that the fat hit the fire when the budget speech was made. The public criticism made the Congress feel that it had been misled into agreeing to something that was potentially damaging to its supporters. There was nothing that could have been considered an attack on Hindu commerce or any particular industrialist.[53]

In his reply to Bhabha on 14 March, Wavell said that the budget proposals were not circulated in advance and while it was impossible for all members of the cabinet to grasp all the detailed implications, 'the general policy of taxation must be the responsibility of the Cabinet as a whole'.[54] He said that nothing that was said in any of the meetings indicated any general disapproval of the taxation policy and he therefore considered it correct to say that the proposals were approved.

This was a desperate move to deny responsibility, but Liaquat was not wrong in claiming that the budget was the responsibility of the entire cabinet and not his alone.[55] Naturally, the budget was supported by the Muslim League and even the socialists in the Congress were happy with what they considered a 'poor man's budget'[56]. It was, however, a fact that neither Nehru nor Matthai had seen the text of the budget before it was read in the assembly.[57] According to Matthai, Liaquat in his speech seemed to assume the role of a 'Tribune of the People' launching a fiery crusade against the oppressors of the poor, principally Hindu businessmen in this case. Matthai believed that in the conditions of early 1947, the taxes were logically justified. However, they produced a psychological impression, which added to the depressing factors already at work.[58]

Matthai's name came to be associated with it because of what he calls his 'rumoured responsibility[59]' over some of the more objectionable features of the budget. There was another feature in this budget that led to an outcry from Congress members led by Patel. Liaquat had mooted the idea of setting up an Income Tax Investigation Commission to probe cases of tax evasion by companies. It was alleged that the budget proposals were primarily aimed at Hindu business leaders.[60] Since Matthai was among those who had approved the proposal, he had to for a time face the ire of indignant Congressmen. As Matthai noted,

> I became for a time very unpopular with the Congress for my connection with this Budget. It fell to me later as Finance Minister to abolish both the capital gains and business profits taxes and to reduce the burden of the super tax and to my surprise I found I was even more unpopular with the Party than in 1947 [61]

Matthai was the only non-League cabinet minister to defend the budget in public. In his speech in the assembly, he argued that in spite of the new proposed taxes, the burden of direct taxes on industry was in reality Rs 40 crore less than the burden in the previous year. He refuted the view that the new tax rates would discourage new investment by lowering the rate of return. He also warned the businessman that if private enterprise put their money into business at much higher rates than the government could allow, then the country would have to seriously consider if continuing private enterprise was in its interest.[62]

Liaquat's now contentious budget proposals, especially those on taxation, were referred to a select committee, which included Matthai. Here too, Liaquat carried his proposals though the business profits tax was modified on Matthai's suggestion in view of the Congress's difficulties. Patel, Rajagopalachari and Bhabha sent Wavell a letter on 16 March saying that they did not subscribe to the view that the budget proposals should be deemed to have been approved. They had not been given an opportunity to express their dissent and refused to accept responsibility for the proposals. They wanted Wavell to convene an emergency meeting of the cabinet before 19 March when the select committee was to re-examine the proposals in the light of the adverse public reaction to them. Wavell demurred and his last cabinet meeting, which was dominated by the Indian National Army case, began as scheduled on 19 March 1947.[63]

***

Matthai says that the Congress–Muslim League coalition, which ruled India from October 1946 to August 1947 was unique and he wondered if any country ever had a government quite like it. He said that they functioned somewhat like a little parliament with two parties, one in opposition to the other, with the viceroy acting as the Speaker. Matthai said that on routine matters of day-to-day administration, there was seldom any difference, nor was there ever any difference on the questions at issue between India and Britain.

> The principal cause of dispute was the administration of the Home Department, particularly with reference to censorship and discipline of the Press. Muslim League newspapers in Delhi were then carrying on a bitter and often scurrilous campaign against Pandit Nehru and Sardar Patel, and the lead in this campaign was generally taken by the official organ of the Muslim League, *Dawn*.[64]

It was a situation like no other. Though the Congress and the League were running the government together, the League continuously vilified the leaders of the Congress in the press. Sardar Patel, who was looking after the home portfolio, was faced with a difficult task. In spite of his strong views about the activities of the Muslim League, Matthai says he showed a surprising measure of patience and restraint. But even the mild steps he proposed from time to time for checking the grosser abuses of the press became the subject of prolonged and acrimonious discussion at meetings of the cabinet. Decisions were often postponed; mild measures were made still milder, and cabinet secrets were often leaked to the press.[65]

The scholarship on Partition and Independence has tended to disregard the interim government. Mainstream, nationalist historiographies in Britain, India and Pakistan have described it in ways that suited their purpose. British writings took pride in the failed attempt at consensus, while Pakistani writers saw it as the final failure of composite nationalism. Indians saw it as an exercise that was shackled by the British on the one hand and the Muslim League on the other.[66] Nehru's biographer, S. Gopal, termed the interim government a 'serious disservice' that Wavell did to India.[67] It was variously called a government of 'friction and mutual antagonism', a 'farce', an 'impossible collective', a 'painful experience' and perhaps the best description of all, 'pride and prejudice'.[68]

It was certainly unique. As N.V. Gadgil, secretary (Congress party, Central Assembly), observed, it was not a coalition in the sense that parties had come together to run the government on either general or particular understanding. The questions he raised were: Could the Congress be considered a party in power? If the Muslim League proposed to function as an opposition, what policy should the Congress follow?[69]

In economic matters, protection for an industry situated in predominantly Hindu provinces was opposed if no corresponding advantage was offered to Muslim provinces. No project of industrial development stood any chance of acceptance if it assumed the existence of a united India. Proposals that happened to benefit the more well-to-do sections of the community were opposed on the ground, seldom openly expressed, that the benefit went mainly to Hindus. The position gradually became so intolerable that when the proposal to partition the country was made as a way out of the difficulty, the Congress leaders in spite of their well-known objections resigned themselves to dividing the country rather than prolong the stalemate.[70]

An Interesting Aside

Lord Mountbatten, who succeeded Wavell as viceroy in March 1947, had been told by London that he should try to ensure that India remained in the commonwealth after Independence. Since the Congress leaders had made clear their intention of severing all connections with Britain after achieving freedom, Mountbatten tried to achieve his objective by planting the seed for this idea in the minority members of the government. He met C.H. Bhabha on 23 April 1947 and told him that it was imperative that India become a member of the commonwealth, as the weapons and equipment used by the Indian Armed Forces was identical with those used by Britain and the USA. If India severed the connection, it would have to either reach out to the Russians or accept a secondary role, with no prospect of modern equipment, particularly in the air force.[71]

Bhabha told the new viceroy that he agreed with him and that he had already discussed the matter with Sardar Baldev Singh, the defence member. Mountbatten wanted Bhabha to discuss the matter with Matthai, and if he agreed, to write a joint letter to the five Congress members in this regard, calling themselves the minority members of the interim government. He wanted his name to be kept out of the whole affair. Mountbatten suggested that they all meet privately at someone's residence to discuss the matter. He and the Muslim League members, would naturally, not be present. Mountbatten said that Bhabha 'seemed to like the idea more and more and got quite excited'.[72] It is not known if Bhabha did as told, but India remained in the commonwealth and continues to be a member to this day.

* * *

When Asaf Ali, who was in charge of Railways and Transport, was appointed ambassador at Washington, a further reshuffling of the cabinet took place. Matthai was shifted to Railways and Transport, as noted before, and C. Rajagopalachari took his place as member for Industry and Supply. Matthai held this difficult charge from 13 January 1947 until 23 September 1948—a period during which the deterioration caused by the war not only reached its peak but was intensified by the terrific dislocation Partition brought in its wake. It is to Matthai's tenure first as member, and later as cabinet minister, for Railways and Transport during the horrors of Partition that we now turn.

7

Minister for Railways and Transport

John Matthai assumed charge as the member for Railways and Transport on 13 January 1947. It was perhaps the worst time to helm the railways, a department that is extremely challenging at the best of times. As luck would have it, Matthai was in charge at unarguably the most critical period in the history of the organization. The Second World War had wreaked its havoc, but worse was to follow: Partition.

Even before the war, the performance of the railways had, to put it mildly, left much to be desired. Gandhi, who was known to travel third class, was highly critical of the travelling conditions. As far back as September 1917, he observed: 'Having resorted to third class travelling, among other reasons, for the purpose of studying the conditions under which this class of passengers travel, I have naturally made as critical observations as I could. I have fairly covered the majority of railways systems during this period.'[1] He said despite his correspondence with the management of different railways about the defects, nothing had been done, and it was time to invite the press and the public to join in a grievance that had for too long remained unaddressed.

Gandhi highlighted the overcrowding ('packing of passengers like sardines') and the filth in third-class carriages.

> Not during the whole of the journey was the compartment once swept or cleaned. The result was that every time you walked on the floor or rather cut your way through the passengers seated on the floor, you waded through dirt. The closet was not cleaned during the journey and there was no water in the water tank.'[2]

He called the refreshments dirty looking, and 'previously sampled by millions of flies'. Referring to the tea as 'tannin water with filthy sugar and a whitish looking liquid mis-called milk', Gandhi said that he could vouch for the muddy appearance of this water but cited the 'testimony of the passengers as to the taste'.[3] His solution for improvement: Let the people in high places, the viceroy, commander-in-chief and others who travel in superior classes, travel third class without previous warning to see for themselves the deplorable conditions that prevail.

But this was before Gandhi became the Mahatma. His security had by then become an important issue. He continued to travel third class, but it is improbable that he did not realize that an entire carriage was filled only with his giant entourage of disciples and followers. Sarojini Naidu said that it cost the country a fortune to keep Gandhi in poverty, or words to that effect.[4] Jinnah once took a dig at him saying that even though he travelled first class, he spent less money on fares because he needed only one ticket![5]

Interim Budget, February 1947

Matthai was the only railway minister to present two railway budgets in the same year. Little over a month after he assumed office, he presented an interim budget on 27 February 1947. He said that it was a unique occasion since it was the first time that the railway budget was being sponsored by a government at the Centre 'reflecting the political opinions of almost the entire House – I might say of almost the whole of British India'.[6] He said that given the vast scale of railway operations and the fact that it was by far the largest industrial concern under one management in the country, it affected not only other government services but also had a profound effect on the industrial situation and the economic stability of the country.

Matthai said that industrial relations had largely been amicable during the war years. After the war ended, a large body of railwaymen who had worked loyally during the war felt that their economic troubles would now come to an end. They now viewed with apprehension the possibility of retrenchment due to reduction in railway activities and the absorption of ex-servicemen. Matthai said that in May 1946, the government had announced the appointment of the post-war Pay Commission with wide terms of reference, which inter alia included, consideration of machinery for the settlement of disputes relating to conditions of service.

The All-India Railwaymen's Federation (AIRF) were, however, not satisfied with the steps taken by the government and on 1 June 1946 gave notice of a strike, which was to commence on the 27th of the same month. The acceptance of the federation's demand would have involved additional expenditure far beyond the capacity of railway finances, and the demands were, therefore referred to the Standing Finance Committee for Railways, for consideration in the light of the additional expenditure involved.

The Standing Finance Committee recommended the grant of interim relief to railwaymen in receipt of a pay of Rs 250 per month and below with retrospective effect from 1 July 1945, involving an additional expenditure in the current financial year of about Rs 9 crore, a recommendation the government accepted.[7]

In order to allay the fears of railwaymen, the Standing Finance Committee also recommended that a high-power committee should be set up, charged inter alia with suggesting practical methods of absorbing surplus staff on the railways. In pursuance of this suggestion, the government set up the Indian Railways Enquiry Committee in 1947. Pending the report of the committee, the government issued instructions to the effect that no employee in service on 15 September 1945 was to be discharged on becoming surplus unless he/she had refused alternative employment pending the consideration of the adjudicator's award by the government. In his speech, Matthai told the House that in pursuance of this policy, the number of discharges that had taken place since July 1946 was 430. Since the end of the war, out of a total of about 9,25,000 railway employees, 37,100 were declared surplus, of whom 29,000 have been provided with alternative employment. Only 8100 were discharged, of which over 4000 were those who had been employed by the railways on behalf of other government departments.[8]

The strike notice was finally rescinded by the AIRF on 21 June 1946, but there were incidents of sudden strikes and stoppages of work in isolated railway centres from time to time. One major strike—that on the South Indian Railway, from August through to September 1946, persisted fitfully for a number of weeks, and although it never resulted in a complete cessation of traffic, it caused considerable inconvenience to the public and substantial loss to the government. Matthai said that such incidents and a policy of 'go slow' would hurt the economy and the workers themselves.[9] He also warned against inflationary pressures saying that substantial increases in the pay level would have to be met by increases in freight rates and this would in turn lead to increases in the prices of commodities, including necessities. The wage earner, he said, could well find himself no better off, while inflation on the other hand had received a fillip.

During his speech, Matthai informed the House about various aspects of the working of the railways: new lines and restoration of old ones, measures for economy and financial control, the regrouping of the railways, revision of the rating structure, restoration of passenger services, manufacture of locomotives in India, and the number of passenger coaches and freight wagons on the system.

Regarding new lines and restoration of old ones Matthai said that a detailed survey had been made of about 5000 miles of new constructions and of about 400 miles of lines that had been dismantled during the war and needed restoration. Survey reports in respect of some of these projects have already been received and were under examination.[10]

Matthai told the House that the Railway Board had already impressed on all administrations the urgent need for effecting economy in expenditure in all possible directions. He said that he intended to start a finance branch on each railway, unconcerned with routine accounts checks, which would be amalgamated with the budget branch of the general manager's office. Matthai said that the necessary detailed investigations to this end had already been taken in hand.[11]

As regards regrouping of railways, Matthai said that while the regrouping of railways for more efficient management had assumed great importance, no firm decision in this regard could be taken in the immediate future for two reasons. Firstly, the railways had not yet recovered from the effects of war, and secondly, several new lines were under consideration and any decision on regrouping would be premature until the investigations were completed and a decision taken as to which of the projects were finally to be taken in hand.[12]

In the course of the previous year's budget speech, mention had been made of the need to revise the railways' goods rating structure. The task, Matthai said, was complex and difficult, calling for extreme caution both in the interests of the public and of the railways. Changes, he said, would in some cases benefit the trade and in others, the railways.[13] He told the House about a new type of 'telescopic' rate to be applied to a few commodities in the future. Meanwhile, the revision of rules and regulations affecting the interchange of goods between the different railways; the routing of traffic; the division of earnings; and the revision of long-standing traffic agreements to bring them in line with the national character of the railways, were all matters that were receiving close attention and satisfactory progress towards finality had been made.[14]

Informing the House about the restoration of pre-war railway facilities, Matthai said that the present passenger train mileage restored ranged from 80 to 90 per cent of the pre-war services on most of the railways. The railways were handicapped by lack of coaching stock, a considerable amount of which was still on loan to the defence department for running military specials. Matthai said that while many had been released, a sizeable balance still remained. He said that the policy of reopening stations and restoring train halts as and when it was possible to do so, would continue.[15]

Locomotives, Matthai said, were being manufactured at the Ajmer workshops of the Bombay, Baroda and Central India (BB & CI) Railway. The first batch of ten locomotives had been handed over to the North Western Railway. Work on another batch of ten was now in hand and an order for fifty-eight passenger locomotives had been placed on these shops. The boilers for the latter were to be manufactured in Tata's Singhbhum shops. (The Singhbhum workshops of the Eastern India Railway were handed over to Tatas on the 1 June 1945.)

It had also been proposed to convert the locomotive repair shops at Kanchrapara into a locomotive manufacturing plant, but this could not be done owing to the fact that the entire capacity had to be used for essential repair work to broad gauge locomotives. A subsequent survey revealed that Kanchrapara shops had no excess capacity and therefore an entirely new production plant at Kanchrapara North, a short distance away from the existing repair shops, had to be planned.[16]

Matthai then informed the House about the number of locomotives ordered from foreign countries and the numbers received. He also told the House about the time frame for the receipt of locomotives, both goods and passenger. He said that by 31 March 1948, they expected to have in service approximately 6100 Broad Gauge (BG) and 2300 Metre Gauge (MG) locomotives as against 5215 and 2064, respectively, in 1939.[17] Similarly, he informed the House about the position of coaches and wagons and the numbers that would be introduced into the system. The Railway Board had also decided that in future, broad-gauge passenger coaches would be 11 feet 8 inches wide, instead of the prevailing 10 feet. By 31 March 1948,

Matthai expected to have in service approximately 14,100 BG and 7800 MG coaching vehicles as against 12,347 and 7309, respectively, in 1939.[18] Matthai also said that a prototype train containing carriages made of metal shells would be placed on exhibition in Delhi in March.

An ever-present anxiety was keeping the railways adequately supplied with coal. Matthai told the House that of the approximately 26 million tons of coal despatched annually from the pitheads, the railways' requirements were about 10 million tons. Thus, fuel economy assumed great importance and a fuel economy campaign was strictly followed. As a long-term policy, the Railway Board was planning to reduce the overall coal consumption by the introduction of lighter rolling stock, both in passenger and goods. As far as new lines were concerned, the board gave the highest priority to those in the coalfield areas. They also explored the possibilities of alternative forms of power and examined the prospects of electrifying 1506 route miles. In addition, the development of diesel electric, gas turbine and other forms of traction were also being investigated.[19]

Budget, 1947–48

Matthai estimated that with the existing rates and fares, the budget estimate of gross traffic receipts for 1947–48 would be Rs 183 crore. The estimate for ordinary working expenses was put at Rs 135.5crore. The appropriation to the depreciation fund was placed at Rs 15.34 crore. Payments to worked lines on the basis of present charges would be Rs 1.6 crore and net miscellaneous receipts, Rs 2.95 crore. Interest charges were expected to be Rs 26.58 crore. The net balance would then be Rs 7 crore, which had to provide for the contributions to general revenues, the Betterment Fund[20] and the railway reserve.

The revised estimates indicated that the contribution to general revenues in the current year was likely to fall Rs 1.75 crore short of the budget estimate of Rs 7.36 crore. Matthai told the House that in view of the heavy commitments of the Government of India, in respect of large development schemes and shrinking revenues and public borrowings, the government had fixed the contribution to general revenues for the next year at Rs 7.5 crore after the loss on strategic lines has been met.

The Betterment Fund was expected to open the budget year with a balance of about Rs 13.8 crore, out of which it was expected to spend Rs 4.1 crore. Expenditure from this Fund was expected to increase rather than diminish in future years and it was considered essential that the appropriation to the fund in the budget year should at a minimum be Rs 5 crore. The railway reserve was expected to stand at Rs 21.5 crore at the end of the current financial year out, of which Rs 5 crore was earmarked for the arrears of maintenance, which had accumulated owing to war conditions leaving a free balance of Rs 16.5 crore. Expenditure from the reserve in the budget year was put at Rs 2 lakh so that the balance at the end of the year would remain practically unchanged.

Given the gap between revenue and expenditure, Matthai said that it was essential to take steps to moderate the decline in earnings. With a fall in the volume of traffic handled, this was possible only by a fare increase in both passenger and freight segments. To ensure the solvency of the national undertaking, Matthai proposed to hike passenger fares by 6.1 per cent for fares above Re. 1 and by 61 per cent increase for fares below Re. 1. The minimum fare of one anna would, however, remain. The yield from this increase is estimated at Rs 4.75 crore.

As far as a fare increase was concerned, an increased charge of 12.5 per cent had already been applied to goods traffic (except for food grains in wagon loads, manures and fodder) and the government was anxious to avoid any action calculated to retard the development of nascent industry or to increase the retail prices of the necessities of life. The yield anticipated from these freight adjustments was expected to be about Rs 5.75 crore, and the incidence of the increase would be so spread as to fall equitably and in just proportion to the ability of the different commodities to bear it.

Matthai said that an exhaustive investigation had been carried out by the board of the data available with railway administrations pertaining to replacements of the various classes of railway assets in past years. The capital at charge of each railway was now being apportioned between the various classes with the use of such records. With the completion of this exercise, it would be possible to calculate the appropriate annual contribution to the Depreciation Fund.[21]

Matthai said that the first full year of peace was drawing to a close and there was evidence that some progress had been made, but the changeover was so great, and its effects on such a vast organization as the Indian railway system so profound, that many challenges had to be faced in the coming months. The unsettling effects of political changes added to the general unrest. But given the goodwill and the exercise of a little patience by the staff and the public alike, the major difficulties were smoothed out in the near future, and they were able to apply themselves to the rehabilitation and development, which all so earnestly desired.

In conclusion, Matthai thanked the staff and officers of the railways for their performance in what had been a very difficult year. 'I wish to take this opportunity to pay a tribute to the loyalty and zeal with which they have discharged their duties under adverse conditions.'[22]

* * *

Matthai was trying his best and it would do well to remember that his portfolio was by no means an easy one, especially given the circumstances when he was placed at its helm. But he was never a politician and even Matthai, 'the archetypal interim coalition figure'[23], had felt for some time that the interim . . . government had ceased to make any appeal to the country'.[24] He wrote to Nehru on 27 June 1947 telling him that now since a new government was to be formed, it would be worthwhile considering its composition on fresh lines. He said that as far as he was concerned, it was not a Congress–League question, but that in the new conditions, there would be little room in the government for men like him, who had no political hold on the people and little political experience and judgement. He confessed that it was for this reason that he felt he had become a misfit in the government and should leave it.[25]

As an illustration, Matthai brought up the contested policy regarding controls. Patel wanted all controls to go, and many in the Congress were inclined to agree with him. Matthai with his 'objective economist's hat' thought this would be disastrous in a time of scarcity. He, however, recognized that the political repercussions of controls could not be ignored and felt that at times like these, he was 'a nuisance and hindrance to government' and anticipated more dilemmas of this kind in the future 'for which you need men who look straight and are not troubled by thought. The upshot of all this is that I feel I must ask you not to consider me for reappointment after August 15th'.[26]

Nehru responded to the letter the same day. While he agreed with Matthai that the interim government had lost touch with the people, he did not agree with his conclusions. His personal inclinations urged him forcefully 'to get out of this government', but he knew the crisis it would cause and had decided to 'stick on reluctantly'. 'We just cannot quit – either you or [me]. The very gravity of the situation prevents this. As for controls, I do not agree entirely with Vallabhbhai Patel.'[27]

* * *

The interim government was 'a complex arrangement of contradictory impulses, individual brinkmanship, petty politicking and ambiguous nationalist positions vis-à-vis the colonial rule'.[28] But it was also in its own way, a landmark of political accommodation and power-sharing, which was inherent in the transition from Empire to dominions in British India. By no means a crowning achievement of unity and fraternity, it was certainly an alternative attempt at sharing and exercising power, plagued as it was by rival tensions between the Congress and the League. It was a kind of dualism tempered by realism. In the advance towards Independence, it was an impulse of consolidation in the face of structural opposition. As historian Rakesh Ankit observes, 'Colonial state apparatus' gradualism and moderation met with the impatient, democratic, and self-determining urges of postcolonial society.'[29]

The legacy of the interim government lived on well after Independence and the political system and economic plan of the 1950s as well as the intellectual life and sociocultural thought drew from this unlikely combine in 1946–47. Ankit believes that if influence is a measure of effectiveness, then the interim government deserves its share of acknowledgement. And if confluence is a measure of consolidation, then the interim government brought British India to its formal end by merging social and political democracy with older imperial strains in a liberal tradition. But as a political instrument of representation, it could neither resolve nor evade the dilemmas inherent in the competing nationalisms of mid-twentieth-century India.[30]

8

The Horrors of Partition

On 1 August 1947, Nehru wrote to Matthai, formally inviting him to join the first cabinet of independent India. He said, 'You have been a tower of strength to us and to me specially and I do not know how I could carry on without you.'[1] Nehru told Matthai that all the existing Indian members would remain unchanged apart from C. Rajagopalachari, who would take office as Governor.

Nehru proposed to send the viceroy only names, and not the portfolios, which could be decided later after discussions among themselves. He thought it desirable for Matthai to continue in the Railways, a department to which he had already given much time and energy. He ended with, 'We are going to have a tough time and will have to face difficult problems. We shall face them, of course, as a united team working together and sharing each other's burdens.'[2] Those were the days when a prime minister used his cabinet colleagues as sounding boards and not as echo chambers.

It is interesting to know what Lord Mountbatten, who succeeded Wavell in March 1947, thought of Nehru's cabinet. Extracts from his personal report give his opinion of those nominated.

I told him . . . that unless he got rid of a lot of top-weights like Rajagopalachari and Maulana Azad, he would find himself greatly hampered . . . that Bhabha and Matthai should both be kept since they were extremely able and fearless . . . that Baldev Singh appeared to me to be unsatisfactory as Defence Member though I realised he was the only available Sikh, that Rajendra Prasad was a dear old man . . . With such a Cabinet the Congress could remain in power for the next few years; without it, it was done.[3]

By early 1947, the main priority of the British was to leave India as soon as possible before anti-colonial politics radicalized and communal violence escalated beyond control. Prime Minister Clement Attlee announced that the British would leave India by 30 June 1948 and sent Lord Mountbatten, who arrived in late March, to oversee the political disengagement. After a series of failed talks, Mountbatten proposed a plan on 3 June which brought forward the date of Independence to 15 August 1947. By June 1947, Pakistan had become a settled fact and the Indian Independence Act was ratified on 18 July and implemented on 14/15 August 1947.

Once the 3 June Plan was accepted, the task at hand was to divide British India and facilitate the departure of the British from India. This meant a division of the army, government staff, properties and a lot else. It also meant a division of the Indian railway system. A Partition Committee was set up to divide the assets and liabilities. It was steered by civil servants, H.M. Patel and Chaudhri Mohammad Ali, and ten expert committees with an equal number of Hindus and Muslims representing the interest of the future India and Pakistan. It was to be an orderly affair, but reality proved otherwise.

No one can better describe the travails of the times better than Matthai himself. Writing about these trying times, he observed:

> I was then in charge of Railways – and was given less than eight weeks in which to complete the arrangements for the partition of the railways. A large unified business concern with a capitalization of approximately £600 million and employing nearly a million people to be split into two separate units within two months seemed to me a fantastic proposition. But orders were orders – and various committees were set up within the ministry each consisting of an equal number of Muslim and non-Muslim officers to work out the details.[4]

Two railway companies—the North Western Railway (NWR), and the Bengal and Assam Railway (BAR) were particularly affected. The NWR served areas on both sides of the newly created boundaries in the western part, and the BAR, in the eastern part of what was formerly British India. The effects of Partition were however not restricted to these two railway systems and were felt across the country.[5]

The Insanity of Hatred

Partition precipitated a bloodbath and a refugee crisis unprecedented in scale and horror. As the deliberations of the Partition Council and the Boundary Commission brought the reality of the impending rupture closer, violence erupted in several places in Punjab and northern India. Partition turned into a humanitarian catastrophe. The violence, unprecedented in its extent and brutality, spared no one: men, women and children of the warring communities all becoming victims of the carnage. It also impacted non-members who resided in the areas engulfed by the violence.[6]

The cycle of Partition-related violence began on 16 August 1946, the day the Muslim League called for 'Direct Action'. It was to mark the formal push towards the achievement of Pakistan through nationwide hartals. In Calcutta, a huge public rally suddenly turned violent as it attacked Hindus and looted homes and property. Hindu retaliation was swift and by 20 August, the violence had claimed 4000 lives, injuring 10,000 others. Police inaction and the scale of the carnage led many to believe that the violence was premeditated.[7]

Shortly after the Calcutta carnage, riots began in Bombay in early September followed by Noakhali and Bihar in October, Garhmukteshwar in UP in November, and North-West Frontier Province (NWFP) in December. By March 1947, the whole of Punjab was engulfed in violence and it was this province that experienced the core of the violence. The violence engulfing the cities of Lahore and Amritsar was immediately followed by riots in Multan, Attock and Rawalpindi. Entire villages were destroyed, corpses of children hung from trees and young girls raped. By August 1947, over 5000 people had been killed in Punjab.

Violence escalated in the province around the time of Independence and the announcement of the Boundary Award[8]. As refugees from all communities began moving across the new borders, violence erupted in the trains carrying them, and in neighbourhoods that had been emptied of residents and filled with the displaced. Delhi was particularly hard hit in this regard, with Hindu and Sikh refugees arriving from West Punjab targeting Muslim residents. This violence left some 20,000 Muslims dead in its wake. The violence was not only retributive in nature; it was also the consequence of routine violence that sought to make space for the influx amid housing shortages. Thousands of Muslims left the city, dramatically changing the culture and demography of the city forever.[9] Partition violence also spilled beyond the boundaries of Punjab to the princely states of Alwar, Bharatpur, and Jammu and Kashmir.

The pendulum of death and destruction swung over a period of many months, both before and after 15 August 1947, across the whole of northern India. Death was everywhere and violent hands were laid on all, irrespective of age or gender. The carnage on the trains coming from Amritsar was particularly gruesome. The trains were packed with thousands of dead bodies and many more were strewn along the side of the tracks. The situation in the reverse direction was equally bad. The trains taking the refugees out of India were deliberately derailed, often with the connivance of the railway staff, so that the passengers could be easily massacred.

Partition violence showed dimensions of ethnic cleansing as rival communities sought to harm, kill and displace opposing communities in ways that made reconstruction impossible at the end of the violent confrontation. Thus, not only homes but businesses were also targeted. The nature of violence also included profaning anything that was held sacred by the other side. Demobilized ex-soldiers of the British Army also played their role in training paramilitary and volunteer groups: The methodical attempt to wipe out entire neighbourhoods and populations depended largely on the actions of volunteer groups, such as the Sikh Jathas and the Muslim tribal parties.[10]

Thus, Partition violence achieved a far greater demographic division than anticipated. Amritsar went from being a Muslim-majority city to one that had virtually no Muslim residents after 1947. Lahore's mixed population gave way to a Muslim majority. Eastern India also witnessed large-scale migration, but partly owing to the lack of large-scale violence, many continued to remain as minority residents in their traditional homes.[11] Most scholars now accept that approximately one million lives were claimed by Partition-related violence. In this enormous crisis, the railways provided the most important escape route. On 18 August, Sir Robert Francis Mudie, the Governor of West Punjab, wrote that some 1,00,000–1,50,000 refugees needed immediate evacuation and that even with 4000 people per train, it would require forty-five trains to move them.[12]

The Railways and the Refugee Crisis

India and Pakistan responded to the crisis by setting up the Military Evacuation Organization (MEO) on 1 September 1947. They planned to move some ten million refugees noting that some two million had already moved between the two dominions. Naturally, the Railways were at the heart of this plan, which required the contribution of twenty trains from India and twelve from Pakistan, with five or six running daily. The trains, known as 'Specials', were to transport refugees free of cost. There were many shortcomings in the actual movement, but the system ran 643 Specials transporting over two million refugees between 27 August and the end of November 1947. The railway companies in eastern India also transported refugees, but the pressure was much less given the staggered migration and lesser violence.[13]

Violence directed at railway stations and trains showed a steady escalation from the autumn of 1947. On 3 August, unknown attackers threw bombs on the Majitha and Fatehgarh Churian stations, north of Amritsar. On 7 August, riots broke out in Calcutta and there was a clash at the Ballygunge railway station. A few days later, a pitched battle at Sealdah station left five dead. Clashes also broke out in Hyderabad, Sind, leading to several injuries. A day after Independence, there were riots at Amritsar station affecting the line going to the new border post of Wagah and disrupting services. The last week of August saw a significant escalation, with the violence spreading to areas around Delhi. Mobs attacked trains and killed passengers. A mob near the Khudian Khas station in Central Punjab attacked a train and several passengers were killed, forcing the railway authorities to suspend services on the Delhi–Bhatinda line. On 31 August, a violent attack at Khanna station on the Frontier Mail resulted in the death of a passenger and the burning of a first-class compartment.[14]

If August was bad, September was worse: Armed mobs attacked trains on a regular basis. Not only passengers but their escorts also had to face the horrific violence, often engaging in hand-to-hand fighting. Violence spread across all of northern and central India. Railway personnel operating refugee trains were attacked on numerous occasions. It is said that most of the trains being taken to Pakistan had Christian and Parsi drivers. Delhi, and areas around it, were among the worst hit. A bomb was even found in the Calcutta Mail at Victoria Terminus (now Chhatrapati Shivaji Maharaj Terminus) in faraway Bombay.

Special trains were routinely attacked and there were many casualties despite armed escorts. On 21 September, there were grisly scenes at Lahore station. The violence in the city escalated when a train arrived with 166 corpses on it. Mobs tried to prevent Hindus and Sikhs from boarding trains bound for India. In what was one of the worst attacks of the Partition violence, a train for Lahore from Delhi was attacked in Beas and Amritsar on 21 September. A massacre took place and when the train finally arrived at Lahore, 400 of the 600 refugees alive were wounded. It was said that the survivors had escaped by pretending to be dead.[15]

Bombay-based journalist D.F. Karaka, who was one of the first journalists to reach the Bergen–Belsen concentration camp, wrote about the train massacres in an article for the *Bombay Chronicle*. He gave a first-hand account of the horrific violence: 'I saw this train myself this morning. The stench was like the stench of Belsen, the brutality is worse than that of the Nazis ... There was a woman sprawled naked. There were children just flung around the place. Compartment after compartment were filled with the dead.'[16] The violence continued into October and November. Under normal circumstances, it would have been classed as horrifying, but compared to the extremes reached in September, it represented a slow de-escalation. While many Indian and Pakistani railwaymen demonstrated individual courage and kindness to survive the carnage, there were also unfortunately those who collaborated with the murderous mobs who attacked trains.

Syloo Matthai narrates how Achamma told her that she had given a necklace with a crucifix to their Muslim bearer who was going to Pakistan to indicate that he was a Christian. Christians and Parsis were generally spared in the carnage. Syloo observes that the Matthai's were a compassionate family with humane values and no prejudices. 'They embodied true Christian values, championed the cause of the underdog and did all they could to ameliorate suffering', she said.[17]

The problems thrown up by Partition were agitating the minds of many important leaders, starting with Nehru. They included the division of railway assets and liabilities, the refugee problem, the future structure of the railways, and perhaps the most important and pressing, the migration of staff across the newly created territories.

During his budget speech on 20 November 1947, Matthai spoke of the problems caused by the transfer of staff, which had 'greatly dislocated and disorganised the railway services of the country'. He said that 1,26,300 had opted for India from Pakistan and 1,08,400 had arrived in India. Of these 10,40,00 had received their posting orders. He added that he had no final information about the number who had opted for Pakistan but tentatively put the figure at 83,000. 'These figures represent a huge problem of administration and of physical movement and the House will realize the strain that this has imposed upon the whole of our railway staff.' Regarding the evacuation of refugees, he said that 2.5 million were moved to, from and within East Punjab. This was the equivalent of the capacity of 800 normal passenger trains, a movement that needed curtailment of passenger services in other parts of the country. 'The latest figure that I have is that the reduction of normal passenger services approximates to 3,800 train miles a day.'[18]

The movement of such a large number of employees posed an enormous challenge to both the Indian and Pakistani railway systems particularly since many of these transfers took place in a very short time span. Matthai estimated it at a mere two and a half months. The problem was particularly acute as different communities had come to dominate separate spheres of work. The Indian railways faced shortages of engine crew and workshop labour. On the other hand, the majority of those migrating to India were clerical staff. It is estimated that there were 18 per cent vacancies in engine crew, and in some railways such as the East Indian Railway, it was as high as 45 per cent.

Railway workshops faced comparable shortages.[19] Pakistan faced a shortage of stationmasters, mechanical, electrical and signalling staff as also doctors. If the migration created shortages, it also created surpluses in certain areas. Though the problem of surplus staff affected Pakistan more, the problem was also significant in India. The disturbances in the north forced many Muslim workers to go to Karachi via Bombay. The huge pressure on Bombay forced the Pakistani transfer office to set up relief camps to house the migrants, and at one time, there were as many as 20,000 in these camps awaiting transportation to Karachi. The shipping constraints only added to the problem.

In addition to the problem of migration, the sudden appearance of international boundaries across what had been a unified railway system created new challenges. Railway workers across seven different railway companies had to coordinate their efforts to set up customs and immigration checkpoints with set protocols for passenger and freight. This was a new set of duties for the railway staff.

Another more serious problem was the maintenance of rolling stock. The abnormal demands of the refugee crisis left the railways with little room to schedule maintenance. The matter was further aggravated with the newly created boundaries cutting off access to supplies and workshops on either side of the border. For instance, the newly created Eastern Punjab Railway in India whose employees belonged to the erstwhile NWR, lost access to the workshop at Mughalpura, which was now in Pakistani territory. Similarly, railway workers on two sections of the NWR in Pakistan lost access to the workshop in Kalka, which was in India.

In the eastern sector, the Indians lost access to the Saidpur railway workshop, which was in East Pakistan and the Pakistanis were left without a broad-gauge workshop, with the Kanchrapara workshop being situated in India. To solve this problem, Indian and Pakistani railway systems entered into a number of agreements to maintain their rolling stock. The Mughalpura workshop offered to service the Eastern Punjab Railway and the Pakistani Railway promised to build coaches and machine timber for the Kalka workshop in India. An agreement similar to Mughalpura was also reached for the Saidpur and Kanchrapara workshops. But the Mughalpura workshop struggled to deliver on its commitments.[20]

Nehru, Matthai and Patel were all seized of the huge crisis caused by Partition. On 18 July 1947 Dewan Chamanlal wrote to Patel regarding the division of railway assets and liabilities. Chamanlal was one of the founders of the All-India Trade Union Congress and also a member of the central legislative assembly. Later, he was India's ambassador to Turkey. The Railway Departmental Sub-Committee on Assets and Liabilities was formed to reach an agreement on the arrangements for ensuring the continuity of train services and the basis of division of locomotives, carriages, wagons, plant and machinery and workshops, as well as on the measure of mutual assistance for repairs in workshops to locomotives, carriages and wagons.

Chamanlal said that the investigation for evaluating the fixed assets located on each side of the boundary had been proceeding for the last twelve days or so on an agreed basis jointly by Muslim and non-Muslim staff, but unfortunately after the results had been tabulated, the Muslim members had gone back on their previous agreement and refused to accept the figures. The method, he said, was admittedly an approximate one and did not aim at working out the value to the last rupee, but the present criticisms of the Muslim members was disingenuous. The argument of the Muslim members was that these figures were unreliable and should not form the basis of division of railway liabilities between India and Pakistan. They wanted the division to be on another basis but made no suggestion in this regard. [21]

On 23 July 1947, Nehru wrote to Matthai about the need for joint discussion on certain problems that had cropped up. More particularly, he wanted to know the solutions to a variety of problems facing the Railways. He said that the Hindu and Sikh workers in the railway workshop in Lahore were on the point of migrating to Delhi. He wanted them to be given some assurance and asked to remain where they were since 'it is not entirely certain which way Lahore will go'.[22] The problem of reorganizing the railways after Partition was also agitating Nehru's mind.

> A part of this system in the North-West and the North-East is cut off from India. What will happen to that part of the North-Western Railway which falls to the lot of India? So also in the east, there is the question of communication with Assam. It may be necessary to undertake some construction programme to connect Assam. We cannot do this on any big scale, but something on a small scale might be thought of.[23]

Referring to a communique that was issued by Matthai about the consequences following Partition, Nehru said that a new administration had been planned for the parts of NWR which India was to maintain. He added that he had 'a horror of adding more and more high officers when the railway administration seems to have quite a large number of these people'. Apart from the costs involved, it would involve the retention of a large number of high British officers. 'Even in the Health Department I feel shocked that there are far too many high officers doing precious little work. It is extraordinary how these people entrench themselves and create vested interests.'[24]

Nehru also touched upon the structure of the railways. He said that if a new central administration was being planned in Delhi, then they would have to keep the accommodation problem in mind. 'You know how difficult it is to get houses in Delhi. Apart from accommodation, even the food situation here will be affected and prices are going up.'[25] Referring to the debate about the divisional system and the district system, he said that he had been given to understand that the divisional system was costly and top heavy and he hoped that Matthai would consider all these matters before final arrangements were made.

Earlier, in the second week of June, Nehru had warned Matthai about the Hyderabad problem. Hyderabad was then flirting with the idea of Independence and Nehru wanted Matthai to be particularly vigilant. 'This applies particularly to the Sholapur-Raichur and Bezwada-Nagpur sections. I hope you will keep this in mind,' he said.[26]

Partition also entailed a large-scale redistribution of railway assets. Referring to the share of locomotives that were to go to Pakistan, Patel wrote to Matthai in early August 1947 adverting to the 121 locomotives destined for Pakistan, but which were still in Sealdah. He wanted them to be moved out before 15 August especially since it meant retention of some 1800 staff there, many of whom had opted to go to Pakistan. He stressed the safety aspect and wanted that the railways should before 15 August be completely manned by staff who had opted for India. In fact, the general manager of BAR had opted for Pakistan along with two other senior officials and Patel wanted immediate steps to be taken to effect the change.[27]

The refugee problem was the most pressing and trying one the country was facing. An examination of the epistolary evidence suggests that there were some sharp exchanges between Matthai and Patel on the subject. All cabinet ministers were under great stress and tempers were often frayed. On 1 September, Patel wrote to Matthai that 'the progress made in securing rail communication is slow and entirely out of keeping with the requirement'.[28] He wanted quick decisions and immediate implementation of those decisions overcoming obstacles with 'will, the direction and the initiative'. He wanted a senior railway official with complete control over all railway resources to work alongside the military officer tasked with organizing the evacuation. He said that evacuation should have overriding priority and the railway official 'should have almost a carte blanche'.[29]

Patel's letter elicited an immediate and an unexpectedly sharp response from Matthai. He said that the main bottleneck in running more trains was the lack of police and army protection. He said that it was a question of protecting the lives and property of passengers and since more trains could not be run without the requisite protection, Patel, as the minister concerned, should apply his mind to solving this problem. Stung by what he perceived to be a rebuke, Matthai said that it was not a question of 'will, direction and initiative'[30] but of protecting the passengers. He was highly critical of Patel's suggestion of a railway official with carte blanche. He said that the nation also faced an acute food, coal and salt crisis, all of which required transport just as urgently as the refugee problem. It was his duty as minister to ensure that these problems also got their share of transport and therefore in the present circumstances, he could not conceive of a more ill-considered suggestion.[31]

Matthai seems to have taken Patel's views on the failures of the railways to heart and a little personally. Clearly, he took offence.

I am sorry to write to you in this strain but your letter obviously calls for plain-speaking. We, as a Cabinet are faced with a crisis of unprecedented magnitude, and much to my regret *I find a growing tendency among Ministers, when they find they are unable to discharge their own responsibilities, to place the blame on others.* (Emphasis added.) It is only by consideration for one's difficulties and a real willingness to render mutual co-operation that we shall survive this crisis.[32]

That even the normally serene Matthai could respond in such a manner shows how much pressure there was to perform, and just how frayed tempers were. In his reminiscences, V. Shankar of the ICS, who was private secretary to Patel, narrates his boss's response to Matthai's broadside. Patel gave Shankar the letter without saying a word. The Sardar had justly acquired the reputation of a man of few words, but even within that narrow compass, as Liaquat Ali Khan so pithily put it, 'he meant what he said and said what he meant'.[33] Whatever he said was always pregnant with wisdom and meaning. Though he was a lawyer by training, he was better known for his common sense, an attribute he seems to have been blessed with to an uncommon degree. This allowed him to reduce the most intricate and complex problems to remarkable simplicity.

Later, when Patel met Matthai, he said, 'You have obviously written it in a temper; I can be provoked into a temper and more easily than you but

I shall say nothing because I know you will have to regret it yourself.'[34] Matthai listened to him gravely and said, 'I am sorry but the complaint you sent me was untrue and I felt that the whispers that go around affect you as well. I find I was mistaken.'[35] There the matter ended. But Shankar says that true to Patel's prophecy, 'Matthai lived to own a complete reversal of his views' of Patel and Nehru when he resigned as finance minister in 1950, a story that is told in some detail in a later chapter. The change in fact was not long in coming: It was Matthai's powerful support in favour of the Hyderabad Police Action that enabled Patel to outvote Nehru.[36]

In September 1947, Nehru wanted Matthai to suggest to the emergency committee, which was to meet in mid-October, that trained workers from the Tata Institute of Social Sciences in Bombay could help with the refugees at the camps. 'If the suggestion is approved, Jehangir Tata can be informed.'[37] The refugee problem continued to agitate his mind and he wrote to Matthai on 17 October after a meeting of the emergency committee telling him about the evacuation of a large number of Muslims from Delhi, asking him to adhere to the plan drawn up by the minister without portfolio, N. Gopalaswami Ayyangar. Ayyangar had drawn up a schedule of evacuation by train, of Muslims migrating to Pakistan and for organizing the movement of Hindu and Sikh refugees, after they had crossed the border into different parts of India. 'What I would suggest, therefore, is that first of all effect be given to the Gopalaswami programme without much deviation from it; secondly, to send the surplus of Delhi evacuees as rapidly as possible leaving a number behind who may be in doubt about their going or who wish to stay. These can be dealt with later.'[38]

On 3 October, Patel wrote to Nehru that Major General Chimni, who was responsible for the evacuation of refugees, had told him on his recent visit to Amritsar that trains should be started at the first possible opportunity since a trainload was equal to ten three-ton lorries and required less escort staff. Patel told Nehru that he had mentioned this to Matthai stressing that they should concentrate on running special trains even for shorter journeys than Delhi to Lahore. He wanted Nehru to tell Matthai about it perhaps not wanting a repeat of the somewhat unpleasant exchange we have alluded to above. 'If you agree, you might ask Matthai to have the question examined, and if necessary, we could have it discussed at the emergency meeting on Tuesday.'[39]

The government was faced with all kinds of problems, including the smuggling of arms and ammunition. Matthai wrote to Baldev Singh, the defence minister, enclosing a note received from the Chief Commissioner of Railways about suspicious happenings in Jubbulpore (now Jabalpur), which was under the command of a British officer, Brigadier Lickman. A number of British officers under his command were leaving for transfer to Pakistan or on leave to stations in Pakistan and there was reason to believe that some of them were carrying arms and ordnance stores in their baggage. Lickman was also planning to order four special goods trains to carry ordnance towards Bombay. Since these trains would have been ordered by Mil Rail, the military wing of the Railways, the railway authorities had decided to run their operations in such a manner which would make it possible to resist the demand for these special trains should such a demand be made. Also of concern was the movement of Muslims to the south trying to get into the Nizam's territory. Matthai wrote, 'We are doing what we can to counter movements of a doubtful character, but there is obviously a limit to what we can do to prevent them.'[40]

During Partition, the problems of the railways put relentless pressure on Matthai. On 16 October, Shankar wrote to H.M. Patel, the defence secretary, saying that the home minister had received a telegram from West Bengal informing them about how the railway staff at Siliguri on the BAR was compelled to stop work and were being subjected to threats by the Pakistani staff. 'Apparently, the Pakistan fiat still reigns there and the earnings of these railways are still being enjoyed by the Pakistani railways.'[41] Shankar wanted inquiries to be made on the subject as soon as possible. In case the local administration had shown unwillingness to transfer the lines to Indian control, the matter should be referred to the Partition Council or to the Pakistan government.[42]

* * *

It is necessary to highlight the role played by the trade unions during this crisis. They could have sabotaged the movement of refugees had they chosen to withhold support, and given the prevailing security concerns, they would have been justified in doing so. Instead, at least on two occasions, the unions assured the government of their commitment to evacuation of refugees despite the dangers involved. S. Guruswamy, the general secretary of AIRF, called upon workers to offer the government their maximum cooperation. Later, the AIRF passed a resolution pledging its full support and called upon its members to offer their services in whatever capacity they were called upon to serve.[43] The railway workers, the union said, would work as a unified and patriotic workforce. This was all the more creditable since many unions were then engaged in difficult negotiations with the Railway Board over pay scales and working conditions and their public support came at a time when the threat of strikes was looming.[44]

The report of the Pay Commission was to be published in mid-May 1947 and on 10 May 1947, Matthai wrote to Sardar Patel giving his suggestions on the publication of the Pay Commission's recommendations and the government's decision on them. After issuing an official communiqué, he wanted Nehru to broadcast a talk in an informal manner on the implications of the new proposals. Matthai wanted the government's decisions to be presented in the form of a human appeal to government employees, including the Railways. The talk would bring out the government's desire to give its employees a fair deal, place on labour a corresponding obligation to render the best service and make a special appeal to railwaymen in view of the acute transport problem that was hindering production. He wanted the talk to be given in Hindustani, with an English translation prepared for subsequent publication in the press.[45]

It is no exaggeration to say that unionization and collective action prevented the collapse of the railway system. While some misguided railwaymen colluded with extremists, the large majority stayed true to their colleagues and the passengers. As author Aniruddha Bose observes in *Shunting the Nation*, 'The long years of collective class-based identities forged through joint struggles throughout the Second World War and struggle for Independence, ensured that railway workers did not fall victim to the poison of communalism. There was no partitioning of the class called railway workers.'[46]

Matthai referred to the massive operation of transporting refugees in his speech introducing the railway budget on 16 February 1948. He felt that the railways had turned the corner and could now look forward to a period of steady progress largely because of the end of the border migration. He observed,

Firstly, there is this very obvious fact that we have come to the end of the period of serious civil disturbances. We have come to the end of the period of these vast refugee movements. The House will remember that altogether during a period of two and a half months the Railways were called upon to move as many as 3 million refugees, which represents the capacity of a thousand passenger trains. That was a terrible strain on the Railways and we have now come to the end of that period of strain.[47]

* * *

The Indian railways faced many serious challenges after Independence. The most immediate of these had to do with staffing. As noted before, a large number of running staff and skilled workshop labour left for Pakistan. Most of the Hindu and Sikh employees who came to India from Pakistan were clerical staff. This created shortages in some categories and surplus in others. The Railways expanded recruitment, intensified training, recalled retired employees, reassigned skilled workers and relaxed promotion criteria to manage the crisis.[48]

Absorbing the refugees proved to be another problem. Many had left all their belongings in Pakistan and the Railway Board sanctioned a two-month advance payment, as also a 'Rehabilitation Advance' equivalent to three months' pay, repayable over thirty-six instalments. Finding comparable positions and ranks was another problem, as was the resentment caused by the newcomers among Indian staff who now had to compete with the migrants. Lack of service and pension records was another serious issue. Even a year after Partition, 14,000 refugees were still waiting to reconstruct their pension records.[49]

The other problem came in the form of management of changes in traffic patterns. These were felt most keenly by those operating the systems adjacent to the territories that had now become East and West Pakistan. Railway workers on the Oudh and Tirhut line had to make adjustments because authorities on both sides of the border insisted on interchange of trains only at designated border crossings. On the western border, workers on the Jodhpur system were told to abruptly stop all train services in July 1948, thereby ending the last operational link between the dominions.[50]

Maintenance of rolling stock continued to remain a major problem as was the shortage of locomotives, coaches and wagons. Engine failures were alarmingly high, and many passenger coaches too were in a state of disrepair. With no normal replacement programme in place thanks to the huge disruption caused by Partition, the Railways found it difficult to deliver services.[51] The demand for both freight and passenger services increased after Independence and this only made things more difficult for the railway system, which was limping back to some kind of normalcy after a year of acute crisis.

* * *

Matthai wrote about his experience in an undated manuscript in the archives. He observed,

> The departure of practically the whole of the British personnel, the exchange of staff numbering nearly a lakh, between India and Pakistan, the division of rolling stock and workshop equipment, the movement of millions of refugees by train, the sudden diversion of heavy traffic to lines hardly equipped for the purpose—these were some of the consequences to the Railways that followed the political changes of August 1947. This difficult situation was superimposed on the rapidly deteriorating conditions caused by the intensive working of the railways during the war with all its reaction on the permanent track and rolling stock; and by the persistent difficulty felt in replacing them.[52]

Matthai said that all officers and staff, now mostly Indian, worked under conditions involving unprecedented strain. He was all praise however for the way in which they had risen to the occasion.

> It is among my few pleasant recollections during this very difficult period that our Indian officers faced by such a situation showed a degree of ability, leadership resourcefulness and tenacity which surpassed my best expectations. Within a year they not merely mastered the situation but succeeded in placing the Indian railways on a footing of progressive improvement and efficiency.[53]

A delicate problem that faced Matthai soon after Independence was to replace the British members of the Railway Board, who found it difficult to adapt themselves to the new situation. Their continuance in service on the existing terms had been guaranteed to them, but Matthai knew that many of them were looking for alternative openings and were anxious to leave. He said that working with such personnel in high positions at a time of unprecedented difficulties was a source of constant anxiety and worry to him. But relief came almost unexpectedly in the form of a departmental crisis, which induced the Chief Commissioner of Railways, Colonel R.B. Emerson, an able and honest but unimaginative Britisher, to send in his resignation, which Matthai promptly accepted.

This was followed immediately by the resignation of another British member of the Railway Board leaving only one British member on the board. Matthai said that he was fortunate in securing as the first Indian chief commissioner K.C. Bakhle, an experienced and able officer, who commanded the confidence of his officers and staff. It was to him that Matthai ascribed the marked improvement that began in the working of the railways within a year after the crisis of August 1947. However, not all saw it as improvement as the debates in the assembly, some of which are discussed in the next chapter, show.

Matthai noted with sorrow that 'officers who for years had worked together as brothers suddenly became rivals and looked at each other with communal eyes'.[54] He said that complicated details of finance and organization arising from Partition were disposed of with a speed and a casualness that were almost unbelievable. Many matters of importance were left over for settlement after Partition became effective. But the civil disturbances that immediately followed it created an atmosphere that was hardly compatible with the method of settlement by conference. He said, 'Speaking from my experience as Minister of Railways for a year since the Partition I cannot help thinking that whatever object motivated these hurried proceedings was achieved at a cost in administrative disorganization, financial loss and human suffering which is beyond computation.'[55]

Many years later Matthai reminisced:

I spent nearly four years as a Cabinet Minister in the first National Government. It was work which was extremely important but which I regret to say I enjoyed only in parts. The trouble with a Cabinet Minister is that he can never call his time his own. I cannot think of a period of equal length in my life when I did less general reading. In fact, the only literature I read consistently was reports of my own speeches which at the time were extremely depressing reading. When I was minister for

Railways, the railways were passing through the worst difficulties of the post partition period and I was the target of a good deal of criticism in Parliament.[56]

In the next two chapters, through an examination of the railway budgets, we see what Matthai did as the minister for Railways and Transport, the problems he faced, the remedies he suggested and the criticism he faced on a regular basis.

9

The Interim Railway Budget,
20 November 1947

On 20 November 1947, Matthai presented the first railway budget of independent India which was for the period 15 August 1947–31 March 1948. In one respect, he made an important departure from previous parliamentary practice. As an experimental step, he decided to abandon the long-standing practice of reading a written speech and to speak extempore with only a few notes for reference. Matthai said that the response he received both from the House and from the press convinced him that the experiment had succeeded beyond expectations. He said he 'had the delectable feeling that I had the sympathy and support of the House for the dismal tale of post partition troubles on the railways which it was my main business to unfold'.[1] He repeated the experiment with similar success in presenting the railway budget in February 1948.

Before the budget was presented, there were discussions on a variety of subjects pertaining to the disturbances caused by Partition, state of coaches and passenger amenities, and the steps the government proposed to take to remedy the many ills faced by the system, already under great strain, first due to the Second World War and then exacerbated by Partition.

Discussions and Deliberations before the Budget

Matthai faced questions in the assembly about whether the government planned to nationalize the Railways, the acute shortage of coaches and the poor condition of existing coaching stock. Inquiries were also made about the new coaches under construction, including ones with a new design.

Matthai in reply said that it was the policy of the government to purchase company-owned railways, where contracts with the companies authorized the government to do so, provided their purchase was justified on administrative and financial grounds. The question of the highly congested Oudh–Tirhut Railway was also discussed. Matthai said that the problems of this railway were a chronic headache for him, and he was making all efforts to improve matters. The shortage, old age and poor condition of locomotives were also commented upon.[2]

Members of the House wanted to know about the provision of electric fans in new coaches. Matthai had to deal with his share of absurd questions: One member went as far as asking if fans would be provided on doors and windows since many passengers were travelling hanging from them! Questions were also raised about many lower-class coaches that were running without lights. In reply, Matthai said that vandalism, theft and the shortage of material had all contributed to this phenomenon, but that every compartment was provided with at least one light.

The provision of drinking water and waterman was discussed as well as the labelling of water as 'Hindu' and 'Muslim' water. Matthai said that he proposed to increase the water hydrants as well as employ more waterman. As regards the communal divide even in drinking water, he said, 'That Sir, is a long-standing trouble. The arrangement still exists but I think what has been altered is the label under which water is distributed.' Another member wanted to know if there was any 'Schedule Caste Water'.[3]

Rustom K. Sidhva, who represented Central Provinces and Berar, wanted to know about the nuisance caused by passengers carrying dogs in the compartment. Matthai said that there were at least four safeguards in this regard. When Sidhva continued his questioning, asking about dangerous dogs, the speaker, G.V. Mavalankar, put an end to what was becoming a somewhat puerile discussion, with a peremptory, 'Next question. Enough of these dogs.'[4]

Questions were also raised about the state of national highway roads passing through big municipalities and if the government planned to undertake cement concreting of national highways where the traffic density was more than 1000 tonnes per day. Matthai said that no road passing through a large town or city had been included in the national highway system. In any case, the responsibility for such urban roads was with the local authority and the provincial governments had been told that it was not proposed to include urban roads in the national highway system.[5] P.S. Deshmukh, the member from CP and Berar, wanted to know the steps that were being taken to build the national highway between Nagpur and Bombay. Matthai said that such a road had been included in the national highway system, but it would be constructed by the provincial government.[6]

K. Santhanam, the member from Madras, wanted to know the effect of Partition on the railway system. Matthai said that the total mileage in India after the separation was 24,565 miles. The calculation of division of rolling stock and locomotives was underway. As regards the estimated loss due to communal disturbance, Matthai put the figure at Rs 2.33 crore for the period 15 August–31 October 1947. He said the movement of refugees by rail started from 27 August, and till 31 October, 12.56 lakh refugees were carried in trains that had crossed the border. In addition, 8.83 lakh refugees were transported in trains within India. The expenses incurred in the running of refugee trains were being charged to the general exchequer.[7]

Interim Budget

In the budget, Matthai outlined some of the problems that they had had to face due to Partition. He dealt with the subject under three heads: Firstly, the operating arrangements that Partition had rendered necessary. Secondly, the important issue of the division of assets and liabilities, and thirdly, certain problems of a current nature that had to be addressed as a result of Partition.

As regards the operating arrangements Matthai said that reciprocal 'running powers' had been given by both India and Pakistan to each other. When one railway ran a train to the border of the other railway, it was likely that due to the territorial division, the terminal points on the border would not have all the facilities necessary for dealing with these trains. Therefore, it became necessary to run the trains beyond the border into the territory of the other railway to points where stabling room, running rooms for staff and other necessary facilities were available. In certain sections of the railway that were completely isolated from the parent railway, 'working powers' were given so that the other railway could be allowed to work such sections under agreed arrangements.[8]

Similarly, workshops that used to work for a certain railway but now fell outside its border would continue to provide facilities as in the past. However, Matthai said that this arrangement had generally proved to be largely unsatisfactory, citing the examples of the Moghalpura Workshop, which served the Eastern Punjab Railway, but which now fell in Pakistan limits, and the Saidpur Workshop, also now in Pakistan, which was to serve the Assam Railway. The Kanchrapara Workshop in Indian territory was to provide similar service for the Pakistan Railway. To obviate trouble due to transhipment, Matthai said that through-booking of wagons and coaches had also been permitted. It was also agreed that there would be no change in fare or freight without prior notice being given to the other railway.

Division of Assets and Liabilities

Matthai first dealt with the problem of the division of assets and liabilities. As regards the division of capital liabilities, he said that the correct basis was the book value less depreciation of the share of assets both fixed and movable that had fallen to each side. Pakistan, on the other hand, thought that the earning capacity of the railway, was the correct method. The matter, he said, was before an arbitral tribunal. Matthai said that if a decision was taken based on Pakistan's principle, then it would get its 7000 miles of railways at 'practically scrap value'.[9]

He said that due to the disturbances caused by Partition, the railways had moved 2.5 million refugees, the normal capacity of roughly 800 passenger trains. Consequently, passenger services in other parts of the country had to be curtailed. 'The latest figure that I have is that the reduction of normal passenger services approximates to 3,800 miles per day,' he added.[10]

Operational Problems

Partition also resulted in the dislocation of goods traffic and this resulted in great congestion. In Punjab alone, thousands of loaded wagons were standing idle. A similar position obtained on other railways as well. Matthai said that the position had since improved but was one which was still of great concern. He lauded the role played by the railway staff in trying conditions and believed that that a word of appreciation was due for the valiant battle that they had waged against terrific odds.[11]

Matthai then spoke of the need to regroup the railways affected by Partition and also the need to link up the Assam Railway, now completely isolated, with the rest of the Indian railway system.[12] He then went on to describe the problems associated with the general movement of goods in the country. The first issue he flagged was the turnround of goods wagons. Wagon turnround[13] remains a performance metric that is monitored to this day. Matthai observed that wagon mobility was adversely affected mainly because the wagon turnround time, which was around nine to ten days in 1938–39, had increased to fourteen to fifteen days in 1947. This resulted in a 40–50 per cent decline in the availability of wagons as compared to the pre-war period. Matthai attributed the decline to civil disturbances that had started in August 1946.

In his speech, he said that while the number of wagons had increased by 15 per cent since 1938–39, an increase in the goods traffic by 20 per cent since 1938–39, had resulted in a slight gap.[14]

Coal movement was another problem. Monthly coal despatches had declined by 16 per cent and this was further exacerbated by civil disturbances in Punjab.[15] Transportation of coal had by then become a major bottleneck. A higher wagon turnround meant an accumulation of coal with the collieries due to the non-availability of wagons. This also affected the working capital of collieries, which in turn altered their production schedules. The slowdown in production also meant retrenchment of labour and attendant social problems.

An important change that occurred in the routing of traffic had to do with the movement of food grains that was imported from America. Prior to Partition, this cargo would land in Karachi. Now it came to Bombay. This exerted significant pressure on the Bombay Port and also the railways, which in turn transported the imported food grain to the hinterland. Another case in point was the diversion of coal traffic from Bombay to Kathiawar. In the past, this was sent by sea, but limited shipping capacity meant that a major portion of this cargo was now carried by the railways.[16]

Locomotives and Engine Crew

Locomotives were also in short supply. Before Partition, India had a total of 8400 locomotives. Of these, 2900 were overage, having outlived their codal life. They could not be replaced instantly as almost all were imported from abroad. In addition, there was a decline in the output of railway workshops due to labour unrest and the non-availability of spares. The number of days to overhaul a broad-gauge locomotive went up from forty days in 1938–39 to forty-eight days in 1946–47, resulting in a decline in output by 20 per cent. Metre-gauge workshops were worse off. The decline in output was 60 per cent.[17]

As per the original plan, all Muslim engine drivers, especially on the East Indian Railway (EIR) who had opted to go to Pakistan were to be relieved by March 1948. However, the riots in Punjab during Partition altered the atmosphere drastically. 'There was tension between Muslim and non-Muslim employees, particularly the engine crew,' Matthai said. This prompted the government to immediately release all the employees who had opted to go to Pakistan (including the Railways) by the end of September 1947. This resulted in a 47 per cent shortage in engine drivers on EIR, a shortage that was directly reflected in the decline in coal transported. A total of 2487 wagons were despatched in a day by both EIR and Bengal Nagpur Railway (BNR) on 29 September 1947. This number came down to 1410 wagons in a matter of three days on 2 October 1947. A national crisis was looming large.[18]

Matthai outlined the three steps he had taken to improve the situation. The first was the decision to elevate junior engine workers, such as firemen, cleaners and drivers even though they did not possess the requisite experience. The second step was diverting a large number of drivers from other sections of these railways to the collieries. The third was speedy recruitment of staff who had opted to relocate to India. With these measures, EIR was able to reduce vacancies to 25 per cent.

* * *

When Matthai presented the first interim railway budget, about 18 lakh tonnes of coal had accumulated at the collieries. Of this, the normal stock at collieries was 8–9 lakh tonnes. About 2600–2700 wagons were being moved daily during that time by EIR and BNR. This was sufficient to move the coal produced in those days (November 1947), but movement of the accumulated coal required an additional 200 wagons per day. Matthai was optimistic that the means that were being devised then were enough to fulfil the requirement in a short time. Given the serious challenges posed by Partition to put the railways back on track, Matthai, while presenting his first railway budget, envisaged a three-year horizon for things to settle down. The reason was simple: The Indian Railways had ordered additional rolling stock from both domestic and international suppliers for its present and future requirements. This, however, was expected to be delivered only after 1948.[19]

On its part, Indian Railways had already started expanding the capacity of its marshalling yards and railway lines; improving the work atmosphere in workshops and with it the output; and deputing a senior railway official to the USA for studying the latest developments in rail transportation. The next most important issue that Matthai had to handle was employees, both labour and superior staff. As noted before, labour unrest had been simmering since May 1946 with the AIRF demanding better pay and better working conditions. The threat of a general railway strike was averted after a temporary settlement was reached in June 1946 giving ad hoc relief. This settlement resulted in the appointment of a Pay Commission, which was given the mandate to resolve labour-related issues.[20] In fact, Matthai had already started discussions with the AIRF soon after taking over as minister, just after Independence. He understood the trust deficit between the labour and management very well and apprehended sporadic flash strikes and go-slow tactics given the general atmosphere prevailing in the days just after Partition.

Indianization of Staff

Finding Indian staff fit to serve in the higher echelons of the railway bureaucracy was Matthai's biggest challenge when he took over. He referred to this as 'Indianization of Superior Staff'. Non-Indians had not been recruited since 1943. Neither did the railways have any plans to recruit more officers after August 1947 other than the technical staff.

Though the government had announced that there would not be any discrimination against non-Indian employees (especially the Europeans), as many as 166 out of the 338 European officers opted to leave the country. With nearly half of the positions held by Europeans falling vacant, replacements had to be identified. It was also imperative to identify a pool of officers and train them to take up senior positions in the hierarchy. Such employees with senior-level experience could not be found at such short notice.

Moreover, Matthai was also expecting additional vacancies at the middle and senior levels in case more Europeans left. Consequently, the then government made an important policy decision regarding replacements for European officers leaving India.[21] Matthai proposed that any future vacancy created by the exit of a European officer would be filled by an

Indian of proven ability irrespective of seniority. The government decided that such a move was in the national interest even if it meant overlooking the prospects of a non-Indian officer who had opted to stay back in India after Independence. This was unavoidable since the government could not prevent any non-Indian officer from leaving.

This policy was first implemented in the Railway Board. Just before Independence, the Railway Board had five members: four Europeans and one Indian. After Independence, the board was reconstituted with six members: five Indians and one European. The sixth was a temporary member entrusted with the responsibility of dealing with refugee-related work.

Railway Finances

The finances of the Railways were under tremendous stress when Matthai took over after Independence. Working expenses were estimated to rise due to an increase in prices of coal and food grains and pay commission proposals. Besides, the adjudicator had ruled in favour of railway staff in matters of working hours and leave conditions.

Matthai said that the reserves stood at Rs 21.61 crore in November 1947. After adjusting the net loss of Rs 16.92 crore, there was a net surplus of Rs 4.69 crore. However, the Betterment Fund and the Depreciation Fund were intact, giving Matthai something to cheer about. He said the Railways would make a net surplus of Rs 4 crore if the status quo continued for another year. His estimate was based on two assumptions: one, an increase in economies and two, a reduction in ticketless travel.

On the subject of ticketless travel, Matthai said that the problem had assumed acute proportions since the refugee problem had started. He said that it was resulting in a loss of Rs 8 crore annually and while measures of a railway character could be taken, he believed that the problem had 'gone much beyond the limits of Railway measures' and now had to be tackled as a law-and-order problem. The problem had been particularly acute in the United Provinces, and he said that he had had discussions with the premier of UP on the subject.[22]

Fare Increase

Matthai increased passenger fares as follows: For first-class tickets, fares were raised from 24 pies[23] per mile to 30 pies per mile for up to 300 miles (first slab). For distances thereafter, the fare was 18 pies per mile plus a

13 per cent surcharge, second class fares increased from 12 to 15 pies per mile for the first slab and thereafter at nine paise per mile plus 13 per cent surcharge. Inter-class fares were fixed at nine paise per mile for mail trains and 7.5 pies per mile for ordinary trains up from the then average rate of 5.47 pies per mile plus a surcharge.[24]

For the lowest class of travel, the third class, fares were fixed at five pies for mail trains and four paise for ordinary up from the then average rate of 3.6 pies per mile. Matthai explained that the differential fares were being charged for mail and ordinary trains so as to not impose an additional burden on the lowest class passengers. With these proposals, Matthai expected first-class revenue to increase 80 per cent, second class and inter class by 40 per cent each, and third class by 33 per cent over pre-Independence fares. Season ticket rates in urban areas were also increased by 50 per cent for the first class, 25 per cent for the second class, 18.75 per cent for the inter class and 12.5 per cent for the third class. In rural areas, monthly season tickets were priced at the equivalent of 12 return fares.[25]

The country was going through a period of transition and Matthai did not propose any general increase in freight rates. However, he made certain internal re-adjustments in freight rate classification: upgrading goods to higher classes, introduction of telescopic rates and a review of station-to-station rates. Coal haulage rates were increased by four annas (25 paise) per ton. In addition, concession rates for steel were also increased by the BNR.[26]

Matthai also proposed the setting up of a Railway Rates Tribunal, an independent judicial body, in April 1948 for an unbiased examination of freight rates. He knew that the decision to increase fares and freight would be unpopular. He concluded his statement by observing that an increase was the only way to avoid a deficit given the circumstances prevailing in those days.[27]

Discussion and Debates on the Budget

Seth Govind Das, the member from CP and Berar, criticized the increase in fares and thought that the third-class fares should not have been increased at all. He then criticized the railways for a lack of passenger amenities, lack of lights in the compartments, scarcity of water in trains and at stations, and overcrowding. He also wanted abolition of the first class. Hussain Imam, the member from Bihar, was more understanding of the fare increase. He said that it was justified since wages had doubled and cost of coal too had increased considerably. He also said that the third-class fare was the lowest in the world, and if more comfortable travel was to be provided to the passengers, there would have to be a further increase in fares.[28]

This view was endorsed by Naziruddin Ahmad, the member from West Bengal, who thought that there was nothing wrong in asking the public to pay for their journey and the cost of transporting goods. He did not think that the railway was being converted into a tax-gathering body. Ahmad, while congratulating Matthai on his speech, said that its excellence may have been due to its synchronization with another happy event: the wedding of Queen Elizabeth II with Prince Philip in London, the ceremonies of which were being actually performed when Matthai rose to speak. 'This may be, cynics may say, a coincidence but I would prefer to call it a happy augury.'[29] Clearly, Ahmad was a fan of the British royal family.

A.P. Pattani, who represented the Western Indian states, wanted to know when the manufacture of locomotives would begin, and the scarcity of spare parts overcome.[30] Prof. N.G. Ranga from Madras wanted more details on the demands for grants which related to the proposed expenditure during the rest of the year. He was critical of the fact that the permanent members of the railway board had been increased to five from three. He did not think that the increase was justified and said that perhaps this was illustrative of the wasteful expenditure in other railway departments as well. While commending Matthai for making the Railway Rates Tribunal a more permanent body, he wanted all stakeholders to be associated with decisions made by the tribunal. Apart from the usual criticism of the poor state of the third class, Ranga wanted better waiting rooms, latrines, raising of platforms at stations and departmental catering in trains and at stations. He cited the example of the South Indian Railway, where departmental catering was a great success. Ranga also raised the issue of corruption on the railway system. He congratulated Matthai on the excellent labour relations but wanted the lower levels of staff to participate more actively with the administration in decision-making.[31]

Rohini Kumar Chaudhuri from Assam bemoaned the fact that since even persons who bought tickets could not be accommodated, it was pointless to penalize those who did not. Matthai, it must be remembered, had said that he would raise Rs 8 crore through penalties from ticketless travel. Chaudhuri also narrated his own unhappy experience while travelling first class. 'I was travelling in a first-class compartment and two of the posts of the bunk broke down . . . The bunk simply collapsed.'[32]

Perhaps the most stinging criticism came from Sidhva, who was also the president of the All-India Railways Passenger Association. He said that every year, improvement was promised but nothing materialized on the ground. His litany of complaints, especially in the third class, included deficiencies in lights, fans, taps, safety catches, planks of the coaches, mirrors and basins, shutters of windows as well as lack of water.

He said that theft of bulbs by passengers had been offered as the main reason for the lack of adequate lighting in the compartments. Sidhva said that this was astounding since the bulbs were manufactured for use only in railway carriages and were totally useless for domestic or commercial use. Moreover, the bulbs were put in a globe that was then locked. It was therefore absurd to suggest that a passenger would first procure the key and then steal a bulb (totally useless to him) and that too in the presence of fifty to 100 passengers. Sidhva then told the House what he thought was the real reason for the missing bulbs: They were being systematically stolen in the railway yards and sold back to the same railway contractor who supplied them.[33]

Sidhva also wanted to know when the protype of the new third-class coach of a train called the 'Silver Arrow' (newly independent India's version of today's Vande Bharat Express) would be introduced on the system. 'I do admit they are very fine. But God knows when we shall see them working on the lines,' he said.[34] Ticket checking too was impossible in the absence of lights and Sidhva said that the excuses of railway officers were not 'tenable for one moment'. He bemoaned the fact that the war had long been over, but conditions were worsening rather than improving. S.K. Patil, the member from Bombay, said that the future of nationalization of other industries depended on the success of the state-run railways. He added that if nationalization was going to go down the path the railways were following it would be a very poor advertisement for future steps in this regard.[35]

Frank R. Anthony, who represented the Anglo-Indian community, said that a number of running staff who had earlier opted for Pakistan now wanted to remain in India and he wanted Matthai to consider the matter sympathetically. He also wanted Matthai to control the vandalism on trains and the theft of coal. More importantly, he was perhaps one of the few members who broke a lance in defence of the much-harried railwaymen. He wanted the public to know the extremely difficult conditions under which railway staff were working and wanted a more public acknowledgement, 'an emphatic tribute which is highly publicised' so that the public could know about the railwayman's 'yeoman service'. He said there was a tendency 'to complain all too generally and all too easily about some incident in a waiting room, or in a refreshment car or in some carriage.'[36] But he wanted discipline to be enforced among the 'inferior staff', whose output in the largest workshop of the EIR was just two man-hours per day. He wanted more interaction between the officers and the staff, but not a petty dictatorship which made the official both feared and hated. But liberality should not be interpreted, he said, to do as one liked.[37]

H.J. Khandekar from CP and Berar raised the issue of separate cups and saucers for 'Harijan' passengers and staff on trains and at stations. He himself had been mistaken for a Mahar and was pointed in the direction of the cup and saucer for the untouchables. He said that he received a reply from the Railway Board, and that too after much delay, saying that it was not obligatory to serve tea on the trains.[38] Khandekar also complained that Matthai was hardly listening to him since he was speaking in Hindi. 'He should try to learn Hindi in free India,' he said, referring to Matthai's unfamiliarity with the language.

H.V. Kamath from CP and Berar raised a point similar to Khandekar's when he referred to 'Hindu and Muslim water' at stations. The nomenclature had now been changed to 'orthodox water' and 'general water', but they still meant the same thing. Narrating his own experience at Allahabad station, he said that the so-called orthodox water was denied him because of his beard. He said, that after considerable argument he 'succeeded in getting even this orthodox water in spite of my hirsute appendage'.[39]

Though the Indian railways has travelled very far since those dark days, Kamath ended with an appeal that remains relevant to this day: 'In conclusion I would like to say that the common man must be made to feel that the railway is his own, that it is a national asset and not merely an instrument of exploitation and oppression.' He wanted the Railways to become an instrument of national happiness and prosperity and hoped that it would become one of the best in the world.[40]

Matthai's Response

In his reply, Matthai said that it was impossible to answer all the questions raised by members, but he would respond to some of the more important problems that were highlighted. He agreed with the need to improve the third class.[41]

He attributed the serious overcrowding to the fact that since 1938–39, passenger traffic had doubled, but the coaches had increased by only by about 10 per cent. Ticketless travel, Matthai said, had greatly aggravated the problem of overcrowding. He said that 'bad citizenship' was only part of the problem. The railways too were to blame since booking offices were inadequate and railway printing presses were not working. Hence, tickets could not be dispensed to even those who were willing to buy them. To ameliorate part of the problem of overcrowding, he said that an additional 800 coaches would be pressed into service, some returned by the defence department, and others which were new.[42]

Matthai agreed with S.K. Patil's concerns about the performance of the railways affecting future nationalization. 'If this large industry which stands out as the typical example of a nationalised concern in the country gives so little satisfaction, then it knocks the bottom out of the case for nationalisation.'[43] Matthai said he was not advocating universal nationalization, but the case had to be considered with reference to the circumstances of each industry. He said that if the railways had been a private concern, then it would have been able to raise fares to cover costs, but as a nationalized concern, it had been unable to do so.[44]

Addressing the concerns of certain members on the question of economy he said that two-thirds of the total working expenses were on staff and labour. Since he did not decide the pay scales, there was no way of reducing salaries. The other way of effecting economy was by a reduction in staff. This too was not going to be easy, given the substantial extension of the liberalization process with regard to working conditions, granting of leave and hours of work. Unable to either reduce staff or salaries, there was nothing he could do to reduce expenditure on an item which was two-thirds of the total working expenses. Referring to the increase in the strength of the board to six, he said that the refugee crisis had necessitated an additional member to deal exclusively with that problem and that this extra post would be abolished within a week's time. He added that twelve superior posts in the board had also been abolished leading to a saving of

Rs 2 lakh per annum and the process of downsizing (rightsizing in today's parlance) would continue.[45]

With regard to economies in the use of coal, Matthai said that the administration was making all efforts to reduce its use of high-grade coal. However, since freight costs contributed greatly to the cost of coal in a vast country like India, even with the use of inferior coal, the freight paid was the same. In fact, with other components like ash in the inferior coal, the Railways were paying freight for a lot of other elements mixed with coal, which had no calorific value. If this argument was accepted, then in some ways, inferior coal was actually increasing costs rather than decreasing them.[46]

Replying to Sidhva's concerns about the introduction of the 'Silver Arrow', he said that many suggestions had been received by them based on the questionnaires sent out and most of them had to do with the doorways, the footboard and the luggage space provided. Matthai, in response to a question from Seth Govind Das, said that the main difference between the 'Silver Arrow' and the old coaches was that the latter was about 10 feet wide, whereas the new one was 11 feet 8 inches, and this increase made a lot of difference as regards the amenities that could be provided inside the coaches.[47]

Matthai agreed with Frank Anthony about the relations between officers, supervisors and labour and wanted the personal contact to be at the level of the district (a railway division in today's parlance) because that was where the primary work of the railways was done (and still is done). He said that he was concentrating his attention on that aspect.[48]

Cut Motions

On 26 November, P.S. Deshmukh brought a cut motion of Rs 100 when Matthai proposed the demand in respect of Demand No. 1 the 'Railway Board'. He had already brought cut motions with reference to comfort of passengers, thefts, and the impossibility of closing and opening doors. His current grievance, for which he had brought the cut motion, was hardly new: overcrowding in trains. He took Matthai to task in very strong language. He said that he had been told by his friends that passengers were 'herded like cattle' or 'packed like sardines'. 'My view is that neither cattle nor sardines – if they were alive – would be able to tolerate the situation which is being forced upon people in the present circumstances.'[49]

Also, passengers were forced to climb in through the windows and that too after having thrown their trunk in first. 'The trunk is a good weapon and once you are able to throw it in you find it easy to get in also.'[50]

He said that the perception was of an irresponsible railway administration and the public had lost hope of any improvement. He hoped that Matthai was not as 'apathetic' as his department and wanted some kind of assurance that things would improve early. He said that the 'lucidity of Matthai's speech or the expert presentation of his case' was not enough and wanted his eloquent words to be translated into comforts for the people.[51]

The cut motion was then moved by the speaker, and it was the turn of B. Pattabhi Sitaramayya, the member from Madras, to speak. He was equally scathing in his criticism calling it humanly impossible to 'execute third-class travel from its first to its last stages'. He complained about how difficult it was to buy a ticket because the booking clerk would come only two minutes before the arrival of the train.

> These people are absolutely like buffaloes under rain. Nothing will move them and they are the lords of the station and they do not see that the government has changed ... It has changed only for the Ministers ... As no chain is stronger than its weakest link, the Minister is no faster than his slowest department official.[52]

He said that the railway officials were looked upon by the public with a feeling of bitterness and helplessness. He wanted Matthai to inject some patriotism, common-sense and decency into the administration. This he said could be done not by departmental reminders but by conferences telling them that the times had changed, and they must also change.

Sitaramayya, in the course of his speech, described the travails of a full journey: the inability to buy a ticket, difficulty of entry first into the waiting room and then the carriage, and difficulty in exiting at the destination because only one gate was generally opened even though the railway staff could easily open the other one. To highlight the general apathy, he cited the case of the Bezwada (Vijayawada) station, where he had been carrying on a correspondence for fifteen years to prevent the channels of urine flowing on to the platform. He wanted them to dig a small drain, but nothing was done. Calling the railway authorities 'an impenetrable mass of human material', he said nothing could move them.[53]

Sitaramayya wanted to tackle the problem of overcrowding by having a double-decker coach, by building 'an upper storey to the third-class carriages as in the tram cars'. In response to this, a member said in jest, 'And then build an overbridge.' Sitaramayya missed the humour (or sarcasm, if you will) saying that there would be a staircase to go up. Seeing Matthai's disapproval, he made a statement that has a grain of truth in it even in present times. 'A layman's suggestion should not be so summarily dispensed with because technical men are hopeless. You should never trust them. As far as possible reject their advice and force a layman's sound common-sense on their (new sense) view.'[54]

Matthai, in response to the cut motion, said he had not been told anything that he did not know, or been deeply conscious of. He said that the travelling conditions of third-class passengers had been agitating his mind for long and he did not want to offer any explanations or put forward any excuses. He wanted, rather, to focus on the practical aspects by which some material improvement could be made. While agreeing with Sitaramayya about a change in the way of thinking, he believed that the question was not really about a 'change of heart', but the situation had to be dealt with on a concrete practical basis. Overcrowding was a function of excess demand (passenger traffic) and inadequate supply (of coaches) and could only be tackled by addressing either or both aspects. He then proceeded to give various statistics about new coaches already introduced, and those on the anvil. 'We have placed as many orders as we are in a position to get carried out. The fabricating and manufacturing capacity of our country is extremely limited . . .'[55]

P.S. Deshmukh, who had moved the cut motion, insinuated that if only Matthai would 'put his heart into the business, he should be able to set the position right within the next few months'. A visibly irked Matthai responded by saying,

> I wish I could. The only thing that I can say in reply to a challenge of that kind is to make him (the mover) a sporting offer. Let him take my place. I have no particular motive for being here except to see that some little service is done and some improvement effected.[56]

Matthai conceded that if the railway staff treated passengers with more patience and consideration, things would improve. They had been used to an entirely different system so far and Matthai believed that if an attitudinal change was to come about, then training was essential. He suggested a corps of railway staff travelling on trains in the capacity of social service workers who 'would bring to bear upon this problem the mentality of social workers rather than of bureaucrat employees'.[57]

Pandit Govind Malaviya, from the United Provinces, brought a cut motion on the question of economy, efficiency and corruption. He expressed concern at the mounting working expenses and the tardy growth in revenues. He stressed the cutting of costs and thought that a regrouping and amalgamation of railways would help. He wanted the nine separate railway administrations to be grouped into three administrations. Apart from efficiency and economy, he showed his concern for rampant corruption in the allotment of wagons. He said that these were being supplied to black marketeers without any record at 'fantastic charges', which the dishonest officers pocketed. The modus operandi was to report such wagons for the time being as untraceable.

K. Santhanam from Madras proposed a cut motion of Rs 1 crore on the question of economy. He wanted all extraneous and superfluous expenditure by the railway bureaucracy to be cut. He said that he knew Matthai could not perform miracles but wanted him to adopt the policy of reducing everything to its normal level. Shibban Lal Saksena, the member from the United Provinces, was unhappy with the way the recommendations of the Central Pay Commission had been implemented and the method of calculating the additional burden on the exchequer. He said that 80 per cent of the salaries had not yet been fixed and what was extraordinary was that in the case of some 1.5 lakh staff, the salary had been reduced. Thus, to say that the fare increase was justified due to the burden of the Pay Commission was patently false. In response to the argument that on the performance of the railways would rest the future of nationalization, he opined that in the past, the railways had been run by a foreign government and therefore the amount earned was not spent in the best interest of the railways. He suggested that the performance of the railways should only be judged from the present period.[58]

Saksena also criticized Matthai for saying that a very high standard was applied while judging the railways, but the same standard was not applied to other industries such as the textile industry. He said that the textile industry was run by capitalists for their own benefit, whereas the railways were run by the government for the benefit of the people. 'I think we have a right to demand from the government a full explanation of everything done and a much higher standard of efficiency,' Saksena said.[59]

Biswanath Das from Orissa said that things would be better if Matthai reflected 'our hearts, our ideals' instead of being guided by his bureaucrats, who he called the 'henchmen of the British Raj' until three months ago. He took exception to Matthai saying that the railways had provided 'cheap services in spite of all-round rise in prices and wages' as long as it was possible to do so. He said that Indian railways had continuously fed the engineering industries in England. The plan to manufacture locomotives in Ajmer in other workshops had not fructified and he wanted those officials (he called them fifth columnists) who had patronized British industry to leave India.[60] He also wanted retrenchment of surplus staff without fear of strikes by socialists and communists. Matthai, he said, in an earlier avatar in Tatas had worked as an 'employer' and he wanted him as minister to also do the same with no useless labour being retained on the system. 'We have gone through the bureaucratic tradition and we must come under the National tradition,' he said.[61]

Anthony attributed the decline in efficiency to the increasing dissatisfaction and frustration among railwaymen. He said that the gulf between officers and subordinates was large, and the railway officials had very little contact with, and no understanding, of the employee or their problems. In the old regime, Anthony said, the official ruled by fear. That fear had now disappeared, and the officers had no weapon with which to substitute it. The employee had come to feel that he could not expect a fair deal from his superiors or a redressal of his grievance.

Anthony said that he was in touch with eighty railway centres, large and small, and knew the feelings of the staff, unlike Matthai, who was getting his information from his officials, who were unresponsive in the extreme. 'So unresponsive is your officialdom today that I find even the sober and stable elements among the railwaymen are being weaned away from their traditions of loyalty and service.'[62] He warned of a 'gigantic paralysis' within six months if Matthai did not put aside his die-hard officials reared in the wrong psychology and reach out to the lower echelons himself and try to understand their grievances and problems. The top management worked on the principle of 'My officers, right or wrong'. Anthony further said that the staff was not entirely unresponsive. 'They do not merely want an increase of wages, so much as they do an increase in understanding.'[63]

In his reply, Matthai said that if working expenses had increased more than the increase in prices, it was because of poor productivity. He said that Anthony had indicated that a change in relationship with the staff was key, and it would result in enhanced output. Matthai said that he was at the head of a million people, and it was impossible for him to be in personal touch with so many employees. He said that the appropriate method of getting in touch with the labour was through their unions, and he was already in touch with them so that each side could better appreciate the other's problems and viewpoint.

> In fact, it is, I think, an unsound thing for the head of the railway administration to contact individual persons in labour except through the organisation which has been set up by labour itself; otherwise, you introduce into your labour organization a disruptive element which will react adversely both on the management and on labour.[64]

As regards the cut motion of Rs 1 crore, Matthai said that with inelastic expenditure on items like staff and coal, the prospects of effecting economy were very limited. But since he realized the strong feelings of the House on the subject of economy, he said he would agree to a cut from 1 crore to Rs 50 lakh. 'Although I see at present no light as regards the possibility of effecting economy, I would put this amount of compulsion on myself in response to the wishes of the House.'[65]

Apart from the budget discussion, there were also other questions, which ranged from the progress of the locomotive factory at Kanchrapara to the manufacture of new coaches expected to be introduced in the current year. A member wanted to know details about the recent emergency recruitment of drivers. Matthai said that of the fifty-two who offered their services, forty-six were retained. As far as the new Silver Arrow coaches were concerned, Matthai said that a new design was in the process of being approved which would have better amenities and more space. A question that came up repeatedly was the abolition of the first class. Matthai said that it was under consideration.[66] He had to field a number of questions on a variety of subjects. These were concerned with standardizing railway equipment, poor quality of coaching stock, loss due to evacuating refugees (Rs 8 crore per annum), payment of claims on goods lost or destroyed and the safety of passengers.

As regards the number of locomotives on the system, Matthai said that it was 6333 and 573 were expected from abroad, and sixty-eight from domestic sources. It had been decided to overturn the decision to make locomotives at the Kanchrapara workshop since otherwise it would handicap the Bengal and Assam Railway considerably.

* * *

It is a little remembered fact that Tata Locomotive and Engineering Company Ltd (TELCO, now Tata Motors) came into being when the workshops at Singhbhum were sold by East Indian Railway to the Tatas. Matthai told the House that the new company had entered into an agreement with TELCO to manufacture fifty locomotives and fifty boilers. A further order of 100 locomotives and fifty-eight boilers had recently been placed with the firm. TELCO had delivered the first locomotive boiler in July 1947. The government had approved the company's scheme for the manufacture of locomotives, and it was required to commence production within a period of two years from the date of receipt of the necessary plant and machinery. No estimate could be made of this date.

Matthai also said that the Ajmer workshops of the BB&CI Railway had been manufacturing locomotives for a few years and production would continue. Orders had been placed for fifty-eight narrow-gauge locomotives, the boilers for which would be supplied by TELCO. Matthai ended on an optimistic note, 'As far as the present position is concerned, it is possible for the government to say that practically all the normal requirements of the Indian railways in respect of locomotives would be met by indigenous manufacture.'[67]

* * *

The railway portfolio has always been a challenging one, and never more so than in Matthai's time. It was clear from his closing statement in the budget that he had formed an opinion of the enormity of the task that confronted him.

> What I have tried to do Mr Speaker, is to give the House a clear picture of the way in which the Railways are functioning under the extremely difficult conditions which prevail today – more difficult than any I had

anticipated in my most pessimistic moments – as clear a picture as I could make of the struggles, the failures, the achievements such as they are, and the hopes of this great national undertaking of *which, for the time being, for no fault of mine, if I may say so, I happen to be the nation's custodian.*[68] (Emphasis added)

The last sentence reveals his sense of desperation and a feeling that he was faced with a thankless job. But he would not be there long. Matthai presented the railway budget for 1948–49 and in September 1949 left to join as finance minister. It is to Matthai's railway budget presented in February 1948 that we now turn.

10

The Railway Budget, 1948–49

A Source of Embarrassment: The Grand Trunk Express

Matthai faced numerous problems during his tenure as railways and transport minister. He was often criticized for, and had to face uncomfortable questions in the assembly, on the unpunctual running of trains. One serious pain in the neck was a train that was perpetually late: the Grand Trunk Express, which ran from Madras to Delhi. Matthai faced much discomfiture when he had to constantly defend and make excuses for the performance of this late runner.

It also became the butt of many jokes. When questioned by the House about the reasons for the late arrival and late departure from Delhi, Matthai gave a number of reasons to show why the matter was largely out of his control. The train was handed over late at Balharshah by the Nizam's State Railway and the entire journey, except for a small stretch between Nagpur and Wardha, was on a single line section. Thus, a train losing its path could rarely make up time. Matthai also attributed the delay to the old age of the locomotives and poor grade of coal. The absence of an overlapping rake and the need to segregate passengers belonging to separate communities given the communal situation in northern India only added to the problem.[1]

Questions were raised as to its detention at wayside stations to give precedence to freight trains. Questions were also raised as to why it arrived only a few hours late in Delhi but was six to twelve hours late when it reached Madras, and the reason for late starts at both originating and destination stations. Matthai attributed the late start to the absence of

an overlapping rake. This had now been made good, and he hoped that it
would make a difference.

H.V. Kamath said that based on the facts admitted by Matthai, it
was obvious that the train was neither 'grand' nor 'express' and wanted to
know if there were plans to give it a more appropriate name. Matthai did
not miss the humour in the question and responded with his own erudite
brand of wit.

> That is a matter, Sir, which I have seriously considered. I may perhaps tell
> the Honourable Member one of the names that I have been considering.
> Rudyard Kipling wrote a poem long ago in which he described Madras
> as 'a withered beldame'. That I think would be an appropriate name for
> the Grand Trunk Express.[2]

Railway Budget, 1948–49

In just a few days over three months after presenting the interim budget,
Matthai presented the railway budget for 1948–49 on 16 February 1948.
He said that since it had been barely three months since he had had the
honour of introducing the interim railway budget, the House would
appreciate that there was nothing new to add. He said that he would deal
with the budgetary position and give the House a few indications of the
directions in which things had changed either for the better or for the
worse. He said that he wanted to spare members the minutiae of financial
and statistical details since in his experience as a legislator 'a budget speech
which is packed with details has invariably the effect of making honourable
members groan almost visibly'.[3]

Financial Position

Matthai told the House that the reality was very different from their earlier
budget estimates and the revised estimates for the seven and a half months
ending 31 March 1948 showed a fall in earnings of about Rs 8 crore as
compared with the budget estimates. Various elements of uncertainty
contributed to this discrepancy: The budget estimates were framed in the
thick of the period of civil disturbances and refugee movements and this
had made it difficult to forecast the probable trend of earnings. They had
to frame budget estimates for a divided India based on their experience of

an undivided India. Also, estimates had to be framed for a broken period, based on their experience for a whole previous year, and Matthai told the members that it was a very difficult matter in actual practice to make 'allowance for those seasonal variations which occur between one period and another in the course of a year'.[4]

There was a fall in both goods and passenger earnings, but other coaching consisting largely of parcel traffic had shown an increase. There was considerable military movement as a result of demobilization and of the movement of troops to disturbed areas. The net drop was Rs 8 crore. There was also a drop in ordinary working expenses, but this was not the result of economy measures; it was because the estimated expenditure for 1947–48 could not be incurred before the end of that year. Thus, the expenditure was not reduced, but merely postponed. All this had resulted in an increase in the net loss from the estimated Rs 2.7 crore to Rs 5.2 crore, the result of which was that they have had to make larger withdrawals from the Reserve Fund, which stood at Rs. 3.8 crore in March 1948.[5]

Matthai expected that in 1948–49, the gross traffic proceeds would be Rs 190 crore. As against that, he estimated that the ordinary working expenses would be Rs 147.15 crore. Deducting working expenses, depreciation and payment to worked lines, Matthai expected to have a net revenue of Rs 32.38 crore. After deducting the liability on account of interest charges of Rs 22.53 crore, they would be left with a net surplus of Rs 9.85 crore for 1948–49.[6]

He said that the House would be relieved to know that he did not intend to increase fares and freights. 'Probably the only redeeming feature of my Budget is that I do not propose on this occasion to pursue this evil tradition.'[7] Regarding the contribution of the Railways to the general revenues, Matthai said that the matter was before a committee of the House and any decision in this regard would be taken when the findings of the committee were received.

Matthai told the House that he thought that the worst was over. 'This does not mean that there is any striking and decided improvement that I can report. What it means is that we have reached a stage where we can go forward expecting steady progress.'[8] Matthai said that they had reached the end of a period of serious civil disturbances and the vast refugee movements. 'The House will remember that altogether during a period of two and a half months the Railways were called upon to move as many as 3 million refugees, which represents the capacity of a thousand passenger trains. That was a period of terrible strain on the Railways and we have now come to the end of that period of strain.'[9]

Operational Problems

The terrible strain caused by the events of Partition were now a thing of the past, but there was a large diversion of traffic, which had occurred as a result of various war developments. A large volume of traffic was moving along routes ill-equipped for the purpose and it was necessary to improve and extend the marshalling yards that were unable to cope with the growing volume of traffic.[10] Matthai said that pending a large extension of the marshalling yards, they had set up an arrangement for a much more intensive and effective supervision of these yards. They had also set up a more effective system of control of train movements. Both these steps had already started yielding satisfactory results with the detention in major yards, such as Asansol, Andal and Moradabad, coming down.

The next factor, Matthai said, was the workshop position. A paucity of locomotives (and the old age of the existing ones) was a serious problem, and the main reason for the current woes of the Railways. In this connection, the importance of workshops assumed great importance. Workshops had suffered from an acute shortage of spares in the past, but now the situation had eased somewhat, with deliveries from the UK and larger orders being placed in the country. Labour was another important aspect. Matthai said that the number of man-days worked in the workshops had improved but unfortunately its productivity left much to be desired. Administrative devices installed with the cooperation of organized labour were seen as a solution.[11]

Matthai said that an improvement in availability of spare parts and productivity had translated into an improvement in the turnround of broad-gauge wagons to 45.9 days from forty-eight days, but a deterioration in the metre gauge from fifty-one days to 60.7 days.[12] The latter metric had deteriorated as a result of serious disturbances in the Ajmer workshop, which was one of the biggest metre-gauge workshops. If the figure for Ajmer was ignored, then even the metre-gauge turnaround showed an improvement.[13]

The staff position had also stabilized by then and there were lesser vacancies, especially in the engine crew in the East Indian Railway, which had created a national crisis in respect of coal movements. When faced with the crew shortage on the East Indian Railway, the total number of wagons that could be sent to the collieries directly on the East Indian Railway and the Bengal Nagpur Railways was about 1400. In November 1947, it had risen to 2600 and as per Matthai, the recent figures showed an increase to 2900.

An aspect that affected the mobility of the system, and ultimately goods loading, was the undue detention to wagons by trade and even by government departments. Matthai observed that there were cases when a large number of wagons came back empty from collieries due to problems in the collieries. This was unacceptable given the difficult position of the railway system. Matthai told the House that they had reduced the free time allowed for demurrage purposes from nine hours of daylight to six hours and that Sundays would also count for the purposes of demurrage. He said that the Railways had been set a target of three hours for placing a wagon for unloading and a maximum of twenty-hour hours detention in a yard.[14]

Matthai said that the operational improvement had to some extent been offset by the disorganization of traffic caused by the policy of decontrol. For example, in food grains, before the introduction of decontrol, all the essential movements sponsored by the government were given top priority and grouped in Class I. When the role of the government reduced, it became necessary to make it possible for private movements to move more freely, and the movements of food grains on private account were given higher priority from Class IV to Class II. There were a large number of indents and the demand for wagons could not be met.

Thus, indents for some commodities were accepted, and some turned down, all of which were in the same grade of priority. This caused resentment among those who could not be served. Matthai said that unregulated movements on private account resulted in cross movements. There were a number of cases where goods despatched by traders to a particular destination were rebooked immediately on arrival and sent on to another destination that was much closer to the original point of consignment. This resulted in a great wastage of transport. He said that perhaps some programme for essential commodities was required and if they found that the policy of decontrol was being nullified by the unnecessary load being put on the railways, it would be necessary to consider fixation of quotas and regulation by zonal control.[15]

Matthai told the House that various line capacity works for doubling (Itarsi–Bhopal, Lucknow– Bareilly, Cawnpore–Etawah and the Moradabad section, among others) had been undertaken and the target for these was March 1949. Similarly, there were plans for the remodelling and extension of marshalling yards, all of which were expected to be complete by March 1949.[16] He also informed the House about the delivery of wagons and oil tank wagons saying that in all, 4720 wagons were scheduled to be delivered by March 1949, but given the strained conditions in India, he expected that only half that number would be delivered. He also said that 146 locomotives were to be delivered in the course of 1948.[17]

Matthai believed that that there was a marked improvement in the prospects of the world food position. Assuming that there was an improvement in the general food position, he thought that a very heavy load would be lifted off the Railways since one of the biggest problems it faced since the end of the war was the transportation over long distances of large quantities of food grains.

Overcrowding continued to dominate the discussion on passenger traffic. The Railways carried twice the number carried in 1938–39, but the passenger train capacity was 14.5 per cent less than in 1938–39. He expected to see a little improvement soon because there was a steady decrease in the average distance travelled by third-class passengers, in technical terms, the lead. If this was the case, the inevitable result would be steadily decreasing congestion. Matthai was hopeful of adding 700–800 coaches in the system, including 400 coaches, which the defence department was supposed to return.[18] Ticketless travel too was discussed again and was seen as a direct consequence of the problem of overcrowding. Matthai thought that the police and the judicial system could not in themselves solve this problem. He observed,

> As I have told the House more than once, this problem of ticketless travel is much more than a railway problem; it is a social problem. It is one of these things, which seem to reflect the gradual decline in the sense of law, which results when big political changes have occurred.[19]

Matthai had spoken of setting up a Railway Rates Tribunal in his previous budget. He told the House that he had found that unless this tribunal was vested with statutory authority, it would not serve its purpose. Rather than establish it through an executive order, he intended to place a Bill before the House to set up a tribunal with a much wider scope than the present Rates Advisory Committee, and more importantly, with a mandatory, and not merely, an advisory jurisdiction.[20] With regard to the Indian Railway Enquiry Committee, he said that it would begin to function in the course of a week or two under Pandit Hirday Nath Kunzru a member from the United Provinces who, he was sure, would bring to bear on this important work his unique knowledge and experience of public affairs.

Matthai thought the Railways had a bright future and he was pained at the allegations and charges levelled against railwaymen in unqualified and widely generalized terms. This greatly discouraged the staff, which was trying to do its best. He gave the example of the recently run Asthi Special carrying the ashes of Mahatma Gandhi to Allahabad in which he himself had the opportunity of seeing first-hand the enthusiasm, loyalty and devotion of the personnel involved in making the effort an unqualified success. He said that he mentioned this fact because it symbolized the new spirit of responsibility that had gradually spread among the railwaymen. He ended by saying: 'There are black sheep, Sir, in every organisation. It is for responsible leaders, when they are inclined to make charges and allegations, to distinguish the few from the many and not to visit upon the many the sins of the few ...'[21] Notwithstanding his best efforts, Matthai continued to face an uphill task. It was generally thought that conditions after Independence were worse than before the war.

Grand Trunk Express Redux

The Grand Trunk Express figured prominently in the budget debate as well. Haji Abdus Sattar Haji Ishaq Seth from Madras moved a cut motion under the demand 'Railway Board' on the late running of trains. Since the Grand Trunk Express was almost always late, and that too by a big margin, it became the focus of attention and ire once again. Seth said that since the war almost all trains were running late, three hours had been added to the old schedules. Despite this, there was no improvement in the running of the Grand Trunk Express. In an earlier discussion, Matthai had said that if things didn't improve, a considerable revision would be the answer.

Ishaq Seth was incensed that a constant revision in timings was the only solution Matthai had to offer and wanted him to take up the matter seriously and institute a departmental inquiry to ascertain the causes of the late running of the train. It was not enough for Matthai to say that there was no use speaking about it since he was already seized of the matter. He also said that whenever the subject of the train came up it, became a matter of jokes or irresponsible talk.

B. Shiva Rao from Madras wanted to rename the train Madras Daily Slow Passenger. When asked for a reason, the standard reason of the Madras and Southern Maratha Railway was, 'The late running is not in our section.' The blame was usually put on the Nizam's State Railway, but later, that too was disproved. Seth called it the most neglected train in India and said that since ministers were not compelled to travel by train with the advent of the airways, there was no improvement. He wanted a full study of the journey to find out where it was getting delayed and wanted Matthai to suggest remedies for the bottlenecks. In contrast, he said that the Frontier Mail, run by the BB&CI, generally ran on time.[22]

The cut motion was supported by Sidhva, a relentless and outspoken crusader on behalf of railway passengers, who had his own complaints: late starts due to problems with coaches or the locomotive, non-availability of either the guard or driver, wasting time enroute by the driver and many more. He said that while he was aware of the quality of locomotives and other related problems, the crux of the matter was that there was no 'will' to run the trains on time. On being questioned by a member as to how he would get the engines to run on time, Sidhva said, 'Let me have the administration. I will show you how.'[23] Another member thought that the railway staff had become irresponsible and just didn't care since they felt that they had a minister who was ready to protect and defend them.

Matthai, in reply, said that the running of the Grand Trunk Express had been a continual source of anxiety to him. Unlike other trains, it was not one single train for the whole journey but was 'tacked on at different points to other trains' and any delay in those would mean more than corresponding delays at successive stages. He said that a full analysis had been done of the train's running over a period of four months, but it was very difficult to draw any generalization from that study. A special investigation would be ordered, and if that too yielded little results, then they would have to consider a change of route of the train. N.G. Ranga from Madras thought that a longer route would make matters worse, but Matthai believed that an alternative route, even if it covered a longer distance, could result in more punctual running of the train.[24]

Sidhva, who had a habit of arguing his point ad nauseam, wanted to know about the late departure of trains, especially the Grand Trunk Express, a point he thought Matthai had not addressed satisfactorily. Matthai said that they had to economize on coaches and so the same rake that came from Madras to Delhi went back again. (Later, as already noted before, there was an overlapping rake.) There was also the question of waiting for armed guards who delayed the train on occasion, a fact to which, Matthai said, he could personally testify. Matthai showed his irritation with Sidhva when he finally said, 'Therefore, Sir, these are questions which require, if I may say so very respectfully, a little more sympathetic consideration than Mr Sidhva in his impatience is prepared to give.'[25]

Matthai said that if the allegations were against him personally, he would not mind. He observed, 'I am aware of the problem in regard to the staff and I want to assure the House that there is nothing that I would leave undone. But that is a different matter from saying that I consider the majority of the railwaymen are not worthy of the position they hold ...' Exhibiting his irritation at Sidhva's constant needling, Matthai suggested that 'my Honourable friend Mr Sidhva . . . should take charge of the Railway Administration, which suggestion, Sir, has my fullest approval and I hope it will be carried out at a very early date.'[26]

In a debate a few months later, in August 1948, Matthai admitted that the Frontier Mail was in many ways the 'Prize' train and their efforts to run it punctually had succeeded to a large extent. Inevitably, the problem of the Grand Trunk Express cropped up again. A member from the United Provinces, Pandit Balkrishna Sharma drew Matthai's attention to a news item that appeared in a Delhi weekly, that a man who wanted to commit suicide by throwing himself on the track of the Grand Trunk Express ultimately died of starvation because the train never came. Matthai, in reply, said, 'With regard to the report in the Delhi weekly, all I can say is that the individual who went and lay in front of the Grand Trunk Express in order to do away with himself chose a very bad train for the purpose.'[27] This incident figured in *Shankar's Weekly* as a cartoon and many years later Matthai wrote about it in an article for the *Times of India*.[28]

Matthai was very fond of Shankar's cartoons, which unfailingly poked fun at the good and the great. Shankar, whose full name was Keshav Shankar Pillai, was a pioneering political cartoonist and *Shankar's Weekly*, which was published from 1948 to 1975, was the Indian equivalent of the UK's *Punch*. Pillai started the weekly after he left the *Hindustan Times* following pressure from the editor, Devdas Gandhi, the Mahatma's youngest son, to stop lampooning Rajagopalachari. It became a platform for aspiring cartoonists across the country carrying the works of prominent cartoonists such as R.K. Laxman, Rajinder Puri, Bal Thackeray and E.P. Unny. Many of Shankar's cartoons were found in some of the newspaper clippings that Matthai had preserved.

Deliberations on the Budget

The deliberations on the budget covered a wide range of subjects, some of a general nature, and others of a more local character. Since it is impossible (nor is it desirable), to place the entire record before the reader, the following paragraphs provide a flavour of the discussions on the general problems faced by the Railways and the concern shown by the members of the House on them.

K. Santhanam while talking about the official railway figures said that he thought that the railway board members did not themselves know where they came from, being dependent on the general managers of the various railways. He said that the board was purely an administrative control organization and left much to be desired in the matter of business efficiency and planning. 'But I wish to suggest that the railway organisation has become like one of the big chariots of South India which millions of people have to drag but no one knows when it will start and where it will go.'[29] He also commented on the 'meagre way' in which the Standing Finance Committee for Railways was compelled to deal with the matters put before it.

Kazi Syed Karimuddin, a member from CP and Berar, spoke about the lack of improvement in the third class and the corruption in the railways. Pandit Hirday Nath Kunzru pointed out a mistake in Matthai's speech. He said that the minister had confused wagon turnround (which he said had reduced to fourteen to fifteen days from a high of forty-eight days) with the period required to repair a wagon. Matthai was quick to admit the mistake, but at the same time said that it was a mistake in a source for which he was not really responsible. Kunzru also wanted Matthai to increase the manufacture of wagons in the country and reduce their cost.[30]

B.V. Keskar from the United Provinces reiterated the corruption in all ranks of the Railways. He wanted the Railways to be used for the general development of the country and society. While agreeing that the Railways should be run as an economic concern, he thought that profits were not all that important. He did not want the Railways to make a great contribution to the general revenues, but 'we expect them to be great arteries in the social development of our country'.[31] Nandkishore Das, a member from Orissa, described the third-class railway compartments as 'air-tight godowns full of human materials' and said that the expectation that free India would bring about a reduction in rates of third-class fares and an improvement in the conditions of travel had been belied. He said that he sympathized with the difficulties through which it had been Matthai's 'unfortunate lot' to pilot the department but thought that the third-class fares could have been spared an increase without any serious consequences on the finances of the Railways.[32]

Matthai said that he was dissatisfied with the parliamentary machinery for scrutiny of railway matters. He thought that each sitting should last for a fortnight and not just a few hours. This would require the board members to spend more time on such matters, leaving aside their day-to-day work. Matthai said that this would require an expansion of the secretariat part of the parliamentary machinery. When questioned about the workload of the Railway Board, Matthai said that they 'have got quite as much work as you could reasonably expect them to do'.[33] Matthai said that detailed scrutiny would require much more data, and the 'statistical equipment' was entirely inadequate.

Matthai said that a mere comparison of operating ratios between countries was not the right way to judge efficiency given the widely differing conditions and contexts between nations. He said he was glad that Pandit Kunzru was going to examine this question in detail and looked forward to his conclusions on the subject. As far as the poor wagon turnround was concerned, Matthai blamed it squarely on overuse and the lack of even minimum maintenance.

Matthai was aware of the constant criticism he and the Railways were subjected to. He said that he had been charged with being the primary cause of the low standard of production in the country. 'Transport is the bottleneck: that is what you find in every newspaper in the country. I have got so used to it that I sometimes regard myself as a living, walking, breathing kind of bottleneck.'[34] Railway transport, Matthai said, depended largely on production of rolling stock, deliveries of which for a variety of reasons were not adequate. He realized that production was not up to the mark because the industrialists too had their share of problems, but to put all the responsibility on transport was a misleading way of stating the position.

Post-war development was being hindered by a shortage of essential materials such as steel, cement and timber. If the Railways embarked on an extensive development plan, it would only fan the fires of inflation. Matthai thought that consolidation and stabilization was the need of the hour. All the key posts in the Railways had been Indianized and Matthai was indignant at the criticism levelled against railway staff and officers. He bemoaned the fact that even his forcing the pace of Indianization had attracted adverse comment. Matthai said that what the Railways was fighting was another kind of war, in some respects more serious than the one that closed in 1945. 'Suppose we were in the midst of a war what would be said of the representatives of the country who spoke of the army in the terms in which railway staff was being described.'[35] There was no doubt that there were some black sheep, Matthai said, but they were in the minority. But Matthai admitted that there had been little improvement in the passenger amenities of the lowest class of passengers despite many promises. He said that the money in the Betterment Fund would be primarily devoted to 'relieving the extraordinarily uncomfortable conditions under which third class passengers now travel'.[36]

Cut Motions

At the next session, which discussed Demands for Grants, Ramnath Goenka, the member from Madras, moved a cut motion under the head 'Railway Board' on the subject of inefficiency. Frank Anthony, while supporting the motion, said that the crux of the problem lay in the lack of discipline among the inferior staff. He said that he had the highest respect for Matthai and the board, but there had been no indication yet of what he called a change of heart. 'The railway worker is essentially good. But today he feels that he is not working with you, but that he is working against you.'[37] H.V. Kamath said that the problem lay in the continuation of the old system of bureaucratic administration.

Ramnarayan Singh, a member from Bihar, got a little carried away. He wanted Matthai to mix incognito with the people, or appoint honest officers to do the job, so as to get a grip on ground realities from which he appeared to be divorced. 'Sir John Matthai, I tell you to go and know things for yourself.'[38] There was no question of a few black sheep, Singh said. There were black sheep everywhere.

Jaipal Singh, another member from Bihar, was the lone voice who spoke in favour of Matthai and opposed the cut motion. He decried the 'venom' that had been poured forth ad nauseam against the railway administration. He said that it was impossible to change things overnight. To be overly critical of all railwaymen was to overlook the good work being done by many in the railway system.[39]

Matthai responded by saying that there was indiscipline and inefficiency in the staff, but he was unwilling to believe that it was prevalent in the 'great bulk of our railwaymen'. He said that his policy was to give the staff a fair deal unless he had evidence to the contrary. Corruption required two parties, and the bribe giver was equally to blame. He was anxious to take every step against corruption but could hardly be expected 'to launch a huge campaign of prosecution and persecution against the men running the railways'.[40]

There were cut motions moved by members on a variety of grievances. They included cut motions by Sidhva on grievances of third-class passengers, Pandit Mukut Bihari Lal Bhargava on the reorganization of the railways, and by R.R. Diwakar on the construction of new lines and restoration of dismantled lines.

* * *

In March 1948, Matthai moved the Railway (Transport of Goods) Amendment Bill to seek an extension of that Act for another year. With the gradual decontrol of commodities, the traffic offered had greatly increased, and the existing transport facilities could not cater to the increased demand. Matthai said that a physical decontrol programme, and a decontrol of movement implemented simultaneously, would lead to serious disorganization. One had to follow the other. He believed that some control was essential to ensure that certain goods could be moved on priority in times of need.[41]

Presently, the central government, under Section 71 of the Railways Act, 1989, can direct the Railways to give special facilities or preference to the carriage of certain goods or a class of goods in the public interest. According to this section, orders are issued by the central government to the railway administration from time to time, for giving priority to booking and movement of particular type of goods in the interest of the nation, the public in general or for industrial development. This was exactly the spirit of the Act whose duration Matthai was seeking to extend by a year.

* * *

Thus far, the discussion has only focused on Matthai as minister of railways. Though this complex and huge organization took up most of his time and energy, he was also minister for transport and in that capacity introduced certain important legislations. One of these was the Road Transport Corporations Bill[42], which gave provincial governments the necessary authority to set up a statutory corporation for development of road transport. While commerce was a subject for the provincial legislatures, Matthai said that a view had been taken by the law officers of the central government that the incorporation, regulation and winding up of trading corporations was the jurisdiction of the central government. Since the central government treated these Road Transport Boards as trading corporations, it was necessary to pass the bill he had introduced.[43]

In April 1948, he moved the Calcutta Port (Pilotage) Bill to provide for the transfer of control over pilotage on the Hooghly River to the commissioners for the Port of Calcutta. Matthai said that it was an anomaly that the port commissioners were responsible for every other matter except the pilots in the Bengal Pilot Service who were under the control of the central government. It was impossible, he said, to exercise proper control from faraway New Delhi.[44] In the same month, he introduced the Bombay, Calcutta, and Madras Port Trusts (Constitution) Amendment Bill to take up the question of providing increased representation of Indian commercial interests on these bodies, given the changed political situation. The Bill, Matthai said, did not have any specific proposals but entrusted the government with the power to issue notifications that would provide for adequate representation of Indian commercial interests.[45]

Railway Rates Tribunal

In August 1948, Matthai introduced the Indian Railways Act, 1890 (Second Amendment) Bill, which referred to two important matters: the constitution and organization of a Railway Rates Tribunal (RRT) and setting up Claims Commissioners for dealing with claims arising out of train accidents.

A little background is in order here. In 1920, the Government of India appointed the Acworth Committee to look into the system of control of rates and fares and for setting up a mechanism for deciding disputes between railways and traders. The committee recommended the establishment of a rates tribunal. In 1926, in consultation with the Central

Advisory Council for Railways, the government appointed the 'Railway Rates Advisory Committee' to deal with certain complaints of undue preference and unreasonable rates. However, its role was only advisory, and the committee was not empowered to take cognizance of complaints unless they were referred to it by the government. The committee continued to function till it was replaced by the Railway Rates Tribunal in 1949.

Pandit Kunzru felt that the powers Matthai had given the tribunal were too wide. The powers of the government would be restricted to the reduction of rates, and it would have to rely on the permission of the tribunal in case revenue had to be raised through an increase in rates. In case this was not adequate, the government would resort to the expedient of increasing passenger fares. He then dilated on the undesirability of divesting the government completely of all power of increasing rates. While he was not denying the need for a statutory body that would deal with complaints from trade and industry, he was against making the tribunal the final arbiter in the matter of a rate increase. He gave the example of the Transport Tribunal in England, whose comprehensive powers were subject to an over-riding provision in the British Transport Act which made it incumbent on the tribunal to ensure that adequate revenues were generated for running the Railways.[46]

Kunzru also raised a very valid point when he said that it was possible that the tribunal may reject an upward revision of rates across the board, calling upon the government to show that the railway administration was being carried out with due diligence. This would in effect be a review of the railway administration and the question here was whether the right body for such a purpose in a democracy should be a tribunal or the legislature. 'So long as there is a democratic legislature . . . it is undesirable to make any committee or commission the judge of the efficiency or economy of the railway administration.'[47] Kunzru said that he supported the motion for the appointment of a Select Committee, something Matthai had already accepted.

K. Santhanam wanted only judges to be part of the tribunal (rather than a judge at the helm and two members, one from the railways, and another from business) and supported the motion that the matter should be brought before the Select Committee. Biswanath Das was against judges becoming members of tribunals, saying lawyers knew nothing about the rates structure of the railways. He wanted this 'loyal worship of High Court judges' to be dropped in future legislation brought before the House. Anthony was against the proposal for Claims Commissioners saying that they would inevitably dance to the tune of the 'executive' that had appointed them. He felt that the settlement of claims for example, bodily harm, should be adjudicated by a judicial body.[48]

Matthai in his reply to Kunzru opined that the Railways had little to lose, and much to gain, if they could secure the support of some impartial authority in matters affecting freight rates. Kunzru said no other department had a similar tribunal. In response, Matthai said that the railway was different from other departments of the government. It was both a business concern, and a public utility placed in a monopolistic position. Was it fair that the government acting as manager should have the final voice in the determination of rates given the fact that every reduction or increase in rates would have a repercussion on the economy? Any sensible tribunal, he said, would look at the issue both from the point of impact on the economy and the solvency of the railways. He was confident that he could convince a tribunal in case he wanted an increase in rates. In case he failed, it was his duty to re-examine his proposals.

The contribution to the general revenues by the Railways in an emergency was another aspect raised by Kunzru. Matthai said that this was a matter for the House to consider. If the existing rates were sufficient to meet costs, would it be fair to increase rates just so that the Railways could contribute to the general exchequer? Matthai felt that certain categories, such as essential public utilities, should be left out 'when charges are made simply for the purpose of adding to general revenue'[49]. Matthai said he had an open mind on the subject and would accept changes if the Select Committee wanted to proceed on other lines. It would, he said, make his job easier. Matthai masterfully summed up why he had given such wide powers to the tribunal.

> It is easy for an organization like the Indian Railways, brought up under traditions which have not altogether been of a wholesome character, to solve its financial difficulties by increasing freight rates rather than by enforcing economies. It would therefore have a restraining influence upon the railway organization to be committed to this position that they cannot increase freight rates unless their proposals are accepted by an independent judicial body.[50]

Replying to Anthony, Matthai said that taking claims arising from accidents to court would only result in a greater delay in their disposal, and he wanted such cases, especially those involving breadwinners, to be disposed of in the shortest possible time.

The Bill was finally passed on 4 September 1948 after making changes suggested by the Select Committee. The Committee omitted the entire section on the Claims Commissioners opining that the disposal of claims raised certain fundamental issues which would require much longer consideration than the Select Committee with limited time at its disposal could afford to give. Pandit Kunzru's views found merit in the eyes of the Committee. It was decided that only the central government would have power to raise the general level of freight rates, but the power to reclassify a commodity in a higher class lay with the tribunal. A few changes in the words in the draft along with some technical changes were also made.

The Railways Rates Tribunal (RRT) was constituted by an Act of Parliament (Central Act 65 of 1948), and it came into being with effect from 4 April 1949, with a bench in Madras comprising a senior judge and two members, with the primary function of ensuring non-discriminatory setting of freight charges and to prevent railway administrations from favouring any particular party. These functions of the RRT are outlined in Section 39 of the Railways Act. However, certain matters, such as classification or reclassification of any commodity, fixation of wharfage and demurrage charges, fixation of fares levied for the carriage of passengers and freight levied for the carriage of luggage, parcels, railway material and military traffic were not within the jurisdiction of the RRT. Consequently, the RRT remained virtually ineffective.

The Railway Claims Tribunal (RCT), on the other hand, was established through the Railway Claims Tribunal Act, 1987, with the objective of adjudicating and providing relief to rail users by payment of compensation against loss, destruction, damage, deterioration or non-delivery of goods entrusted to the Railways for carriage and for death, injury or loss to a passenger in a railway accident or an untoward incident. However, unlike the rates tribunal, these have been functioning quite effectively, even though some benches have a large backlog. The RRT ceased to exist in 2017 and all the pending cases of the RRT were transferred to the RCT.

A Difficult Time

Matthai's woes continued unabated. On 6 April 1948, Muhammed Saleh Akbar Hydari, the Governor of Assam, wrote to Matthai about the intrusion of communist workers among the Bengali personnel of the railway. This had adversely impacted discipline on the railway, and also affected the workers of other industries like tea. He said that the chief administrative officer was 'not by general repute strong enough to cope' and wanted an officer from Madras or Bombay to be posted there, who with the full support of the Railway Board would be strong enough to deal with the subversive elements among the employees.[51] Hydari said that he was very sorry to have to make this complaint, but he thought it his duty to bring it to Matthai's notice so that the latter could take remedial action. He said he was open to having his claims verified by any railway officer Matthai chose to depute for this purpose, and who would receive all assistance from his government.

Nehru in a letter to Patel in early June 1948 touched upon a number of important issues, which included administration in general and the working of the Railways in particular. He said that the administrative set-up all over India was in bad shape. Instead of recovering from the ill effects of the war, they had slipped further down, with Partition and its aftermath only compounding the problem. Corruption, he said, had risen to monstrous proportions. Cloth smuggling was being done on a large scale, with cloth being sent in trains from Ahmedabad to north India, part of the cloth also going to Pakistan. A regular train run by Punjab refugees aided by the mill owners and traders was being run for this purpose with railway officials from Ahmedabad being bribed heavily. Since the profits were so great, it was difficult to check this business by any normal method.[52]

Nehru also said that he had definite information about the corruption in four ministries, one of which was the railways. He agreed with Patel that they had not had great success in handling the Railways but stopped short of putting the blame on Matthai. 'It is difficult for me to say whose fault this is, because conditions have been very bad.'[53] However, he was all praise for Matthai as an economist and thought that he was well-suited for a ministry of social and economic welfare. Nehru had spoken of the need of dealing with economic problems and wanted a minister who would look at the broad economic picture and suggest remedial measures. He was suggesting a ministry of economic affairs and thought Matthai would be the perfect candidate for the job. 'He is a man of the highest integrity and of very great ability. He is an economist of high standing as well as an industrialist . . . His reputation is very high in the country and abroad.'[54] The public, Nehru said, would generally approve of him.

In early July 1948, Patel circulated a note to the cabinet on the economic conditions in which he had been critical of the role played by the Railways. In it he said that Lord Mountbatten in a note had commented adversely on the functioning of the Railways. Matthai in his letter dated 9 July rebutted Patel's claims. He said that he had discussed the matter with Mountbatten and discovered that the note circulated by Mountbatten had been based on feedback given by a disgruntled British officer who Matthai had sacked. Matthai said that during the course of the conversation Mountbatten practically withdrew the comments made in his note. He then quoted from a letter the former viceroy had written to him just before he returned to England.[55]

> The firmness with which you have handled matters connected with your onerous portfolio has been a source of admiration to me and to many others. You and your Ministry could well be proud of the way in which you have kept the transport and railways of the country going in spite of the difficulties with which you have been beset.[56]

Patel was unconvinced. He replied the very next day saying that it was not his intention to minimize Matthai's contribution but merely to draw attention to the fact that despite the latter's best efforts, conditions were bad. 'This is a general complaint on this matter, and I thought it would only be fair on my part to give expression to this feeling.'[57]

* * *

Matthai had to answer several questions, most of them inconvenient, when he was in charge of the Railways. Since there was no effective opposition, every member of the House, including members of the ruling party, had assumed the responsibility of being a custodian of the public's welfare. Such was the ethos of the times. Matthai for his part had developed his own strategy in tackling Parliament. He said that his own relations with Parliament were of the friendliest character throughout his term of office. Members often disagreed with him, but whenever they did so, they seemed to be moved more by sorrow than by anger.[58]

According to Matthai, the secret of the right handling of Parliament lay in three things. Firstly, the House should have no reason to doubt that one's attitude to it was one of genuine respect, and this had to be reflected both in demeanour and speech. 'Human beings organized in groups are much more susceptible in these matters than individuals,' he said.[59] Secondly, the House should be treated with the utmost candour even if the facts presented happen to show one in a bad light or are likely to expose one personally to criticism. 'A democracy is indulgent to faults provided it is convinced of the sincerity of the person concerned.'[60] Thirdly, in putting forward a case to the House, one must show that he has a complete mastery both of the facts and of their implications. Any slip on this account can result in lasting damage to one's prestige.[61]

Matthai said that he used to spend many hours preparing for the question hour. He wanted not merely to get his answers right but also to become fully conversant with the subject matter and its background. Matthai observed:

> It enabled me to secure a firm grip on important details relating to the working of my ministry which otherwise might have escaped me altogether. Secondly, it helped more than anything else to set my relations right with the House by giving members the feeling that I took even their minor activities seriously and also that I knew what I was talking about.[62]

***

Matthai demitted office as railways and transport minister and joined as independent India's second finance minister on 23 September. How Matthai took R.K. Shanmukham Chetty's place and his tenure as finance minister, form the subject of the next section.

PART III

11

Finance Minister

An unusual feature about the Congress-led governments from September 1946 to July 1956 was that none of their finance ministers belonged to the Congress party. Liaquat Ali Khan, Sir R.K. Shanmukham Chetty, John Matthai and C.D. Deshmukh held this portfolio with two out of the four associated with political parties who opposed the Congress. Matthai became independent India's second finance minister after Chetty, who resigned under a bit of a cloud.

R.K. Shanmukham Chetty: India's First Finance Minister

In 1946, Nehru chose Sir R.K. Shanmukham Chetty, industrialist and erstwhile Dewan of Cochin State, as his finance minister. Despite not being from a Congress background but the more conciliatory Justice Party, Nehru picked him as India's first finance minister, since he believed that an industrialist outside the regular Congress fold might help reassure Indian industrialists nervous with the socialist rhetoric of the Congress. Chetty had studied economics at MCC, and later pursued law, but he never became a practising lawyer. He joined the family business and later took to politics. He was elected a legislator of the Madras Presidency legislative council in 1920 and later joined the Swaraj Party in 1923. The following year, he was elected to the central legislative assembly, serving as its deputy president (1931–35).

There was no denying Chetty's capabilities. He had represented India at the Imperial Economic Conference held in Ottawa in 1932 and signed a trade agreement (something that did not please the Congress very much)[1]. In 1934, he became president of the central legislative assembly but quit the assembly when he lost the election in 1935. He became Dewan of Cochin, serving in that capacity for six years, from 1935 to 1941. He represented India at international forums too. He was an Indian delegate to the League of Nations in 1938 and also at Bretton Woods in 1944. Chetty also served as president of the Indian Tariff Board and was a constitutional adviser to the Nawab of Bhopal.

It appears that Gandhi had a high opinion of Chetty's understanding of economic matters and recommended him to Nehru.[2] The other contender for the post was Matthai (who was in fact Nehru's first choice), but Patel did not want Matthai because he had agreed with Liaquat's suggestion to set up an Income Tax Investigation Commission. Matthai had been in general agreement with Liaquat's budget proposals, and this did not endear him to Patel, who thought that Liaquat's real motive was to ruin Hindu businessmen and industrialists.

Patel's opposition to Matthai, and Gandhi's support of Chetty's candidature, effectively put paid to Matthai's chances of becoming the finance minister. The choice of a non-Congress man as the finance minister reflected the non-partisan thinking of the Congress leadership. They thought that Chetty was the best man for the job, and cutting across party lines, appointed him to the post. This is something unthinkable in today's times. Also, Chetty's appointment, given the background of the Ottawa Pact, came as a complete surprise to most people. Nehru's private secretary, M.O. Mathai, thought that Patel selected Chetty because he thought he would be pliable and do his bidding.[3]

On 26 November 1946, Chetty rose to present his first budget. He noted its historic nature and the tragedy of Partition that shadowed it. The interim budget was largely concerned with the economic problems of separation of the assets of the two new nations, and in particular the ways to fund an army that was being demobilized and divided. Chetty was worried about inflationary pressures that had been suppressed during the war but were now on the verge of bursting out thanks to the surpluses that people had accumulated, and the low supply due to a lack of industrial investment. His speech aimed at encouraging industrial production, news that was welcomed by the stock market. The Tata Deferred, a popular share at the time, duly shot up in the post budget session.[4]

Chetty's second budget, and the first full budget of the country, was dominated by two tragedies: the influx of refugees in the aftermath of Partition who had to be provided for, and the assassination of Gandhi barely a month before. It was perhaps the only budget speech ever to end with a reference to a hymn, Gandhi's favourite 'Lead Kindly Light'. Chetty eloquently said, 'The next step is enough for us if it is illuminated by the star of our ambition and fortified by the faith in our destiny.'[5]

Shanmukham Chetty's Resignation

Chetty, however, was not destined to lead those next steps. Not long after presenting his budget, he resigned on 17 August 1948, after just a year in office in circumstances which have never been made entirely clear. M.O. Mathai thought that Patel was responsible for Chetty's exit from the cabinet. According to Mathai, Patel persuaded Chetty to delete a few names of Gujarati businessmen and industrialists from the list of those who were to be proceeded against based on the findings of the Income Tax Investigation Commission. When this became known, there was a furore in Parliament and Patel found himself in a tight corner. 'He kept quiet and let down the man who did his bidding, and did not lose a wink of sleep in the process. Nehru asked for and received Chetty's resignation.'[6]

V. Shankar had a somewhat similar version except that there was no mention of Patel having asked Chetty to withdraw the names. He merely said that Chetty withdrew the names of five prominent industrialists who were to be investigated. (The names included Ahmedabad mill-owners, Ambalal Sarabhai [the father of space scientist, Vikram Sarabhai] and Kasturbhai Lalbhai.) This he said was done without reference to the cabinet and without the knowledge of Nehru or Patel. Nehru said that he would stand by Chetty, if, as he had assured him, he had acted on the advice of his department. Patel called K.R.K. Menon, the finance secretary, with the relevant file before he was to attend a party meeting at Parliament house. It turned out that the official view was opposed to the withdrawal and the proposal had originated from Chetty himself. Patel called Chetty and said that under the circumstances, he would not be able to support him. Nehru too was of a similar opinion, leaving Chetty with no option but to resign.[7]

These have been the generally accepted versions of what happened, but the truth is rarely simple. Recent scholarship has given a slightly different colour to the episode. A.K. Bhattacharya in his book on finance ministers of India has opined that there is no corroboration of M.O. Mathai's account in official records. While the original cause stemmed from the Income Tax Investigation Commission and its inquiries into the tax arrears of industrialists, he says that the crux of the controversy was that some cases under investigation had been withdrawn by Chetty just before the government introduced an amendment to the relevant law, making withdrawal of cases subject to approval by the commission. The issue here was a technical point as to whether the finance ministry should have moved for withdrawal of cases before introducing the amendment that would allow such withdrawals only after obtaining the commission's prior approval.[8]

Chetty told Nehru that he had done no wrong. The cases pertained to a period well before the amendment had been mooted. In a letter to Nehru, he said that a number of cases had to be sent to the Commission before 31 December 1947 as per the old Act. Since time was short, it was not possible to make a detailed examination of whether there was a prima facie case against each of them. It was therefore decided that such cases would be withdrawn after a detailed examination if no case was found. This, he said, was exactly what had been done in all the cases. Oral instructions had been issued to withdraw the cases on 19 February 1948, although a written order was issued later, on 12 March 1948. Chetty said that such issues assumed importance only when the bona fides of the minister were in doubt. Nehru, it appears, had assured Chetty that his bona fides were not in doubt. However, at the end of a Congress party meeting on 13 August 1948, Nehru announced that he would like to review the matter and take a decision. Chetty ended his letter by saying that he was placing his resignation in Nehru's hands so that he could take a decision without any embarrassment.

Nehru accepted the resignation the next day. He said that while he still had no doubts about Chetty's bona fides, he was guilty of an error of judgement. There should have been no withdrawal without reference to the commission since Chetty had already piloted the bill in the cabinet and it was on the point of being introduced in the assembly. Calling it a discourtesy to the assembly, Nehru said that a 'certain degree of misapprehension' had arisen and Chetty had done the right thing by resigning.[9]

Taking Charge of the Finance Ministry

K.C. Neogy held temporary charge of the finance portfolio from 17 August but was anxious to be relieved of the double charge so that he could devote all his time to the commerce ministry, in which he was more interested. Little over a month later, Nehru managed to convince Matthai to accept the portfolio. Matthai said that Nehru had turned to him as a last resort after all the others had refused the post. He observed, 'The Prime Minister then turned to me as a last step and almost in despair. I tried hard to resist because I had already begun to feel tired of politics and was not too enamoured of taking up a new post and making a fresh start.'[10]

Nehru also enlisted the support of Rajagopalachari in trying to convince Matthai, who recalled that Rajagopalachari, who was then governor general, sent for him one morning and 'pressed upon me by parables and by metaphysical arguments the importance of responding to the call of public duty'.[11] Rajagopalachari also told Matthai to bring Achamma to the meeting.

> In inviting me to meet him, he insisted for some reason (that I was not able to gauge) that my wife also should be present at the meeting. Probably he thought as a man of experience and ripe wisdom that women responded to duty better than men. If so, he was right because in the end I accepted the offer and so began the last phase of my life in the national government.[12]

Matthai's assessment of the man most Indians know as Rajaji makes interesting reading. After praising his many qualities (intellectual gifts, idealism, administrative and diplomatic skills, to name a few), Matthai thought that he was still a complex character whom it was not easy to analyse. It is the latter part of his assessment that tells us what he really thought of him.

> But when all is said and done and every allowance made for his abilities and achievements, he remains a puzzle and a disappointment . . . If he laboured for the public good, he seldom lost sight of what was good for himself. If he believed in freedom, it was freedom from other people's rule rather than his own. If he championed the constitutional methods of parliamentary government, he also knew how to manage it by pulling the many strings that lay to hand in its lobbies and ante-rooms. Mr Rajagopalachari has travelled a long way in the course of his public life, but he remains, and is likely to remain an enigma to his countrymen.[13]

It was Matthai's support of the commission that made Patel oppose his candidature as finance minister. Now ironically, it was the same commission that had proved to be Chetty's undoing. What did Matthai think of the controversy that resulted in Chetty's exit? Matthai thought that Chetty was 'more sinned against than sinning', and that he saw nothing in the papers relating to the subject of his resignation, which reflected in the least on his integrity and sense of honour. He observed, 'Politics is often a messy business and when you are in the thick of it, it is so easy not merely unwittingly but even when acting with the best of intentions to get besmirched in its turbulent and muddy waters.'[14]

Nehru had all along wanted Matthai as the finance minister and now he had finally got his wish. Matthai took charge on 23 September 1948. In a letter to the chief ministers of states in October 1948, Nehru said that the finance portfolio was in some ways the most important one and he was very pleased that Matthai was in charge of it. It was to be an eventful tenure and one which also had a premature ending, with some degree of hurt and ill feeling on either side. But we are getting a little ahead of our story.

When Matthai started his tenure in the finance ministry, the economy was yet to recover from the adverse effects of the Second World War and Partition. Inflation was on the rise and India had to rely on higher food imports, which put a great strain on its foreign exchange resources. It was, Matthai said, a problem of too much demand and too little supply. While the purchasing power in the hands of the community had increased significantly as a result of the war, the available supply of commodities in the post-war period was not sufficient to meet the increasing demand. Difficulties in transport and distribution accentuated the shortages.

Food imports had risen to 2.8 million tonnes in 1948–49 from about 2 million tonnes in 1947–48 as a result of crop failure. Floods in Bihar and the United Provinces, famine in Gujarat and Rajasthan and cyclone damage in Bombay were threatening to push up the imports to 4 million tonnes in 1948–49. The chief problem facing the government at the time was the steep rise in the prices of food grains which followed the decontrol of food in December 1947.

According to Matthai, it was Gandhi who was principally responsible for this 'bold and spectacular' step[15]. Opinion, both in the cabinet and in the country at large, was sharply divided on the issue. Matthai and

N. Gopalaswami Ayyangar strongly opposed decontrol of food. Hearing of this, Gandhi sent for them, wanting to understand from them the real logic of control. Matthai explained in simple language the familiar economic arguments for maintaining control. Gandhi listened patiently and attentively. Ayyangar endorsed what Matthai had said and added some arguments of his own. After they both had finished, Gandhi told them that he wanted them to know his point of view.[16]

Gandhi's reply, Matthai said, had little reference to any of the arguments they had urged, but dealt with the problem 'entirely on the moral plane' pointing out with much earnestness the dishonesty and corruption that control had brought about and his determination to do everything in his power to put a stop to it. It was obvious that their arguments had made no difference to his way of thinking. Matthai said that with Gandhi, it was a case not of reasoned argument but of intuition. 'Dr Rajendra Prasad was then Food Minister and as a devout and loyal disciple of the Mahatma was prepared to accept his intuitive rather than other people's reasoned conclusions.'[17]

However, it was an essential part of Rajendra Prasad's proposal for decontrol that a substantial reserve of food grains should be built up as soon as possible which was to be used for checking price rise. Matthai observed, 'This however was found impracticable because of the failure of the crops during the following year and decontrol had then to be carried out without the antidote provided in the original scheme.'[18]

However, the government faced with a strong public agitation against the sharp and widespread rise in prices decided to resume control of food. This was the first of a series of steps Matthai took to counter inflation. A definite programme of anti-inflationary measures was adopted towards the end of 1948 which had some effect in preventing a further rise but was of little effect in bringing down prices. Matthai said that it had become imperative to prevent as far as possible the further creation of purchasing power in the hands of the community and to take all measures to stimulate production. Matthai imposed additional duties on certain luxury articles such as liquor, tobacco, motor cars, and silk and art silk fabrics. In addition, he levied an excise duty on super-fine cloth.[19]

The government assumed additional powers to make provisional assessments of income tax on the basis of returns submitted by the assesses. Matthai also revived a system of interest-bearing deposits for income tax, which had been introduced in 1943. It was also decided to postpone refund of deposits of excess profits tax for a further period of three years and place a temporary limit on the amount that was distributed as dividend by public companies.[20]

If controlling inflation was paramount, no less important was the need to give a fillip to industrial production. Matthai reduced the import duty on machinery and certain industrial raw materials and abolished the import duty on cotton yarn. New industrial concerns commencing production in the next three years were given a tax holiday for the first five years up to a limit of 6 per cent per annum on their capital. Matthai also liberalized the rules regulating depreciation.[21]

In an address Matthai gave to the Associated Chambers of India towards the end of 1948, he described government's policy as primarily one of stabilizing prices. This statement gave rise to a great deal of criticism and there was a general demand that something more drastic should be attempted. In consequence of this, Rajagopalachari, during a visit to Bombay in early 1949, tried to allay criticism by laying more stress than Matthai did on the second objective of their policy, namely the gradual lowering of prices. This created the impression that government had revised their policy and that the governor general's visit to Bombay was utilized by the government for announcing it.

Matthai's position as the finance minister and Rajagopalachari's position as constitutional head of state both came in for sharp criticism. When Parliament met for the budget session, Matthai was asked to explain what had occurred. Matthai in the course of his reply said that there had been no change whatever in the policy of the government and that all that had happened was that Rajaji, with his mastery of lucid and simple prose, was able to explain his point of view more clearly than he himself could. Matthai recalled, 'Late that evening Mr Rajagopalachari rang me up from Government House to say that he thought I was developing into a seasoned politician.'[22]

The Sterling Balances

As far as the external financial position of the country was concerned, there had been a sharp decline in the sterling balances held by the RBI when Matthai became the finance minister. The growing difficulty in the financing of imports from the hard currency areas and the emergence of

Pakistan as a foreign country for currency purposes with the separation of its currency from that of India, had all been a cause for worry. The sterling balances which had reached a peak of Rs 1733 crore at the end of 1945–46 declined by Rs 121 crore to Rs 1612 crore during 1946–47. This reduction was due mainly to the large imports of food, but there were also substantial imports of other goods to satisfy the pent-up demand of the war years and a certain amount of repatriation of British capital.[23] But what were these sterling balances? Some background is in order here.

Accumulation of Sterling: The Background

At the start of the Second World War, India owed Britain over £360 million, a debt that it had accumulated since the mid-nineteenth century for expenditure incurred on the so-called 'home charges'. These charges included interest on debt, interest paid to the railway companies as annuities, expenses of the Secretary of State's office in London, cost of stores for India, and pension and furlough payments to British civil and military officers. The war, with its strong and direct stimulus, marked a turnaround in the fortunes of Indian industry hitherto held back by the colonial government. Indian factories churned out a variety of war materials; the army expanded as did the civil and semi-military administrators recruited for the war effort.[24]

As a result of this war-related expenditure, India grew out of its debt, which reduced to £240 million in 1940–41 and till 1943, the accumulating sterling balance was used to offset India's long-standing debt. Once the debt was wiped out, Britain began to pay for its war-related expenditure in India in sterling. Under the Defence Expenditure Plan of February 1940, Britain agreed to pay for the reorganization of the Indian Army, for the costs incurred to maintain British armed forces in India, and for the deployment of Indian troops beyond the subcontinent. Not only did India repay a debt accumulated over three quarters of a century, by the end of the war, it had amassed a staggering £1.3 billion balance, becoming, along with Egypt, one of Britain's largest creditors.

Whenever it purchased goods and services in India, it made payment in terms of sterling that was credited to the account of the RBI in London. Against these balances, the Reserve Bank printed paper currency which was placed at the disposal of the government for making payments. However, it was not as if the accumulating sterling was available to India for buying goods and services in the UK or elsewhere. While the Government of India received an asset in the form of sterling which was not immediately usable, they had to find the rupee resources for meeting that expenditure. The government financed a substantial part of the expenditure through currency issue and unsurprisingly, the result was inflation.

Purshotamdas Thakurdas (a very active member of the central board of the RBI) and his other colleagues on the board wanted no restriction on the time, place and manner of utilizing these assets. They wanted the issue to be resolved multilaterally at Bretton Woods so as to ensure convertibility and an early liquidation of the sterling balances. Another demand was the abolition of the Empire Dollar Pool, in which India's dollar earnings were put in the name of helping the war effort and which were not available for India's use. When the war ended, Indian business demanded an adequate allotment of foreign exchange, particularly dollars, for replenishing stocks badly depleted by the war. The UK, who headed the sterling area also had to consider the interests of other areas and seemed to India to be unduly chary of sparing dollars. The RBI strongly supported the Indian plea, and the clamour only grew with the passage of time.[25]

The central board of the RBI lost no time in urging the segregation of India's contribution so as to conserve dollar earnings for post-war reconstruction and development. During the period September 1939–March 1945, India's net contribution was of the order of $300 million. An extreme proposal mooted in some quarters was that India should withdraw from the Empire Dollar Pool forthwith and hold its dollar earnings separately. The situation was complicated by a lend-lease arrangement with the USA. There was every probability of India's favourable balance with the USA being drastically reduced, if not changed into an unfavourable one, if the amount of lend-lease assistance to India was taken into account.[26]

A series of negotiations led to the creation by the British Treasury of a Reconstruction Fund, into which $20 million would be credited annually to be held by the Reserve Bank in a dollar account with the Bank of England. But this failed to satisfy both public opinion in India and potential exporters to India and USA. The relevant announcement in February 1944 by the finance member explained that the fund would be apart from, and in addition to, India's current dollar requirements, which were met from the Empire Dollar Pool. Deshmukh, the RBI governor, was anxious that some part at least of India's past contributions to the Pool should be made available to India.[27]

Deshmukh had been opposed to India's continuance in the Empire Dollar Pool given that India's contribution of surplus dollars to the Pool were not necessarily going to be available to her as a reserve for the future. He had suggested that the favourable balance that India would have with the USA after 1 January 1946 should be earmarked for future needs and should be excluded from any other allotments of foreign exchange which may be agreed upon in view of India's contributions to the Dollar Pool up to 31 December 1945. Initially in favour of an immediate withdrawal from the Pool or the sterling area, Deshmukh later expressed the view that this should not take place till the International Monetary Fund had started operations. India had a lot to gain from the various monetary agreements made by the British government.[28]

Negotiations on the Sterling Balances

The first official discussions between the governments of the UK and India on the sterling balances did not take place until February 1947 when a British delegation led by Sir Wilfred Eady, permanent secretary in the Treasury accompanied by Cameron Cobbold (later Lord), deputy governor of the Bank of England, visited India in early February 1947. The Indian side was headed by V. Narahari Rao, the finance secretary. The other senior members were Sir Raghavan Pillai, joint secretary, commerce department, Choudhary Mohammed Ali, financial adviser, military finance, Braj Kumar Nehru, joint secretary in the finance ministry, and Keith Roy, private secretary to the Finance Member. The RBI was represented by J.V. Joshi and Ram Nath.[29]

Braj Kumar Nehru of the ICS wrote about these negotiations in his memoirs. His father, Brijlal, was Jawaharlal Nehru's first cousin. Since Brijlal's father, Nand Lal, died young, the former was brought up by Motilal Nehru. B.K. Nehru said that he had been insisting on a guarantee against the devaluation of sterling because devaluation would in effect be equivalent to writing off of these debts. But no one among his seniors had the gumption to ask for an exchange guarantee for sterling, and it was left to B.K. Nehru himself to raise the issue with Cobbold. Cobbold said that the Bank of England could never even contemplate such a guarantee. He observed, 'Sterling was sterling; there was no question of its value being judged in terms of any other currency! The IMF, in short, be damned!'[30]

It was finally agreed that the existing arrangements would continue on the understanding that an early settlement would be reached providing for a ceiling on withdrawals for current expenditure, the regulation of capital transfers and other related matters. The British acknowledged the sacrifices made by India and also agreed not to question the prices charged for war supplies.

In April 1947, Liaquat Ali Khan proposed the names of Matthai and Jawaharlal Nehru as two members of the cabinet to serve on the proposed sterling balances delegation. In his reply on 21 April, the prime minister said that it was impossible for any cabinet minister to go abroad for a lengthy period. Apart from the routine workload, which was considerable, the Constituent Assembly was also meeting frequently at the time and those who were taking an important part in its deliberations could hardly afford to be away for a long period.

Matthai, who held the railways portfolio, was an obvious choice given his economics background. But Matthai, according to Pandit Nehru, was reluctant to go since he expected a great deal of trouble in his department, the Railways.[31] In the end, Matthai did not go, and when the next round of negotiations took place between 9 July and 25 July 1947, in London, Rao led the Indian delegation, and once again, the opposite side was led by Sir Wilfred. The other members of the delegation were B.K. Nehru, Keith Roy and H.D. Cayley, deputy controller of exchange at the RBI.

In view of the political changes in India, the scope of the talks was restricted to arrangements to be made for a period of six months in order to help India tide over her balance of payments deficit. These talks were important as the basic principles and mechanism relating to the execution of all subsequent agreements evolved at this time. The concept of two accounts, one from which India could draw freely from, and the other a blocked one, was agreed upon. The RBI's balances with the Bank of England were accordingly designated No.1 and No. 2. On the date of the agreement, the No. 1 Account was to be credited with £65 million less all amounts spent between 15 July and the date of the agreement. (The account was actually opened with £39 million as the value of the Bank's sterling assets was £1134 million, £26 million less than the notional figure of £1,160 million on which the initial calculation had been based.)[32]

Account No. 2 was opened with £1095 million, which were the remainder of the sterling assets. These were to be utilized for specific purposes only where the transactions were of a capital nature or involved a one-time payment. The Government of India consulted Deshmukh before signifying their assent to the terms negotiated by the Indian delegation. However, India had to accept the unfair figure of 1 per cent per annum on the blocked balances.[33]

The first interim agreement ended the fears that part of the balances would be written off. However, India had to accept a limitation on its right to use them since the strain on the rundown British economy would have been too much to bear if India had been allowed to spend them without limit. But a surprise was in store for India. Barely a week later, the British government repudiated the convertibility clause of the Anglo–American loan agreement. The denial of convertibility changed the character of the agreement since the pounds released were no longer usable for what India wanted to buy. B.K. Nehru recalls that Eady had said 'Watch your dollars'[34] as they were saying goodbye. He had not understood the warning then, but now it all fell into place. This change necessitated another delegation to renegotiate the amount which would be convertible.

Ultimately, India's current earnings of sterling as well as the amounts released under the agreement were not rendered inconvertible, but the British government made an appeal to India to minimize her dollar expenditure.[35] In January 1948, a delegation from the UK led by Sir Jeremy Raisman visited India for further negotiations for releases from 1 January 1948. The Indian side comprised Rao and Cayley of the RBI. The negotiations led to the extension of the earlier agreement on the same basic principles. However, Partition necessitated separate releases for Pakistan's account.

Negotiations with the British government were renewed in London in June–July 1948 with the aim of securing a long-term settlement to cover at least three years with adequate safeguards for later years. The delegation was led by Finance Minister Chetty and included Deshmukh, V.K. Krishnamachari, T.T. Krishnamachari, Purshotamdas and FICCI President Lalji Mehrotra. Deshmukh was accompanied by P.J. Jeejeebhoy, deputy controller of exchange at the RBI, and P.S. Narayan Prasad, director of monetary research, as his advisers. Among the subjects discussed was the price to be paid by the Government of India for the purchase of UK's military stores and installations in India on 1 April 1947, and a tapering annuity to meet the sterling pensionary and provident fund liabilities of the Government of India. A settlement of the amount to be released from the sterling balances for current use and the convertibility of a portion of this release into a multilaterally convertible currency was also discussed.[36]

The negotiations resulted in an extension of the agreement of August 1947 (with some modifications) for three years up to June 1951. A fresh release of £80 million from the No. 2 Account was to be made for the whole period, to be made available in annual instalments of £40 million each for the two years ending 30 June 1950 and 30 June 1951. No transfer was made for 1948–49 in view of the balance already available in Account No.1.

The arrangement was to be worked flexibly with the British government agreeing to make advance transfers in case India found it was running short of foreign exchange (i.e. if the balance in Account No. 1 fell below £30 million.) India was to pay a sum of £100 million in full and final settlement of the cost of military stores and India agreed to pay £147.6 million and £20.5 million for the central and provincial pensions, respectively, in return for which they were to receive from the UK over the next sixty years tapering amounts for paying the pensions as they fell due.[37]

There is an interesting aside to the negotiations. According to B.K. Nehru, Chetty had bought a housing factory in England for £1 million on that visit. When Chetty was leaving for London, he had gone to say goodbye to Pandit Nehru. The prime minister told him that houses were desperately needed for the refugees from Pakistan. He had heard that there were factories in England that produced readymade houses and wanted Chetty to buy one. Chetty being a businessman knew better but duly obliged. Even at that time, sycophancy trumped national interest. The factory that was set up in New Delhi never produced a single house.[38]

When it was time for the next round of negotiations in June 1949, Matthai had succeeded Chetty as finance minister, and it was he who led the Indian delegation to England, a subject which is discussed in the next chapter.

12

Matthai's First General Budget, 1949–50

In his first budget (1949–50), Matthai showed concern for inflationary pressures. The answer to the problem of inflation and high prices, according to Matthai, was to increase the supply of commodities to meet the existing demand, and until this position was reached, to control the distribution of essential commodities.

Financial Position

As regards investment, Matthai said that it had been stagnant and there had been little flow of money into government loans or into industrial concerns. This stagnation, according to him, was due in large measure to the prevailing uncertainty in regard to matters affecting industrial development and prospects. His own view was that with the huge potential demand in this country for both consumer and capital goods, there was bound to be a wide field for private enterprise for many years.

As far as the import policy was concerned, its main aim was to regulate trade in a manner which while keeping in mind the needs of the country, ensured that the overall deficit in India's balance of payments on current account did not exceed the ceiling on the drawal of sterling balances agreed to by India at any time. Matthai said that while the overall balance of payment position was on the whole satisfactory, India's balance of payments with the dollar and hard currency countries was causing great concern. In the past, India's dollar deficit was financed by the central reserves of the sterling area, but from January 1948, the UK refused to carry this responsibility and also limited the convertibility of sterling.

Despite the maximum possible limitation of imports from the hard currency areas, India had a deficit of $45 million in her balance of payments with these countries for the period April–September 1948. The deficit for the next three months, for which preliminary figures were available, was expected to be $48 million. The purchase of food grains was largely responsible for the deficit that far exceeded the convertibility allowed by the UK. The deficit was met by loans from the International Monetary Fund from which (since March 1948), India had borrowed $92 million.[1]

Matthai confessed that this chronic dollar deficit was causing the government great anxiety. He said that they intended to negotiate dollar loans from the International Bank for Reconstruction and Development (World Bank). But these loans would be available only for financing the purchase of equipment for developmental projects and not for current expenditure. One ray of hope was that in the future, India would need to import less food and would be able to divert food purchases to the soft currency areas.[2]

Matthai estimated the deficit for the current year at Rs 1.55 crore against Rs 2.14 crore provided in the budget. The revenue receipts were estimated at Rs 338.32 crore against the budget estimates of Rs 255.24 crore. The total expenditure that year was estimated at Rs 339.87 crore, an increase of Rs 82.49 crore over the budget estimate. Of this increase, defence accounted for Rs 34.35 crore and civil estimates for the balance of Rs 48.14 crore. The expenditure on defence during the year was affected by the continuance of the operations in Kashmir, the extent and duration of which could not be foreseen at the time of budget preparation. The unforeseen deterioration in the situation in Hyderabad which led to the police action in September 1947 added to the expenditure.[3]

The increase of Rs 48.14 crore in civil expenditure was mainly due three reasons. Firstly, a new provision of Rs 20.75 crore was made for meeting pre-Partition liabilities for which no provision was made in the budget. Secondly, the expenditure on the relief and rehabilitation of refugees, earlier budgeted at Rs 10.04 crore, was now expected to be Rs 19.45 crore. Thirdly, the expenditure on the subsidising of imported food grains and the payment of bonuses to provincial governments on internal procurement was expected to exceed the original budget by Rs 12.05 crore.[4]

Income-Tax Investigation Commission

Matthai devoted a few paragraphs of his speech to the work done by the Income-Tax Investigation Commission. He said that the commission had been assigned two duties. The first was to investigate and report on the adequacy of the existing laws and procedures for the assessment and collection of taxes. The second was to investigate specific cases referred to the commission by the central government. The commission had spent a great deal of its time on the first and had recently submitted its report in which it had made recommendations on many points of law and administration. These recommendations were now being examined and Matthai hoped that it would be possible to place a bill before the House at its next session. As regards the investigation of specific cases, Matthai agreed that progress had been tardy. He cited lack of officers and staff and the need to gather data and collate it, as reasons for the slow progress. He assured the House that now with the necessary infrastructure in place, cases would be disposed more expeditiously.[5]

Matthai unveiled plans for the starting of basic industries essential for national development. Among them were a telephone factory, setting up of a shipping corporation, the setting up of new steel works and factories for the manufacture of wireless equipment, synthetic oil, machine tools, cables, diesel engines and heavy electrical equipment.[6]

Financial Estimates

Coming to the estimates for the next financial year, Matthai estimated the total revenue at Rs 307.74 crore and the expenditure charged to revenue at Rs 322.53 crore, leaving a deficit of Rs 14.79 crore. He outlined how he expected to deal with the substantial deficit, which in the present inflationary conditions it was inadvisable to leave uncovered. The problem before him, he said, was not merely that of raising the additional revenue to cover this deficit. He also had to consider the adjustments in taxation necessary in the light of past experience. Matthai summed it up quite pithily when he observed: 'Fiscal policy is not an end in itself but has to subserve the ends of national policy and in a transitional period like this it is essential to keep the working of the taxation system under constant review and readjust it in the light of changing circumstances.'[7]

Matthai felt that apart from inflation, the greatest challenge facing the economy was the stagnant capital market. He attributed this state of affairs to a lack of confidence and a deep fear of the future. Unless conditions that encouraged savings and investment were created, the industrial expansion of the country was bound to be delayed. Matthai said that he had kept this fact in mind while formulating his tax proposals.[8]

Tax Policy Changes

Matthai proposed three important tax policy changes. The first was to abolish the capital gains tax. He said that at the time this tax was introduced, it was expected to yield a large revenue, but experience had proved otherwise. Its psychological effect on investment, had however, been markedly adverse and in the present circumstances, he considered the retention of this tax ill-advised. The loss of revenue was estimated at Rs 1 crore.[9] Matthai reduced the income tax on the lowest- and medium income-earning individuals arguing that this class had been severely hit by inflation and deserved some relief. He also reduced the super tax on both earned and unearned income by varying the rates.

Chetty, in his budget, had given a concession to companies with an income of Rs 25,000 and below, by reducing their income tax to half the usual rates. After carefully reviewing the position, Matthai had concluded that while the concession should be maintained, it should take the form of a rebate of half the corporation tax, and should be limited to public-controlled small companies that were not branches or subsidiaries of bigger companies. The second change related to the taxation of incomes of privately controlled companies which did not declare their dividends in India. He proposed that all corporations, whether Indian or foreign, should continue to be treated as companies, but a further super-tax of one anna should be paid by those privately controlled companies that did not distribute their profits in India.[10] To encourage replacement of assets expeditiously, Matthai decided that depreciation allowance at double the ordinary rate would be allowed for all new plant and machinery installed during the five years from 1 April 1948.

On the indirect taxes front, Matthai withdrew the earlier export duties on oilseeds and vegetable oils and offered customs duty relief on several raw materials imported by industry. To encourage civil aviation, he reduced the duty on aviation fuel by half. While most of Matthai's tax hikes were well received, the one that received the most criticism was his decision to increase the tariff on postal services. Other indirect tax increases, such as higher duties on liquor, fabrics containing silk, glass and glassware, photographic appliances, stationery articles cutlery, metal furniture, motor spirit and clocks and watches were by and large well-received. His decision to impose higher excise duties on petroleum products, tyres and cotton cloth also did not face much opposition.[11]

At the end of it all, Matthai said that the final effect of his proposals was to convert the prospective deficit into a small surplus of Rs 45 lakh. He was apologetic about the increase in taxes.

> It is not pleasant for a finance minister to appear before the House with a record of deficits and proposals for additional taxation but a finance minister is as much the creature of circumstances as anyone else . . . In laying fresh burdens of taxation, the House will accept my assurance that I have done my best to secure that they are equitable and that no section of the community is made to pay more than its fair share.[12]

Deliberations on the Budget

The debates that followed in the House after the presentation of the budget were generally critical of Matthai's proposals. Pandit Hirday Nath Kunzru doubted if measures like the abolition of capital gains tax and reduction of super tax would instil confidence in the business community and lead to greater productivity. He said a stage had been reached when it was necessary to decide if free enterprise was to be given a free hand or if the country was going to opt for a socialistic economy. It was this uncertainty that needed to be cleared up first.[13] In this connection, T.A. Ramalingam Chettiar, the member from Coimbatore, said that the main reason for lack of investment was the uncertainty regarding nationalization in the minds of the businessmen. No one would be willing to invest in an enterprise if he feared that it would be taken over by the government.[14]

K.T. Shah was critical of Matthai's 'heavy pontifical style' and 'the assurances ex cathedra', which he doubted were of much value. He said that it was a pity that even after so many years, the war was 'still trotted out to tell us why the situation is so depressing and why deficit is inevitable'.[15] He said that the budget displayed no art of budgeting since there were wide variations in the estimates. He accused Matthai of a lack of close attention and precision and said that while he was in no doubt about the finance minister's abilities, the old Matthai, who was meticulous in details, had changed in the 'sleepless nights and sleepy days' that it was his fate to undergo.[16]

Shah criticized the relief given to industrialists and high-net worth individuals. 'Without charging Dr Matthai with any lack of intellectual honesty, I do believe that Dr Matthai himself does not believe that this is an equitable budget which he has presented.'[17] He said that such a budget was acceptable from a person whose great sympathy for the capitalist or industrialist class was well known but unacceptable from a former economist. He was also scathing in his criticism on the hike in postal fares. He said that Matthai had restored the wartime rate of 9 pies even though the finance member at the time, Jeremy Raisman, had introduced the 6 pies postcard. He said that if Matthai's only excuse was unforeseen circumstances, and if it was to be judged on its contents and not on Matthai's personal knowledge and integrity, it deserved to be condemned unreservedly.[18]

Pandit Mukut Bihari Lal Bhargava, the member from Ajmer, called it a rich man's budget. He criticized the hike in postal rates and the imposition of a levy on motor spirit. He also felt that enough steps were not being taken to fight inflation. C. Subramaniam from Madras agreed that inflation was not being tackled satisfactorily. He said that the capitalists had been given enough relief but still wanted assurances. They had not risen to the occasion and were apprehensive of nationalization. If private enterprise did not come up to expectations, it would have to be replaced by an agency that might perform better.[19]

B. Shiva Rao, also from Madras, wanted the defence estimates to be examined by a separate subcommittee of the Standing Finance Committee, which he hoped would lead to the development of a full-fledged estimates committee. He also said that the quantity and quality of work done in the secretariat had deteriorated and wanted members of the cabinet to take note of this serious issue. Inefficient persons were being reinstated, and the capable ones were only waiting to retire.[20]

The postal hike was also criticized by M. Tirumala Rao, a member from Madras, who felt that the advantage of quick delivery of mail would benefit only the business community. Every little item of tax would hit the poor man and give him a handle to proclaim that this was not a Congress government but a government of the rich people, by the rich people and for the rich people. Ramnath Goenka echoed this view saying that the budget had proved that the finance minister was not a friend of the common man. He also said that it had failed to give a definite direction to the economy and did not 'indicate either the present economic or financial plans or the future plans in relation thereto'.[21]

The postal hike and levy on coarse cloth came in for universal criticism as did the abolition of the capital gains tax. Almost everyone thought that there was nothing in it for the common man. Mihir Lal Chattopadhyay from Bengal said that Matthai knew that letters in the rural areas were not going to be carried by air, so justifying the hike under the pretext of air transportation was not befitting a man of his calibre. Khandubhai K. Desai from Bombay said that there was nothing in the budget to enthuse the common man nor did it have any foresight. He said that relief had been given to those who did not deserve it. [22]

The lone voice of praise and support for Matthai's budget came from Annie Mascarene, the member from Travancore State, who while agreeing that the postal hike was a 'most unkind cut', felt that the budget had been forced on Matthai by circumstances and given the current situation, his budget was what the country needed.[23] B. Pattabhi Sitaramayya, who spoke later, insinuated that Mascarene's support of Matthai was coloured by communal feelings: '. . . the honourable Annie Mascarene, with true Christian sympathy for the Finance Minister has showered ample encomium on the Finance Minister.'[24] K. Hanumanthaiya, from Mysore, criticized the neglect of agriculture and called it the 'agriculturists-nowhere budget' and the 'incentive-to-industrialists' budget. He blamed it on the fact that very few ministers visited villages and knew the problems and difficulties of the rural people.[25]

Homi Mody, who had been Matthai's colleague in Tatas, provided some much-needed humour in his address, and indeed, no less could have been expected of him. He started by saying that he hoped his friend Matthai was not unduly depressed over the criticisms that had been lavished on his budget. Matthai, Mody said, need not worry since a perusal of the budget debates of the past few decades would show that 'much the same things had been said without doing any damage to anybody'. There was no such thing as a perfect budget, nor would there be one till men learnt to live without the army, the police, the secretariat and above all cabinet ministers. 'But till that time the Finance Minister must make up his mind that he is there to be criticized and condemned and that no consideration will be shown to him,'[26] he said. Other finance ministers would have done well to keep this advice in mind.

Personally, Mody said that he did not stand to benefit since he would have to 'pay a lot more for my cigars, wines and other little things with which I solace myself in a world in which everybody is so harassed and unhappy'.[27] He also took a dig at the members of the House.

> There are economists; there are lay critics. The only difference between an economist and a lay critic is this: an economist is right on his facts and wrong in his conclusions, while a lay critic is wrong on both. There again my honourable friend has much reason for comfort when he feels particularly depressed by some virulent criticism of his economics.[28]

Taken as a whole, Mody said that he found the budget to be sound. However, while praising the speech for its vigour and lucidity, he said that there were gaps which needed Matthai's attention. He said there was no exposition of monetary policy in the budget. The policy the government proposed to follow in the matter of regulating currency and credit was of fundamental importance, according to Mody. He also wanted more accuracy in budgeting. A budget whose expenditure and income 'was out by 60, 70 or 80 crores is not a budget'.[29]

He said that the industrial community had a duty to the country which it had to fulfil. 'After all we are not fair-weather sailors; we have to take the lean with the fat.' He showed his concern for inflation, the refugee problem, and above all drew Matthai's attention to the conflict in policies between the Centre and the provinces. 'The Centre gives subsidies for food, but items of daily consumption are being taxed by the provinces.'[30] The burden of the criticism of some other members was a familiar one: they were against the hike in postal rates and thought that the budget favoured the big industrialists.

Matthai's Reply

Matthai, in his reply to the debate, explained the fundamental principles behind his budget. He said that he had told himself that he would produce 'an orthodox, routine, straight-forward budget'. He said that the country had been buffeted about for two years and what it needed was rest and recuperation for convalescence. 'The period will not be long, but that period is essential if the country is to get back its health.'[31]

Regarding inflation, Matthai said that it was a function of money supply on one side and goods and services on the other. He had been accused of doing little to draw away the abundant supply of money from circulation. Matthai said that due to hoarding, there was a lot less in circulation, and it would be a mistake to judge the quantity of money in the system from currency note issue and bank deposits. The amount of superfluous money was therefore much less than what it was thought to be. Whatever money there was, only a little was going into industrial investment because of the risks involved. The real problem was to divert the money back from consumer goods into the investment market. In the end, he said that increased production was the only panacea for the problem of inflation.[32]

In more general terms, Matthai said it was important for members to realize that the economy had been severely damaged by Partition and his priority was to set the wheels of production moving again. Rebutting the argument that his budget had a pro-capitalist bias, he said that all he had done was to give tangible evidence of the government's desire to assure industrialists of the immediate future and that if they invested their money in the business of production, the government would safeguard their interests. Matthai said that despite these assurances, if the business community still did not respond, then there was something fundamentally wrong with the business community as a whole.[33]

The hike in postal rates, more specifically the postcard, had attracted the most flak. Matthai said that the cost of the postcard would work out to 8.2 pies and he had proposed only 9 pies. This he said was not a new rate—the price of the postcard had been 9 pies for nearly fifteen years until February 1946. Another proposal that attracted criticism was the excise duty on coarse cloth. The reason for imposing that duty, Matthai said, was the abolition of the salt duty, which had resulted in a loss of revenue. Reimposing the salt tax was out of the question since it had 'a symbolic significance which we of this generation cannot afford to ignore'.[34]

He observed that if the principle of an excise duty on an article of universal consumption was accepted, then there was no reason for making a fuss over an excise duty on cloth. He went on to say that the average incidence of excise duty on cloth per head was less than half the average incidence of salt duty. Further, the duty on cloth would give protection to the handloom industry. He told the House that the excise duty on sugar would apply only to mill-made sugar and not to *gur* or *khandsari*.

There was no denying that the scathing criticism of his budget had hurt Matthai. In a subsequent debate on the passing of a grant for interest-free and interest-bearing advances in mid-March, Matthai made his hurt known. He said that the House made generous promises to the spending ministries regarding additional funds, but when the finance ministry tried to raise the money for implementing the generous assurances, the attitude of the House suddenly changed.

> The House curses me, swears at me, throws stones at me . . . I have come to the conclusion that in any modern governmental set up the life of a Finance Minister, like the proverbial policeman's lot is a very hard one and so he sits here in his little corner of the House, listening to these criticisms, subjected to these attacks, and looks for all the world like a maimed dog, licking his wounds all the time.[35]

A motion was tabled to refer the finance bill to a select committee of the House. There were detailed deliberations on 21 and 22 March at the end of which the motion was adopted.

* * *

Matthai had a trying time defending his first budget, but there was more criticism in store. On 1 April 1949, he wrote to G.D. Birla about the criticism of the budget in the *Eastern Economist*, which was owned by the Birlas. He said he had received a letter from a 'well-known Englishman in London' and quoted from it.

> I have just returned from lunching with [Jeremy] Raisman and he showed me a copy of the *Eastern Economist* in which the comments on your speech seem to be particularly severe. We were both surprised at this, especially in view of what your budget has done for the business community, and wonder why this particular line is taken. We were very interested in the comments on your income-tax estimates, as the representatives of the business community had always urged that a reduction in tax on business would in fact stimulate activities and, in the end, increase the net yield! Now that you have assumed that this may be so in your budget, they criticize you for doing it.[36]

Using somewhat strong language, Matthai went on to say that the erratic and superficial comments of the journal had had a demoralizing influence on economic thinking in the country and done a great deal of harm to India's interest abroad. Matthai sent a copy of his letter to Sardar Patel, who replied on 3 April 1949. He said that even before his letter had been received, V. Shankar, his private secretary, had noticed the criticism and spoken to Birla about it. Patel said that he too had had a word with Birla on the subject and the latter had hinted to his editor to take 'a more balanced view of things'. According to Patel, Matthai had Birla's full support. Patel bemoaned the lack of discretion.

> It does distress me to find that our people here or outside have not yet appreciated the virtue of silence and do not try to cultivate it. But I suppose this is one of the many lessons of democracy which we, as a nation have yet to learn, but on that account, we need not be deterred from, or discouraged in, doing our duty.[37]

Matthai and Negotiations on the Sterling Balances

In June1949, Matthai held discussions with the British government in London. He was accompanied by Deshmukh, who was to relinquish charge of the post of Governor in June but acceded to Matthai's request to accompany him as adviser. As a result of the negotiations, an additional £81 million was made available for 1948–49 for which there had been no provision in the earlier agreement. Moreover, the annual releases for 1949–50 and 1950–51 were raised to £50 million. The arrangement of keeping £30 million in Account No.1 was to continue. Insofar as convertibility was concerned, the quantitative restrictions on the right to draw dollars was removed, but India agreed to keep her dollar imports during the twelve months ending June 1950 down to 75 per cent of the imports during the calendar year 1948. This ceiling was ultimately removed in September 1950.[38]

Matthai observed:

> In a market which had been depleted of goods, the scramble for imports aided by large sources of hidden money resulted in a serious drain on our exchange resources. The situation was rendered worse by the fall in our

exports caused by the high level of internal prices. It became therefore necessary to open negotiations with the United Kingdom with a view to securing large releases from our sterling balances than had been agreed to in the previous year. I went to London in June to conduct negotiations. Meanwhile the continuous drain on the dollar reserves of the sterling area led the U.K. Government to call a conference of Commonwealth Finance Ministers to discuss the situation. This conference was held at about the same time as our negotiations regarding the sterling balances.[39]

B.K. Nehru has an interesting anecdote about the drawing down of the sterling balances by India. A Commonwealth Prime Ministers' Conference was held in May 1949 which Pandit Nehru attended. From there Nehru sent a telegram to Matthai enclosing a copy of an aide-memoire given to him by the chancellor of the exchequer, Sir Stafford Cripps. This aide-memoire, worded in the most intemperate language possible, accused the Indians of consistently breaking treaty obligations by drawing down their balances far in excess of what they were permitted to do.

The prime minister wanted an immediate reply so that he could personally hand it over to Sir Stafford before leaving in the next few days. Matthai was in Bombay discussing matters with Deshmukh and Benegal Rama Rau, the RBI governor-designate, when the telegram arrived. Matthai became very agitated and wanted an explanation from B.K Nehru about the so-called breach of faith. B.K. Nehru told him that they had broken no faith and took the next plane to Bombay armed with the draft of a letter from Matthai to the prime minister explaining the situation. It was couched in language which was almost as foul as that of Sir Stafford. The last sentence of the draft was: 'Please explain the position to Stafford Cripps in suitable terms.'[40]

When Matthai and the rest got to know the true facts, they 'got equally excited in the opposite direction'. Matthai was especially agitated since it was his actions that were being questioned. He too was greatly upset at the wording and the tone of Sir Stafford's communication. As a result, he changed nothing of the draft except to cut out the last three words: 'in suitable terms'. He said, 'What d'you mean in suitable terms? Has Stafford Cripps used suitable terms? Let the Prime Minister use whatever terms he likes.'[41]

Photo courtesy of Vivek Matthai

Young Matthai

Photo courtesy of Vivek Matthai

Achamma and John Matthai

Photo courtesy of Vivek Matthai

Matthai family circa 1930s

Duleep, Valsa and Ravi

Valsa Matthai

Tatas' boardroom

The cabinet after the Muslim League joined the interim government in October 1946

The first cabinet of independent India at lunch

The cabinet after Independence. Matthai is fourth from right

Matthai inspecting the Asthi
Special, which carried Gandhi's
ashes to Allahabad

Matthai in conversation with
Devdas Gandhi before departure
of the Asthi Special

Matthai inspecting the site for the
Kanchrapara locomotive workshop
with officials

Matthai being shown the new
signalling cabin in Andal Yard,
West Bengal

A cartoon on the condition of the Railways

Matthai inspecting a coach of the Bengal and Assam Railway that had been vandalized

Matthai in his office

(L to R) Homi Mody, Achamma and J.R.D. Tata

(From L to R) Achamma, J.R.D. Tata and Homi Mody

Homi Mody speaks as Matthai covers his face. In all probability, Mody had said something very funny

Jamshed Bhabha presenting a memento to Matthai as Lady Navajbai Tata looks on

Signing the Constitution. On Matthai's right is Sardar Patel

Sardar Patel greeting Matthai as Achamma looks on

Achamma with Lord Mountbatten and Lady Edwina Mountbatten

Matthai with Homi Bhabha (on his left)

Achamma with
C. Rajagopalachari

Matthai with M.C. Chagla

THE SELECT COMMITTEE ON THE FINANCE BILL HAS
GRACIOUSLY GIVEN A LITTLE TAX RELIEF FOR LOWER
INCOME GROUPS. FEEDING THE
ELEPHANT WITH A LOLLIPOP!

A cartoon from *Shankar's
Weekly*, 2 April 1950

Cover cartoon of *Shankar's Weekly*,
12 March 1950

'Ask, and It Shall Be Given to You', *Shankar's Weekly*, 12 March 1950

'Annual Fashion Parade', *Shankar's Weekly*, 26 March 1950

'He Cannot Escape Now', *Shankar's Weekly*, 26 March 1950

'At the Crossroads', *Shankar's Weekly*, 30 April 1950

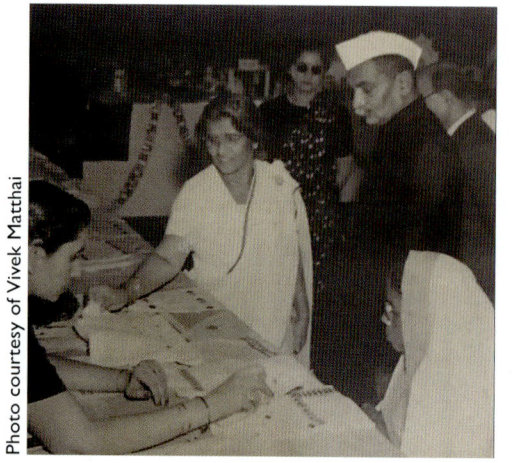

Achamma with Rajendra Prasad

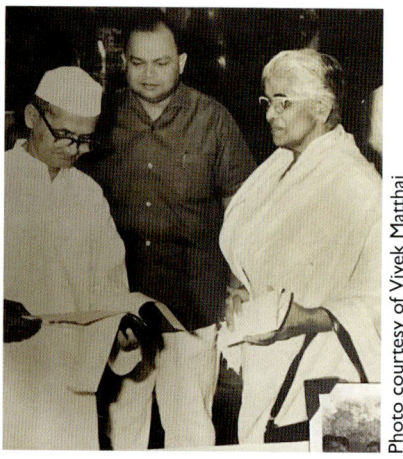

Achamma with Lal
Bahadur Shastri

Signed photo which Nehru gifted Matthai

Ornate box gifted by
Nehru to Matthai

Inside of the box gifted by
Nehru

With the Court of Governors and directing staff of the Administrative
Staff College of India (ASCI), Hyderabad

Matthai at the ASCI, Hyderabad

As vice chancellor of
Bombay University

Matthai with A. Ramaswami Mudaliar,
his predecessor as vice chancellor of
Kerala University

Addressing a convocation
of the Maharaja Sayajirao
University in Baroda in
October 1956

Addressing the Rotary Club,
Bombay, 1956

Ravi and Duleep Matthai

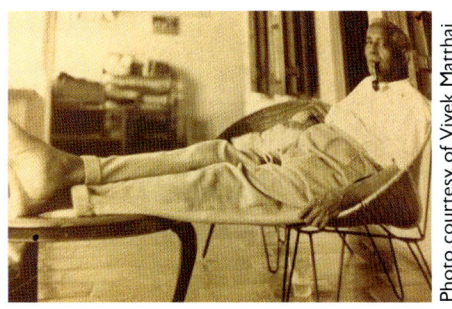

Relaxing with a pipe

Marriage of Ravi and Syloo

Syloo with Achamma

Shaking hands with Nehru after receiving the Padma Vibhushan
in 1959. To Matthai's right is G.L. Mehta, also a Padma
Vibhushan recipient

Nehru and Achamma under a portrait of Matthai at Kerala University, Trivandrum

Matthai's funeral. J.R.D. Tata is also seen behind Ravi

Matthai's last journey

Special cover in honour of Matthai

Duleep's son, Arjun, and his wife Gini

(L to R) Radha, Ashok, Syloo, Cooma and Vivek Matthai

(L to R) Radha, Vivek, Syloo, Phiroze, Ashok, Nitya and Cooma Matthai

Syloo Matthai

The letter was carried by Vijaya Lakshmi Pandit, the prime minister's sister and India's ambassador to the US, who was leaving that night for London en route to Washington. When the prime minister returned from London, he summoned B.K. Nehru and upbraided him as to the language used in Matthai's letter. He said that it was obvious that it had been drafted by B.K. Nehru since 'the language was yours, the style was yours and, in any case, nobody could have known the facts but you'.[42] He wanted B.K Nehru to avoid such language in future since it could cause embarrassment. B.K. Nehru says that his loyalty to Matthai, his minister, prevented him from telling the prime minister about the sole change Matthai had made in the draft put up to him.[43]

The last series of negotiations on the sterling balance covered a period of six years from 1 July 1951, on the expiry of which the No.1 and No. 2 Accounts were to be amalgamated. Discussions were held in this regard between Deshmukh, who succeeded Matthai as finance minister and the chancellor of the exchequer towards the close of 1950, and a broad agreement was reached on the size of the annual releases. It provided for an immediate transfer of £310 million from account No.2 to Account No.1 to be held by the RBI as a currency reserve. The agreement also permitted an annual drawal of £35 million for each of the six years including the flexibility of carrying forward undrawn releases to later periods and limited advance transfers.[44]

The Incident in Allahabad

In the second half of 1949 (this is an estimate, the actual date is not known) Ravi, Matthai's younger son, got into trouble when he was an MA student at Allahabad University. Driving in an inebriated state, he ran his car over a pedestrian and killed him. According to M.O. Mathai, the young man was arrested by the police. Matthai, in his distress, approached Nehru with an appeal to save the boy. M.O. Mathai observed, 'I am afraid John Matthai came to the wrong person; Nehru would never interfere with the course of justice. The PM expressed his sympathy. John Matthai was deeply disappointed and hurt. This coloured his subsequent attitude to the PM.'[45]

According to Mathai's version, Matthai, having failed with Nehru, rushed to Patel, who was eager to put him under his personal obligation.[46]

Patel rang up Govind Ballabh Pant, chief minister of the United Provinces, and asked him to release the boy at once and send him under police escort to New Delhi. The next day, when Ravi reached Patel's house, the latter rang up Matthai and asked him to come to his residence. On his arrival, Patel told him, 'I have a surprise for you,' and had Ravi brought to them. He told Matthai to get the boy out of the country as quickly as possible. Ravi was then quietly sent abroad for further studies. Nothing more was heard of the case against him.[47]

M.O. Mathai is admittedly a less than watertight source, but we have corroboration about this incident from other sources.[48] In fact rather than flee, Ravi picked up the body, put it in his car and surrendered to the police. He then went to the house of Tej Bahadur Sapru, the famous lawyer and freedom fighter, who was a friend of his father. Sapru reportedly said, 'Why did you go to the police? You should have come here straight!'[49]

At the end of it all, Ravi was sent to Balliol College, Matthai's alma mater in Oxford, where by his own account, he had a good time. Soaked in history and tradition, Oxford held Ravi in its thrall. He read politics, philosophy and economics and also took part in extracurricular activities becoming president of the Oxford Majlis, the second-oldest society at Oxford after the Oxford Union. Ravi said that his father was very keen that he go to Oxford and chose both the college and the course. He recalled with self-deprecating humour, '... I don't think he regarded me as particularly bright. So, he chose the subjects which he thought a person of my somewhat limited capability would be able to cope with.'[50]

13

Devaluation of the Rupee

Before Matthai could present his second budget, he had to deal with another crisis: the devaluation of the rupee. Closely linked to the issue of the sterling balances was the devaluation of sterling in September 1949, and the decision to devalue the Indian rupee that was linked to it. The devaluation of sterling came like a bolt from the blue and took Matthai and the Indians by surprise.

Matthai, in his speech on the motion of devaluation in the Constituent Assembly in the first week of October 1949, told the House that on account of the severe drain upon the dollar resources of countries in the sterling area, there were rumours about the ability of the pound sterling—the master currency—to maintain its exchange value. He said that he had attended a conference of commonwealth ministers at the end of July 1949 in London to discuss the situation arising out of the severe strain upon the resources of the sterling area. According to Matthai, the resolutions framed at that conference were to provide the basis for forthcoming talks with the US and Canada. He was categorical that the question of devaluation was never discussed at the conference; in fact, there was no reference whatsoever to it.[1]

But rumours of devaluation had been in the air for some time. The conference of commonwealth finance ministers was announced on 29 June 1949, and on the same day, Nehru wrote to V.K. Krishna Menon telling him that Matthai would attend the conference, and that he was sending the letter he was writing, through him. Nehru said that there was a chance that the question of devaluation of sterling would be discussed. 'I do not know much about these matters. But it seems to me that it would be very injurious to us if we accept any such thing and thereby drag the rupee down too.'[2] Nehru also told Krishna Menon that Matthai did not like travelling. 'Matthai dislikes wandering about and leaving home. He is not at all looking forward to going to England and disturbing his normal routine. I do not think he has met Attlee or Stafford, certainly not the latter. You will of course introduce him to them.'[3]

Matthai said that the commonwealth countries were not represented at the talks in Washington between Britain, USA and Canada, but it was understood that the chancellor of the exchequer would argue the case for the sterling countries based on the brief prepared at the Commonwealth Ministers Conference. Matthai asked Deshmukh who was the Indian ambassador-at-large on matters of external finance in Europe and America to be present in Washington before these talks, as an informal observer. Matthai was of the view that the decision to devalue the pound had already been taken before the British delegation left for London.[4] Deshmukh, in his memoirs, says that the joint meeting of the Bank and Fund in 1949 had special significance as devaluation of currencies was in the air. Even though Sir Stafford Cripps, the chancellor of the exchequer, had stoutly denied any intention to devalue, the world had learnt to discount such disclaimers, and it was believed that devaluation would take place, although by how much was not clear at the time.[5]

A Bolt from the Blue

The first information about the devaluation was received in a message from Prime Minister Clement Attlee to Pandit Nehru. The message was received on Friday, 16 September at 2 p.m. and Nehru gave it to Matthai as soon as he got it. Almost at the same time, Matthai received a message from Washington that Benegal Rama Rau, the RBI governor, who was in Washington for a meeting of the World Bank, was flying back to Delhi. Having seen Attlee's message, Matthai realized that Rama Rau's sudden flight back home was linked to the news of the devaluation.

A cabinet meeting was fixed for 10 p.m. on the same day, since the RBI Governor's plane was expected to land at around 8 p.m. and it was thought that his presence would help the cabinet to arrive at a decision on the subject. Unfortunately, his flight was delayed by eight hours, and he arrived only on the next morning, by which time the decision to devalue the rupee to the same extent as the pound had already been taken. Another cabinet meeting took place at 10 p.m. on Saturday, at which Rama Rau informed them of the discussions in Washington. What he told them only served to confirm that the decision taken the night before was the correct one.

Matthai, who claimed to have an inkling of the devaluation, told the House that he had not dismissed the possibility of a devaluation completely even though the British had categorically denied any intention to devalue. He had, he claimed, prepared for such an eventuality and had arranged for technical advisers in the government and in the RBI to make a detailed and exhaustive study of the problem. Their recommendation was that in case the pound was devalued, then the rupee should be devalued to the same extent. He told the House that Deshmukh gave him the same advice, an opinion in which the RBI governor also fully concurred.[6] Deshmukh recalls in his memoirs:

> It was at this juncture that Sir Stafford Cripps, obviously greatly depressed, called us representatives of Commonwealth Governments and announced that the sterling was to be devalued by thirty per cent. I cabled to India and recommenced that we agree to go along with the pound sterling and received instructions accordingly.[7]

Matthai said that the commonwealth finance ministers' conference that he had attended was a somewhat tame affair. The subjects discussed at the conference were not new and simply formalized what had previously been taken for granted by the different countries. The one issue that troubled everyone 'and on which everybody at the conference silently sought for light, namely the rumoured devaluation of sterling and its possible consequences, was not even mentioned at the Conference'. Sir Stafford repeatedly denied (and with great vehemence) the slightest possibility of devaluation. Matthai said that the devaluation came just within two months of the conference, and Sir Stafford not merely continued in office, but made it his business to extol the benefits of devaluation.[8]

There is no denying that Matthai had not only been caught off-guard but also felt a little let-down by his British counterpart. He realized that parliamentary government based on the principle of collective responsibility was unworkable without a large measure of compromise. He knew that this necessarily implied ministers having to make statements in public which did not accord with their convictions, as he had himself realized at his own cost. But he felt that one must draw the line somewhere.

Matthai had learnt to like and respect Sir Stafford during their meetings at the commonwealth conference and someday hoped 'to hear from his own mouth sharing as I do his faith in the ultimate verities of life how he reconciled within himself so vast a contradiction between utterance and action'.[9]

Matthai said that he received hardly twenty-four hours' notice of the British government's decision to devalue sterling before coming to a decision regarding the value of the Indian rupee. 'The delicate nature of the issue, I have no doubt justified the secrecy in which it was shrouded, but I have never yet reconciled myself to the action of the British government in keeping it secret from the Chancellor's opposite numbers in the Dominions.'[10] He said that Washington knew of the decision, as did Ottawa, long before New Delhi, although India was more intimately concerned with its consequences than either of them.

The Bombay market, Matthai said, hummed with the news for several days before Nehru received Attlee's message. The right course for the chancellor to have followed would have been to fix another meeting in September where he could have reported on the result of his Washington talks on the various matters discussed at the July conference and 'which incidentally would have enabled him to convey to us personally the devaluation decision'.[11]

According to Matthai, one unfortunate result of the secrecy and suddenness with which the decision was taken was that it made it impossible for him to discuss the question with Pakistan before each country committed itself to a final decision regarding its own currency. He observed,

A country's currency like its national flag tends to become a symbol of honour and prestige and decisions once taken are difficult to alter because economics get intermingled with indefinable considerations of national prestige. That is the position which Pakistan and India have now reached. As far as we are concerned, I am convinced that however difficult the decision was at the time we took it, we have done the right thing in devaluing the rupee to the same extent as sterling. The results so far have justified our decision. It was moreover in line with the decision taken by practically every country in the sterling area barring Pakistan and had besides the full approval of the International Monetary Fund.[12]

B.K. Nehru's Version

B.K. Nehru, who was part of the sterling balances negotiating team which Matthai led in 1949, has his own story to tell. At the goodbye dinner after the 'captains and kings' had departed, Wilfrid Eady told him that though the chancellor had assured them that there would be no devaluation of sterling, they as civil servants had to be prepared for every eventuality. If at some stage it was decided to devalue, the civil servants should know what to do. He said that considerable thought had been given to this both within the British Treasury and the Bank of England, as to how this most unlikely possibility was to be handled. Eady kept reassuring him that it was unlikely that such circumstances would arise but at the same time asked him to see Sir George Bolton at the Bank of England, who would brief them on the theoretical plans that Britain had made to deal with a devaluation, which, once again he was quick to reiterate, was a highly unlikely possibility.[13]

When B.K. Nehru met Sir George, the latter spoke about the hypothetical devaluation in great detail, including giving dates in September 1949 and about when the IMF would ratify the decision. He even hazarded a guess as to the rate after devaluation: He said it would be $3.20 or even $3 to the pound. B.K. Nehru says that this was so obvious a forewarning that on his return, he reported the conversation in full to Matthai, who refused to believe that sterling would be devalued. Matthai said that if there had been any proposal, Sir Stafford, who was an honest man and a friend, would have told him. B.K. Nehru's argument that it was impossible for a finance minister to admit to anybody that there was going to be a devaluation of his own currency, fell on deaf ears. He observed, 'But even the ego of a man like him would not accept that so great a secret could possibly have been conveyed to a mere civil servant.'[14]

Contrary to Matthai's statement in the Constituent Assembly debate, B.K. Nehru said that Matthai initiated no action to examine the fallout of a devaluation, and the steps India should take in case of such an eventuality. It is difficult to say at this distant date whose version is correct. Matthai was known for his unimpeachable integrity, but on the other hand, there appears to be no reason for Nehru to fabricate stories. Nehru also seems to have got his dates mixed up. He said that the telegram announcing the devaluation came on 21 September; Matthai in his speech had said it was 16 September.

By the time the devaluation actually took place, B.K. Nehru was transferred to Washington and as noted before, RBI Governor Rama Rau, who was in Washington for a Fund-Bank meeting, left that city precipitately. The new rate was $2.80 to the pound and Sir George told B.K. Nehru that apart from the exchange rate (Bolton had indicated $3), the long notice should have helped India prepare its response. When Sir George asked B.K. Nehru why his warning had not been heeded, the latter told him that he had not been believed. B.K. Nehru observed, 'This he himself could not believe!'[15] If B.K. Nehru's version is to be believed, then there is little doubt that Matthai had been caught napping.

Deliberations in the Assembly

Matthai told the House that he had informed Ceylon and Pakistan about the devaluation but had received no response from the latter. Matthai released an announcement in the press on 19 September, a Monday, about the devaluation and the concurrence was received from the IMF by the finance ministry on the same day. However, since Monday to Wednesday were all bank holidays, the new rate became effective only on 22 September 1949.

Matthai said that while he appreciated the difficulties faced by the British government, he found it strange that there was no mention of devaluation at the commonwealth ministers conference which was convened for discussing the dollar situation. 'I cannot help thinking that in a matter which so vitally affects the whole economy of every country in the sterling area, steps should have been taken to arrange for a secret meeting of the Finance Ministers of the Commonwealth countries before this decision was sprung upon them . . .'[16]

Matthai told the House that there existed a case based on economic facts for the devaluation of both the pound and the rupee, but he would have liked to have more time for deliberation on the subject. It was a decision not born out of logic but thrust upon him by the compulsion of events. He said that there was no other option open to India but to devalue since 75 per cent of exports was with the soft currency areas and in case they did not devalue, Indian exports would have been hard hit. Since the sterling balance was not an infinite source, the only way India could maintain a healthy trade balance was by promoting exports. 'That then is the main reason. May I put it like this? We took this decision in the main as a defensive measure.'[17]

He then went on to explain that India was a member of what was called the sterling area, and as long as India was part of the sterling area, it had to honour the objective of that area, which as he understood it, was to 'achieve a balance of trade at the highest possible level, partly by expanding exports and partly as a temporary measure—if that was necessary in order to restore equilibrium—by reducing imports also'.[18] The essence of the sterling area was that all the hard currency resources earned by the members of the sterling area were pooled and all the members of the sterling area had the right to draw upon the central reserves for meeting their deficits in respect of dollar resources. It was in India's interest to remain in the sterling area, since unlike in the past when it was a net contributor to the pool, it was in the present day, a net beneficiary. After the UK, it was India who made the biggest demand upon the central reserves. Hence, it was in India's interest to remain in the sterling area.[19]

Matthai warned that it was quite possible that India would not have access to the resources represented by the central reserves of the sterling area. He said it was time that the country 'marshalled its resources and put its whole pattern of trade on a basis which would enable it to go without this adventitious aid'.[20] If the need for devaluation was accepted, then there was an equal ground for suggesting that there should be devaluation in equal measure. As it is, he said, the level of prices was higher in India, and if added to that there was an appreciation of the rupee, it would seriously handicap India's exports.[21]

India devalued to the extent the Britian did, but curiously Pakistan did not. The price of their exports was inelastic, and devaluation would have reduced their incomes. Matthai told the House that he thought that Pakistan's decision lacked economic justification. Pakistan's economic condition was not fundamentally different from those of other countries in the sterling area to justify what was in effect an appreciation of their currency.

Pakistan's favourable balance of payments was due largely to two factors: first, the export of raw cotton and jute to India and, second, its low capital imports given the fact that its industrialization programme had yet to take off. Given the appreciation, Indian manufacturers would be compelled as a matter of self-preservation to refuse to buy raw jute and cotton from Pakistan. According to B.K. Nehru, Pakistan's failure to devalue started a trade war (with India being the aggressor), which lasted well over a year.[22] He narrates how when a year after the devaluation he met Sir George Bolton again and in the course of the conversation asked him if he had not given the Pakistanis the same information he had given the Indians. Bolton responded with a categorical 'no' saying that he could not think of any Pakistani who would not have made money if he was privy to such information. B.K. Nehru observes, 'This I thought was a most unfair remark. There was no difference then in the standards of integrity between civil servants of India and Pakistan.'[23]

Analysing what he thought would be the future trend in Pakistan's balance of payments, given the fall in the export in cotton and jute and the impending industrialization which would involve the import of capital goods, Matthai argued that Pakistan's decision not to devalue was the result of not economic, but other, considerations. Matthai approvingly quoted *The Economist* of London in this regard. The magazine had called it a 'temporary aberration' attributing it to psychological causes that included a sense of injured pride. Also, the temptation to demonstrate the superiority of their currency over the Indian currency had been too strong to resist.[24] Matthai also said that economic forces would make it increasingly difficult for Pakistan to maintain the new ratio.

Matthai told the House that since the question of the exchange rate was linked with certain issues arising out of the payments agreement between the two countries, there was no decision to announce a new rate or to alter in any way the Indian decision on the devaluation. Referring to the effects of the devaluation on the Indian economy, Matthai said that the position was still obscure. 'There are far too many uncertain factors and I hesitate to lay down any dogmatic or categorical proposition.'[25] However, he did venture to state a few broad conclusions which were necessarily of a tentative character.

Analysing the balance of payments with the US, Matthai said that India's exports mainly comprised jute and tea, both commodities being demand and supply inelastic. Thus, devaluation was unlikely to lead to any quantitative increase. On the import side, he wanted to stop the import of food grains as early as possible, reduce the imports of motor vehicles, and to divert the purchase of machinery and other industrial products as far as possible to soft currency areas.[26]

As far as the balance of payments position with UK was concerned, he said that the goods exported to India by the UK using US material would necessarily show some increase. With the increasing demand, which was going to be placed upon the soft currency areas because of the higher dollar prices of these goods, there was 'likely to be an increased pressure of demand upon soft currency areas which could raise to some extent the prices of goods imported from soft currency areas'.[27]

Matthai also discussed the effect of the devaluation on the convertible portion of India's sterling balance. While he admitted that there would be some loss, the loss was not likely to be as large as a straightforward application of arithmetical percentages would suggest. The loss would depend on the extent to which India could divert purchases to the sterling area, on the difference in prices, and on the money value that they set upon the difference in quality and periods of delivery. He observed, 'The real test in these matters is not currency, but the things currency buys.'[28]

There had been fears about an attempt to scale down the sterling balances, something which was stoutly resisted by Purshotamdas Thakurdas and others. Matthai, during the course of his speech, adverted to Sir Winston Churchill's speech to the British Parliament regarding the scaling down of the sterling balances. He said that the demand for scaling down the balances was based on the plea that India owed a good deal more than it had contributed so far towards the war expenses of the allied countries. Matthai said that India's share of the war expenditure was a matter of definite and deliberate agreement between the two countries made at a time when Churchill was the prime minister. 'Every penny due from us under the present agreement has been paid . . . I maintain therefore in fairness, there is no justification for the demand which is being repeatedly made by certain sections of public opinion in the United Kingdom.'[29]

The sterling balances, Matthai said, were a result of an improper use of the provisions of the RBI Act, which linked the rupee with the sterling, sterling securities being used to that extent as reserves for Indian currency. It was the sterling balances that were at the root of the inflation in India. He said that if there had been an Indian government at the time of the war, then the cost of goods supplied by India to the UK would have been met by goods supplied to India, especially capital goods, by rupee loans raised in India or by gold. If these did not meet the cost of supplies required, the supplies would have had to be restricted to that extent. This, he said, would have spared India the terrific inflation it inherited. India was not a party to the declaration of the war, whatever its merits, and it was unfair to now saddle a national government with additional expenses.[30]

After briefly touching upon the price level, he told the House about the various steps taken, and proposed to be taken, after devaluation. He ended with a word of warning: He said that devaluation should be viewed as a timely warning about the fact that India had been living beyond its means, both internally and externally.

Debates and Criticism

K.T. Shah, in the course of the debate, spoke of the betrayal by the British and how Matthai had been led into a trap by Sir Stafford, who till the very end said there would be no devaluation and then suddenly did what he had been denying all along. He accused Matthai of underestimating the injury that had occurred and said that nothing in the finance minister's statement had shown that import of either food grains or capital goods could be curtailed. Speaking about the link with sterling, he said that even though technically there was no connection with sterling since the relevant RBI Act had been amended, the psychological link still remained, and this was affecting the behaviour of those in authority. He said that the decision to devalue would benefit only the British in their standard of living or in their industry.

Using strong language he observed, 'It has no concern with us . . . if anybody lives in the hope . . . the belief that we are going to benefit from it. I should regard him a candidate for an asylum and not for an Assembly.'[31] He added that devaluation was of little use if there were competitive devaluations. Referring to Britain's difficult position he observed, 'Here is a country which must necessarily depend upon trade and depend upon Empire. While the Empire was there it was able to levy an unseen invisible tribute from that Empire in one way or the other.'[32] Referring to the sterling balances, he bemoaned the reduction in the purchasing power of the balances and wanted a third-party guarantee for conversion into gold or dollar equivalent, and wanted no more contact with the British.

Pandit Thakur Das Bhargava from East Punjab believed that devaluation was the only option open to the government. He believed that Matthai had done the only thing possible at the time and that devaluation was done not to placate Britain but as a sovereign act by the government in the interest of the country. 'Our government, in self-interest alone agreed to this course. There was no other course open to government, and I want that this assembly should approve of this action of the government.'[33]

Prof. N.G. Ranga from Madras wanted to know what steps Matthai had taken to reduce imports and increase exports if, as he said he had had had an inkling of the devaluation. He wanted to know about the probability of converting the sterling balances into dollar exchange. T. Prakasam, also from Madras, said that even though India was free, it was still 'tied down in the currency business to Great Britain'.[34] He asked why India had devalued to the same extent as Britain and wanted the extent of devaluation to be reduced.

Pandit Nehru said that the country could not continue living beyond its means and that to that extent the devaluation had been a wake-up call. He wanted the country to concentrate on capital goods and the machine-making industry which would facilitate industrialization.[35] He wanted the members of the House to confer with the finance minister so that ideas could be shared by both parties. 'Now the members in this house are important not only as being members of Parliament, but as links with the people in the country, and it is quite essential that the house should cooperate fully in all the steps that we may take.'[36]

Khandubhai K. Desai said he supported the devaluation because it was inevitable but wanted the best to be made of a bad bargain 'and pave the way for the economic recovery of the country'.[37] H.V. Kamath adverted to the great haste (within twenty-four hours) with which India had devalued. He said that West Germany had taken a week to devalue and if India was indeed as independent as it claimed to be, the decision to devalue could have been postponed for a while. He cited the example of the government in Bonn, who made it look as if the decision had been theirs and not because the pound had been devalued. 'That is my chief quarrel with the decision,' he said.[38]

Biswanath Das from Orissa said that England had behaved 'most tyrannically, mischievously' against India and he could not support Matthai in his dismissing the 'British perfidy, the wickedness of Sir Stafford Cripps in the way he did'. He referred to a cartoon in *Shankar's Weekly* that showed Sir Stafford swimming with a gleam of merriment on his face, with Matthai standing with the water almost near his lips—almost sinking under the strain of devaluation. He said that the criticism of other members was 'mere talk, all in the air, all in the stratosphere' if it did not suggest a practical approach to the problem.[39]

M. Ananthasayanam Ayyangar from Madras wanted the government to have a minister for economic affairs and wanted Matthai to appoint a standing committee to examine all issues arising out of the devaluation since the Standing Committee on Finance was already overburdened.[40]

In his closing remarks at the end of the debate, Matthai said that what was required was not more proposals but the ability to implement them. The so-called economic problems of the day were not in reality economic problems but 'deep down they resolve themselves into problems of efficiency and honest administration'. What was required was not intellectual analysis or more planning for big projects but the need to 'settle down to the drudgery of good honest administration'. For this, Matthai said coordination was important, not only between ministries but also between the Centre and the provinces.[41]

According to Matthai, there were three important directions in which the government had to move. Firstly, it had to curtail public expenditure. Secondly, it had to control the price level, and thirdly, increase the productive capacity of the economy. He agreed with Pandit Thakurdas Bhargava that one could not get away overnight from the commitments which history had made for the country. He said that it was difficult to build up trade connections and due to historical reasons, much of India's trade had been with countries in the sterling area. He said it would be a mistake to do anything that would destroy a long-standing relationship but what was needed was to try to reduce the proportion of trade with the sterling area by building up connections in other areas.[42]

K.M. Munshi from Bombay raised the issue of inefficient tax administration impacting savings and investment and ultimately production. Matthai said at present the tax officers had been unable to establish anything like a satisfactory liaison with the public and it was one of his aims to have some kind of organization that would give officers 'the right attitude with regard to the question of dealing with the public'. Matthai also told the House his intention to reduce direct taxes as soon as he could and to ensure that taxes were collected promptly and efficiently.[43]

* * *

India's next devaluation came in June 1966 when Indira Gandhi was prime minister. She devalued the rupee by over 57 per cent against the dollar and the decision was announced in early June by the finance minister, Sachindra Chaudhuri. The moves for this devaluation began many months earlier when Lal Bahadur Shastri was prime minister and T.T. Krishnamachari, the finance minister. In March 1965, the government entered into a standby agreement with the IMF to bolster its foreign exchange reserves to meet its demands for imports and to finance the Third Plan. It was around this time that it was hinted that perhaps India should consider a devaluation of the grossly overvalued rupee, to solve its chronic foreign exchange crisis, though there was no reference to this when the agreement was concluded. Devaluation had, however, been in the air in official circles in Delhi, but Krishnamachari was violently opposed to the idea. Some of the 'adamantine quality' of his opposition came from the manner in which George Woods, the president of the World Bank, had proposed the devaluation to him at the annual meeting of the Bank–Fund in Tokyo in September 1965. Woods had given the impression that he was issuing an ultimatum: 'Devalue or no money.' This got Krishnamachari's back up and he vowed never to devalue.[44] When he resigned, Chaudhuri was appointed finance minister, and he did the needful.

14

Matthai's Second General Budget, 1950–51

Matthai's second and last budget speech made history for two reasons: First, he was presenting India's first budget after it had formally become a republic, and second, it was delivered from memory. To the great consternation of the staff of the finance ministry, Matthai refused to allow them to prepare the usual formal budget speech for him to read. K.R.K. Menon, the finance secretary, related how anxious he and his officers were at Matthai's intransigence. Matthai discussed the budget in great detail with his secretariat the day before, made a few notes and then went home. Menon, however, prevailed upon him to make only the first part of his speech extempore and allow the printing of the second part.[1]

Matthai started his speech confidently and except for a cursory look at a chit he had in his pocket continued to speak for nearly three hours without recourse to any aide-memoire:[2] ' . . . I propose to allow myself today the freedom of speaking somewhat informally on the matters covered by the Budget, instead of delivering a set address as is usually done on occasions of this kind.' He set out the reasons for the unconventional character of his speech in his peroration. The budget, he said, was a human document that exercised the emotions of millions of people all over the country. 'I think therefore it is appropriate that its presentation to the people's representatives in Parliament should be somewhat less impersonal than has been customary with us hitherto.'[3]

The lack of a written budget speech put the journalists present in a quandary. Had a Press Trust of India reporter not taken down the extempore part of the speech in shorthand, there would have been nothing in the next day's papers. It was an unprecedented performance and one that has never been repeated by any finance minister. But there is a parallel outside government. For many years, legal luminary and taxation expert, Nani A. Palkhivala, spoke entirely from memory when he gave his views on the union budget at The Cricket Club of India's Brabourne Stadium in Mumbai. A hugely popular talk attended by many thousand people, it was said that there were two budget speeches, one by the finance minister and the other by Palkhivala.

The Budget

Matthai announced the government's decision to request the House to set up an Estimates Committee to scrutinize the expenditure of each department of the government and of the government as a whole. He said that the expenditure being examined by an independent authority set up by the House would act as a deterrent to extravagance in public expenditure, and that there was a distinction between the work of the Standing Finance Committee and the work of the proposed Estimates Committee. The Standing Finance Committee was concerned with specific proposals of expenditure by each department of government, but the Estimates Committee's business would be to make a comprehensive examination of expenditure in relation to the resources available to government.[4]

State of the Economy

Matthai said that the economy continued to face many challenges and inflation remained a serious problem. He attributed the latest bout of price rise to international developments and observed that the world was apprehensive about another outbreak of war, which could fuel a price rise. 'Taking our own country, we are necessarily affected by all these international forces. India today has far more points of contact with the outside world than she had at the end of the first war.'[5]

Matthai argued that the problem of inflation was linked to the critical question of production. He said that there has been a substantial increase in various important industries: steel, cement, coal, heavy chemicals, paper and generation of electricity, but the same could not be said for two very important industries, namely cotton textiles and jute manufactures. In both these cases, the limiting factor was the supply of raw material, particularly as a result of the deadlock that had arisen in the trade between India and Pakistan. The situation had necessitated greater import of raw cotton. As far as jute was concerned, production of raw jute had shown an improvement and there were enough stocks to last until the end of the current jute season.[6] Matthai considered the food grains position to be encouraging. Higher production and procurement had ensured that there was no cause for anxiety. One of the factors that had assisted this increase in performance was the improvement in railway transport and the improvement in the labour situation.[7]

As regards the money market, Matthai said there was no cheer either in the short-term or the long-term markets. He refused to subscribe to the common view that stagnation in the investment market was because 'capital today is on strike'.

> I have looked into this matter with some care, and I have come to the conclusion that there is no foundation for this allegation. The position of the investment market can be fully and intelligibly explained with reference to such factors as increased costs, reduced margin of profits and unstable economic and psychological conditions which, if they had prevailed in any other country, would have resulted in exactly the same situation in the investment market . . .[8]

Since July 1949, there had been signs of revival of confidence, but the genuine investor was holding aloof because 'he has not got the measure of confidence which would justify his putting what little he has into investment'.[9]

On the question of foreign capital, Matthai said that he considered it necessary not merely for the purpose of supplementing our own resources but for the purpose of instilling a spirit of confidence among investors. He said that 'capital from foreign countries must hereafter be looked for not in the shape of fixed interest-bearing loans and bonds, but in the shape of equity capital on the basis of joint participation on strict business considerations without any political strings attached to it'.[10] Therefore, it was necessary to provide reasonable conditions of security and fair treatment for those who are willing to take the risk of investing their money in India. He referred to Pandit Nehru's statement made in the past year in this regard: 'The statement that the Prime Minister made last year still represents our policy in this matter and I believe that the terms and conditions outlined in that statement ought to provide reasonable security for foreign investors.'[11]

Matthai also decided against renewing the Dividend Limitation Act, 1936. He gave three reasons. First, with the fall in the level of profits, the limit fixed by the Act was practically inoperative. Second, it had failed as an anti-inflationary measure and third, it had a 'disproportionately depressing effect' on the investment market.[12]

On the question of the country's balance of payments, Matthai said that there had been an improvement in the sterling balances in the last seven and a half months. He refuted the accusation that a large quantity of luxury goods was being imported under the Open General License saying that such goods amounted to not more than 1.5–2 per cent of the total imports.[13] He added that there was an improvement in the balance of payments, but there was no room for complacency. He warned that a balance of payments, which was based on a drastic reduction of imports, and by continued releases of accumulated balances abroad, was an unhealthy balance.

A healthy balance was the sort of balance that one attained at the highest possible level of imports as well as exports. He observed,

If you look at the present size of our sterling balances, making allowance for an adequate reserve against our currency in foreign assets, and assuming for the time being that the releases would be more or less at the average rate of the past two years, our sterling balances are not likely to last us more than six or seven years.'[14]

Therefore, Matthai said, it was of the highest importance that they should begin to plan for an external economy that would be self-balancing. And that could be done only by a stimulation of exports.

Summing up the economic position, Matthai said that while the situation was still replete with dangers and called for the utmost care and watchfulness, there was no cause for undue pessimism. He said that the government had been widely criticized for the way in which it had handled the economic situation, but he welcomed such criticism for two reasons. First, it had a stimulating effect on members of the government, and second, it provided a kind of safety valve for 'the suppressed emotions of people which, but for this outlet, might someday burst and break up society'. He then rather dramatically said: 'Mr. Speaker, even they serve whose business is just to get shot.'[15]

Taxation

With regard to fresh taxation, Matthai decided to undo some of the increases in postal rates which had been unpopular with both citizens and members of the House. The rates for telephone services were also reduced. In direct taxes, he abolished the business profits tax whose revenues were falling. The maximum rate of income tax was reduced from 31.5 per cent to 25 per cent and the rates on lower slabs were also reduced by almost similar margins. Matthai raised the tax exemption limit for an undivided family. A slight increase in the corporation tax was neutralized by a reduction in the maximum income tax rate. He removed the distinction between earned and unearned income for the levy of super tax and the maximum super tax rate was reduced from the earlier range of 56.25–62.5 per cent to 53.12 per cent, which was to be levied only on incomes above Rs 1.21 lakh.[16]

The Planning Commission

Matthai also announced the creation of an institution which would have an important bearing on his own future: the Planning Commission. Early in the session, the President had announced to the House that a Planning Commission would be set up. Matthai said it was necessary to undertake a review of the existing programme of development and the existing schemes of production. Public opinion too was demanding a different kind of approach to the whole problem of development. As we shall see in a subsequent chapter, the Planning Commission was Nehru's idée fixe. Matthai said the Planning Commission would consist of Nehru as chairman and Gulzari Lal Nanda as deputy chairman. C.D. Deshmukh, Gaganvihari Lal Mehta and R.K. Patil were to be members. (There was also a fourth member whose name was to be announced later.) N.R. Pillai, the cabinet secretary, would function as the secretary of the commission and he would be assisted, as deputy secretary, by Sardar Tarlok Singh, deputy secretary in the finance ministry.[17]

Revenue and Expenditure

With regard to the revenue and expenditure of government, Matthai said that in 1949–50 he had estimated a total revenue of about Rs 323 crore and a total expenditure of Rs 322.5 crore, leaving a small surplus of about

Rs 49 lakh. The revised estimates now showed a total revenue of a little over Rs 332 crore and a total expenditure of a little over Rs 336 crore, thus converting the token surplus of Rs 49 lakh into a deficit of Rs 3.74 crore. He said he regarded this small deficit with a sense of relief since there was a time, in the course of the year, when he expected to be faced with a deficit of much bigger dimensions. Defence had increased from an estimated Rs 153 to Rs 170 crore in the current year, which was inescapable, and customs duties went up by Rs 9 crore and the difference between the two gave exactly the measure of the deficit.[18]

At the existing level of taxation, the total revenue for 1950–51 was estimated at Rs 347.5 crore and the total expenditure at Rs 337.88 crore, leaving a surplus of Rs 9.62 crore. On the expenditure side, in 1949–50, the revised figures of defence expenditure showed an expenditure of Rs 170 crore. Matthai said that he was providing for 1950–51 an expenditure of Rs 168 crore for defence. This represented 50 per cent of the expenditure, but Matthai qualified his statement by saying that these figures held good only on the assumption that no abnormal developments would occur.[19]

The civil expenditure estimates for 1950–51 showed an increase of Rs 3.83 crore. Matthai said that before members questioned his much-vaunted economy campaign, he wanted them to know the real position. The figures included many items of expenditure which had not found a place earlier. They included the administration of states taken over as chief commissionership, privy purses of Indian rulers and special items, such as relief of displaced persons, food subsidies and expenses of the coming election.[20]

Matthai said that he considered the present level of taxation in the country as uneconomic in the sense that the economy of the country could not bear it. He was clear that the effect of the present level of taxation was not disinflationary but positively inflationary. If one took the line that the solution to the problem of inflation was production, then a very high level of taxation (which reduced the margin of saving and the amount available for investment) was in fact a potential inflationary force. He also said that he would have liked a fundamental revision of the tax structure but had refrained from doing so because the economy was still in the middle of a very difficult period of transition. It was for this purpose that the government had set up a committee 'to inquire into the whole question of national income and its distribution'.[21]

Deliberations and Discussions

The debate on Matthai's second budget was comparatively less heated, perhaps because he had proposed no additional taxation. Pandit Thakur Das Bhargava called it a featureless budget but lauded Matthai for not including populist features which played to the gallery. [22] B. Shiva Rao praised him for being more accurate in his forecasts and for reducing greatly the difference in the original estimates and the revised estimates.[23] However, he believed that Matthai should have produced in his budget speech 'a picture of the special conditions of this country'. Frank Anthony was upset about what he called the 'irresponsible and extravagant misdirection of public finances' and the 'squander-mania' of the government.

The now common charge of it being a capitalist's budget was made by D.S. Seth, who said that the budget had been designed to serve the interests of mill-owners, industrialists and big businessmen. Ramnath Goenka, while praising Matthai for his integrity, made a similar accusation saying that they had given away Rs 15 crore (the loss on account of reduced taxation) to the 'haves'. He also raised a point that has much relevance also for the present time. He said that the middle class was the backbone of the investing public and asked Matthai to explain how the tax relief to the higher classes was likely to encourage investment.[24]

Khandubhai K Desai called it an 'accountant's budget' and said that the masses had been left entirely in the cold.[25] The budget proposals were also criticized for the departure they made from the programmes of the Congress party. J.N. Hazarika from Assam praised the budget because tax relief to the wealthy had not resulted in a deficit.

R. Velayudhan, the member from Travancore-Cochin, congratulated Matthai on his budget but wanted more clarity on the direction of the economy. Was it to be a capitalist one or a socialist one? He said that the current position was a confused one. The capitalists said that the government did not know how to run a capitalist government, nor did it know how to run a socialist government. He wanted men like G.D Birla and A.D. Shroff to find a place in the Planning Commission saying that their acumen should be used to benefit the country.[26]

A lot of the criticism was centred on the 'lot of the common man'. G. Durgabai from Madras referred to the common man as the 'man in the street', something which Matthai was to poke gentle fun at in the course of his rejoinder to the debate. This did not go down well with the members of the House though Durgabai herself attached little importance to it. (We will come to what Matthai actually said later in the narrative.) J.B. Kripalani, popularly known as Acharya, said that Matthai's speech presented a picture that was bright as the rose and colourful as the rainbow, but these when subjected to analysis would turn out to be something else. He had also told a story about a man who had joined government service with the aim of showing the effect of such service on the brain. (His sarcasm backfired; Matthai neatly turned the tables on him in his rejoinder.)

S. Ramaswamy Naidu from Madras recognized the difficulties involved and patted Matthai on the back. '. . . It is a budget framed mainly with the idea of getting the ship of State going and not subjecting it to any hazardous manoeuvres.'[27] Joachim Alva, from Bombay who though appreciative of Matthai's speech, said that after going home, what looked like an excellent cake with rich cream and milk at the top had hard grain crust below.[28]

Matthai's Reply

Matthai gave a good exhibition of his wit and keen sense of repartee in his reply to the debate. It was obvious that he was not going to suffer criticism for its own sake. His responses were rich in sarcasm, and some were even personal in nature. He was certainly not pulling his punches. Pandit Kunzru had likened him to a man groping in the dark. In response, Matthai said that this was an understatement. He said that he was not groping in the dark but was in fact driving 'a ten-year old jeep along a narrow mountain road over a steep precipice on a moonless night'.[29] Given the current situation in the country, there was nothing else to do but 'grope my way in the impenetrable darkness that surrounds the financial world today'. He called Pandit Kunzru's criticism 'platitudinous'. Pandit Kunzru, Matthai said, was nothing if not platitudinous, and that is why he was such a respectable figure in the House. Acharya Kripalani was hoist by his own petard. Matthai said: 'The point of the story was to elucidate the precise effect of government employment upon the condition of your brain. As I listened to Acharya Kripalani, I said to myself that the learned Acharya is getting ripe for a government job.'[30]

Responding to B. Shiva Rao, who wanted him to present 'a picture of the special conditions of this country', Matthai said that if he was able to produce a picture of only the economic conditions, then it would be a little more than a finance minister was ordinarily able to do. To paint a social picture, given India's infinite variety, was beyond him even if he had the leisure Shiva Rao had. 'The painting of a social picture, I would leave to people who have developed the true U.N.O. mentality. I am not one of those.'[31] This was a dig at Shiva Rao, who had led the Indian delegation to the United Nations General Assembly from 1947 to 1950.

The one rejoinder which hit a slightly queer pitch was his response to Durgabai's concern for the 'man in the street'. Matthai said that most of the speeches were made on behalf of the common man, but Durgabai varied the theme and spoke for what she called the man in the street. Matthai said, 'Now she is greatly disturbed about the conditions of the man in the street. Now I should like to advise Shrimati Durgabai that she should not worry to the extent she does about the man in the street. There is nothing whatever in the budget which occasions worry on that account.'[32]

On the face of it, there appears to be nothing objectionable about what Matthai said, but perhaps what may have caused it to appear so was the fact that Durgabai was single at the time.[33] The constant reference to the man on the street was misconstrued even though that would never have been Matthai's intention. But what Matthai said did not go down well with the House and some members wanted an apology. Durgabai would later marry, and very well too. In 1953, she married C.D. Deshmukh, who had by then succeeded Matthai as finance minister. Today, they would have been considered the numero uno power couple of the times, but both were far too grounded to think of themselves in such terms.

But there was a silver lining here. Matthai had been 'unthinkingly discourteous'[34] as Deshmukh called it in his memoirs, but he said that it was only after this incident that he first heard about Durgabai. A gentleman to the core, Matthai would never have intended any discourtesy. He apologized later and Durgabai, for her part, made no fuss about the episode. ('Durgabai had shown much forbearance according to press reports,'[35] Deshmukh said.) Durgabai also referred to this incident in her memoirs when she wrote: 'There was an uproar in the House and some members asked Dr Matthai to apologise to me for using those unworthy words. I said that there was no need for Dr Matthai to apologise and that he meant no offence.'[36] A little later, Sardar Patel, who sat in the front bench, came to Durgabai and said, 'You are a noble and generous-hearted woman. I appreciate what you have said.'[37] When the news of Deshmukh and Durgabai being affianced became public, it created a minor sensation.

Matthai told Deshmukh with a twinkle in his eye, 'That is a very powerful alliance.'[38]

Matthai didn't spare Anthony either. Making a somewhat personal attack on him, he said:

I listened with interest to the speech that he made on the perils of extravagances committed by government . . . Then I had a close look at Mr Frank Anthony while he spoke and to me it was amazing that an honourable member with his sartorial set up and with his corporeal dimensions should hide behind this very pleasant exterior a heart that is pining for the simple austere life.[39]

Satish Chandra from Uttar Pradesh had said that there was a fundamental difference between his and Matthai's outlook because he was born at the time of the Russian Revolution, whereas Matthai was born in the Victorian era. In response, Matthai observed,

I have been doing a little research on the chronology of such matters . . . Karl Marx died in the eighties of the last century; Joseph Stalin was born in the eighties of that century; I was also born in the eighties of the last century. There is obviously a common galaxy of stars that guide our lives.[40]

Reacting to the accusation that cottage industries had been neglected, he said that whatever the ideals and outlook with which India had started as an independent state, it was necessary to preserve that independence. This could only be done by an effective defence organization which, in turn, was predicated on large-scale industrial development. Matthai observed, 'You cannot build it on the economy of three acres and a cow.'[41] Matthai was also criticized for not following Gandhi's philosophy and ideals. He observed,

Those who reduce the economic philosophy of Mahatma Gandhi to the cheapest variety of western socialism are doing very much less than justice to him . . . If Mahatma Gandhi stood for anything it was first the need of developing to the fullest extent the potentialities of the individual . . . If that is the right ideal of the Congress, for the life of me I cannot see anything in the budget which is inconsistent with that.[42]

Later, the member from Vindhya Pradesh, Manoolal Dwivedi, went as far as making a highly communal allegation. He said that the spirit of Gandhi was in agony because 'an apostle of Jesus from beyond the seas imposes and displays a hue of Jesus of this land in an otherwise skin'.[43] Matthai did not dignify this remark with a reply, treating it with the contempt it deserved.

Matthai had been criticized for his Rs 15 crore of tax relief, which he believed his critics wanted spent on developmental and social welfare schemes. In his defence, he said that rather than spend it on capital expenditure, he had assumed that using it to stimulate the investment resources of the country would yield better results. He also denied that production meant only industrial production. Only 10 per cent of the total provision for capital expenditure was devoted to industrial production.

In conclusion, Matthai said that the country was going through a grim time, and it was time to 'look realities in the face' and now when faced with hard problems, it was a question of self-preservation. 'I suggest very respectfully to the House, that we must be prepared to compromise, we have to temporise, he said.[44]

* * *

Matthai resigned three months after presenting his budget over differences he had with Nehru regarding the Planning Commission, something which ironically, he himself had announced in his budget. The most significant feature of the composition of the Planning Commission as initially announced by Matthai was the absence of the finance minister as a member. (Later, the finance minister was included as a member.) This was inconceivable for an apex body tasked with reviewing and charting out the economic development of the country and clearly showed Matthai's opposition to the idea. His opposition to the Planning Commission and his subsequent resignation form the subject of the next chapter.

15

An Unhappy Interlude

While Nehru and Matthai had had their disagreements in the past, it was their disagreement on the role of the Planning Commission that brought matters to a head and led to the latter quitting office on 31 May 1950. Power is a potent glue, and sticking to it, a universal characteristic of politicians, but this certainly did not apply to Matthai. In any case, he was a technocrat and not a dyed-in-the-wool politician.

Matthai had also opposed Nehru on the signing of the Liaquat–Nehru Pact (8 April 1950), something which was not so well received even during Nehru's own time. As per the pact, refugees would be allowed to return unmolested to dispose of their property, abducted women and looted property were to be returned, forced conversions would be derecognized and minority rights confirmed. Syama Prasad Mukherjee, who was minister for Industry and Supply, resigned from the cabinet as a sign of protest. Even Law Minister B.R. Ambedkar was critical of the pact. In his own resignation on 27 June 1950, he condemned the insensitivity shown by Nehru against the afflictions faced by the Hindus of East Pakistan.

Nehru, Trone and Matthai

According to historian Rakesh Ankit, it was an individual and an institution that made the widening differences between Nehru and Matthai unbridgeable.[1] In the autumn of 1949, Solomon Abramovich Trone, an engineer, came to India on Nehru's invitation. Trone, however, is conspicuous by his absence in the history of the Planning Commission that focuses on Fabian Socialism and the Russian inspiration for planning. Born in Latvia to Jewish parents, Trone migrated to the US in 1916. He rose through the ranks of General Electric (GE) becoming its director in 1931.

Trone was involved in an electrification drive in Soviet Russia in which GE participated. In the 1940s, he was associated with the Kuomintang government in China and the Allied Reparations Commission in Europe. Between September and November 1949, he wrote five memoranda in which he emphasized the role of the Indian state as a producer of basic goods and services as well as a regulator of private and provincial undertakings with a national industrial plan and a clearly defined social purpose.

Trone believed that the way to achieve this social purpose was by having a person with power and authority at the helm, someone who could act as a coordinator. In his second memorandum, prepared after a survey of major industrial establishments in Bengal and Bihar, Trone proposed that a small central planning agency directly attached to the prime minister be set up without delay. It would consist of a few carefully selected members well acquainted with planning. It was this agency that would fix priorities, evolve a unified national plan, coordinate activities and make the plans a reality.[2]

After eastern India, Trone visited the southern, central and western parts of the country. He thought that the schemes overlooked the bigger unit which was India. He discovered that the people thought the Congress wavered in its economic and political policies, and this estranged the industrialists, labour and the middle class. The peasant was also out of the active field. But he found that the people had great faith in Nehru personally.[3]

In his last memorandum on 'Planning and Planning Machinery', dated 21 November 1949, Trone gave the example of the Labour government in England taking on the capitalist class, who by withholding investments, closing factories and refusing to pay taxes on past profits had tried to force the government into acceptance of their laissez faire policy. He believed that Indian capitalists were only out to make quick profits. Trone thought that the solution lay in an all-India plan of a 'managed mixed economy' that was sufficiently controlled to ensure equity.[4]

Ankit observes, 'Fleshing out his vision of the social-minded body with "an engineer, an economist, an administrator, a businessman and an expert on rural economy", Trone insisted on it being invested with sufficient authority and autonomy, by being responsible directly to the Prime Minister.' He wanted the body to be called a small 'brain trust'. Writing separately to Nehru, he told him that he alone, and not the Congress, enjoyed the love and confidence of the people. Trone, however, did caution against 'over-centralisation' and wanted the Planning Commission to reflect regional aspirations and diversity. He wanted Nehru to directly communicate with the people through the radio to ensure enlightened public opinion and continuous popular interest.[5]

While Nehru was completely taken by Trone's views, Matthai did not share his enthusiasm. He told Nehru that Trone's stay would not serve any useful purpose. Given the present conditions, it was impossible to do any real planning since the Indian economy was like a 'damaged ship'. Matthai, in his letter to Nehru, observed, 'At a time when our main job is to repair a damaged ship what we want is not able naval architects but experienced, competent workmen.'[6] The reformer of 1944 was now more interested in conserving than redesigning the economy.

Nehru responded by defending planning as 'a positive active policy', giving the example of the planned progress made by England, Germany, Italy, Soviet Union and Japan since the war. He said that apart from the USA, most countries were in the position of damaged ships. Clarifying that this did 'not mean spending more money than one can afford', he elaborated on the benefits of taking risks and enthusing people. Planning was important to offer the people a clear picture so that they do not 'have a sensation of being asked to labour and to suffer with no promise of reward in future'.[7]

Nehru dismissed the planning hitherto attempted in India by various departments, provinces and princely states, calling those attempts a large number of separate schemes with little relation to each other and with no bigger picture involved. Nehru said there was no common outlook, no clear objective and no coordinated approach. Matthai cautioned that the expenditure on existing plans already amounted to Rs 2500 crore and he would not advise adding to the plan unless it was indispensable.[8] Nehru said that the human aspects of planning, such as unemployment, were missing from these plans. The human aspect was necessary for a democratic government dependent on the goodwill of large number of people, who made insistent demands. He thought that people would be prepared to put up with any kind of discomfort provided they knew the objective.[9]

Nehru recalled appointing an advisory board for planning in September 1946. In 1948, he set up a statistical unit of the cabinet apart from its economic committee. He wanted something more definite and was impatient for larger and more fundamental policies. In these, he rejected traditional and static methods and wanted a full cabinet discussion before he went to America in October 1949. Wanting to combine popular appeal with a definite plan, Nehru was critical of the government, which thought too much in terms of money and less in terms of its connection with the people.[10]

He wrote to Matthai about the inadequacy of the Indian capitalist class charging them with having no vision or the capacity to do anything big. It was against this background that Nehru invited Trone, who he thought would be of great use and who he wanted to keep in India for a number of years. He thought that economists lacked the human outlook to economic problems. A little later, Nehru wrote to Matthai that if he himself did not understand the objectives clearly, how could they expect the public to understand it. He wanted to retain Trone in India, but Matthai continued to oppose the idea.[11] Nehru, reiterated that they should try to profit from his wide experience, and said he had decided to ask Trone to carry on. Matthai must certainly have felt slighted: Nehru had appointed Trone and extended his tenure not only without his approval but also against his advice. Matthai also felt a lack of support from both his cabinet colleagues, as also the Congress rank and file on a range of issues, revealing his lack of a political base.

Nehru, and indeed the Congress, had been convinced of the need for planning for many years. On 29 September, Nehru wrote to Matthai that he felt that an attempt at a planned approach was essential. This did not mean spending more money than the country could afford but would result in a clearer vision of how economic and social objectives could be achieved. It would also allow them to view the whole scheme realistically and objectively and result in a coordinated effort. However, he wanted a full discussion with the cabinet on the subject and did not want to set up a planning authority in a hurry. 'In the meantime, it was my desire to prepare the ground for this planning authority in some way or other. Even that idea I am now giving up to some extent, as I do not wish to rush my colleagues without their having the fullest opportunity for consideration and discussion.'[12]

According to C.D. Deshmukh, the principal matter that occupied Nehru's attention was not the devaluation of the rupee or monetary problems so much as planned economic and social development. He said that during the last two months of 1949, he had participated in many informal exploratory discussions on planning for development with officials. Nehru had not then assigned any responsibility to Deshmukh in the matter. Matthai for his part kept away and showed no interest in the subject. Deshmukh says that this attitude 'surprised me not a little' coming as it did from one of the signatories of the Bombay Plan.[13] Matthai's indifference notwithstanding, the Planning Commission was constituted on 15 March 1950: Nehru's idea was now a reality.

Deshmukh believed that the actual experience of financial and economic administration, coupled with the grim reality of post-war inflation that forbade experimentation, were the reasons for Matthai's changed views on planning. Deshmukh, for his part, thought that planned development was necessary. He observed, 'We never discussed the matter, but had he asked for my advice I would have urged some considerations in favour of planned development, especially as India had paid the price of inflationary finance by devaluing the rupee.'[14]

Matthai's Resignation

Matthai's last day in office was 31 May 1950. In his letter of resignation to Nehru, Matthai had written that the Planning Commission as it was then constituted was not competent to handle the technical details of existing plans. He said that the need of the hour was to decide the priority of the existing plans and to place them technically on a basis that would enable them to be carried out. The commission, Matthai said, was unlikely to be useful in both cases.

The reason given for setting up the Planning Commission was that the government preoccupied with day-to-day administration had little time for thinking and planning ahead. But, Matthai said, as things stood, the Planning Commission was asking for a voice in discussing current economic problems and had with Nehru's approval been associated with the cabinet in these discussions. It had tended to not only become a 'parallel cabinet' but increased the discussions inside the government as a result of which there was a delay in arriving at decisions on immediate problems. 'In my opinion, Cabinet responsibility has definitely weakened since the establishment of the Planning Commission. For these reasons I consider the Planning Commission not merely ill-timed, but in its working and general set-up ill conceived.'[15]

Patel sent Matthai an affectionate letter in which he expressed his sorrow at Matthai's departure from the cabinet. He said that it had been a pleasure to serve the government alongside him. 'Your sincerity of purpose, clarity of views and the ability, experience and intelligence, which you brought to bear upon our manifold problems, always commanded respect and admiration.'[16] Patel said that it was with a genuine feeling of regret and loss of a distinguished and valued colleague that he was writing the letter to him and he hoped that Matthai's services would be available to the country in the future also. He also lauded Achamma's social work whose 'selfless zeal in all humanitarian causes have endeared her to all and sundry not only in the Capital City but also outside'.[17]

This was not the first time that the subject of Matthai's resignation had come up. Differences with Nehru on economic policy had prompted him to put in his papers in December 1949. Nehru requested him to continue till 26 January 1950. Later, they had a long conversation in March 1950, when Nehru told Matthai that their differences were not such as would prevent them from working together. Nehru told him not to press his resignation.

But Matthai felt that he had not been treated with propriety and communicated his unhappiness to President Rajendra Prasad telling him how hurt he was. The President in turn told Nehru about it, and on 3 May 1950, Nehru wrote to Matthai to assuage his feelings. He said that he was very sorry to learn that he had caused hurt to him,

> . . . because you are the last person whom I would like to hurt or to give an impression of any discourtesy on my part. When you wrote to me two or three months ago offering your resignation, I begged of you to carry on till the end of the Budget session at least when we could consider the matter. You were good enough to agree.[18]

Nehru said that he had hoped Matthai would continue, and their differences toned down, but unfortunately, they had not only persisted, but in fact become more intense. 'That did not lead me to respect you or like you any less, but it did distress me,' he wrote.[19] Nehru then spoke about how apart from his own viewpoint, he also represented the Congress's viewpoint and its policies. He said that he himself had gone through a period of mental anguish and had thought of retiring but had been talked out of it by his friends. He noted that staying on as prime minister meant furthering such policies, policies which went against Matthai's way of thinking and thus was likely to create some friction. Nehru said that he had gradually got 'half-converted' to the idea of Matthai leaving the cabinet much as he disliked it. Nehru said that he had hoped to the last that Matthai would continue, but he realized that the deep differences in regard to the policy to be pursued made this difficult. 'Hence when you put forward some arguments in favour of your not continuing in office, I could see that these were valid grounds and I told you so. It was only after our talk yesterday that I decided more or less finally.'[20]

Matthai had agreed to Nehru's suggestion that his name would be included in the new council of ministers with the statement that 'Dr John Matthai expressed his wish not to continue in office, but he was requested to continue in his present office till the end of this month and he had kindly agreed.' He said that cabinet formation had always been done in a hurry and they were pressed for time because of Sardar Patel's imminent departure for Bombay and the South and so something had to be done before he went away. There never was any question of being discourteous to him and he would hate it if he thought so. The real point Nehru said was that 'our approaches have progressively widened' and what was important was not so much personal relations but the public context.[21]

Nehru thanked him for his contribution during a period of great crisis in the country. 'Whether you were a Congressman or not, you were one of the most important members of the Cabinet to whose views we attached greatest importance. Your going away will leave a gap which cannot be filled adequately.'[22] Matthai responded in a letter on 4 May in which he wrote about the hurt caused by Nehru's remark that he would prefer Matthai leaving the cabinet and his suggestion that he accept a less important ministry. He wrote that Nehru had been 'neither as fair nor as candid with me as I had a right to expect from you as a colleague'.[23]

On the same day, Nehru replied to Matthai's letter and spoke his mind. Nehru said that he had read his letter with some distress and that it pained him to think that he had done anything to have hurt him or that he had, as Matthai had written, not been candid with him. He said that there was no question of his having any less faith in his ability or integrity notwithstanding the differences of opinion between them in the recent past. About the hurt caused to Matthai, Nehru said:

It surprises me that you should have thought that I would suggest something to you that was derogatory to your dignity or that I should have imagined that you would remain in Government for the sake of a job and drawing a salary from it. Even a person totally lacking intelligence knows that you can any day earn much more and have a less troubled time than by remaining in Government.[24]

Nehru said that he had made the suggestion in good faith and only with the idea of retaining him in the cabinet, since friction caused by differing viewpoints would disappear if he was given another portfolio. He wrote: 'Perhaps it was a foolish thing to say on my part. But it was said merely with a desire, a selfish desire if you like, of prolonging our association in Government, if that was possible. I have often told you how much I valued it.'[25] Nehru confided in Matthai that he himself was debating whether to continue in government or not. He said that he had begun to feel more and more that the ideals he stood for and had worked for more than a generation were fading away. 'I was wondering how I could serve them better, in Government or outside, and I had nearly come to the decision that I should resign. This decision had gradually grown upon me and had finally been caused by events in East Bengal.'[26]

Nehru felt 'that certain principles for which we had stood should be followed and that so long as I was Prime Minister', otherwise he had no business to be prime minister. Nehru said that while all this had little to do with Matthai directly, it indicated 'that I was passing through a state of great mental anguish and was feeling that our government as a whole had strayed from what I considered the right path. This was partly on the communal issue and partly on the general economic issue.'[27]

Nehru told Matthai that he had become aware of a 'growing estrangement between you and me'[28] in the past few months. He said that he did not know what this was due to, 'for differences in policy need not lead to estrangement between colleagues' and he did not know what to do about it. Nehru noted the heated exchanges when Matthai opposed him but 'in spite of this, I valued your presence in the Government so much that I could not reconcile myself to your leaving it, though many doubts arose in my mind as to how far this collaboration would be fruitful'.[29]

Nehru, always conciliatory, wanted the association to continue but was a little doubtful about how things would turn out since 'some of your public speeches did not seem to me in keeping with that policy and I wondered what would happen in the future, when we had to take this matter up more definitely'. He thought it would 'be rather absurd for the Prime Minister and the Finance Minister to say things in public which did not fit in with each other'.[30]

He said that all these thoughts had been troubling him for the last few months, and he did not know what more he could have told him when they spoke last in March of that year. He said that Matthai's letter indicated the measure of the estrangement and 'which has even led you to impute certain motive or idea to me which you would hardly have done, if you had had any faith in my bona fides. I am sorry for this'.[31] He ended with, ' . . . all good wishes to you and again my gratitude for all your kindness during these past three and a half years'.[32] It was clear that Nehru was trying his best to ensure that the break did not result in bad blood, but Matthai, set in his stirrups for war, was unrelenting and inflexible.

On 8 May 1950, Nehru confided in V.K. Krishna Menon. He said that he was distressed about Matthai because he liked and admired him for his ability and honesty, but for some odd reason, he had gone further and further away from him during the last eight or nine months or more. Nehru said that they had differed on many important matters of policy, and even in some relatively small matters Matthai had been very stiff.

Indeed, he has sometimes been on the verge of discourtesy to me. The Finance Ministry and the Economic Committee of the Cabinet have functioned as independent units. Naturally I have not approved of this. But, as we were always thinking of reorganisation, I allowed them to carry on. Matthai speaks a different language now and certainly appears to have moved away from his original mooring. That is so in regard to economic matters. That is so also surprisingly in regard to the communal situation. During the recent crisis, he was practically at one with Syama Prasad Mookerjee.[33]

Nehru told Menon that it had become increasingly difficult to work with him but yet he did not want to part with him. When some ten days ago or so, he had spoken to him in a frank, but friendly manner Matthai had become rather annoyed.

He has gone about saying that I have not treated him fairly or candidly and have pushed him out. I have tried to explain to him in as gentle language as possible that there is no desire on my part to push him out, but circumstances had arisen which made it a little difficult for contrary policies to be pursued at the same time.[34]

Nehru had also confided in Govind Ballabh Pant a few days before. 'Matthai is entirely opposed to the Planning Commission . . . He thinks that it is not only a waste of money and energy but something worse . . . This will mean continued friction.'[35]

* * *

The differences in opinion between Nehru and Matthai, however, did not prevent the niceties of social behaviour from being observed. The Delhi Provincial Congress Committee organized a farewell on behalf of the citizens of Delhi at the Constitution Club on 21 May for two outgoing ministers, Matthai and Jairamdas Daulatram, the food minister. Nehru was generous in his praise referring in particular to Matthai's role in tackling economic and financial problems, the rehabilitation of millions of refugees, Indo-Pakistan trade and the situation arising out of devaluation. Matthai, Nehru said, was a pillar of strength to the government and had contributed in no small measure to raising its prestige and adding to its strength.[36] Describing Matthai as someone who had no political ambition, Nehru said that he was aware that it was only Matthai's personal regard for him that had led him to accept a cabinet position and he was grateful for this consideration.[37] Nehru described the office of a minister as a 'bed of thorns'. He said he did not know of a more difficult job and wondered why people wanted to become ministers. 'This is a prison house – a bed of thorns.'[38]

'We regret to leave him. Yet we are confident that wherever he may be and to whatever sphere of work he might go he will continue to be useful to this growing democracy of ours,' Nehru said.[39] In this, Nehru was remarkably prescient, since as we shall see, Matthai notwithstanding his somewhat unhappy exit from the cabinet, would serve the government in other capacities as well.

Achamma was also present at the function and Nehru acknowledged the outstanding work she had done in the field of social work. Nehru said that her silent work in the field of rehabilitation of women and children had endeared her to countless refugees.[40] He agreed with one of the other speakers, Deshbandhu Gupta, MP, that she should continue to be in touch with her work in Delhi. Achamma warned against the spread of tuberculosis and spoke of the plight of discarded wives among refugee women.[41]

Matthai, in his reply, said that he had not only an interesting but useful and enjoyable experience as a member of the first national government. He felt that future historians would write that the Nehru government had come out of the trying times not only unscathed but with positive achievements to its credit. Matthai said that there were difficult times ahead, which would require calm and balanced judgement for their solution. 'They will require a great deal of moral courage and a strong determination not to attempt anything sensational but to pursue always first things first.'[42] Obviously, Matthai just could not help himself when he made that veiled reference to the Planning Commission and the need to give priority to urgent problems. Matthai's speech, however, ended on a light note. Referring to the eulogistic references to his wife's work, he humourously remarked: 'It is extremely good for a husband to be reminded that he subsists not in his own right but as his wife's husband.'[43]

Towards the end of May, Sardar Baldev Singh, the defence minister, hosted a party at Delhi Gymkhana's Rose Garden to bid farewell to the Matthais. It was attended by both Nehru and Patel. Nehru was about to leave for Indonesia and Patel, noticeably improved in health, had just returned after his health cruise in the Indian Ocean and official visit to Travancore–Cochin. At the party, many emphasized Achamma's splendid work for social organizations during her stay in the capital. This led to Matthai saying in jest that he probably was the one nobody wanted.

* * *

Matthai also intended to resign from Parliament and had written to Nehru informing him of his decision. In his letter dated 28 May, Nehru said that he was sorry Matthai had decided to resign from Parliament because he thought that his 'presence there would have been of value and even your criticism will help'.[44] Matthai had enclosed a draft of his proposed statement to the press along with his letter. Nehru was non-committal.

I am returning to you your draft statement to the press. I can hardly say anything about it, as it is for you to decide what you should say. The reference to differences in regard to important matter obviously leads to another question as to what these important matters are. There is likely to be speculation about them. I suppose that can hardly be avoided.[45]

16

The Matter Escalates

On 1 June 1950, Nehru gave a speech in Trivandrum during the course of which he made a reference to Matthai's resignation and his statement in the press in which he said that his resignation from the cabinet was due to certain differences with the prime minister on important matters of policy. Nehru said that one normally did not talk about cabinet secrets but that he wanted to clarify what these matters were since people tend to make 'the wildest and most incorrect guesses'. He said that the differences were largely concerned with the appointment and the purpose of the Planning Commission. Matthai was not opposed to planning in general but thought that given the stringency of resources, it was not necessary or desirable at this stage to have such a body. Nehru said that it was because resources were limited that it was necessary to have a planning body that would ensure that scarce resources were not wasted. He said both he and the Congress were committed to the establishment of such a body and had repeatedly given assurances in Parliament that they would appoint a planning commission.[1]

Matthai's Statement on Resignation

Matthai issued a statement on 2 June which was in essence a response to Nehru's speech in Trivandrum. Matthai told the Press Trust of India that his 'attitude to the Planning Commission' was only one of the main reasons for his resignation. He said that his other differences with Nehru were over the 'vital question of control over government expenditure' and his grave misgivings in regard to the Indo–Pakistan Pact and he had 'anticipated the gradual disillusionments that recent developments have produced'.[2]

The differences over the Planning Commission, he said, were not only over its setting up but also in regard to its working. 'I consider the Planning Commission not merely ill-timed but in its working and general set-up ill conceived,' he declared. Matthai felt that it was tending to become a 'parallel Cabinet' and thought that cabinet responsibility had 'definitely weakened' since its establishment. He was also critical of the fact that the deputy chairman, a paid government employee, presided over its work while the finance minister was only an ordinary member. He also thought that the association of the commission with the cabinet in the discussion of current economic problems was an unsound arrangement. Matthai thought that it would weaken the authority of the finance ministry and 'gradually reduce the Cabinet to practically a registering authority.'[3]

Worse was to follow. Matthai was certainly not pulling his punches. He maintained that the Planning Commission was 'totally unnecessary' and in fact hardly qualified for its work. He said that what was required at the present juncture was drawing up of priorities for existing plans something which the Planning Commission 'is not competent to handle'.[4]

Discussing his other differences with Nehru, namely the question of expenditure control, he said that the present budgetary position 'is more difficult than at the time I presented the budget'. He deplored the general tendency amongst the various ministries to disregard the authority of the Standing Finance Committee and said that some of the greatest offenders were the ministries directly under the control of Nehru. When departures from accepted practice were approved by the prime minister, 'it has a demoralising effect on other departments of Government and the Finance Minister's position is unnecessarily made difficult,' he added.[5] Matthai listed no less than twenty cases from the period April–February 1950 in which government expenditure had been incurred by Nehru's external affairs ministry and Patel's states ministry without the approval of the Standing Finance Committee.

Matthai also adverted to his differences over the Indo–Pakistan Pact of April 1950, which dealt with the security and rights of minorities arguing that while a policy of appeasement was inevitable under the circumstances, vital national interest should not be compromised on that account. The government was a trustee of the people and had no right 'to sacrifice without adequate consideration and sufficient justification the interests of those committed to its care'.[6]

Understandably, there was a flurry of activity in response to Matthai's broadside. Nehru, who was taking a short break sailing on *INS Delhi*, sent a telegram to Sardar Patel on 4 June saying that he did not propose to reply to it till he returned. However, he wanted Patel to clarify that there was constant and almost daily interaction with the cabinet on the Indo–Pakistan Pact and every step had been taken with almost unanimous cabinet approval. 'I do not remember Matthai objected at any stage except long before conversation with Liaquat Ali Khan started.'[7]

The matter seems to have been further complicated by Maulana Abul Kalam Azad jumping into the fray. He issued a statement on 3 June in reply to Matthai disregarding Patel's advice not to do so, saying that the Planning Commission had no executive powers, and its functions had been clearly defined as that of an advisory body whose recommendations would be subject to cabinet approval. He added that the prime minister had always sided with the finance minister on the question of expenditure control. Regarding the Nehru–Liaquat pact, Azad said that this was the first time he had become aware of Matthai's opposition to it.[8]

On 3 June itself, Patel had written to Azad advising caution. He asked him not to make a statement since he thought the matter was best dealt with by Nehru since it appeared that the matter was 'rather personal between him (Matthai) and the Prime Minister'[9]. He said that it was inappropriate for an individual minister to make a statement, and particularly so if there were factual inaccuracies.

Patel pointed out two in Azad's statement: the first concerned the time when the 20 per cent cut in expenditure was imposed. Nehru was away in America at the time and Matthai could easily contradict Azad by saying that the whole thing was completed before the prime minister had returned. The second had to do with Matthai's opposition to the Indo–Pakistan Pact during cabinet meetings. Patel wrote to Azad: 'I recall several times when Dr Matthai did express his opposition in emphatic language. In fact, we were all surprised at Dr Matthai taking so much interest in the discussion over this issue.'[10]

Azad, as noted, chose to ignore Patel's advice. In his own letter to Patel on 4 June, he said that since Matthai had not only questioned the establishment of the Planning Commission but tried to show that it was not only useless but injurious as well, he had felt obliged to intervene. 'Personally, I consider it to be a very important work and I am deeply hurt if any one tries to ridicule it.' He also rebutted the Sardar's claims about factual inaccuracy on the 20 per cent expenditure cut. He said that the proposal had come up before the cabinet in the presence of the prime minister. While a few ministers, himself included, had opposed the cut, the prime minister had sided with Matthai and requested all ministers to support the finance minister during the present financial crunch. The matter was then referred to Patel, who was to give a decision in the matter after calling for details, which he did.[11]

Strangely, despite Azad's unadvised intervention, he seems to have genuinely regretted Matthai's departure. Before the matter had escalated, he had sent for K.R.K. Menon, the finance secretary, who was known to be close to Matthai in early May. Since Azad was not particularly fluent in English, Humayun Kabir translated his Urdu into English. Azad asked Menon: 'Why are you allowing the great man to retire? Please ask him to become vice chancellor of Delhi University.' Menon, who was the first to know of Matthai's resignation, met Matthai and conveyed Maulana's offer, but Matthai had had enough. He refused and after resigning went to Kashmir for a holiday. Patel was the only member of the cabinet who saw him off at the airport, reaching just as the plane was about to take off.[12] In fact, it was Shankar who had made the arrangements for his stay in Kashmir at one of the houses of the Maharaja of Kashmir. On 10 May, Matthai wrote to thank him. 'I have seen the details of the arrangements you have made and consider them excellent.'[13]

On 4 June, Nehru wrote to Matthai from *INS Delhi*. He said that he had always wanted to avoid controversy and had avoided the subject at a press conference in Delhi but some Madras newspapers reacting to Matthai's statement 'drew rather extraordinary conclusions, and asked for further explanations'. Nehru said that since Matthai had issued a longer statement, it was necessary for him to deal with 'these matters' in greater detail. He regretted the tone of Matthai's statement and the assumption underlying it that he was guilty not only of wasteful expenditure but also of bartering away vital national interests. He said these were serious charges and did not merely refer to differences in opinion but 'something deeper'. Nehru said that it appeared as if he was completely irresponsible and unsuited for the position he now occupied. If this was Matthai's opinion of him then 'it is clear that either you should have continued in Government or I'.[14]

Nehru said that when Matthai had sent him his brief statement meant for the press, he did not realize all that lay behind it. He said that perhaps it would have been advisable, in the circumstances, if Matthai had indicated to Nehru then or earlier what he felt about these matters. 'It may be that I might have been able to remove certain misconception. So far as the Planning Commission is concerned, I shall not say much here except that I do not think you have been quite just to it in some way.'[15]

Nehru said that at no time had there been any question of the Planning Commission functioning as a parallel cabinet. Regarding Matthai's reference to refer to the warrant of precedence and salaries, he said he would have been glad if Matthai had drawn his attention to these matters at some earlier stage.

> As I have told you and the Cabinet on several occasions, I attach, in existing circumstances, very great importance to a Planning Commission. Apart from that, the Congress Working Committee had practically directed me to go ahead with such a Commission and if I myself disapproved of this direction, as I do not, the only alternative for me was to resign.[16]

A Point of No Return

Matthai had referred to the interference of the Planning Commission in the work of the government and more particularly to its advice on cotton policy! Nehru thought it unfortunate that Matthai should have referred to something which was a cabinet secret since cabinet secrets were not normally discussed in public. He also said that he failed to understand how taking the advice of experts could be considered an interference with governmental working and if consultation with others was prejudicial to national interests.[17]

One of the main issues that seems to have upset Matthai was the erosion of control by the finance ministry and disregard of its authority. He thought that ministries under the prime minister's control were disregarding the authority of the Standing Finance Committee and thus setting a bad example to other ministries. Nehru observed, 'I do not know which ministries you refer to other than the External Affairs Ministry. I do not control any other ministry directly, unless it is the Scientific Research Department which is not a Ministry.'[18]

There was also the disagreement over the embassy in Dublin. When it was decided that the high commissioner in London would also be the ambassador in Ireland, the Standing Finance Committee agreed only to the travelling expenditure of the high commissioner as part of the economy campaign. Later, the cabinet agreed to provide building and staff to the embassy in Dublin not only without the approval of the Standing Finance Committee but against its recommendations. Later, referring to this incident, Nehru told Krishna Menon that the finance ministry had no particular objection to the Dublin expenditure, but it was Matthai who objected to the last. This was the kind of approach, Nehru said, which he had had to face for many months. 'I have often differed with Sardar Patel but I have never had arguments about petty matters with him . . . But Matthai appears to have developed a peculiar antipathy to what I do or say. Why I cannot imagine.'[19]

Referring to this, Nehru wrote to Matthai that whatever the merits or demerits of that decision, 'it took place long after your decision to resign and therefore could not have influenced it.'

> You give this example as typical of many cases. I do not, for the moment, remember other cases coming either from External Affairs or the Department of Scientific Research, which in any way went against the decisions of the Standing Finance Committee. In any event you had not drawn my attention to any such cases previously and I did not even realise that you had such a general grievance against me or my Ministry.[20]

Nehru said that Matthai should have made some reference to this matter at some stage before making such a general charge. He said that he had made all attempts to reduce expenditure and wanted to know of any particular instance when the external affairs ministry or the Scientific Research Department went against the wishes of the Standing Finance Committee. The other major point of disagreement was with regard to Matthai's disapproval of the Indo–Pakistan Agreement of last April. While this agreement was being considered, and while the talks with the Pakistan prime minister were going on, the cabinet met almost daily to discuss the issues involved. Nehru said that he did not remember a single instance during these meetings of Matthai objecting to what was being done.[21]

As regards interference with economic and financial policies, Nehru said that he did not think he had 'interfered to the lightest degree with your conduct of our financial or economic policy'. Apart from writing a letter to him on the eve of the Budget, he had not in any way interfered with the budget process. 'You refer to this controversy having been forced upon you. I hardly think that is a fair statement ... I tried to say something in as friendly a way as possible, because of the wrong inferences that were drawn. Your reply to what I have said is not very friendly and evidently proceeds from a deep-seated feeling of resentment and irritation.'[22]

Nehru thought that there was 'unfortunately a personal equation also involved, which is evident enough from the tone of your statement'. He said that he had sensed for some months past a certain tension 'and sometimes the treatment you accorded me verged on discourtesy. Respecting you as I do, I did not say anything about it although I was pained by it.'[23]

On 4 June, Nehru also wrote to Deshmukh, who was a Planning Commission member, about Matthai's statement. He wanted Deshmukh to make a brief statement about the Planning Commission. On the same day, he wrote to C. Rajagopalachari how his holiday at sea had been disturbed by Matthai's statement. 'Now Matthai has come out with something which displays a bitterness of mind which surprised me.' Nehru also confided in his favourite, V.K. Krishna Menon, telling him how Matthai had made a 'major issue' of the small expenditure on the Dublin Embassy, his vituperative attitude to the Planning Commission and his differences over the Indo–Pakistan Agreement.

> You will have some idea from all this what a vast difference in approach there has been between Matthai and me, even in regard to matters which were not directly his concern ... As a matter of fact, Matthai's general behaviour towards me has verged on discourtesy ever since I came back from America.[24]

On 5 June, Nehru had sent a cable to Patel. 'Matthai's statement insulting to me, derogatory to Cabinet, improper for ex-Cabinet Minister, inaccurate and full of bitterness. It is clear that this matter cannot rest where it is and public controversy cannot be avoided.'[25] He also said that at no stage had Matthai spoken out against the Indo–Pakistan Agreement. 'I am amazed at [the] impropriety of Matthai's behaviour.'

The same day, Patel cabled back saying that Matthai's statement had 'created little adverse public relation'. He said that the *Statesman* had called it 'unedifying' and criticized him both on procedure and on merit.

He believed that Azad's statement had queered the pitch somewhat, otherwise the matter may have blown over by the time Nehru returned. Patel did not want to fan the fires saying that any statement from him would only keep the controversy alive. He had therefore decided to say nothing, preferring to wait and watch. As far as Matthai's criticism of policy was concerned, he said that both he and other cabinet colleagues had the impression that 'he was critical of policy on more than one occasion though he eventually agreed to give it fair trial'. This was, Patel said, exactly the position Matthai had maintained on the Indo–Pakistan Pact though 'I agree that the language used is not quite representative of the trend of his views in the cabinet.'[26]

On 8 June, Nehru wrote to Patel from Madras thanking him for his letter and the enclosures 'in connection with the nuisance that Dr Matthai is making of himself'. Disgusted with Matthai's intemperate utterings he said: 'Compare Dr Matthai's behaviour with the silence preserved by Lord Wavell on his being recalled, in spite of the provocation he had to launch out against the policy which resulted in Mountbatten replacing him. How much have we yet to learn!'[27]

Endgame

Nehru was rattled and also deeply hurt by Matthai's attack on him and the institution he held very dear: the Planning Commission. He told his sister, Vijaya Lakshmi Pandit, about it, complaining that the unseemly controversy had interfered with his holiday, and he would have to 'face all this trouble' when he got back.[28]

The correspondence between Nehru and Matthai continued, with the tone of the letters becoming more bitter. On 17 June, Matthai wrote that he was not surprised by Nehru's letter of 4 June and that if his 'statement proceeds on the lines of your letter, I should have no alternative to making a counter statement'.[29] Matthai thought that cabinet responsibility had been weakened by the members of the Planning Commission being given the same place in the warrant of precedence as cabinet ministers and their salaries and allowances being fixed in accordance with those of the cabinet ministers. In reply to Nehru saying that he was bound by the decision of the Congress Working Committee, Matthai said that this was hardly relevant and if the Prime Minister was to be bound by the decision of 'the party caucus in so important a matter to the extent you presume, there is an end to Parliamentary Government as one knows it'.[30]

Nehru had accused Matthai of revealing cabinet secrets, the issue being the control of raw cotton. Matthai replied that one of his reasons for not making specific references was to keep cabinet secrets. But the cabinet decision about control of raw cotton had been published and ceased to be a secret.[31]

On the Planning Commission, Matthai said:

> The Prime Minister's position as the chairman of the Planning Commission and now the Finance Minister's as a member essentially differentiate it from an ordinary advisory body. A recommendation to the cabinet by a committee, which include the two most important members of the cabinet, as far as economic matters are concerned, ceases in effect to be an advisory body.[32]

On their deteriorating personal relations, Matthai admitted using 'strong expressions in the heat of argument, perhaps to the point of discourtesy', before revealing what had hurt him the most:

> ...my discourtesy has been only in speech. You have shown me discourtesy in action of a kind I never expected ... At your instance, I withdrew my resignation twice, first in December and then in March. You asked for my resignation in April without a single convincing explanation ... Am I wrong in thinking that [I] deserved more courteous treatment?[33]

In his reply on 27 June, Nehru said that he found it surprising that Matthai had chosen to continue in a cabinet of which Nehru was the head when he had such a poor opinion of him since there was no 'common ground left for us to work together in a Cabinet'. 'Normally a member of the Cabinet who feels that way about his Prime Minister has no further place in that Cabinet.'[34] He said that it was his affection and respect for Matthai that had allowed him to continue since there had been 'a growing sense of estrangement from you' and that 'troubled me greatly'.[35]

Claiming 'some knowledge of parliamentary government', Nehru argued that 'if a party has gone to the country on the basis of a programme, its first duty is to follow that'. Moreover, 'parliamentary government, after the British model, also consists in the Prime Minister having a very special responsibility'.[36] Nehru regretted that the break should have happened with 'impropriety' and set a bad example in our public life.' He regretted that differences of opinion had affected their personal relations. 'For my part, I would rather forget recent happenings and remember the three years and more of pleasant companionship in the course of which we faced together many difficult situations. I shall always be grateful for that.'[37]

What Went Wrong?

Matthai returned to the Tata fold and was welcomed back with open arms by J.R.D. Tata. It was ironic that the principal drafter of the Bombay Plan had resigned over planning. What went wrong? By February 1950, Matthai's taxation proposals were a cause for worry for Nehru. The public and the party both felt that while the interest of particular groups had been attended to, the vast majority were more unhappily situated. Moreover, the desired reduction in the army, with a view to effecting economy, had to be postponed given the growing crisis over East Bengal. This upset Matthai, and his budget, and he resigned again in March 1950, with Nehru again asking him to continue. There were many minor pinpricks too over the last many months. One of them was the transfer in 1948 of Arthur S. Lall, who was trade commissioner at the High Commission in London, back to India with no prior warning and without consulting V.K. Krishna Menon, the high commissioner. Nehru wanted such transfers to be made only after obtaining the reaction of the embassies concerned.[38]

Matthai had his share of detractors. M.O. Mathai thought that as finance minister 'John Matthai was not much more than a calculating machine'. He lacked the social consciousness, compassion and vision so essential in the finance minister of an underdeveloped country. Added to this was his complete lack of political understanding. Mathai observed, 'It is recognised that a liberal person will tend to become conservative after working in financial administration, and a conservative person tends to become rigid. John Matthai belonged to the latter category.'[39]

Mathai also believed that John Matthai was a little out of date, unaware of the new thinking in economics. As a man set in his views, Matthai disliked taking advice from economic advisers within the Government of India. One of them was P.J. Thomas, an economic adviser in the finance ministry from 1942 to 1946. A Balliol man like Matthai, he had a DPhil from Oxford, and was professor of economics, first at the University of Ceylon, and then for fifteen long years at the University of Madras from 1927 to 1942. Matthai also detested Gyan Chand, an economist who was adviser to the Planning Commission and of whom Nehru thought highly of.[40]

Referring to the rift, Matthai observed:

The rumours of my possible resignation from the Cabinet began in the autumn of 1949. They arose from certain differences of opinion between the Prime Minister and myself regarding the question of making the payment of compensation for the acquisition of property a justiciable issue and these differences came to light at an informal meeting of members of the Congress Party in the Constituent Assembly. I was then battling hard against the growing demoralisation in the investment market due to uncertainty and nervousness regarding government's economic policy—and I felt that unless some judicial remedy was provided in the Constitution investment might be seriously affected and the flow of foreign capital which we were then endeavouring to encourage would become impossible.[41]

Matthai says that he was left with the feeling that the prime minister and he, who till then had almost instinctively seen and appreciated each other's point of view on practically every issue that arose in the course of their work, were beginning to drift apart. 'Already I felt that a cloud was slowly forming between us—at first no bigger than a man's hand but later to assume considerable dimensions and preventing us from perceiving and understanding the workings of each other's mind.'[42]

Matthai attributed the rest of the tension to the fact that as finance minister, he was then faced with what he thought was an approaching collapse of the economy and had primarily to bring to bear upon problems as hard-headed and realistic an outlook as he was capable of. 'It was no use fighting phantoms when you were so near disaster.'[43] Nehru, he said, was preoccupied with the approaching general election and the imperative need of presenting a programme to the country that would rally the country to the Congress party. He said that it was a perfectly legitimate stand for the leader of a great political party to take on the eve of what was going to be the severest trial in its long and eventful history. Matthai observed, 'Although he never confided to me the fears and anxieties that lay at the back of his mind, I was pretty certain that I read him right.'[44]

> Between the immediate problems that troubled me and the remoter problems that troubled him, there was a wide gulf made up of conflicting approaches, ideas, perceptions, situations which neither of us in spite of our personal regard for each other and the comradeship born of three years of strenuous work in a common cause was able to resolve.[45]

Matthai believed that when Nehru in his approach to the problems of government laid more emphasis on formulating a programme for the future than on providing solutions for immediate difficulties, he was following the instincts of the true politician rather than the man of affairs intent on fulfilling the job in hand. Matthai spoke of the many long arguments he had with Nehru about the question of setting up a planning commission at a time when conditions were so fluid that no data of any permanent value could be collected, and when the general scarcity of money and materials made it difficult to implement any new plans.

> I failed to appreciate his insistence on the proposal except as a concession to a widespread but uninformed political demand and a useful plank in the party platform for the coming elections. *In spite of every desire to understand him, I could only explain it by the known habit of statesmen, when action becomes difficult, of getting busy with intentions.*[46] (Emphasis added)

Unlike Patel, who was a hard-headed realist, Nehru loved abstract argument and delighted in 'drawing generalised inferences from situations which offered the slightest provocation to his nimble deductive mind'.[47] Whenever in the course of a discussion, the trend of argument led in the direction of concrete conclusions and brought him close to the point of decision, his mind would wander back to 'the Elysian fields where argument took the form of a long procession in irregular formation, of ideas which did not necessarily help towards decisive action.'[48]

Later, Matthai analysed the reasons for his fallout with Nehru and his exit from the government. He said that the main business of a party organization is to watch the trend of public opinion from the point of view of its own continuance and that of the government in power, and to adjust both policy and administration to secure this end. Among these

constant shifts and manoeuvres for position, a non-political member of
the government like himself was at a disadvantage however much his work
was appreciated by the vast body of neutral opinion in the country. Matthai
was a minister who did not belong to the ruling party and a rift started
forming between him and the Congress organization. Nehru, like Gandhi,
combined political idealism with political expediency, and Matthai perhaps
could not or did not want to respond appropriately. He observed,

> If my resignation was prompted in the first instance by my differences
> with the Prime Minister I was influenced also, perhaps not altogether
> consciously, by the widening rift between me and the party organization
> and by my inability to sense its reactions and adapt myself to them.
> On closer analysis I sometimes felt that my differences with the Prime
> Minister were themselves a result of this lack of responsiveness on my
> part to the changing moods of the party.[49]

Matthai was candid enough to admit that he himself was responsible to a
large extent for the rift with Nehru. When I asked Syloo if Matthai was
bitter about how things had turned out between Nehru and him she said
that there was no bitterness but only a feeling of regret. She believed that
her father-in-law had nothing personal against Nehru and admired him
despite their differences.[50]

The one-party membership of the assembly after Independence had
also become obvious to Matthai. It was composed entirely of the members
of the Congress party or those who were nominated by it. The European
group, the official members and the Muslim League legislators were
no longer present. Matthai noted that the disappearance of opposition
deprived the treasury benches of any special incentive to put forward their
best in debate. The larger legislative output came at the expense of detailed
discussions.[51]

There was also a criticism that in its outward forms, the assumption
of office by the Congress made no difference. Matthai seemed to concur.

> Coming to office . . . we assumed all the trappings, tokens and symbols
> of the Imperialism that preceded us. The slogans and their expressions
> present a contradiction too glaring to escape observation . . . The present
> parliament of India is composed of members of one party subject to
> the control of a well-disciplined party organization. Real criticism of

the government is seldom heard. This tendency is aggravated by the submissive and generally uncritical press.[52]

* * *

Matthai aired his views on the Planning Commission six years later in a talk he gave to the Rotary Club, Bombay. He said that he had never been happy about the institution of the Planning Commission and the place assigned to it in the structure of government. He felt that such a body ought to be a body of experts subordinate to the cabinet but 'through adventitious circumstances into which I do not want to enter, the Planning Commission has become a body of amateurs with whom for all practical purposes final decision rests in matters of economic development'.[53] As a result, he said, many ministers concerned with economic affairs had lost their initiative and sense of responsibility.

It was not only Matthai who was unhappy with the importance given to the Planning Commission. In late December 1953, Nehru wrote to the commerce and industry minister, T.T. Krishnamachari, about the strained relations between the commerce ministry and the Planning Commission. He said that the ministry viewed the Planning Commission as an unnecessary intrusion and that even the secretary, H.V.R. Iengar, had been rather casual in his dealings with it. Nehru wrote that though it was only an advisory body, it had been very useful. 'It is not fair to it to produce an impression that it is not wanted or not to give it all the cooperation that it may need.'[54]

Many years later, Iengar gave his views on the reasons for the change in Matthai's thinking on planning. He believed that a couple of years in actual administration had given Matthai glimpses into the extent to which political power had corrupted the politicians in India something which must have come as a shock to a sensitive and honest man like him. It must also have destroyed one of the foundations on which the Bombay Plan was based, namely, that the state would be run by men of undoubted integrity who could be trusted with enormous power.[55]

Most of Matthai's fears about the Planning Commission proved to be well-founded. By the end of the 1950s, the early euphoria with planning had disappeared. Critics such as J.B. Kripalani and Rajagopalachari openly showed their displeasure, and the latter, who later founded the explicitly anti-socialist Swatantra Party, wrote to Nehru about his frustration with the hegemony planning enjoyed: 'I fear a church is growing round the God of planning,' he said.[56]

However, planning remained the master narrative and while the earliest Plans boasted of some successes, by the late 1960s, the mood was somewhat more sombre. Droughts, wars with China and Pakistan, and the shortcomings of the Plans themselves, led to repeated economic crises. Nehru was the Planning Commission's symbol and essence, evocator and voice. Its reputation suffered after his demise and its influence started waning. The finance ministry started gaining ground after every crisis, and much more so after the license-permit raj gained ground. Still, the Planning Commission survived into the era of market reforms and liberalization, and it was only in 2014, after the Narendra Modi government came to power, that it was abolished and replaced by the NITI Aayog (National Institution for the Transformation of India).

* * *

Matthai's successor was a reluctant C.D. Deshmukh, who was offered the job after Patel, who disliked both Gopalaswami Ayyangar and T.T. Krishnamachari, disapproved of their candidature. Patel, who as we have seen, expressed a genuine feeling of regret and loss at Matthai's departure, had a high opinion of Deshmukh, who as finance secretary of CP and Berar in 1935, had helped Patel and Pattabhi Sitaramayya in drafting an award for equitable distribution of development expenditure in that province's annual budget. Patel was pleased with Deshmukh's work, and when he met Deshmukh again, a decade later, reminded him of this happy conclusion and asked if he could do anything for him.[57] Little wonder then, that Patel decided to accept Deshmukh's 'advice and talents' as finance minister.

Seeking the People's Mandate

As a cabinet minister, Matthai had been elected to the Constituent Assembly from the United Provinces. It is said that Nehru asked him to sign on a nomination paper and before he knew it, Matthai had become a member of the Assembly.[58] Still, Matthai remained largely apolitical even as a member of the cabinet. Though he was invited to attend meetings of the Congress Working Committee, he was never a member of the Congress party. Matthai, thus, was largely without political influence and owed his position solely to Nehru's high opinion of his abilities and integrity. As already noted, after resigning as finance minister, he also resigned from Parliament and rejoined Tatas as director-in-charge of TISCO.

During the first general election, a large number of his supporters and well-wishers prevailed upon Matthai to try his luck at the hustings. By October 1951, Matthai seems to have made up his mind to contest the election from the Kottayam constituency of the erstwhile Travancore–Cochin State. What made a largely apolitical person with a serene disposition want to enter the rough and tumble of an electoral battle? The answer lies in a letter Matthai wrote to the bishop of the CSI Church in Kottayam, C.K. Jacob. The latter held Matthai in great esteem from the time Matthai had been a tutor at MCC, an institution of which the bishop was also an alumnus. When the bishop received the news of Matthai's intention to contest, he invited him to stay with him.

Writing to him from Bombay on 5 October 1951, Matthai said that he had had so little contact with Travancore in the past that he was looking forward to the opportunity of serving the people should he get elected. He also said that Kottayam held a special interest for him because of its association with his family. His reasons for offering himself as a candidate were made clear in a letter he wrote on 15 October 1951.

> I have strong feelings that we have reached a position in the country where men with no party-ties or inhibitions who are able to bring a fresh mind to bear upon public problems have a vital contribution to make . . . I have no doubt where the call of duty lies for me but at the same time the thought of the time and effort required for a contested election somewhat deters me.[59]

It appears that Matthai thought that he would be elected unopposed. He had informed Nehru about his intention to contest the election and hoped that the Congress would not oppose him. The *Malayala Manorama*, a leading daily, wrote a long editorial on 4 October 1951. The thinking at the time was that people like Matthai should be elected unopposed. This feeling may have given Matthai the impression that there would be no opposition to his candidature. Nehru wrote back to say that he personally would like to see Matthai elected unopposed, but he was not sure if the Congress high command would agree with him.[60] It was a diplomatic reply, and a somewhat disingenuous one. Nehru would certainly have known what others thought of the matter, and he was very much part of the Congress's high command. Perhaps, he didn't want to go out of the way to help Matthai after all that had passed between them.

Matthai also wrote a letter addressed to the bishops of Kottayam explaining the reasons behind his decision to stand for election. He said that the exigencies of official work had kept him out of the place of his origin but in the closing stages of his working life, 'it is natural that one should feel a desire to be brought into close contact with the interests of the State and its people.'[61] He said he felt like the proverbial 'prodigal son' longing to return before his days were done. He said that he was standing as an independent candidate because he believed that if one's motive was service and not office, then freedom of speech and action were essential and therefore there should be no restriction on one's judgement except the true interest of the people.

Bishop Jacob's brother-in-law, Prof. P.C. Joseph, was the principal of CMS College and he played host to Matthai in the bishop's absence. Joseph thought that Matthai had none of the qualities required to be a successful politician.[62] What was more, he was contesting as an independent candidate with limited resources. He tried to talk him out of it but could not change Matthai's decision; he and his wife, in fact, ended up proposing and seconding Matthai's name. Matthai was registered as a voter in New Delhi. Since his number in the electoral roll was required to complete the filing process, Matthai requested for, and ultimately got, the number, after a few anxious moments.

After filing his nomination papers Matthai started holding meetings in and around Kottayam. He had been out of touch with Malayalam for many years and came a cropper when he tried to speak the language during his election campaign, getting confused between the dialect spoken in Malabar (with which he was familiar) and that spoken in Travancore. But help and support for his electoral battle came from many quarters. There were also numerous invitations from colleges and cultural institutions to make speeches.

The candidates included Justice Gopala Menon of the Travancore–Cochin Praja Party, a local party, formed by the planters. He was the elder brother of K.P.S. Menon, the ICS officer who had worked closely with Nehru. Gopala Menon knew Matthai well and wanted to meet him. The two met at the residence of Joseph when the latter invited him for tea. There

were also two Congress candidates in the field: Prof. C.P. Mathew and P.S.
George. Mathew was a professor of philosophy who had taught at the
MCC. He was one of the founders of Union Christian College, Alwaye, in
1921, and later became its principal from 1947 to 1952. Like Matthai, he,
too, was a Syrian Christian and held Matthai in the highest regard. In fact,
he told the *Malayala Manorama* that he had filed his nomination yielding
to pressure from New Delhi. It was obvious that Nehru's communication
to Matthai was just empty words. George, an advocate from Quilon, was
aligned with Sir C.P. Ramaswami Aiyar, the Dewan of Travancore, who
was known to be unsympathetic to the Syrian Christians and also opposed
to the idea of Independence. Many in the Congress thought that fielding
him as a candidate would send the wrong message.[63]

That Matthai commanded universal esteem is apparent from the fact
all the candidates met him before filing their papers. In fact, Justice Gopala
Menon withdrew his candidature before the scrutiny of the papers took
place. The scrutiny of the nomination papers took place on 30 October
1951 in the office of the district collector. Matthai went to the collector's
office accompanied by his brother-in-law, John Jacob, and his lawyer. Little
did he know at the time that great disappointment lay in store. His papers
were rejected on technical grounds on an objection raised by George who
had represented that Matthai was a paid employee of the Tatas, a company
in which the government had shares, and hence ineligible to stand for
election. The objection was upheld by the returning officer and Matthai's
nomination was rejected.[64]

Matthai contested the decision in the high court, perhaps the first
election petition to be filed in a high court in India. A case was also filed
by one of Joseph's friends who had been one of the other proposers apart
from Joseph and his wife. The high court said it had no jurisdiction in the
case and advised Matthai to approach the Election Commission. Nothing
came of it and in the end Mathew, the Congress candidate, won by a large
margin. (The Congress had decided to field only Mathew; George the
other Congress candidate was dropped.)

Matthai left for Bombay on 10 November 1951 entrusting Joseph
with money to settle legal bills. There was some money leftover which was
used by Joseph to commission a portrait of Thomas Matthai, Matthai's
father, who had been headmaster of the then CMS High School. Matthai
was unable to find a suitable painter in Bombay and so the task was

entrusted to a painter from Kerala. The painter took an inordinately long time to complete his commission and the painting was unveiled by Achamma only in November 1960, more than a year after Matthai had passed away.[65]

With the wisdom of hindsight, it was perhaps a blessing in disguise that Matthai's nomination was rejected. He would have found it difficult to win the election against a determined Congress party and was spared the loss of prestige that a defeat in his own home town would have brought. There is a certain irony about this since back in 1945 Matthai had been unofficially invited to contest as a Congress candidate from Bombay. Sardar Patel had written to J.R.D. from Poona on 9 October 1945 asking him to persuade Matthai to stand as a candidate from one of the two seats of the Bombay City General Constituency. He said there would be no difficulty in winning both seats. He told J.R.D. that he would be doing the country a great service if he could persuade Matthai to stand for election as a Congress candidate.

> His services in the Central Assembly at this critical juncture would be of immense value. If he would accept a Congress ticket, I would see that there is no difficulty in winning the seat in the elections. As the date of nominations is drawing near, I would request you to send me a reply as soon as possible. I have written this on my own behalf, but if you agree, I will place it before my committee.[66]

It is not known what transpired, but J.R.D. would certainly have conveyed the request to Matthai who must have refused. In any case it made very little difference since Matthai found himself in Wavell's cabinet the next year.

World Conference of Christian Youth

In 1952, Matthai was elected chairman of the Indian Committee of the World Conference of Christian Youth held in Kottayam in December 1952. Attended by 300 young men and women, the conference considered the problem of human relations in the light of moral and spiritual values embodied in Christianity. Money for the conference was raised by a performance of Felix Mendelssohn's oratorio, *Elijah*, in Bombay.

Among the delegates was Robert Hawke, popularly known as Bob Hawke, who went on to lead the Australian Labour Party and who became prime minister of Australia (1983–91). A socialist at heart, he attended a communist rally which was being held in Kottayam at the time. Hawke collected communist literature which he took back with him to Australia, and which was confiscated by the customs department. His protests brought him a measure of fame at the time.[67] Like Matthai, he was also an Oxford man. In 1953, he went to Oxford on the back of a Rhodes scholarship to do a PPE (Philosophy, Politics and Economics). Later, he switched to a Bachelor of Letters since he discovered that he had already covered much of the same ground in his BA in Australia.

PART IV

17

The Taxation Enquiry Commission

Within a year and a half of Matthai's abortive attempt at becoming a member of the Lok Sabha, he was called to the service of the country once again, this time as chairman of the Taxation Enquiry Commission. That finance minister C.D. Deshmukh chose his immediate predecessor was surprising, given Matthai's exit from the cabinet over the Planning Commission, a body in whose formation Deshmukh had played a key role. But the relationship between the two had always been a cordial one. Deshmukh was one of the members of the sterling balances delegation in 1949 which Matthai had led.

When Deshmukh's term as RBI governor ended in August 1949, he planned to go to England to be with his English wife, Rosina, and to try to re-establish contact with his estranged daughter, Kiki. But when a sudden stroke caused Rosina's demise, Deshmukh found that his reason to stay on in England had disappeared. It was then that Matthai offered him the post of financial ambassador to USA and Europe, his main job being the negotiation of a wheat loan of two million tonnes. Deshmukh accepted and in early September went to Washington, D.C. He was called back at the end of 1949 to discuss the devaluation crisis. In his memoirs, Deshmukh observed, 'Despite the events leading to his resignation John Matthai and I remained friends. At my special request, he accepted the chairmanship of the Taxation Enquiry Committee I appointed in 1952 . . .'[1]

It appears that Nehru had some reservations about Matthai's appointment. In his reply to Deshmukh's letter dated 16 January 1953 telling him about his intention to make Matthai chairman, he said that while Matthai was an 'excellent and experienced person', he doubted if his appointment would be welcomed by all sections of the people. He said that the question of taxation had social implications, with politics and economics being interrelated 'and they produce gradually a changed social outlook in considering all these matters'.[2]

Nehru felt that Matthai, though not a big industrialist like the others, would inevitably be influenced by his connection with big industry. 'It is because of this that I feel that Dr Matthai, good as he is, might not bring that viewpoint and would function in rather orthodox grooves with an inclination towards big industry.'[3] Nehru favoured K.C. Neogy, a former cabinet colleague, who had become chairman of the first Finance Commission in 1951. Nehru wanted Deshmukh to appoint members to the Commission who would represent both the 'new approach' as well as those who represented more orthodox viewpoints. In the end, Deshmukh managed to convince Nehru, and Matthai's appointment was made public. Matthai told a newspaper that he was beginning to get the feeling that this was probably the heaviest work he had ever undertaken. He had also begun complaining: 'I am getting a bit old and a bit tired.'[4]

It is necessary to understand the circumstances under which the Taxation Enquiry Commission was appointed. Finance ministers of the post-war period were torn between the needs of a developing economy and the extremely limited resources at their disposal. Almost all current resources were exhausted by the normal demands of administration and defence. State governments were crying out for larger outlays on health, education, irrigation and the like. The political pressure of vested interests limited the scope of direct taxes; and inflation added to the unpopularity of the whole range of indirect taxes. Finance ministers did not know where to seek additional sources of revenue.

At the Helm

For some years, there had been a persistent demand both in the legislature and outside, for a systematic inquiry into taxation. As far back as 1946, the Government of India had decided that such an inquiry should be conducted, but this decision could not be implemented owing to impending constitutional changes. Since Independence, more urgent preoccupations were given priority, but the idea was never dropped. While presenting the budget for 1953–54, Deshmukh said that the government had decided to set up a compact commission to conduct a comprehensive inquiry into taxation. He said that he was pleased to announce that Dr John Matthai 'has accepted our invitation to be the Chairman of the Commission'.[5] The other members were Vaikunth. L. Mehta, former finance minister of Bombay and till recently a member of the Finance Commission, Dr V.K.R.V. Rao of the Delhi School of Economics, K.R.K. Menon, secretary, finance ministry, B. Venkatappaiah, a former finance secretary of the Bombay Government, and finally Dr B.K. Madan, economic adviser at the RBI. Sardar Indrajit Singh, a former commissioner of income tax, was the secretary of the commission.

The commission started functioning on 1 April 1953 with terms of reference that were very comprehensive and covered all aspects of taxation: central, state and local. It was to examine the incidence of taxation on people and states, the suitability of taxation for mobilizing resources for the reduction of inequalities and development, the impact of taxation on capital formation and its use as a fiscal instrument to deal with inflation and deflation.

Deshmukh also told the House that it was the government's intention to associate two foreign experts on taxation and public finance with the commission 'so as to make available to the Commission such expert advice as they may require from foreign experience'. The Commission would also be free to co-opt additional members for short periods while considering specific problems. He expected the Commission to start functioning from April and complete its work in about two years. 'I am sure that the labours of the Commission would assist in laying the foundations of a taxation system best fitted for the development of the economy of the country on a firm and sound basis.'[6]

With Independence, the cry for rapid economic development became shriller, but the issue of how such development was to be financed remained a thorny one. There was a limit to which the expedient of deficit financing could be resorted to. The last Taxation Enquiry Commission had been set up in 1924 and much had changed in the economy and polity since then. At that time, customs duty formed the main part of the central government's revenue, while land revenue was the main source of the provinces. Salt duty and excise duty on liquor constituted the second major source of revenue for the central government and provinces, respectively. Now thirty years later, customs duty had declined in importance, the salt tax had been abolished and excise duty had also declined thanks to the introduction of prohibition in some states. The importance of land revenue declined, and sales tax now emerged as the principal source of revenue.[7]

The world had gone through the Keynesian revolution in public finance and Keynes's prescription, considered revolutionary at one time, had become part of the new orthodoxy. The Commission needed to study how far the tax system needed to be modified to meet the needs of development and a growing economy.[8] Since the economy was subjected to serious and prolonged inflationary pressure from 1943 right up to 1951 when deflationary pressures set in, the government took the opportunity of including in the Commission's terms of reference an examination of the use of taxation as an instrument for dealing with inflationary and deflationary situations. The economic system, completely distorted by prolonged inflationary pressures and grotesque in its inequities, had subjected the populace to extremes of suffering. Thus, the Commission was also tasked with examining the suitability of the present system of taxation for reducing inequalities of income and wealth. Associated with this was the technical examination of the incidence of central, state and local taxation on various classes of people and in different states. The whole system of taxation was to be rationalized so as to make it an effective instrument for development and equity.[9]

Initially, K.R.K. Menon, the finance secretary, was not included as a member because it was thought that as secretary, he would have to examine and comment on the report from the side of the government. But Matthai insisted on his inclusion and wrote to Nehru requesting that he be appointed.[10] On 8 April 1953, the Commission issued a press note inviting the views of individuals and organizations on the issues covered by the terms of reference. In July, a detailed questionnaire was sent which was followed by a supplementary one. By October 1953, most of the replies were received.

The members undertook a tour of six months and discussed the issues with ministers and members of the state legislature. They also took oral evidence. Matthai seems to have adopted a procedure similar to the one followed by him in the Tariff Board. Always correct in his behaviour, Matthai, who was a stickler for protocol, expected the same treatment in return. His visit to Madras is a case in point. Matthai visited all state capitals and wrote letters to all chief ministers informing them of his visit. As chairman, Matthai had the rank of a union minister. He wrote a letter to Rajagopalachari, who was chief minister of Madras, but received a reply from a secretary to the Madras government. When Matthai visited Madras, he held discussions with the secretary and ignored Rajaji. Later, Rajagopalachari realized his impropriety and apologized.[11]

Each member was tasked with studying and reporting on a certain subject. Menon worked on central taxes; Venkatappaiah on state and local taxes; V.K.R.V. Rao and Madan on the economic aspects of taxation and V.L. Mehta on state finances. Matthai coordinated the activities of all the members and a draft report on each subject was discussed by all members, thereby facilitating the preparation of the report in a relatively short time.

The Report: Some Recommendations

Taxes: Central and State

The central revenue was mainly derived from three sources: income tax, customs and central excise duties. The Commission recommended clubbing the income of husband and wife and even the whole family since the percentage of people paying income tax was very small. They did not think that it was the right time to introduce a gift tax.

The Commission recommended the elimination of complex rates in central excise duties. As far as individual commodities were concerned, they thought that there was no case for reducing the duties on manufactured tobacco, coffee and motor spirit but recommended an increase on packaged tea, kerosene, sugar and matches. The commission recommended a modest increase on cloth but thought that there was no scope for increasing the tax on steel ingots and tyres.

An important recommendation was the use of the tax system to give a fillip to small scale and cottage industries. One of the recommendations of the Commission led to the introduction of central sales tax, which had been a long-standing demand of business.[12] The Commission noted that dealers in centres such as Bombay, Delhi and Calcutta had to seek registration under the sales tax acts of almost all the states. They had to send returns, get their accounts examined, be assessed by an officer of each state and finally make payments in accordance with such assessment.[13] While business wanted sales tax to be centralized, the states were understandably opposed to it. The Commission had to devise a method that was acceptable to both the states and the business community.

By the time of the Commission's enquiry, sales tax had become an important tax in the states. The growth of sales and central excise both relying on a common commodity base created problems of coordination of tax policy. Sales tax law was complex and at times also ambiguous.

Tax evasion was another problem. The Commission was very critical of sales tax. Their analysis showed that the kinds of sales taxes existing at the time were selective, single point, double point and multipoint sales taxes. The Commission examined the scope for a purchase tax but found it to be impractical. In any case, the sales tax thanks to its yield and flexibility had come to occupy a large and independent place in the financial system.[14]

The Commission, recognizing the need to expand the tax base so that additional revenue for development and social welfare needs could be found, considered a 'general sales tax' for this purpose.[15] It also considered abolishing sales tax and extending other duties instead but found that it was not possible to do so. 'The merit of sales tax as a major source of revenue is that it is dispersed over a number of goods . . . customs and excise apply only to a strictly limited portion of the industrial output that is sold within the country.'[16]

The Commission recommended that sales tax should continue to be a state tax but that inter-state sales and cases where the incidence of taxes impinged administratively on the businessman and consumers of other states should be the concern of the central government.[17] It recommended the creation of an intelligence section in every sales tax department and a sales tax tribunal in every state. The creation of an Inter-State Taxation Council to introduce uniformity in the matter of sales tax law and procedure was another of its recommendations.

As far as agricultural tax was concerned, it recommended a tax on agricultural income in excess of Rs 3000 a year. The Commission was also highly critical of octroi and wanted it to be eliminated from the system but recognized that it could only be a long-term aim.[18] It noted with approval that the excise policy in general encouraged temperance. The excise on alcohol was an important source of revenue for the states. It noted that the tax on transfer of property was a suitable item of taxation and wanted court fees and registration fees to reflect the expenditure incurred by the state for performing that service.

Taxation Policy and Administration

One of the terms of reference of the Commission had been to look into aspects of increasing production accompanied with distributive justice. It observed that there was a feeling that in the current situation, production should take priority over an improvement in distribution. In this connection, the Commission maintained that the country could no longer afford to leave the problem of equality to the 'automatic functioning of economic and social forces' and the 'attainment of a wider measure of equality' must 'form an integral part of economic development and social advance'.[19] 'The demand that the instrument of taxation should be used as a means of bringing about a redistribution of incomes, more in consonance with social justice, cannot be kept in abeyance,' it observed.[20]

Discussing the need for capital gains tax, the Commission averred that while distributive justice made a strong case for such a tax, it tended to have an adverse psychological effect on investment. They thought that heavier annual taxation of property and transfer of property might help in this matter.

Incidence of Taxation

The Commission estimated that indirect taxes absorbed 3.6 per cent of per capita total expenditure and amounted to 5.7 per cent of the total cash purchases. The average incidence of central excise duties in relation to cash expenditure was worked out at 1.5 per cent. On the whole, the conclusion of the Commission was that the rural classes, for various reasons, were escaping their fair share of taxation.

In 1950–51, land revenue, as a proportion of the gross value of agricultural output, was only 1 per cent, and of the net value, 1.2 per cent. Taking the income-tax and the land revenue together, the Commission concluded that the tax system was progressive only for the urban groups with expenditure levels over Rs 300 a month. Hence, there was greater room for increased taxation of higher rural incomes. Though the Commission warned that its general review of the incidence of taxation was hardly perfect, and should therefore be treated with caution, a detailed reading of the Report shows that it was about the best that could have been attempted from the data available.[21]

The Commission noted that per capita tax was not only larger in the urban sector but increased with the degree of urbanization. It found that the incidence of both central and state taxes was higher in the urban sector, with the rural–urban difference being more pronounced in sales tax than in central excise. After studying the tax incidence, the Commission came to the conclusion that increased taxation on rural incomes would correct the one-sided picture of incidence which at present was skewed in favour of urban areas.[22] The presence of a large non-monetized sector in the rural economy showed good potential for taxation.

The Commission believed that the co-operative form of organization was the best suited for large-sector economic activity and recommended greater tax concessions to certain types of co-operative societies. In the opinion of the Commission, there was great potential for expansion of co-operative activities and they saw tax concessions as the way to achieve such expansion.[23] As far as the method of financing local bodies was concerned, it was in favour of grants-in-aid. One of the drawbacks of local bodies was the inefficiency in tax administration. They wanted all municipalities to have qualified chief executive officers vested with statutory powers, selected and appointed by the government. It had little confidence in village panchayats undertaking activities involving production and distribution activities and thought that these would be better managed by the co-operative sector.

The Commission emphasized the need for improving and strengthening the tax machinery, particularly the one dealing with income tax. Tax evasion was a serious problem, and the Commission recommended granting the power of entry and search to income-tax officers. It wanted the penalty for tax evasion to be enhanced to three times the amount of tax evaded. An important recommendation related to the creation of the All-India Taxation Council, the main objective of which was to be the coordination of tax policies, tax legislation and tax administration between the centre and the states and among states. It would be served by a permanent secretariat in the form of a Tax Research Bureau attached to the finance ministry.

With a view to accelerating development of various industries, the Commission discussed at length the incentives required and found that relief was necessary to both expand existing industries and also set up new ones. It recommended a development rebate on investment in plant and machinery. For the mining industry, for example, the Commission recommended that exploration expenditure, which resulted in tangible assets, would be admissible for depreciation and that which resulted in intangible advantages would be amortised.[24]

It also recommended a tax holiday for six years for industries of national importance. The Commission realized that the concessions they had recommended constituted a new and important departure in tax policy and wanted a review after five years with a report being placed before Parliament.[25] In addition to the recommendations for boosting the growth of industry, the Commission also made far reaching recommendations relating to stimulating savings and investment.

Character of Expenditure

Though the Commission was concerned with taxation, it could not ignore the fact that the character and distribution of public expenditure modified the economic effects of taxation. It pointed out that a wise, beneficent and progressive system of public expenditure could raise both the capacity, as well as the willingness of the people, to pay taxes. It was critical of the extravagant, irregular and infructuous expenditure of the government. While agreeing that expenditure in India had been moving towards beneficent expenditure 'it cannot be said with equal certainty that it is moving also towards economy and efficiency'.[26]

The Commission suggested the appointment of high-powered bodies to deal with the system of expenditure, which had been undergoing chaotic changes owing to the pressure of circumstance. There was need for both fundamental and factual analysis. Non-development expenditure was still substantial. Taking a broad picture of the current public expenditure of all governments in India (1953–54), the Commission showed that out of each rupee of the total expenditure, nearly ten annas were spent on non-development purposes and the remaining six annas, almost equally divided between social services and economic development. This, however, did not take into consideration capital outlays which were relatively small before Independence, owing to the restricted role of government in economic development and social welfare.

The total capital outlay was now rising rapidly, and it was therefore necessary to keep non-development expenditure as low as possible. In the long run, this increasing development expenditure was likely to increase the taxable capacity of the people. At the time, however, the role of public expenditure in the Indian economy was modest. Estimated at Rs 1170 crore for 1953–54, the combined expenditure of the central and state governments and local authorities was only 11 per cent of the probable level of national income.[27]

Foundations of Tax Policy

With regard to the long period, the Commission had valuable suggestions to offer. The broad lines of a sound and progressive tax policy that it laid down, guided the budgets of the central and state governments in future. Its conclusion that the problem of equity could no longer be left to the automatic functioning of economic and social forces, and its emphasis on the fact of an appreciable degree of avoidable inequality in incomes and wealth was widely welcomed. More effective tax enforcement and additional taxes on luxury consumption and widening of the taxation of wealth and property provided possible means for the reduction of inequalities. But if any considerable addition had to be made to public revenues, some contribution must come from the mass of people through taxes which had a wide base. This was in fact the justification of the new excises.

Above all, there was the imperative need for raising the volume of taxation. Indian tax revenues were 7–8 per cent of the national income and this proportion was lower than many countries, including some in South-East Asia. In the opinion of the Commission, the existing structure of the Indian taxation system did not fully tap the taxable resources of the country and there was a justification for some increase. It was also desirable to cover at least a part of the capital account through taxation. However, the Commission did not suggest that the development programme be wholly financed by taxes.[28]

The Commission was of the view that deficit financing for one or two years might not upset the stability of the economy, but in the long-term, the Commission warned that deficit financing of a quantitatively significant magnitude would result in inflation with speculative elements gaining ascendancy and distorting the pattern of development and retarding capital formation. With regard to the correcting of inflationary and deflationary pressures, the Commission had rightly arrived at the conclusion that the possibilities of the Indian tax system as a corrective for deflation were limited. But for checking inflation, it had possibilities. These matters, however, lay beyond the taxation system. When such pressures develop, the Commission opined, it is the whole fiscal and monetary mechanism which goes into operation and mere changes in taxes cannot go far.[29]

Ceiling on Incomes

Perhaps the most radical suggestion of the Commission was a ceiling on incomes. It referred to the wide disparity in consumption levels, which had a demoralizing effect on the masses. In the opinion of the Commission, the disincentive effect of higher taxation on the will to work on the part of higher income groups was generally exaggerated. It was necessary to have a ceiling on personal incomes on the basis of a reasonable multiple of the per capita income or family income. The multiple might well be thirty of the prevailing average family income. The Commission did not suggest the ceiling for immediate implementation, but nevertheless it considered it important that the government should strive for it by stages in a realistic manner and as part of an integrated approach along several directions.[30]

The Commission had also considered certain additional forms of taxation such as an annual tax on total wealth at a low rate as a complement to income tax. But while these suggestions could be made use of in future, the Commission did not recommend them for immediate adoption. In the opinion of the Commission, additional sources would be found in an increase in the rates of income tax, partially offset by some reduction in the corporation tax and with additional reliefs for savings and investment Other ways to offset this included an increase in excise taxes, increase in non-tax revenue through adoption of suitable price policies and moderate land revenue surcharges.[31]

The Commission was praised for its concessions to companies which were considered the best part of the report. But there was criticism as well. The *Capital*, a Calcutta based journal, wrote, 'The theory that consumption must be restrained and investment encouraged is, in general sound. But the transformation only takes place through the process of saving and investment and especially personal savings. But it is exactly personal savings that the Commission wants to stop.'[32] While welcoming the tax concessions, it opined that they would be but small comfort if they came packaged with a plan in which there would be 'no more savings, no more enterprise and precious little expansion of consumer markets'.[33]

* * *

The recommendations of the Commission would figure in the budgets that Deshmukh presented. The Commission submitted its report to the government in December 1954 before the deadline assigned to it. Deshmukh praised the report calling it a massive and historic document covering the entire field of taxation with recommendations that covered a very wide field. He hoped that the states too would study the recommendations confessing at the same time that he had had little time to examine the report in its entirety. Still, he made a series of changes in taxes in keeping with the Commission's recommendations in the budget for 1955–56. He raised the duty on sugar quite steeply, rationalized the rates of cotton cloth and included many new items under the excise regime. As far as direct taxes were concerned in keeping with the spirit of the commission's recommendations, he raised the exemption limit for individual income tax but phased out tax relief for higher incomes.

In his budget for 1956–57, Deshmukh implemented other recommendations of the Commission. The Commission had recommended that there should be no time limit for opening cases of tax evasion. Deshmukh, was then in the process of redrafting the Taxation on Income (Investigation Commission) Act of 1947, to enable the government to reopen old cases. This had been the subject of litigation in the past, with the Supreme Court ruling against the government. The issue of how the government was to investigate tax evasion became a somewhat controversial subject after Independence and proved to be a thorny issue for all finance ministers. Deshmukh told Parliament that the powers of search and seizure which the Investigation Commission had would now be given to the income tax department in keeping with the recommendations of the Taxation Enquiry Commission.[34]

On the whole, in thinking out a suitable and progressive fiscal machinery for an active and high-level economy based on welfare conceptions, the Commission arrived at conclusions which played an important role in shaping the budgets of the future for a decade, if not for a generation. Apart from its analytical aspects, the report brought together a wealth of data and the enormous amount of research was in itself commendable.

18

Rejoining the Tatas

After his resignation from government, Matthai rejoined Tatas as director-in-charge of TISCO and was welcomed back with open arms. His Tata connection became stronger when J.R.D. made him chairman of the Sir Dorabji Tata Trust, the first non-Parsi to hold that post. Matthai was chairman of the Trust from 1951 to 1957. He was also the chairman of the governing board of the Tata Institute of Social Sciences (TISS) from 1951 to 1956 and at the helm of the Court of Governors of the Indian Institute of Science (IISC), Bangalore. In the last two years of his life, he was the chairman (1957–59) of the governing council of the Tata Memorial Centre, the cancer hospital in Bombay, in which he passed away in early November 1959.

Sir Dorabji Tata Trust

Tata Institute of Fundamental Research

Matthai had a long association with the Sir Dorabji Tata Trust. He was a trustee in 1944 when the Cambridge-educated theoretical physicist Homi J. Bhabha's proposal for an institute for fundamental research was approved by the Trust. Bhabha had first broached the topic about his institute with J.R.D., who was known to be receptive to new ideas. On 19 August 1943, Bhabha wrote to him saying that lack of proper conditions and financial support had hampered the development of science in India. He believed that those who chose a scientific career were not being given the necessary facilities for conducting research.[1]

In his letter, Bhabha pointed out that if Indian science was to progress, far greater financial support was needed for 'pure' or fundamental research, something that was unlikely to yield any immediate economic return. In his reply on 2 September 1943, J.R.D. Tata said that if Bhabha put up a concrete proposal backed by a convincing argument, there was a very good chance that the Sir Dorabji Tata Trust and the Sir Ratan Tata Trust would respond.

Bhabha was also friends with Rustum D. Choksi, a trustee of the Sir Dorabji Tata Trust, and his brother, J.D. Choksi, the legal adviser to the Tatas. Rustum had been a professor of Latin and English at Wilson College in Bombay when he succeeded Dr Clifford Manshardt as a trustee of the Sir Dorabji Tata Trust in 1941.[2] He became the managing trustee in 1950 and served in that position till 1980. An erudite, self-effacing man with considerable personal charm, he not only helped Bhabha shape his proposal but also gave him inside information on what the trustees were thinking. His patient persuasion played no small role in getting the Trust to approve Bhabha's proposal.

Choksi was opposed to the idea of the Trust being reduced to a lending institution. Indeed, the trustees had always been concerned about the need to make a distinction between its grant-making activities committed to social development ('constructive philanthropy') and run-of-the-mill donations to alleviate distress. From the beginning, it was clear that the Trust would not fritter away its resources on many projects but focus on supporting the founding of a few institutions that individuals with foresight were unable to establish due to a lack of resources.

Bhabha placed a formal proposal before Sir Sorab Saklatvala, the chairman of the Sir Dorabji Tata Trust, after Choksi guided him on how to present his scheme to the trustees. On 17 February 1944, Choksi wrote to Bhabha asking him to submit a scheme to the trustees along with a personal letter to Sir Sorab. He advised him to send the scheme as a draft, which Bhabha could finalize once he received Sir Sorab's opinion.

Choksi informed Bhabha that he had sounded out the trustees and graded their response.

Have seen bosses D, T, S and M in that order, 3rd and 4th [are] somewhat non-committal. Following algebraic symbols denote reaction in the same order – b+, a, c+, c. All the details you shall have later – perhaps in person. May suggest in your letter that you'd come to Bombay to unfold, explain to Sir S and co-trustees, if they wish.[3]

D stood for Sir Ardeshir Dalal, T referred to J.R.D. Tata, S was Sir Sorab Saklatvala and M was John Matthai. Matthai ranked last in Choksi's assessment of the trustees' degrees of enthusiasm about Bhabha's proposal. Cautiously conservative at times, perhaps he was not convinced that they should place their trust in the abilities of only one man, however capable. Anyway, in the end, he seems to have been persuaded by Choksi and the other trustees. It was Choksi who laid out the first clear policy on the kind of work the Trust ought to be doing, stressing the pioneering nature of its work, and the need to keep that reputation intact.

On 12 March 1944, Bhabha wrote his now famous letter to Sir Sorab from Bangalore submitting the scheme for what became the Tata Institute of Fundamental Research. Bhabha's proposed institute was based on a model that focussed on the individual—in this case, him. Citing the example of the Kaiser Wilhelm Society, which believed in first picking an outstanding man and then building an institution for him, Bhabha suggested that the Trust fund an institute based around him. It had never been done in India before and Bhabha reassured Sir Sorab that outstanding schools of research had been built in the UK in the same way, and he saw no reason why the same could not be done in India.

As for fears about it being a one-man show, Choksi argued that earlier, too, the trustees had supported Dr Manshardt to build TISS. Finally, on 14 April 1944, the trustees discussed the proposal and gave it the green signal. This decision of the trust was in keeping with the Tatas' vision of providing what India needed. With Independence on the horizon, the Trust now also saw its role as contributing to nation-building. Choksi had stressed the pioneering nature of the institute, and it was this emphasis on supporting the unconventional that became the nub of the argument in support of Bhabha's institute. The Trust's support of Bhabha is usually couched in terms of support for science but as oral historian Indira Chowdhury points out, it was also a result of the 'reconceptualization of philanthropy' in India.[4]

The Rural Thrust

In December 1951, some six months after he had resigned as finance minister, Matthai, while presiding over a convocation of TISS, announced that the Dorabji Tata Trust, whose activities were hitherto confined to urban areas would now turn its attention to village reconstruction, a new and valuable avenue for pioneer service. In fact, Matthai had wanted to work in the rural areas but didn't know where and how to start. He got the chance when Professor D.R. Gadgil, director of the Gokhale Institute of Politics and Economics, Poona, suggested the village of Devapur, some 90 km from Satara in Maharashtra (then Bombay State).[5]

The village, which was deep in the interior, received barely 25 cm of rain annually and faced drought on a regular basis. Into this village, which lacked even a school teacher for a long time, came a person called Bhaurao Patil, who though not highly educated himself, came with a burning passion to educate the children of Devapur. He requested for, and got some land, for a hostel in which children irrespective of caste would reside. He was convinced that the only way to break the caste system was to have young children live and eat together.[6]

Bhaurao showed the area to Gadgil who, in turn, suggested it to Matthai. Matthai and Rustum Choksi, now the managing trustee of the Dorabji Tata Trust, visited Devapur to get an idea of what they were getting into. Since the village was a few miles off the nearest motorable road, the last lap of their journey was made in a festively decorated bullock cart. Matthai not only took Devapur under his wing, but on the advice of the villagers also took eight other neighbouring villages for development. The Trust started a subsidiary called the Rural Welfare Board (RWB) for this purpose. It consisted of an agricultural expert, a cattle specialist, an accountant, a commerce graduate and a graduate from TISS. N.D. Godbole, the secretary of the Trust, was overall in charge of the RWB.[7]

The first priority was to stop soil erosion and for this, they constructed contour bunds on the land. Sisal was grown on the bunds, but this proved to be less than successful because the goats developed a taste for it! This activity of making bunds resulted in employment for about 400 people.[8] Over the next five years, 1952–57, the villages got drinking water wells, schools, dispensaries and community centres. A change in the cropping pattern, cattle breeding and introduction of Merino sheep were some of the other innovations undertaken over the years. Suffice it to say that the Devapur Project, which was the first integrated rural scheme undertaken by a private agency in India, became a textbook case for development. Later, the RWB took up projects at Mulshi (Poona district) and at Mithapur (Amreli district) in Gujarat. It is possible that Matthai's foray into rural development, provided at least part of the inspiration for his son, Ravi's, famous rural university experiment in Jawaja, Rajasthan.

International Institute for Population Studies

The first institute for population studies, not only in India, but in the entire developing world, was the brainchild of Matthai. It helped that J.R.D. was the first prominent Indian to espouse family planning. He thought that India's population would double in fifty years (it doubled in forty). When J.R.D. spoke to Nehru about the importance of curbing the population soon after Independence, he was told, 'But, Jeh, population is our strength!' A few years later, in 1951, he broached the subject again, but his pleas fell on deaf years. At that time, India's population was just 361 million, but Nehru thought that India's human capital would be a huge asset and politely ignored him. This however did not dissuade J.R.D. from pursuing a campaign to promote family planning for forty years.[9]

In December 1954, when Matthai was chairman of the Trust, he suggested to the health minister, Rajkumari Amrit Kaur, that a school of population studies be started in association with TISS. The aim was to train people who would carry out population studies for the universities or government. He also thought that the United Nations (UN) would be interested if its facilities were made available for this part of Asia. The UN officials showed keen interest. In July 1956, the central government approved a joint undertaking with the Trust for a Demographic Centre for Training and Research with the collaboration of the UN, who would supply the expertise. The recurring expenses would be largely met by the government, with the Trust contributing one-sixth of the cost of running the Centre for five years.[10]

The Centre was housed in TISS till it got its own premises. From the beginning, it was expected that the new Centre would work on a co-operative basis with not only TISS but also the Gokhale Institute in Poona, Bombay University's School of Economics and Sociology, and the Indian Cancer Research Centre, Bombay. The Sir Ratan Tata Trust gifted land in Chembur for the new Centre. In July 1970, its name was changed to the International Institute for Population Studies (IIPS) to reflect the importance and wider scope of demographic studies. After having played a role in its founding and helping to run it for fourteen years, the Trust felt that its role as initiator and sponsor had ended, and it withdrew financial support that same year.[11] That same year, J.R.D. helped to found with other industrialists the Family Planning Foundation in New Delhi, which received generous assistance from the Sir Dorabji Tata Trust.

Today, the IIPS serves as a regional centre for training and research in population studies for the ESCAP (Economic and Social Commission for Asia and the Pacific) region. The institute was declared a deemed university in August 1985, a recognition that facilitated the award of degrees by the institute itself and paved the way for its further expansion as an academic institution. It is the hub of population and health-related teaching and research in India and has trained students from different countries of the Asia and the Pacific region, Africa and North America over the years.

Fostering a Corporate Identity

In spite of its paternalistic policies, TISCO had its share of labour problems. The trade union movement had gathered momentum, and it was hit by a flash strike in 1920 that stunned the management. Another followed two years later and yet another in 1924, when Gandhi, Rajendra Prasad and C.F. Andrews came for mediation. Among his responsibilities as chairman, J.R.D.'s responsibilities was to deal occasionally with the fiery president of the Tata Workers' Union, Abdul Bari. By the early-1950s, Tatas 'faced an identity crisis evident both in the vacillations over labour policy and the fraught relationship with the Nehruvian state'.[12] Fifty years after the death of the founder, Jamsetji Tata, there was little institutional memory of the early days. There was criticism from insiders that the group had strayed from its roots. The new generation would have to be educated about their past so that they could be part of a shared corporate identity.[13]

It was in this context that in 1952, Matthai proposed putting together a book on the progress of industrial development in India in which the Tatas 'would form the main skeleton'[14]. Such a task would normally have been assigned to the public relations department, but Matthai wanted it to be a high-class exercise in economic scholarship with no resemblance to propaganda. The research work was done by the Department of Economics and Statistics of Tata Sons who had assisted with the preparation of the Bombay Plan and brought out *Tata Quarterly*, a review of economic trends and financial data. The mandate was to produce a sober, straightforward, factual account that not only brought out what private enterprise had achieved, but what it could still do, if run with a full sense of responsibility. While setbacks were not to be ignored, it was important to 'not embarrass our position in the context of present or future activities'[15], Matthai observed in an outline of the proposed monograph.

The book, *House of Tata*, was completed in November 1954 and along with a general overview of the Indian economy had subheadings dealing with finance, personnel, philanthropy and so on. The aim of the entire exercise was to enhance the group's legitimacy as a national and global institution. Naval Tata, the father of future Tata chairman Ratan Tata, who would go on to become deputy chairman of the group, while summarising the thesis of the book said that the Tatas through their benevolent activities propagated socialism to strengthen capitalism. This was a concession to Nehru's socialist rhetoric and also a reflection of his own views. J.R.D. never used such language.[16]

The Tata Administrative Service

The second step in the process of constructing a shared corporate identity was the Tata Administrative Service. By the 1950s, the number of foreigners in key positions had reduced and each Tata company developed its own methods for the recruitment of specialized workmen. Later, a number of outstanding specialists were moved to higher administrative positions even as their areas of expertise remained the same. One of J.R.D.'s key concerns was how to safeguard Tata values and collective interests as the Tata companies expanded. He wanted a superglue that would ensure that even as the group's companies continued to grow, they would retain the essential Tata ethos. The idea was to build a foundation for a common and distinctive Tata culture. He wanted this culture to be characterized by a spirit of consensus and the authority that flows from technical knowledge, apart from leadership qualities of a high standard.[17] That glue would be the Tata Administrative Service, but before that came into being, there were a few hits and misses.

J.R.D. established the Superior Staff Recruitment Committee in 1948. It consisted of a small team of senior executives that would assess and recruit people. It included Homi Mody, Ardeshir Dalal, Matthai and J.R.D. himself. The word 'superior' was intended to convey that the personnel selected would not only be highly qualified but also bring that extra something in the form of initiative and energy. The committee selected three new recruits but sadly all of them left within two years. It was thought that lack of guidance and attention had contributed to their early departure from the Tata companies to which they had been assigned.

For a while, J.R.D. became the butt of jokes among his colleagues, but his disappointment did not affect his conviction that it was still the right thing to do.[18] His own experience when he first joined Tatas as executive assistant to John Peterson, an ICS officer, planted the idea that the Tatas needed something like the ICS for the Tatas. Peterson was the role model J.R.D. had in mind. He realized that as the Tatas expanded, they would need a prestigious management school of their own which would be the main source of their top executives.

In keeping with this line of thinking, J.R.D. relaunched his idea as a more structured Tata cadre. The committee studied the management-trainee programmes of companies such as Hindustan Lever and the recruitment schemes and training processes of the large multinational oil companies. The members realized that for a diversified conglomerate like the Tata group, a simple management-trainee programme would not achieve the objectives J.R.D. had in mind.

By 1956, apart from the recommendations of the Superior Staff Recruitment Committee, J.R.D. also studied administrative cadres in Britain and France apart from of course, the IAS, the successor to the ICS in India. He recognized the value such a cadre could have for Tatas: It would be the cohesive force ensuring that all the companies were fully aligned with the values and ethos of the Tata group. The members of the new service would move between companies and such mobility would benefit both them and the group as a whole. Drawing his inspiration from the IAS, J.R.D. called his cadre the Tata Administrative Service (TAS). Freddie Mehta, an LSE-trained economist, was the first to join TAS in 1956 and went on to become chairman of the Forbes Forbes & Campbell group heading seventeen companies.

A Staff College

An important step in forging a shared corporate identity was taken in 1956 when what eventually became the Tata Staff College had a modest start. The Tatas hired the Turf Club in Poona for a month and Tata directors and distinguished experts were asked to share their experiences with young and middle-aged Tata officers. Long before the Indian Institute of Management was set up in Ahmedabad in November 1961, J.R.D. had with the help of Matthai and Professor Rustum D. Choksi, decided to set up a Staff College. In 1964, the lawyer and landowner, F.E. Dinshaw's home, which had wide grounds, was made the base for a permanent Tata Management Training Centre. The fabulously wealthy Dinshaw had lent money to the Tatas and was a kind of lender of the last resort for the group. From 1924 to 1926, he lent Rs 2 crore to bail out TISCO and Tata Hydro. In the 1930s, this loan was ultimately converted into equity of 12.5 per cent in Tata Sons. In 1936, this stake was bought by Shapurji Pallonji Mistry from Dinshaw's heirs.[19]

In his inaugural speech to the second session in December 1956, Matthai said that the new college would foster a 'corporate sense' among different group companies to ensure the survival of the Tata 'tradition.' They would also in the process become public advocates for business countering the socialist agenda of the Congress party. The rise of state-run institutions like the IITs and IIMs meant that the privileged role of the Tatas as providers of expertise and technical training was greatly eroded. Rather than pioneering new industries, Tata was now destined to 'fulfil a very important purpose, namely to provide the right atmosphere and the right tradition which is a very important thing nowadays, because there is a great deal of criticism against the way in which business is being run'.[20] The mission of the college was to impart the Tata tradition to all Tata companies.

* * *

Matthai was very particular about his morning and evening walks, each for an hour. Before he joined the Tatas, the board meetings used to take place after office hours. But Matthai had to have his evening walk and so he requested J.R.D. to hold the meetings earlier. Every evening, Matthai could be seen walking briskly down Bombay's Nepean Sea Road in his khaki shorts.

When the Matthais returned from New Delhi, they stayed at the Taj Mahal Hotel for many years. According to Syloo Matthai, Achamma wanted to devote her time and energy exclusively to her social work and wanted to be spared the burden of setting up and running a home. The supportive John Matthai agreed.[21] The venue of Matthai's evening walks then shifted to the Oval Maidan where, according to Syloo, he took three rounds, never more and never less. Syloo narrated with a chuckle how her father-in-law had even bought shorts and a T-shirt for Achamma! 'I don't think she ever wore them and that's hardly surprising,' she added.[22]

Punctuality was another of his traits. He would leave office at exactly 5.30 p.m. and was known to follow a fixed daily routine. After an early dinner at 8 p.m., he would retire for the night at around 9.30 p.m. Little wonder then, that Matthai didn't like travelling, a fact, as we have noted before, even Nehru had commented on in a letter to Krishna Menon.

Matthai never travelled for mere pleasure even though as Tata director, he was entitled to foreign travel at company expense. His trips abroad were only for unavoidable work. Matthai paid for stationery and material used for personal correspondence from his own pocket and gave his secretary an imprest of Rs 100 for this purpose. As a member of the viceroy's executive council, Matthai was eligible to draw an outfit allowance. Nehru asked them not to do so since most of them wore khaddar. One of the members had already drawn the allowance, and Matthai was quite vocal about his disapproval.

When he wrote a series of article for the *Times of India*, he declined a generous payment from the newspaper for his labours. Matthai himself favoured dark-coloured suits, and when the occasion demanded it, a *bandhgala* (closed neck formal suit). He was always appropriately dressed but was never a dandy. As we have already seen, Matthai believed in calling a spade a spade, perhaps taking things to an extreme at times. He never did anything which would place him under an obligation or embarrass him at a later date. Anything that impaired his impartiality or affected his reputation for honesty was anathema to him.

Matthai preferred to stay at home and read. He was a voracious reader and was rarely seen without a book, even at the dinner table. He subscribed to *The Economist* of London and was always well informed about the world economic situation. As noted before, he liked the cartoons and caricatures appearing in magazines and collected them in a file. The ones in *Shankar's Weekly* were his favourite. He was very fond of the cartoon that poked fun at the late running of the Grand Trunk Express and the story of the disappointed lover who died of starvation, something we have already encountered in an earlier chapter.

Bonhomie and Camaraderie

The Tata board room was a cheerful place. With the likes of Sir Homi Mody regaling the other directors with his wit, it could have been nothing else. Sir Homi was known to muffle his 'moral in mirth' and his exchanges with Matthai, the apotheosis of dignity, enlivened Tata meetings with a welcome levity. While Matthai was known to adopt a serious mien, he was not devoid of a sense of humour. Certainly, he was far more susceptible to enjoying and even contributing a joke than the austere and stern, Sir Ardeshir Dalal, of whom R.M. Lala said: 'No humour escaped his lips and seldom did his perpetual cigar yield place to a smile.'[23]

Matthai was a perfect foil to the irrepressible Sir Homi, whose wit and humour have provided many amusing Tata anecdotes. Sir Homi, while bidding farewell to Matthai, said that while both of them had a very high opinion of each other, there was a difference insofar as his colleagues were concerned, because they always looked up to Matthai. Sir Homi observed, 'He has got many natural advantages: face, figure, manner, voice, all that and invested with an air of profundity in everything he said. Even if Dr Matthai said "Good morning" it sounded like a Papal benediction.'[24]

Sir Homi addressed Matthai as 'Brother John' and the Tata lunch table was witness to some heady badinage between the two. The lunch table was also served with 'a sprinkling of smutty jokes',[25] but the general level of discourse was of a very high level. National issues were discussed leaving no doubt that Tatas belonged to the nation. And Sir Homi, who his biographer, D.R. Mankekar, called a 'licensed jester on the stage of Indian public affairs'[26], was in reality a serious-minded personality of intelligence, integrity and courage. Sir Homi was also perhaps one of the very few people who could take liberties with Matthai. On one occasion while having lunch, they received the news that a friend had passed away. 'Brother John,' inquired Sir Homi, 'what do you think you and I will be doing when we are dead?' After removing the cigar from his mouth, Matthai replied in his deep baritone, 'Roasting I suppose.'[27] Matthai smoked both a pipe and a cigar. He was known to say, 'I work on a pipe and relax on a cigar.'[28]

On another occasion, the story goes, that Matthai entered Sir Homi's room in Bombay House and started smoking a very foul-smelling cigar. Sir Homi's response to this odious intrusion was: 'Will you please go to my bedroom and smoke your cigar to drive away the mosquitoes.'[29] For his part, Matthai admired Sir Homi's sense of humour, remarking that one could not work with Sir Homi without feeling that 'life was every bit worth living and that it was a pleasure to work with people who combined zest for work with a sense of humour.'[30]

Sir Homi was also the father of two famous sons: the parliamentarian Pilloo, who regaled Parliament with his wit, and the peerless man-manager Russi Mody, who had worked under Matthai in TISCO and of whom he was very fond. As director-in-charge of TISCO, Matthai had occasion to deal with a young Russi, who was then a somewhat 'restless, anti-establishment character'.[31] J.R.D. once asked Matthai what he would have done if he was Russi's age. Matthai replied that he would have been a revolutionary.[32]

When Matthai was dying of cancer, Russi met him at the Tata Memorial Hospital (TMH) in Bombay. It was obvious that Matthai was on his deathbed, but as Russi was leaving, he said, 'Get well soon.' Matthai gripped his hand and said, 'Russi, have I gone down so much in your estimation that you think I am such a fool.' Russi, who was very fond of Matthai, says that he couldn't say much at the time because he was on the verge of tears.[33] In his condolence letter to Achamma after Matthai's demise, he said that while no words would soothe her sense of loss, he wanted her to know that her husband would be missed by 'hundreds of young men like myself who received a helping hand from Dr Matthai on more than one occasion'.[34]

Russi Mody went on to have a storied career with TISCO and was its managing director (and then chairman) for many years. Unfortunately, hubris overtook him, and he was sacked from Tatas on 19 April 1993, a month before his retirement. His exit was a sad day in the history of Tatas. No chairman had ever been forced to resign, leave alone dismissed. He had been undone by his arrogance and the feeling that he was indispensable. After all, it was Russi who had once said, 'There are only three great men who have come out of Harrow—Jawaharlal Nehru, Winston Churchill and Russi Mody.'[35]

19

A Man for All Seasons

Chairman, State Bank of India

The State Bank of India (SBI) came into being on 1 July 1955 in terms of the State Bank of India Act, 1955, and all the assets and liabilities of the Imperial Bank were transferred to SBI in terms of this Act.[1] Matthai was prevailed upon by Deshmukh to become the first chairman of the new entity. Ever responsive to a call for service to the nation, Matthai accepted. It is inconceivable that a former finance minister would accept such a post today. Matthai had high self-esteem but no false ego, and this was perhaps why he accepted an appointment that most others would have considered infra dig.

In early May, Deshmukh wrote to J.R.D. requesting the services of Matthai. He said that RBI governor, Benegal Rama Rau, had sounded Matthai at his instance asking him if he would agree to accept the part-time chairmanship of the SBI. Matthai had indicated his willingness for the same. But a re-examination of the workload had led them to believe that a part-time chairman would be inadequate to deal with the enormous amount of 'spade work that would be necessary if the policy and attitude of the Bank is to be rapidly reoriented on desired lines'.[2] He wanted J.R.D. to 'facilitate Matthai's accepting the whole-time responsibility we contemplate and to remove whatever difficulties there may exist so that he can join the new Bank on the 1st of July'.[3] The Tata chairman who rarely, if ever, turned down an appeal for help, duly obliged.

When Matthai was appointed as the first chairman of the new SBI, J.R.D. wrote to him to express his unhappiness at losing him. He said that he had hoped that Tatas would have had the benefit of his wise counsel for some more time even if only in a part-time capacity, but since the work he was going to do was of national importance, 'we should not stand in the way.' He was happy that Matthai had decided to remain chairman of the Sir Dorabji Tata Trust and the trustees would continue to have him as a colleague. He ended with: 'It has not only been a privilege but a great personal satisfaction to have you with us all these years. The Firm and I personally have been the gainers.'[4]

Matthai was fully conversant with the history of the nationalization of the Imperial Bank having answered questions in Parliament on it as finance minister. In the course of the debate on the RBI Bill in September 1948, demands were made for the nationalization of the bank. The issue of nationalization came up once again on 1 February 1949 when Matthai, in reply to a question said that given the economic climate of the country at that time, nationalization was not feasible. But he did give an assurance that the Act would be examined to see how it would be possible to 'enable it to render the fullest possible service in the most suitable manner'[5] and to remove some 'unsatisfactory' features of the bank's working without nationalizing it. The board of the Imperial Bank discussed the issue in April 1948 and passed a resolution that nationalization was totally unjustified and that no material benefit could be expected to accrue to government, the country and the shareholders from such action.

The views of the Imperial Bank's board were communicated to the government through RBI Governor Deshmukh, who in a memorandum for the RBI board, wrote that the nationalization would be a serious mistake with nothing to be gained and much likely to be lost.[6] The matter died down at that time, but the demand for nationalization continued and led to the appointment of the Rural Banking Enquiry Committee (RBEC) under Sir Purshotamdas Thakurdas in November 1949. The need for pooling the savings of the rural areas to make them available for increasing production had assumed importance after the devaluation of the rupee in 1949 and the government had decided that one of the best ways of stimulating investment was through the extension of banking facilities in the rural areas.

Matthai's statement about removing the 'unsatisfactory' aspects of the Imperial Bank's working had led to a series of consultations between the RBI, the government and the Imperial Bank on the subject. Matthai and RBI Governor Rama Rau attended a meeting of the central board of the Imperial Bank in Bombay in October 1949, where a proposal to appoint the

Imperial Bank's chief executive officers after government or RBI approval met with vehement opposition from the Imperial Bank's board. Since informal consultations failed to resolve the impasse, Matthai and Rama Rau decided to refer this matter to the RBEC which the government had decided to set up. Purshotamdas attempted to produce by negotiation with the Imperial Bank a scheme that might secure its cooperation in the promotion of rural banking. As part of this scheme, he and Rama Rau promoted the idea of the Imperial Bank having a non-executive chairman appointed with government approval. This proposal was supported by A.R. Chisholm, managing director, and a few other directors of the Imperial Bank, and approved by both Matthai and Deshmukh.

The RBEC submitted its report in May 1950. The RBEC was in favour of the Imperial Bank, which was for all practical purposes a state-sponsored institution, retaining, and in certain circumstances extending, its pre-eminent position in treasury arrangements. However, in the committee's view, the patronage it received from the state justified the popular expectation that the bank would develop as a national organization. But nationalization was not the best means of achieving this objective. It was necessary in the country's interest that the Imperial Bank retained its commercial character, and 'existing restrictions on its business were quite sufficient' for the proposed ends. The case for bringing the bank under more effective public regulation would be met by the government resuming some of the powers over the institution which it had allowed to lapse upon the formation of the RBI. Whatever the final means adopted, the committee felt they should not be such as to promote official or political interference in the routine working of the institution.[7]

The measures that the committee proposed involved, chiefly, the reconstitution of the top management of the bank. Two alternative proposals were advanced in this connection. According to the first, the managing director and deputy managing director of the bank would be appointed with the approval of the Government of India, which would also have the right to demand their removal from office if they ceased to enjoy its confidence. In addition, the committee suggested restoring the pre-1935 authority of the government in the bank's affairs, whereby its nominee on the bank's board had the power to seek postponement or review of decisions bearing on the national policy of the government. In order to make government representation on the board more effective, its nominees were also to have seats on the committee of the central board.[8]

Alternatively, as agreed informally earlier, the RBEC suggested that the central board of the Imperial Bank should be reconstituted on the pattern of other commercial banks, with overall policy and general superintendence being placed in the charge of a chairman, whose appointment would be subject to government approval, and a board of directors, two of whose members would be nominated by the government on the recommendations of the RBI. The day-to-day functioning of the bank was to be entrusted to a general manager who would not have a seat on the board. Responding to other criticisms of the functioning of the Imperial Bank, the committee recommended granting fuller representation to various regional interests on its local and central boards. It also suggested the opening of one or two more local head offices to redress regional imbalances in its operations.[9]

But rather surprisingly, the Imperial Bank's management decided to repudiate the earlier informal understanding and reject the recommendations of the Purshotamdas Thakurdas committee. Rama Rau, in a memorandum dated 18 December 1950 to his central board, referred to the fact that the RBEC had nowhere in its report recommended 'even by implication' any steps that could be regarded as constituting nationalization of the bank. The governor opined that if the powers vested in the government and the RBI were 'exercised properly', it would be 'difficult, if not impossible', for the bank to adopt any policy that was detrimental to national interests. He instead chose to favour the alternative suggested by the RBEC that the constitution of the bank should be changed on the model of that of the other commercial banks, placing the overall policy and the general superintendence of the bank in the charge of a chairman whose appointment would be subject to the approval of the central government.[10]

By April 1951, steps were initiated by the RBI, in consultation with the government, to amend the Imperial Bank Act to provide a machinery that would enable the government to have fuller information regarding the day-to-day working of the bank and thus make fuller use of the powers already vested in the government.[11] The proposed legislative changes were eventually postponed probably because the government preferred to wait for a more propitious time to carry them through. Meanwhile, the Imperial Bank's role in promoting banking in rural areas had come under sharp focus. The role of the bank in relation to the needs of the planned development of the country also came under close scrutiny. Rama Rau thus felt that the time had arrived for considering the issue of nationalization or radical changes in the bank's constitution from the point of view of planned development of the country.[12]

It became necessary to re-examine the whole issue from the point of view of development of banking and credit facilities after the report of the All-India Rural Credit Survey Committee (AIRCSC) appointed in August 1951 to consider the lines on which credit facilities were to be extended in rural areas was published. It consisted of A.D. Gorwala (chairman), Professor D.R. Gadgil, B. Venkatappaiah and Dr N.S.R. Sastry as members, the last-named being the member secretary. Venkatappaiah had not only been a key member of the RBEC but was also strongly pro-nationalization. The committee submitted its report three years later, in December 1954.[13]

The AIRCSC recommended the nationalization of the Imperial Bank and government's acceptance of the proposal were first made public by the finance minister, C.D. Deshmukh, in the Lok Sabha on 20 December 1954 during his speech on economic policy. But by far the most important recommendation was the scheme of a State Bank of India by amalgamation of a number of banks including the Imperial Bank.[14] The objectives of the bank were briefly stated in the preamble to the State Bank of India Act, 1955, as 'the extension of banking facilities on a large scale, more particularly in the rural and semi-urban areas, and for diverse other public purposes'.

The central board of the new SBI was to consist of a chairman and a vice chairman to be appointed by the central government. A.D. Gorwala, a respected ICS officer, was in the reckoning for the post of vice chairman, but his candidature was vetoed by Nehru, who felt that Gorwala was opposed to government policy on many fronts. Nehru was apprehensive that his appointment could lead to opposition from Parliament, and it would be unfortunate if the good effect generated by Matthai's appointment was undone by a controversial appointment. In the event, the vice chairman's post went to Vaikunth Lal Mehta, a former finance minister in the government of Bombay. S.K. Handoo, managing director of the Imperial bank, was retained in the same capacity as one of the managing directors in the transformed entity. The post of the second managing director was filled by M.R. Bhide, joint secretary in the ministry of food and agriculture, who was put in charge of cooperation and rural banking, a field that was new to the bank. Gorwala was appointed a member of the central board as the government nominee.[15]

Every officer and employee of the Imperial Bank (except the managing director, the deputy manager director and other directors) became an officer and employee of the SBI on and from 1 July 1955 and continued to serve with the same rights and privileges as before. The second step of the SBI scheme, namely, the takeover of state-associated banks, would take another five years.

Matthai's Tenure

The establishment of the SBI started a new chapter in the history of banking in India. The bank started to function under the direction of a central board and three local boards at Bombay, Calcutta and Madras. The local boards were initially appointed by government, and consisted of men of outstanding ability and experience in various fields of economic activity. Thus, stalwarts such as R.G. Saraiya, Sachindra Chaudhuri, Professor D.R. Gadgil, H.M. Patel (nominated by the government) and B. Venkatappaiah (nominated by RBI), joined luminaries such as Sir Vithal Chandavarkar, Badridas Goenka, S.V. Ramamurthy and A.D. Gorwala on the board of the bank. Leading this eminent group was Matthai.[16]

Matthai was in office for less than a year, but he set in motion schemes which came to fruition after his departure. The new SBI had an obligation to open 400 new branches during the first five years. As a first step, 100 were identified. The amalgamation of the associated banks also received his attention and at the first annual general meeting of the bank, he said that they were examining the feasibility of taking over some of the minor state-associated banks and had already made a beginning in this regard.

Matthai realized the importance of credit to small-scale industries as also the important role the SBI had to play in this regard. He believed that the SBI had an important role in planning and coordinating the activities of various credit agencies. Matthai said that planning for such a scheme had already been taken up and a pilot scheme for providing credit to small-scale industries had been drawn up. The experience gained from this pilot project would then be used to draw up a general scheme for providing credit in a coordinated manner by the SBI and other institutions.[17] The

Eastern Economist reported that all in all, there was a general feeling that management had 'achieved success in removing the apprehensions created by the change in the status and character of the bank'.[18]

Matthai's tenure ended prematurely when he resigned on 19 June 1956, less than a year after taking up office, over the issue of payment of bonus to the 'non-award' or supervisory staff. He asked for and was granted a month's leave. The government wanted the bonus to be confined to the 'award'[19] staff and such members of the 'non-award' staff drawing a salary not exceeding a certain figure. Matthai wanted to continue the practice of paying bonus to all the non-award staff, but he was overruled by the government. He was also upset about the attitude of the government in demanding a drastic reduction in the 'preposterously high' salaries and perquisites of its senior officers. He viewed these rulings from the government as a growing tendency to undermine the autonomy of the bank.[20] A stickler for precedent and protocol, Matthai also resented the growing tendency of ministers to answer questions relating to the SBI in Parliament and objected to the fact that the government was issuing directives to the bank.

Matthai summed up his own feelings succinctly in an address to the Rotary Club in Bombay in June 1956. He said that there was a convention in the British House of Commons that interpellations regarding public corporations, like directives, should apply only to matters of policy. But in India, at the present stage of public corporations, Matthai said, an unjustifiable measure of latitude had been allowed.

> The wide interpretation placed on public interest leads Ministers to assume a degree of responsibility for the working of public corporations which constitutes an abuse of the right to issue directives and to answer questions in Parliament. In certain matters with which I happen to be personally acquainted, replies by Ministers have not been merely unwarranted but almost invariably factually inaccurate.[21]

Writing about Matthai's exit from the bank in his memoirs, Deshmukh said, 'We had irreconcilable differences of opinion on the issue of the grant of bonus to the officers (firmly opposed by me). Also, he was not really at home in the new job and resigned – but without any bitterness.'[22] By the end of September 1956, the first central board had lost three of its key members. S.K. Handoo, the managing director, had put in his papers a week before Matthai without assigning any reason. He was given leave preparatory to retirement from October 1956 till his retirement in 1958. Sir Vithal Chandavarkar, who had been a director of the Imperial Bank since 1945 and a member of the SBI central board since the inception, also resigned in August 1956 without assigning any reason. The bank, however, continued to make steady progress.[23]

Vice Chancellor, University of Bombay

In March 1955, a few months before he was appointed chairman of SBI, Matthai was appointed vice chancellor of the University of Bombay. (It was an honorary post at the time.) Like his tenure at the SBI, his stint as vice chancellor too ended prematurely with his resignation on 23 February 1957, shortly after he had led the centenary celebrations of the university a few weeks before. Given his high contacts and influence in the business world, Matthai was able to raise a substantial sum of money for the celebrations.

A Storm in a Teacup

Matthai's tenure ended soon after the centenary celebrations when he resigned over a controversy regarding the age of retirement of the post of rector in the university, a post to which the retiring registrar, S.R. Dongerkery, was to be appointed.

On 17 August 1955, the university Senate passed a resolution appointing a rector for a period of five years; no age limit was specified. It appears that others were aspiring to the post and lobbied for a shorter tenure of three years. On 6 September, Matthai wrote to the Governor of Bombay, Harekrushna Mahtab, who was the chancellor of the university opposing the reduction in the tenure. He said that since it was a new post 'the person holding it will hardly have time to prepare the ground to render fullest assistance to the university and the vice chancellor'.[24]

Matthai also pointed out that a shorter tenure would lead to 'unhealthy scramble at frequent intervals' and though the present University Act had helped to check competition for office 'the evil has not by any means been eradicated.'[25] He followed this up with another letter on 8 September reiterating his views.

It would be a mistake for the tenure of the Rector not to be somewhat longer than that of the vice chancellor. It would be an advantage to a vice chancellor to have at least for a limited time the assistance of a Rector who has had experience of working with a previous holder of the office.[26]

However, it appears that despite Matthai's opposition, the government decided to reduce the tenure. Matthai wrote to Mahtab once again on 8 December expressing his inability to accept the decision of the government. It had been indicated to Matthai informally that the government was prepared to accept a tenure of five years officially, provided the person appointed was willing to vacate the office on Matthai's retirement, or at any other time indicated by the government withing the five-year period. Matthai wrote, 'I regret I cannot agree to this arrangement because what it will do in effect is to uphold publicly the principle of autonomy while surrendering it privately without the knowledge and approval of the university.'[27] At the end of the letter, Matthai offered to resign, asking that he be relieved by the end of the month or latest by 14 January 1956.

Mahtab replied a few days later on 11 December saying that he wanted to discuss the matter personally with Matthai but could not do so because of other commitments. He said that he was going to Orissa for two weeks, but on his return, he would take up the matter in the first week of January and dispose of it finally. Regarding Matthai's resignation he wrote, 'In the meanwhile, I would request you kindly not to allow your mind to play with the idea of resignation.'[28]

Later, Mahtab and Matthai had a private chat on the subject and the matter seems to have been amicably resolved. We find Mahtab writing to Matthai on 2 January 1956 telling him that the statutes had been duly sanctioned and that he had accepted the recommendation to appoint S.R. Dongerkery, the registrar, as rector. The age of retirement, which was sixty, would remain: There was no intention to revise it in respect of a person holding the office of rector, that subject being a matter for future consideration.[29] Matthai communicated the Governor's decision to Dongerkery, who accepted the terms. On 3 January, Matthai wrote to Mahtab asking him to announce the appointment immediately since there had already been a great delay in making the appointment. He also withdrew his resignation in view of the agreement reached.[30]

But the matter that appeared to have been resolved took another turn when a letter written by Mahtab's secretary on 3 January 1956 to Dongerkery queered the pitch. In it, he wanted the age limit of the rector to be fixed at sixty. Matthai was quick to respond. The next day, he shot off another letter to Mahtab saying that a change in the age would require him to take the matter back to the Senate, which he was unwilling to do because 'one amendment will lead to others' and it would also make it necessary for him to tell the Senate that the government's action violated the university's autonomy and the Senate, if it had any self-respect, should reject the government's suggestion. Matthai said that Mahtab's letter of 2 January was a correct record of what happened at the meeting between the two and this letter should be accepted as the official statement of the government's decision. He wanted the letter written on 3 January by Mahtab's secretary to be cancelled.[31]

The sanction of the chancellor to the statutes was communicated by a letter dated 5 January 1956 from the Governor's secretary to the registrar. In that letter, Mahtab also made a suggestion that an amendment might be made to statute 100A at an early date providing an age limit of sixty years for the rector as was the rule for other officers. The letter of 3 January 1956 was treated as withdrawn, but the issue of the retirement age remained a grey area. The matter lay dormant till November 1956, when it was placed before the Syndicate again who decided that Matthai should approach the chancellor again.

The matter flared up again in February 1957 when the matter was placed before the Senate and ultimately ended with Matthai's resignation. By that time Sri Prakasa had succeeded Mahtab as the Governor and in that capacity was the new chancellor. Matthai was greatly distressed at what he perceived to be political interference in his work and in an emotional speech to the Senate on 23 February, his last as vice chancellor, declared that ever since he had assumed charge, he had never been so exercised in his mind about the status, honour and freedom of the university as he had been during that time. He said that as vice chancellor, he had had to discuss the matter of the rector's term with both the chancellor and the ministers of the government, switching back and forth between them. He said, 'If the University is to preserve its academic freedom and maintain its dignity and honour, it is necessary that this system should be stopped not merely in Bombay, but throughout the country.'[32]

After his impassioned speech, the original resolution of having a post of rector with no age limit was unanimously accepted by the House. Never one to mince his words, Matthai was reported as publicly saying that the system of making governors the chancellors of their respective states should end since it provided a channel for political influence to work its way into the universities.[33] The matter received wide coverage in the 24 February edition of the *Times of India* and this was presumably when the new Governor first heard about it. Even though Sri Prakasa had been in office from mid-December 1956, Matthai had not thought it necessary to brief him on the subject.

The newspaper reported that the matter received the attention of the Syndicate only in November 1956. The Syndicate asked Matthai to write to the chancellor asking him not to press the advice of a change in retirement age for the rector as it was an amendment that was unlikely to be passed. The news report also said that a letter had been addressed to the chancellor which had yet to receive a reply. It was reported that the Syndicate had on 2 February 1957 decided to place before the Senate a motion on the subject which had reference to previous correspondence with the chancellor.[34]

Understandably upset, Sri Prakasa wrote to Matthai on the same day telling him that it would have been better if the matter been 'brought directly to my notice' before it was proceeded with and got publicity in the press. He noted Matthai's admonition that the chancellor should mind his own business but believed that the clearing up of a possible misunderstanding was part of that business. Sri Prakasa said that his office had not received any letter on the subject and therefore the question of replying to a non-existent letter did not arise. He then outlined the sequence of events in detail and expressed regret that the 'proceedings of yesterday should have taken the form that they did'. 'I have a feeling that in case you had informed the Senate of your own earlier concurrence to the age limit as suggested by my predecessor, the Senate would have agreed; and even if they had not, there would certainly not have been that acerbity in the proceedings that the press has reported.'[35]

Sri Prakasa said that he did not want the public to think that all these incidents 'happened in my time'. This, would not matter, he said, if the records had shown that his predecessor had left any cause for complaint, which he clearly had not, the matter being finalized in discussions with Matthai. The fact that Matthai had withdrawn his resignation itself showed that the matter had been satisfactorily resolved. Sri Prakasa wanted Matthai to put the facts before the public so that the misunderstanding could be cleared up. He also said that he would wait for an authentic copy of the proceedings of the meeting on 23 February with a 'certain amount of eagerness'.[36]

Matthai's reply on 25 February solved the mystery of the missing letter. The letter, Matthai said, had been addressed to the education minister and law minister and not the chancellor. Matthai said that since he had been asked by the Syndicate to approach the chancellor again, he decided first to discuss the matter with the education minister, Shantilal H. Shah, since he knew from past experience that the chancellor usually discussed these matters first with the minister concerned. In it, Matthai said that since the Senate had already voted against applying the age limit to the rector, it would now not be in a mood to reopen that question. Given this fact, he wanted Shah to explain the position to the chancellor and inquire whether he still wanted the suggestion to be conveyed to the Senate.[37] Strangely, Matthai chose to keep the chancellor completely out of the picture, in effect, asking the minister to do what he himself should have done.

The fact that the letter dated 11 January was addressed to the minister and not the chancellor had been made clear in the printed agenda placed before the Senate. Matthai followed it up with a reminder on 21 January. He also told Sri Prakasa that the documents in his possession did not tell the full story. There were conversations which he had had with both Mahtab and Morarji Desai, the chief minister, which had an important bearing on the matter but of which necessarily there was no record. Matthai admitted that Sri Prakasa himself did not come into the picture because all the incidents had taken place in his predecessor's time.[38]

Sri Prakasa was miffed and understandably so. Matthai had inexplicably kept him in the dark about the entire affair and he said as much in his letter dated 26 February. He wanted Matthai to take steps to correct the media item by stating categorically that the letter had been addressed to the education minister and not to the Governor.

As for the autonomy of the university, he said that he himself had been so keen on it that when he was chancellor of Madras University, he had allowed full freedom to the vice chancellor even when the latter had referred matters to him. The vice chancellor was however very meticulous in keeping the chancellor informed of everything. 'If I could have been privileged to have the same opportunity with you, I am sure you would have had no grievance,' Sri Prakasa said. Matthai, he said, had failed to inform him even when he did not hear from the education minister.[39]

Sri Prakasa also said that though the issue was one between the university and the chancellor's office, personalities could not be entirely kept out of the picture.

> . . . the emotion with which you are reported to have spoken, and the language that you are reported to have used, do clearly denote to me at least that the question was not being discussed on a purely academic basis, but it did actually refer to those personally who held the offices concerned.[40]

He also said that if a friendly suggestion was construed as an attack on the autonomy of the university, and the Governor referred to in the language that was used, then he would have to ask the government to relieve him as chancellor since the university had no need for him.

Sri Prakasa thought that Matthai's conversation with Mahtab on the subject had given the latter enough reason to believe that there was no opposition to the suggestion about the age limit of the rector. Sri Prakasa said that Matthai only later changed his views in his letter to the education minister in his letter of 11 January 1957. He said that he would have liked the matter to be cleared up during Matthai's tenure, but if that was not possible, he would pursue the matter himself to vindicate the dignity of his office.[41] Matthai's reply on 1 March was brief but there was no doubt about its import. He would fight to the end. He said he would see what steps the Governor took to 'vindicate' his office. If such action took the form of a public statement, then he would also 'reply in the same coin'.[42]

Nehru, in a letter to Sri Prakasa on 2 March 1957, expressed his unhappiness at Matthai's behaviour. Sri Prakasa had also written a letter to the President on 1 March about Matthai's 'very ungraceful and wholly uncalled for public statement' about the Governor. Nehru wrote to Sri Prakasa that he thought Matthai was 'objecting to some letter that your secretary had written about the Rector's age. Now, I find that it was a matter dealt with by Mahtab. However, this does not make much difference, but in a sense, it makes it a little easier for you to say something about it'.[43]

Nehru then proceeded to unburden himself about Matthai and his pernickety behaviour.

Dr Matthai has a very definite trace of utter crankiness. He goes off the rail sometimes completely. He did that when he had to leave our Cabinet. He did this again on a very silly occasion when I was made an honorary Member of the Bombay College of Surgeons, etc. Also, in regard to the State Bank.[44]

There is little doubt that Matthai had over a period of time become rebarbative and prickly. Oversensitive in most matters, it had become difficult to conciliate him.

Nehru asked Sri Prakasa to deal with the matter as he saw fit but not 'allow this matter to rest where it is'. He said that he was in agreement about the autonomy of universities but to call a suggestion by the chancellor an interference was absurd. In any event, it was highly improper to publicly condemn the action of the Governor. Nehru asked if Matthai had disagreed with the Governor on any other issue and wanted Sri Prakasa to explain the matter to the new vice chancellor, and to also write to him officially pointing out the impropriety of Matthai's statement.[45] Matthai's resignation brought to an end this avoidable, and somewhat unpleasant, episode.

* * *

Matthai aired his views on university administration when he delivered the sixth convocation address of The Maharaja Sayajirao University, Baroda, in October 1956 well before the controversy with the Governor. He could hardly have prophesied at the time that it was in defence of these very principles that he would resign as vice chancellor of Bombay University. Matthai said that the application of a democratic system of government to university administration had academic consequences which called for careful consideration. While there was no questioning the fact that the chief governing body of a university should be representative of the best public opinion, he said that in the agencies of the university which dealt with academic work, there was no room for representation of public opinion.[46]

The legislature in which public opinion is represented is exclusively concerned with matters of general policy, but the day-to-day work of the administration and its technical and professional activities are exclusively for the executive whose selection is based on their knowledge and experience and not on their representative character. The academic work ... must be left to the teachers ... and neither the public nor the government should have any voice in it.[47]

He also believed that there was an unfortunate tendency for the elective principle to be applied in appointments to academic bodies. 'The elective principle ... is in universities attended with results which tend to demoralize the teacher and degrade his profession.'[48]

Matthai also touched upon a subject which is perhaps even more relevant today than it was in his time and it is testimony to his prescience that he commented on it at the time he did. He said that although technical and scientific studies had assumed greater importance, he thought that it was equally important to produce graduates with 'balanced judgement and cultured minds who not merely possess knowledge but know how to use it and who understand the art of living in the sense of getting out of life the best and most enduring enjoyment'.[49]

He said that even America, which had the highest level of technological and scientific education, had thought it necessary to introduce the humanities and cultural studies as a corrective to the narrow specialism of scientific education. As to the role of government he observed: 'But to those who value true education and realize how human values languish and be destroyed when Governments combine politics with science to force the pace of development, the time has come to utter a warning of the danger ahead.'[50]

The Controversy over Honorary Fellowships

Matthai's resignation was not the only controversy during his tenure. The College of Physicians and Surgeons, Bombay, had decided to confer honorary fellowships on Nehru and Morarji Desai, the then chief minister of Bombay, and this proved to be a subject of disagreement between Nehru and Matthai. Although the college was under the jurisdiction of the university, Matthai was not consulted and so he took umbrage. He was also, in principle, against public figures holding high office to accept such honours. He wrote to both asking them to refuse the honour. Nehru said that he had refused the offer a number of times in the past and had now agreed because he did not want to continue to be discourteous. All universities gave honorary degrees to public figures and he himself had received many from universities all over the world. He did not think that an Oxford or Cambridge doctorate lost its value because they granted it *honoris causa* to public figures.

> I wish all universities and like bodies would stop giving honorary degrees, except on grounds of pure merit. But as this happens to be almost a universal practice, it is difficult to become too virtuous about it and for me to refuse it. It makes no difference to me. I have received a dozen doctorates ... I wish you would agitate to put an end to this practice.[51]

As a postscript he added: 'Winston Churchill is of course a great man, but he is neither a surgeon nor a scientist. Yet he is an honorary FRCS and FRS. So also, others.'[52] Morarji's reply was brief and to the point. He said that he agreed with the views Nehru had aired in his letter to Matthai, and had decided to accept the honour. He said that he too had refused on a number of occasions and now had decided to accept in the face of persistent requests.[53] In his reply to Nehru on 28 May 1956, Matthai said that he would not have objected had both Nehru and Morarji not held high government positions 'which enable you to confer favours upon people'.

Matthai said that the occasion for his writing as he did was that a similar suggestion had been made to him in Bombay University by certain members of the university, 'mainly of the opportunist class that unfortunately find their way into every academic society and I set my face firmly against it.' So, when he received notice of the holding of a special convocation of the College of Physicians and Surgeons in the very heart of the university's jurisdiction, he naturally felt a little let down. He said that he was well aware of the practice in other countries but said that he still attached importance to this distinction in the present conditions of the country. 'When we are a maturer people democratically, the question may assume a different aspect,' he said.[54]

Matthai did not let the matter rest there. He had not taken Nehru's intention to accept the honorary degree well and followed it up with another very strongly worded and somewhat unpleasant letter to the prime minister. Matthai said that he had made inquiries about the college in question and had concluded that the college had unduly relaxed its standards of medical education, and this was hampering the efforts made by the university to maintain reasonable academic standards.[55]

He said that Nehru's and Morarji's accepting the honour without so much as the courtesy of a previous consultation with the university (or the health ministry) had in his judgement weakened the hands of those who were striving to maintain academic standards. He ended with, 'I regret to say that in so doing you have done a disservice to the cause of university education.'[56] The oversensitive Matthai had overreacted again. He seems to have taken the rejection of his advice personally. Still, it reveals his courage in speaking truth to power, something which is conspicuous by its absence in the present day. It also redounds to Nehru's credit that such dissent was viewed in the right spirit: There was no attempt to threaten and bludgeon those with differing viewpoints into submission.

A Missed Chance?

Matthai's somewhat unhappy tenure ended with his resignation, but it is possible that he may have missed out on a chance to bring pioneering high-level management education to Bombay University. This is even more ironic given the fact that the institution, which was supposed to come up in Bombay, became what we know today as the Indian Institute of Management Ahmedabad (IIMA), an institution in which his younger son, Ravi, was to play a defining role.

In 1955, a decision was taken to establish an institute of management when the central government established a committee under T.T. Krishnamachari to examine the issue. Universities in India were modelled on the British model and had remained oblivious to the development of business education in the USA. In 1953, the All India Council for Technical Education (AICTE) recommended the teaching of management at universities. It also recommended the setting up of an administrative staff college in India. The government created a Board of Management Studies in the Ministry of Education, and in the period 1953–57, seven institutions (including Bombay University) offered part-time diplomas approved by the board. But these catered only to the needs of lower management and lacked both depth and rigour. Nor had any university established connections with industrial and commercial concerns for research or study.

In 1956, the government decided to set up the Administrative Staff College of India (ASCI) at Hyderabad. Matthai became the chairman of the first eighteen-member Court of Governors, which included several senior civil servants and leaders from business and academic communities.

The erstwhile palace of the Prince of Berar at Bella Vista became the campus of the new institution.

On 18 May 1956, ASCI was registered as a society under the Societies Registration Act 1860. General S.M. Shrinagesh was appointed as the first principal of the college on retiring as army chief. He took charge on 8 May 1957 after a six-week stint at the Administrative Staff College, Henley-on-Thames, in England to study the organizational set-up, method of work and details of courses at the behest of the Court of Governors . Academic activities started in 1957 on 6 December, a day that is celebrated each year as ASCI Foundation Day. ASCI quickly became an institute of national importance with international standards.

Meanwhile, the Ford Foundation had also become increasingly active in the field of technical and management education in India. The Foundation had established an office in New Delhi headed by Douglas Ensminger. By 1958, it was playing an important role in establishing institutions such as the Indian Institute of Technology Kanpur.[57]

In March 1955, Ensminger held talks with the Indian and the US governments regarding aid for the establishment of institutions of higher learning in management and technology. The initial dialogue took place between representatives of both governments and the University of Bombay. Matthai was the vice chancellor, and the famous economist Prof. C.N. Vakil headed the department of economics. Both responded favourably to the idea. In early 1957, two Harvard Business School professors, Richard Meriam and Harold Thurlby, came to India on the invitation of the Ford Foundation to prepare a report on the establishment of such an institution. Their report, submitted a little later, recommended a business school on the American model and, more importantly, stressed complete independence of the university system.[58] Unfortunately, by then Matthai had already resigned. Still, it would be reasonable to assume that the idea of an autonomous institution which was not under the control of the university would not have appealed to him.

There, the matter rested for over a year till it was revived in mid-1959 following discussions between Ensminger and the new vice chancellor of Bombay University. Fresh correspondence resulted in the University of California, Los Angeles (UCLA), replacing Harvard Business School as a potential collaborator. In late 1959, associate dean, George W. Robbins, visited India and prepared a report.[59] This and other events leading to the establishment of the IIMA are discussed briefly in the Epilogue which deals with Ravi Matthai's seminal contribution to management education in India. As the first full-time director of IIMA, he continues to be a revered figure in the history of the institute.

National Council of Applied Economic Research

The roots of the National Council of Applied Economic Research (NCAER) lay in Nehru's early vision of a newly independent India needing independent institutions as sounding boards for the government and the private sector. It was the result of a realization that a scientific analysis of the problems facing the country was necessary. The focus of NCAER's work was on generating and analysing empirical evidence to support and inform policy choices. It was perhaps the first think tank in India to combine rigorous analysis and policy outreach with data collection capability, especially for household surveys.

The NCAER was established in 1956 as a public–private partnership, both catering to and funded by the government and private industry. The Ford Foundation provided financial support in the early years, combined with support from the finance ministry and Tata Sons. NCAER's first governing body included cabinet ministers and the leading lights of the private sector, and included C.D. Deshmukh, J.R.D. Tata and Asoka Mehta. It was only appropriate that Matthai should become the first president of the new institution. He had as his Director General P.S. Lokanathan, whose acquaintance we have already made in regard to the Bombay Plan. Matthai gave him a freehand, and Lokanathan's scholarship, combined with his experience at ECAFE, proved to be invaluable in the earlier studies undertaken in the form of techno-economic surveys of the states.

The economic research was to follow a multidisciplinary approach and Matthai wanted the council to be independent of government. The institution had the cooperation of the Stanford Research Institute, California. The NCAER was to act as an unofficial coordinating agency by maintaining close links with research institutions in India in related fields. It marked a major step in the introduction of applied research in understanding the economic problems of India.

Nehru laid the foundation stone for the current campus on 31 October 1959. More than five decades later, on 27 July 2013, Prime Minister Manmohan Singh laid the foundation stone for the new NCAER India Centre that was inaugurated in August 2019. This gave a greatly needed boost to NCAER's infrastructure and the new office tower was appropriately named John Matthai Tower, in honour of its first president. It is perhaps the only example of civic memorialization that honours the memory of a long-forgotten stalwart.

Vice Chancellor, Kerala University

On 1 January 1958, Matthai became the first vice chancellor of the University of Kerala. The university traces its origins to the University of Travancore, founded in 1937, in the erstwhile princely state of Travancore. It came into being by a promulgation of the Maharaja of Travancore and Sir C.P. Ramaswamy Aiyar, the then diwan (prime minister) of the state, was its first vice chancellor. It is said that the government made an unsuccessful attempt to invite Albert Einstein to be the first vice chancellor.[60]

The earliest origins of the university may be traced back to two institutions of modern learning in Kerala: the University College, Trivandrum, and the Trivandrum Observatory. When the University of Travancore was founded, the departments of the college became university departments. They switched back again when the University of Kerala was established in 1957. The University College still retains its connection with the university as an affiliated college. The Trivandrum Observatory, which was founded in 1838, became a part of the Travancore University but was administered as an independent government institution for a while. It is now the oldest institution under the Kerala University.[61]

Many years ago, when the Maharaja of Travancore was thinking of establishing a university at Trivandrum, he had asked Matthai for his opinion on the feasibility of setting up a university. There is an amusing anecdote associated with their meeting. Since Matthai was a Westernized person, the Maharaja realized that in all probability, he would have to shake hands with him. Matthai was a Christian, and since Christians were equated with Shudras, it was thought that any physical contact with him would pollute the royal. According to custom, any contact with a Shudra required a bath to restore ritual purity. It was therefore decided to fix the meeting at the unearthly hour of 5 a.m. so that the Maharaja could have his usual bath after shaking hands with Matthai![62]

Even before the formation of the state of Kerala, there was an attempt at establishing a composite university for the Malayalam-speaking people and in this Cherian Matthai played an active role as director of public instruction of Cochin State. He wanted the university to be located at Alwaye or Trichur and reached out to educationists seeking support for the university. Sadly, none was forthcoming. Kerala's first government was a communist one and the education minister Prof. Joseph Mundassery belonged to Trichur. He had been on the lookout for a suitably eminent Keralite after A. Ramaswami Mudaliar's term ended to become vice chancellor and soon zeroed in on Matthai, who was also a resident of Trichur at the time.

Matthai was unwilling to join; it is possible that his not-so-happy experience in Bombay played a role in this hesitance. It was only when his friend Prof. P. C. Joseph appealed to his sentiments saying that the university had been very dear to his late brother Cherian that Matthai agreed. It is pertinent to note that despite Matthai's right-wing predilections, Kerala's first communist chief minister, E.M.S. Namboodiripad, accepted him as the newly formed Kerala University's first vice chancellor. Nor did the fact that the communists were in power deter Matthai from accepting the position. Both respected each other irrespective of their ideological differences. Deshmukh had by then become chairman of the University Grants Commission (UGC) and extended all help to Matthai. Deshmukh and his wife, Durgabai, visited him at Trichur and Deshmukh in his first John Matthai Memorial lecture recalled 'with poignancy the visit my wife and I paid to him and Smt. Matthai at their newly completed home in Trichur during my visit to the Kerala University and its widely scattered institutions'.[63]

During Matthai's short tenure, two engineering colleges, one arts college and a training college were started and new courses of MD, MS, BDS and B.Lib.Sc were introduced. Three new posts of professors were introduced in education, economics and botany apart from a number of posts of readers and lecturers. The departments of chemistry and statistics were expanded and, more importantly, a three-year degree course was started. Matthai's other achievements included the introduction of grant-in-aid to private colleges and the revision of pay scales of private college teachers through UGC schemes. On 31 October 1959, a mortally ill Matthai resigned his post. He would die two days later, on 2 November, of cancer of the liver at the Tata Memorial Centre, Bombay, the cancer hospital of which he was chairman till his death. The revision of pay scales only took place after Matthai's death.[64]

John Matthai Centre

After the death of his brother Cherian Matthai, John Matthai inherited a vast eighteen-acre estate and a palatial house from his brother. According to Syrian Christian custom, female members were given their share at the time of marriage. Since all the other brothers had passed on, Matthai became the sole inheritor of his brother's property. However, Matthai shared the income from the property among his relatives and even gave his private secretary, Ramakrishna Iyer, a share for helping with the correspondence regarding the estate. When Iyer protested saying he had done nothing special to deserve it, Matthai said, 'Am I entitled to the share? I too have not earned it.'[65]

It was in keeping with this philosophy of her husband that Achamma gave away the entire estate called Matthaipuram for a nominal Rs 5000[66] to the University of Calicut in the mid-1970s. She wanted it to be made into a centre for economics. Matthai would certainly have approved. It is now known as the John Matthai Centre at Aranattukara in Thrissur district which houses a School for Economics and also a School of Drama and Fine Arts. Situated at Laloor, a suburban village, 5 km away from the heart of Thrissur, the cultural capital of Kerala, the large property abounds in greenery and massive trees with picturesque paths running through them.

It was set up in 1976 as a regional centre of the Calicut University under Prof. M.A. Oommen and offered courses in economics, management and associated disciplines. The School of Drama, the brainchild of the poet Vayala Vasudevan Pillai, was a later addition. The John Matthai Centre is now referred to by its acronym, JMC. It is quite possible that with the passage of time, students will forget its full form! Matthai, at best, remains a shadowy figure for the new generation. A bust of Matthai was unveiled in 2017 in front of the building to keep his memory alive. It is not generally known that the JMC is housed in the property which once belonged to him, and was donated by his family.

The large house with its spacious balconies running around the top floor has remained unchanged to this day. Matthai accepted the offer to become vice chancellor of Kerala University on the condition that he would work from a home office, and one of the rooms in the palatial house was converted into the vice chancellor's office. There is now a plaque outside that room which reads: 'Dr John Matthai functioned as vice chancellor of the Kerala University from this room during Jan.1, 1958 to Oct. 31, 1959.'[67]

The JMC has now expanded well beyond economics and dramatics. There is now a School of Management Studies, a Centre for Computer Science and Information Technology, the Calicut University Teacher Education Centre and the Inter-University Centre for Financial Economics/Financial Engineering. It celebrated Matthai's 138th birth anniversary in 2024 with a memorial lecture and a two-day international seminar. In 2022, it issued a special cover and stamp to honour Matthai on his 136th birth anniversary, a function his grandson, Vivek, also attended.

National Book Trust

Matthai was also the first chairman of the National Book Trust (NBT) when it was set up in August 1957. Perhaps, nothing could have been more appropriate given his love for reading and writing. The objectives of the NBT are to produce and encourage the production of good literature in English, Hindi and other Indian languages and to make such literature available at moderate prices to the public. An autonomous body then under the Ministry of Education and now under the Ministry of Human Resource Development, its objectives are to produce and encourage the production of good literature in English, Hindi and other Indian languages and to make such literature available at moderate prices to the public. Its activities include organizing book fairs and seminars and take all necessary steps to encourage the reading habit. Matthai, as its first chairman, played an important role in moulding its future given that he was involved with the Trust in its formative years.

Fertilizers and Chemicals, Travancore Ltd (FACT)

After Matthai retired in Trichur, the Government of India requested him to join the board of directors of FACT, Alwaye, as its chairman. Matthai accepted it in an honorary category. Among the board members was K.R.K. Menon, former finance secretary. Matthai was chairman for two years (July 1957–July 1959). When he joined, the company had a loss of Rs 30 lakh. When he demitted office, the company had not only wiped out the loss but made a marginal profit. He also continued to be vice chancellor of Kerala University at the same time.

20

Eventide

Matthai left Bombay to settle in Trichur, and in mid-1957, J.R.D. Tata wrote him a touching letter. He said that throughout the years they had been together, Matthai had been a wonderful source of strength and comfort and someone to whom he could always turn when troubled or uncertain about any matter and 'get advice which would never compromise on fundamentals, particularly where the prestige of the Firm and the country was involved'.[1]

> When we said goodbye at the aerodrome last month, I found it impossible to express my thoughts, but I think you knew or sensed that I was deeply moved at seeing you go and come to an end our 17 years' association which had meant so much to me. Even though you abandoned me to my fate twice during these years, your absences were provisional; I could look forward to welcoming you back some day, and in the meantime, you always seemed still to be one of us and close to me.[2]

J.R.D. said that Matthai would be missed by all and that he personally would feel more alone. He expressed regret that Matthai had chosen to settle so far away. 'I wish, at least, that you had settled somewhere more within reach!' He ended on a note of humour. 'Homi (Mody) is worried about what will become of you under the Communist influence in your part of the world. He fears that all the years it took him to save your soul will be wasted!'[3]

Matthai responded with equal warmth:

> How good of you to write. I spend my time . . . doing a certain amount of desultory reading. I am discovering good books deserve to be read many

times over and can be a continuing source of pleasure . . . I enjoy reading and also thinking. But the prospect of writing frankly bores me. Will you let me say that in surveying the past, there is no period that gives me such unmixed satisfaction as the time I spent with you in the firm. I wish in some way, some time I could repay the debt.[4]

Padma Vibhushan

In January 1959, Matthai found himself in the honours list when the government awarded him India's second highest civilian award, the Padma Vibhushan. Thereby hangs a tale. On 14 January, Nehru had written to Matthai telling him that they planned to honour him with the Padma Vibhushan.[5]

Matthai, who thought he was being given some sort of title, wrote back on 17 January declining the honour. 'I trust you will not misunderstand me if I say that I had a strong sentimental objection to accepting titles . . . and I would respectfully ask you and the President to excuse me from accepting the title you have so graciously offered me.'[6]

Nehru wrote back clarifying the issue. 'We are forbidden to give titles by our Constitution. These are just awards involving no addition to the name of a person. Perhaps you might reconsider your decision on this basis?'[7] His doubts cleared, Matthai sent his acceptance to Nehru in a briefly worded letter two days later. It was a timely recognition since by the end of the year, Matthai passed away.

A Fatal Illness

Matthai lived a very active life and had no serious health problems. After leaving Tatas in 1957, he wanted to retire completely but was persuaded, as we have noted, to accept the vice chancellorship of Kerala University. In 1958, he suffered frequent bouts of exhaustion but carried on thinking it would pass. It was only in early 1959 that he realized that something was seriously amiss. He went to Bombay for a thorough medical examination. He was admitted to the Tata Memorial Hospital and the worst fears of the doctors were confirmed when he was diagnosed with cancer of the liver. An operation was performed, but the cancer had metastasized and the doctors could do nothing to save him. His condition worsened on

1 November 1959, and he passed away the next day, with his wife and two sons, Duleep and Ravi, by his side.

His body was taken to St Thomas Cathedral in the Fort area the same day and a memorial service was held the next morning. He was buried in the Sewri cemetery, which is also the resting place of the likes of F.W. Stevens, who designed Victoria Terminus (now Chhatrapati Shivaji Maharaj Terminus). The epitaph on his grave, selected by Achamma, has the following lines from the famous hymn 'O Love that wilt not let me go' by George Matheson: 'I give thee back the life I owe/that in thine ocean depth its flow/ may richer fuller be. The offices of Tata Industries, Bombay University, Tata Institute of Fundamental Research (TIFR), TISS and Tata Memorial Hospital (TMH) remained closed as a mark of respect on 2 November. The Tariff Commission passed a resolution mourning his death and closed for the day. Other government organizations with which he was associated also passed resolutions and closed their offices in his memory.

Deshmukh was one of the many high-profile visitors who visited him in hospital. A tone of goodbye lay in the parting. Nothing maudlin, but the sober knowledge of the finiteness of existence. Deshmukh observed, 'It was a sad parting as, although no word was said, it was perhaps realized all round that this was a very serious illness.'[8] Matthai had expressed a wish that Deshmukh should succeed him as chairman of the Court of Governors of ASCI. His wishes were respected and Deshmukh succeeded Matthai as chairman. He acknowledged the work done by his predecessor, 'gratefully conscious of the splendid work that John Matthai had done in guiding the development of that institution in its difficult early years'.[9]

One of the first to condole his death was Nehru, who still retained a lingering ember of fondness. He visited him in hospital in October when told that the end was near. 'I have learnt with sorrow about the death of my old colleague Dr John Matthai. His severe illness from a dreadful disease had partly prepared our mind for the end. Nevertheless, it is sad that a man of his eminence in so many fields of public activity should have left us.'[10] He sent a telegram to Achamma: 'Deeply grieved to learn of John Matthai's passing away. Please accept the expression of my sorrow and deep condolences.'

Edwina Mountbatten sent a telegram on 5 November 1959: 'Please accept our heartfelt sympathy and understanding on your great loss.' Birla sent a telegram the next day: 'Please accept my condolences and sympathies on the death of Dr Matthai. We have lost the services of a great son of

India.' Walchand Hirachand, Morarji Desai and Maniben Patel, Rajendra Prasad, Jivraj Mehta and Y.B. Chavan also sent their condolences. S. Radhakrishnan, G.B. Pant and many others sent telegrams.

On 11 November, J.R.D. wrote to Achamma forwarding a copy of the resolution passed by the Director of Tata Sons and Tata Industries:

> There is no man I respected, loved and trusted more than I did John and, although I saw him rarely – too rarely – since his final retirement in Trichur, it always gave me a feeling of comfort and inner strength to know he was there and I could turn to him in case of need. His loss has left me all the poorer and lonelier and I shall miss him deeply . . . May you find some measure of consolation and comfort in the love and company of your children and grandchildren and in the knowledge that John cannot but be happy wherever he is, for no man I know described more than he, peace, happiness and the blessings of God.[11]

He said that her letter to him and Thelly had touched them deeply. He wrote, 'Please remember dear Achamma that you are and will always be one of the Tata "family" . . . And please always remember that at any time you pass through Bombay, the Cairn is your home there.'[12]

The Lok Sabha condoled his death on 16 November, and this was duly conveyed to Achamma by the secretary of the Lok Sabha secretariat M.N. Kaul. V.P. Menon wrote on 29 November condoling his death. 'To tell you the truth your letter made me and my wife very unhappy . . . If there is anything we can do to help you in any way you need only just write to me.'[13] C.D. Deshmukh and Durgabai sent a telegram: 'Deeply grieved at your tragic bereavement. Our hearts go out to you and your sons in profound sympathy. May God give you fortitude to bear your loss.'

In a handwritten note, Indira Gandhi sent Achamma her condolences on 3 November 1959, a day after Matthai had passed away.

> . . . But I wish I knew what to say. However expected it is, the passing away of a loved one is a shock. Words of sympathy can offer only meagre comfort. And yet there is nothing else one can offer . . . All those who knew Dr Matthai and his work mourn with you.[14]

The *Times of India* in its editorial observed that Dr Matthai would not compromise on what he considered to be matters of fundamental importance. 'In the death of Dr John Matthai the nation has lost a great public servant and an uncommon man. For more than four decades he served his country with distinction displaying a versatility rare in this age.'[15]

Achamma and J.R.D. stayed in touch and the former offered to pay part of the expenses incurred during Matthai's last illness in her letter of 8 April 1961. On 21 April 1961, J.R.D. wrote to her in Trichur in which he politely declined the offer. 'It was intended from the start that we should bear these expenses and the account has been closed long ago. I am touched however by your kind offer.'[16]

* * *

In his life, John Matthai cultivated many gardens. He started life as a lawyer and a minor civil servant and later became a professor, an administrator, a banker and a minister. He did not stick to law for long, his high moral standards coming in the way of pursuing a legal profession as a means of livelihood. In fact, his steadfast adherence to principles throughout his life led him to forsake many lucrative offers. He could never countenance falsehood and hypocrisy, regardless of the level where he encountered it.

Since he had been a director of Tata Sons, and had also been associated with numerous companies as a director in the course of his career, Matthai was dubbed a businessman in most of the obituary notices which appeared in the press. But he could hardly be called a businessman in the way it is understood today, or for that matter even in his time. That appellation would apply to him only if the word business is dissociated from many of the attitudes and values which usually go with it. His counsel and advice were eagerly sought and highly respected in Bombay House since J.R.D. knew that Matthai's advice would never compromise on fundamental values. Matthai had always respected human dignity and did not believe in violating it or in tolerating any violation. He brought an air of learning to the business world. A vision without blinkers, his erudite and enlightened mind soared above the immediate and the present, and this was apparent in his sagacious advice and wise counsel whenever it was solicited.

His most outstanding contribution while he was with the Tata Sons was his work on the Bombay Plan which gave concrete shape to the urge for economic development and made a vast advance on the very tentative work of the pre-war National Planning Committee of the Congress. Matthai brought his deep scholarship to everything he worked on. He was nothing if not thorough and laborious. But his mind was not one which admitted of snap decisions. It was a powerful, searching mind which grappled simultaneously with numerous variables but only after it had reduced these variables to manageable proportions, shorn of the non-essentials. The variables themselves, however, were not abstract entities, but parts of reality. He seemed to delight, not in abstract theory, but in grappling with facts, and reducing them to order, searching out the interrelations between them. He had a sure feel in his own way of rural India and of agriculture, and it had always been his dream to retire to Kerala and spend his last years in experimenting with peasant cultivation on a co-operative basis.[17]

Matthai's ministerial appointments were unusual, the administrative challenges he faced were formidable, and his exit from government unexpected. He was the target of much criticism in both his cabinet posts. He faced it with self-deprecating humour though on occasion his retorts could be sharp since he did not suffer fools or hypocrisy gladly. He was in charge of the railways at one of the most trying times in its history and faced the horrors of Partition and the subsequent bifurcation of the railway system. When he took charge of the finance ministry, the steep rise in prices of food was his biggest worry. He favoured the resumption of controls and was proved right in the end.

In his attitude to material things, Matthai was detached without being otherworldly. He remained firmly grounded in solid earth when other men of his age turned to religious or spiritual pursuits. Matthai could have retired comfortably, laden with honours, to enjoy well-deserved peace and quiet, but he was never one to reject a call for public service. When Deshmukh invited him to become chairman of the newly formed SBI, he accepted. It was neither money nor honours he was seeking. In fact, for a man who had been in charge of the finance portfolio, this was an assignment far below his stature, but Matthai believed that he had something to contribute and did not let the official hierarchy interfere with his spirit of public service. That eventually the government could not utilize his services to the best advantage is another story.

Matthai had the distinction of presiding over the destinies of many institutions during their infancy. Apart from the SBI, he was, as we have seen, the first president of ASCI, the first president of NCAER and the first chairman of NBT. In 1953, he chaired the Taxation Enquiry Commission, which sought, by devising an appropriate tax structure, to give shape and body to the socialistic pattern of society which India had adopted. The Taxation Enquiry Committee's report was primarily the work of a man who believed in the fundamentals of a new economic order, although in the shaping of it, he found himself out of sympathy with its main architect, Jawaharlal Nehru.[18] For sheer variety of offices, formal and informal only C.D. Deshmukh, his successor as finance minister, could boast of a greater variety of associations.

What about Matthai's views on socialism and the role of the state? Socialism, according to Matthai, was a difficult concept to define. Its theory had been variously explained and there was little agreement as regards its practice in countries which had adopted it. It was not a definite creed or type of organization but rather a way of life, an attitude to society which aimed at the widest practicable diffusion of social justice by methods which were appropriate to a democratic country. As for the role of the state, Matthai warned against a 'tendency to overestimate its potentialities of use' and said that it should not be made to carry a bigger burden than it could bear. He said that while the while the individual in a well-ordered state under good leadership could stand a great deal of discipline, there was a limit beyond which the individual would begin either to languish or to rebel. In the light of India's experience in the eight years after Independence, he believed that there was greater need for objectivity on the part of both planners and statesmen.[19]

Matthai was a man of great integrity not merely in its narrow sense, but in the wider intellectual sense. His impartiality, sound judgement and unfailing courtesy made him a respected man in all circles. He disagreed, and disagreed quite vehemently, with Nehru on the Planning Commission. Perhaps he overreacted, but Matthai never hesitated in speaking his mind. As Nehru had pointed out, both to Matthai and to his other correspondents, Matthai's extreme irritation, even antipathy, seemed to have its roots elsewhere, something he was unable to identify. It was this feeling that led Matthai to go public with his grievances leaving Nehru with no choice but to defend himself. Nehru had been quite conciliatory, even friendly, in his communication with Matthai. In February 1950, he had sent him a photograph of his and signed it 'In Friendship'. Nehru had offered the peace pipe, but Matthai for some reason, refused to take a puff. Some years after the resignation, the ice did not break, but it started to melt, leading to Matthai's subsequent appointments in the Taxation Enquiry Commission and the SBI.

Matthai came into his own as an educationist as vice chancellor of Bombay University. It was by no means a distinction crowning a distinguished career, but he brought to that office unprecedented dignity in that institution's centenary year. We have already noted that he was a zealous advocate of untrammeled university autonomy, suggesting that it would be better if Governors ceased to be chancellors of universities. Far from being a personal reflection on the incumbent in Raj Bhavan (though Matthai, perhaps, failed to make that clear, causing some hurt), it was the testament of an educationist averse to political poaching in the realm of university education.

Perhaps we should let Deshmukh have the last word with his masterful estimate of Matthai in the first lecture of his John Matthai Memorial lecture series. Deshmukh said that he admired Matthai,

> . . . as one of India's most cultured products, endowed with a rare combination of qualities, a perceptive and thoughtful mind, a sobriety of judgement in regard to men and affairs, a rare concern for principles, a delightful sense of humour with the soupcon of cynicism natural to a man of the world, scholarliness with its flame kept by regular reading, and fluency and cogency of expression which profoundly influenced those who heard him.[20]

Epilogue

Matthai's Sons

Ravi

Bombay, as we have already noted in an earlier chapter, was one of the probable locations for an institute of management. Talks in this regard had already started when Matthai was vice chancellor. The associate dean of UCLA, George Robbins, came to India and presented a detailed plan. Robbins proposed an autonomous institute (he wanted an autonomous society under the Societies Registration Act 1860) and proposed that the scope of activities, include teaching, research and consulting. His report also outlined the number of students to be admitted over a ten-year period, the criteria for admissions and the evaluation of student performance. It also made detailed recommendations on how the faculty was to be developed.

The Robbins report was accepted in principle by the Planning Commission in 1959 and in mid-1960 the ministry took several steps towards its implementation. However, there were two significant points of departure from the Robbins report. The report had recommended one institute, but the government decided on two. Initially, it seemed that the locations would be Bombay and Calcutta, but by September 1960, it became clear that the second location would be Ahmedabad. This happened due to a variety of reasons. A lukewarm response from Bombay University and the Maharashtra government, the role played by the Gujarat government, and the support of local businessman like Kasturbhai Lalbhai, a prominent millowner who put his faith in Vikram Sarabhai, were all contributory factors.

Sarabhai, the scion of a famous family from Ahmedabad, is best known as the founder of India's space programme. A cosmic-ray physicist who did his tripos and then his PhD from Cambridge, he succeeded

Homi J. Bhabha as chairman of the Atomic Energy Commission on the former's demise. He was also an institution builder par excellence, being associated with many institutions in Ahmedabad as founder or a central figure. Foremost among them are the Physical Research Laboratory, the Ahmedabad Textiles Industry's Research Association (ATIRA) and IIM Ahmedabad (IIMA).

IIMA came into existence in December 1961, with Sarabhai as the honorary director, a post he would hold for three-and-a-half years. He was responsible for the institution's autonomy. It was run by a board that was accountable to a society and not directly to the government. It was decided not to have it set up by an Act of Parliament (a requirement to award degrees), as otherwise that would have placed it under the supervision of Parliament. This is why the IIMs only award a diploma and not a degree. Wanting only the best, Sarabhai also insisted on having Harvard Business School (HBS) as a partner. His getting the famous architect, Louis Kahn, to design the building was another masterstroke. All that remained was to find a full-time director.

Collaborating with Sarabhai in the IIMA project were three other remarkable individuals. The first was Kasturbhai Lalbhai, the founder of Arvind Mills and a textile magnate, who embraced the idea enthusiastically and even contributed to the costs of building in the early stages. The second was Prakash Tandon, the first Indian chairman of Hindustan Lever, who had wide experience both in the public and private sectors. He became chairman of the IIMA board after the chief minister, Jivraj Mehta, demitted office.

Last, but certainly not the least, was Kamla Chowdhry, Sarabhai's friend and companion, who had a doctorate in psychology from Michigan University and was associated with Sarabhai in ATIRA. She played no small role in conceptualizing IIMA with Sarabhai. Married to an ICS officer who was posted in Pakistan in the 1940s, she was widowed just three months after marriage when her husband was shot dead by a man he had tried in his capacity as district magistrate. The accused thought that he could escape the sentence by killing the judge. Kamla knew Sarabhai's wife, Mrinalini, from their Shantiniketan days, and was warmly welcomed into the Sarabhai fold when she moved to Ahmedabad. But that came with its own set of problems. A certain intimacy developed between her and Sarabhai and this ménage à trois took its toll on everyone.

Since Sarabhai was only honorary director, the task of actually running the institute fell on Chowdhry, who was designated as coordinator of programmes. She was assisted by an administrative officer. Sarabhai wanted her to be designated as deputy director, but the board disagreed. They thought that the task of finding a full-time director would be complicated if a deputy director was already running the show. Not unsurprisingly, Chowdhry felt a little let down. The search for a director continued, but no one suitable was found. Many thought that Tandon and Sarabhai were purposely dragging their feet so that the post could ultimately go to Chowdhry. Then suddenly quite out of the blue in 1965, Tandon and Sarabhai settled on a young man with no serious academic credentials or experience: Ravi Matthai, John Matthai's younger son.

Ravi Matthai was just thirty-eight at the time and had a BA (Hons) from Oxford. On his return from Oxford, he joined Messrs McNeill and Barry, a managing agency firm in India. In 1957, he became chief executive of Kilburn and Company. He was a corporate executive for twelve years, but his heart was in an academic career and when the offer of senior professor came from IIM Calcutta (IIMC) in 1963, he was happy to accept. When Sarabhai and Tandon met him, in 1964, Ravi was teaching at a workshop for executives held in Srinagar. Impressed with his clarity of thinking and confidence, they seemed to have decided almost immediately that their search had ended. Ravi was of medium build, but he oozed personality, and people could not help noticing that there was something different about the way he carried himself. Ravi then met the representatives of HBS at IIMA and the head of the Ford Foundation in India. Both immediately approved the choice and IIMA wasted no time in making its offer. But Ravi was reluctant to accept because he had just joined IIMC and had also been sent to the Massachusetts Institute of Technology for training. The IIMA board persisted, and Ravi finally joined the institute in August 1965.

It must be noted that unlike many others in important positions, John Matthai did not believe in promoting the careers of his children. Ravi never used his illustrious father's name or connections to further his career, nor did he ever advertise his family background. Ravi's corporate life had little in common with his father's; what was passed on, however, was a set of values and fierce integrity.[1]

When Sarabhai told his wife Mrinalini that he had found someone called Ravi Matthai from Calcutta to become the new director, he found to his surprise that she knew who he was. It turned out that the Swaminathans (Mrinalini's family) and the Matthais were family friends. Mrinalini would spend a night at Calcutta with the Matthais en route to Shantiniketan, where she was studying. John Matthai, Mrinalini said, was her idea of an ideal man. 'He and his wife Achamma, were very dear friends of our family and I always thought that he personified everything one would like in a man and I hero-worshipped him.'[2] She remembered Ravi too, who had on one of her visits proudly proclaimed that he could sing 'Vande Mataram' from memory and had proceeded to sing it with noticeable patriotism. She told her husband that Ravi was just the right man to build IIMA. Mrinalini recalled in an article written after Ravi's premature demise, 'When I met him again his face was still the same. He was still the eager boy who sang "Vande Mataram", so full of ideals, so full of plans for the future. And I was really happy when I heard that he was going to take up this great institution.'[3]

Director of IIMA

When Ravi joined as director, he found that many aspects of the flagship Postgraduate Programme (PGP) were the source of discontent among students. He streamlined the PGP and dealt with student disturbances by having long chats with students, using his great persuasive powers to convince them. That he was also a transparently sincere person also helped. His other challenge was getting industry to accept the PGP. It was Ravi and his colleagues who did the hard work of selling the PGP to industry.

A key decision that Ravi took after becoming director was to end the collaboration with HBS. The reasons were never made clear, but perhaps he felt that the collaboration was not benefitting the institute the way it should. HBS was not doing enough by way of sending faculty. What is more, there was no reciprocity: IIMA faculty could not teach at HBS. Nor was there any collaboration in research. Ravi also discontinued IIMA's participation in the Integrated Training Programme at Harvard. He wanted faculty training to be need-based: some faculty could go for a PhD, some for an MBA and not all to HBS. Both were controversial decisions which were debated at the time (and perhaps still are), but Ravi had the courage of his convictions to see them through.

Ravi's greatest strength lay in his people skills. Practically no one knew him personally when he first came to Ahmedabad, but his amiable personality and unassuming nature won him friends almost immediately. His unerring judgement of people and his skill in managing them contributed in no small measure to his success. He devoted much effort to recruiting faculty, which more than doubled in his time, with many returning to India from abroad. He was very good at selling IIMA to Indian academics in the US and persuading them to return. This was one of his biggest contributions to the fledgling institution. IIMA was cash-strapped when Ravi joined, but he managed to persuade the central government to loosen its strings and soon funding ceased to be an issue. That he did this without compromising on the autonomy of the institute is worth noting.

It was also under Ravi that IIMA developed its sectoral focus by setting up centres for agriculture and education. Sarabhai and Ravi both believed that IIMA should develop expertise in other sectors such as agriculture, education, banking, trade unions and government systems. The centre for agriculture came up in Ravi's time and, in due course, the two-year programme in agriculture. During his tenure, IIMA commenced its Fellowship Programme in Management (FPM), as its doctoral programme is known.

IIMA developed an enviable reputation for excellence, and it is a tribute to the culture Ravi established that this reputation has endured. IIMA's success can be ascribed to the culture that was created in its formative years when Sarabhai and Ravi were at the helm and remains a distinguishing feature of the institute. IIMA is a prime example of how an organization's culture can become a differentiator and a source of competitive advantage.

What is this IIMA culture? Its three pillars were autonomy, faculty freedom and faculty governance. Autonomy refers to freedom from outside interference. Faculty freedom includes both freedom of expression and also operational freedom. These elements were carefully fostered by Sarabhai and Ravi in their time, and it proved to be an enduring contribution. Faculty governance is another important distinguishing feature of IIMA. All important decisions, and certainly all academic decisions, were taken by the faculty.[4]

This decentralized governance model was conceived by Sarabhai and given practical shape by Ravi. Hierarchy was all but absent and junior faculty could speak as freely as senior faculty. This brought out the best in everyone and also helped in developing a strong peer culture. Faculty attended each other's classes and discussed cases. They also commented on each other's research. First names were used to address people reflecting the egalitarian culture.[5] The director was 'Ravi' to his colleagues.

Ravi believed in consensus and participative decision-making. There was no autocratic way of doing things and he believed in persuading rather than dictating. And he was as much willing to be persuaded as to persuade. Open to new ideas, Ravi never thought in terms of stereotypes. While he was open to the ideas of others, he balanced these against his own inner convictions. But if consensus rather than conflict was the watchword, there was little doubt about who was in charge. It was Ravi, and he did not hesitate to impose his will when the situation demanded. The doctoral programme and the introduction of the agriculture programme are cases in point.[6]

It is important to note that as director, Ravi focused mainly on policy matters, discussions on which he actively involved the faculty. Once the policy was decided, he played no role in the actual implementation: Ravi did not believe in micro-management. He delegated authority but never responsibility. As he observed, 'In my concept of delegation, I don't have to enter the kitchen to find out whether the rice is burning, but I must have the sense to know if it is burning.'[7]

A noteworthy feature of Ravi's administrative style was the absence of elaborate rules and regulations. He believed that each case was unique and hence rules were of little use. Nor was he one for following precedents. 'I am not bound hand and foot by precedents. Following a precedent very often is nothing but the perpetuation of an earlier mistake.'[8] The other element was the absence of administrative authority for activity heads and area heads. They had no authority to dictate but had to persuade their colleagues. In this atmosphere everyone could express their creativity without being stifled by needless rules and excessive authority. It was precisely this atmosphere that led to a feeling that all were equal partners in institution-building and led to an environment that was conducive to the achievement of excellence.

It is also important to take into consideration individual personalities in the establishment of a new culture. IIMA's culture is a result of not only of the principles described above, but also the personalities and managerial abilities of Sarabhai and Ravi. The former was a charismatic leader and the latter a gifted manager and leader. This explains why the culture and processes they put in place have endured for so long.[9]

Perhaps Ravi's greatest contribution to the system was his insistence on the principle of a single term for the director. In January 1972, after seven years at the helm, he resigned as director. Ravi was only forty-five and at the peak of his powers. Very few were aware that one of the conditions when he accepted the job was that he would stay as director only for five to seven years. It was an act of renunciation that was rare then, and perhaps impossible to encounter in today's times, when even octogenarians in their dotage still cling to positions of power. But Ravi clarified that while he was resigning the post of director, he would like to continue as faculty, something he did for twelve years, never asking for any special concessions or ever interfering in any manner with the management of the institute.

What were Ravi's reasons for resigning? He believed that as an organization evolves, it needs different styles of leadership, a fresh vision and different structures. As he wrote in his letter of resignation, he did not want 'the individual in charge to become the ideologically vested focal point of no change'[10] and wanted a new incumbent with whom vision was not a vested interest, thereby providing a fresh point of view from which the institute could move forward. He said that in each major stage of development a change of style was desirable and the institute may need to change the trajectory of its development. If that were to be the case, then others with more suitable styles would be required. What Ravi was trying to convey can perhaps be best summed up in his own words: 'Many institutions in India have suffered either from instability due to frequent changes of the chief executive ... irrespective of institutional needs, or have suffered from stagnation as a result of the perpetuation of an individual who becomes the institutionalised image of a no-change continuity, once again, irrespective of institutional needs.'[11]

After resigning, Ravi received numerous lucrative offers from government and the corporate sector but spurned them all. As Tata stalwart, Sir Jehangir Ghandy, told a faculty member when Ravi was still the director: 'Ravi can put on a piece of paper the position and the emolument he would like to have, fold the paper, and give it to us. We would say "yes" to his terms before looking at the paper. But your director wants to remain a school master.'[12]

When Ravi was asked about his future plans on the day he handed over charge, he said that he would like to develop a university of applied learning. He was as good as his word and devoted himself to a unique experiment in rural education in the arid Jawaja block of Ajmer district in Rajasthan. Jawaja village is 70 km from Ajmer and the block at the time comprised 200 villages with a population of 80,000. But before we come to Ravi's famous Jawaja experiment, let us take a look at his thoughts on management education which have a direct bearing on what he tried to achieve in Jawaja.

Management Education: Progress and Problems

Ravi stressed that the context of knowledge was of great importance in the early stages of training people in various sectors. If a district official was to be trained in the use of control systems using the example of Bhilai Steel Plant, then it would make little sense to him. 'If therefore the people managing the processes of a sector are to be trained, the teaching material that goes into their training should bear heavily on the context in which they function.'[13] He believed that the research work done in any sector should not only provide a basis for better policy-making and problem-solving but should also be developed into teaching material. He also stressed the need to develop an indigenous body of knowledge.

> This does not stem from emotional patriotism. There are enough xenophobic noises in the country without adding to them. The need for indigenous materials is a necessary part of the structure we are trying to evolve on the assumption that learning is accelerated by the contextual relevance of what is being learnt. The need stems therefore from commonsensical practicality.[14]

Ravi advocated a few broad-based institutions which would cover a wide range of sectors and serve as the country's centres of excellence He called them the Indian academies of applied knowledge whose role would be to create knowledge, develop acceptance of the use of this knowledge in the sectors to which they catered, develop relevant teaching materials, train intensively a small number of managers who would act as multipliers, and build teachers and researchers in relation to both academic fields and to the relevant sectors. He said that there would be two multiplier effects: The first would be the early output of highly trained managers who would train people under them. The second effect would be the centres of excellence themselves becoming institution builders. He observed, 'To get even to this stage will take time and the restraint of deliberate patience. But I wonder, whether in our circumstances, crash programmes aimed at large numbers don't tend to crash.'[15]

His idea was to build a body of knowledge about the operations of each sector: knowledge that was relevant to, and could be used by policymakers and managers of that sector, and other sectors as well. The idea was to build channels through which this knowledge could be transferred across the boundaries of sectors so that they could see in this knowledge an integrated view of India's economy. Ravi realized that this was an ideal situation which may never be realized, but he thought that the implication of what he called a 'University of Applied Knowledge' was something worth thinking about.[16] He believed that resolution of problems required an interdisciplinary approach. A problem occurs in a context. If problems are to be resolved, then one must understand the context in which those problems occur. Ravi observed, 'To my mind it is very necessary that in developing applied knowledge we should do so rather on the basis of an interdisciplinary and intersectoral approach, and my thesis, my advocation is that I think we should be developing what I call universities or academies of applied knowledge.'[17]

Just as there was a need to develop and transfer knowledge across sectors, so it was necessary to transfer operational knowledge between the sectors and the government since the government was concerned with all sectors of the nation's activities. Also, there were research institutions which were far too removed from the world of practice to be able to bridge the communication gap: He wanted a study to be made if a chain of organizations from fundamental research to the production of goods and services was required which would ensure that the gaps between successive organizations in the chain were not so great as to inhibit the transfer of knowledge.[18]

He gave the example of the Council of Scientific and Industrial Research (CSIR), which was criticized for doing nothing to raise the standard of living of the people. Ravi attributed it to the large gap between the laboratories themselves and the people who could use that knowledge. He said, 'One raises the question whether in fact there is a gap in communication that is so great that the scientist in his laboratory cannot talk to the product development officer in the country.'[19]

The Rural University

Ravi concluded that the problem of primary education could be addressed only by relating it to the economic activities of the villagers. The Rural University was nothing like a traditional university. It was about informal rather than structured learning, and its basic objective was to link rural development with rural education. Rural education could only be relevant to rural development if it involved economic activities of the area. The Rural University was not an organization in a structured sense; it was an idea. The catalysts for the experiment were a team of outsiders called independent volunteers, who would meet the villagers and help them formulate ideas for improving productivity and generating more income. Local teachers and village-level officials would also be part of this Rural University. Ravi and his colleagues comprised the core team.[20]

How would the learning take place? It was basically learning by doing. In Ravi's words,

> They recognise others as members of this community by their having given of themselves to others and others of themselves to them . . . They learn technologies, how to manage their affairs, how to create bridges of mutual help between individuals and groups. They learn about societies beyond the limits of their past experiences, of institutions and processes which will enable them to establish links with the world beyond their immediate environment. They learn about urban and metropolitan markets, about supply and demand, of products, design and pricing. They learn to cost their activities and keep accounts. They learn about financial institutions and the banking habit. They learn about government systems, educational and research institutions, and in establishing links with them they learn from their experiences as to how these links can help them grow . . . They learn that the autonomy of others to build themselves is only as real as is their regard for the autonomy of others to build themselves. All this they learn by doing.[21]

Ravi emphasized that the development of rural India would occur not through mere target-oriented plans but through the development of people. He called the university 'a locator, enabler, provider and organiser of learning wherever the opportunities for learning might exist or may be created'. These could be a villager's hut, a teashop, around a well, a government office, a bank counter or a shop. Learning could occur just about anywhere, with all members of this 'university' involved in learning and helping others learn.[22] One of Ravi's greatest qualities was his capacity to listen to others, even the so-called 'illiterates' and to respect their views. He readily acknowledged that it was in fact he who was learning. But that was his innate modesty. Ravi gave the villagers much more than he got.[23]

Ravi was aware of the somewhat abstract nature of his concept. If anyone connected with this was asked a question about belonging to a university, they would be surprised. 'They are unaware of being "institutionalised" because they have not been 'organised'.[24] They were aware of only having shared an experience for which there was no label. Then why use a label at all? Ravi said that a label was required to give the idea an identity to which reference could be made 'to provide a visible link between those who have this common bond, and may be, to throw a phrase, perhaps not particularly original, into the educational dovecot with the hope that some fluttering occurs'.[25]

Since Ravi realized that there were a host of problems with the educational system, instead of trying to change the school system directly, he tried to bring about changes in the village community, which in turn might transform the school system. Integrating economic activities with rural education would give it a new meaning. Education would be provided not only in vocational skills but the entire gamut of business activities.

The problems Ravi faced and the details of the Jawaja experiment are beyond the scope of this brief epilogue. Ravi devoted the last eight years of his life to this project and wore himself out in the process. He suffered his first heart attack in 1977 but never slackened his pace. He drove a five-tonne Tata truck to Jawaja and back numerous times, shared dak bungalows with his colleagues, ate at dhabas and became more accessible as a person. He played raga 'Malkauns' on his flute and once asked a volunteer to teach him to play the guitar to see if he could play raga 'Bageshwari' on it.[26]

What did Ravi think he had gained from the experiment? He was unconcerned at the lack of material outcome since for him, the Jawaja project was an open-ended experiment from which he and his colleagues kept learning. Success or failure was not relevant. What was important was the learning from live situations so that concepts and strategies could be varied in further experimentation. An approach imposes its own constraints, and Ravi thought it necessary to start a series of experiments in which other approaches could be tried out.

Was the experiment a success? Many people at IIMA dismissed it out of hand and thought that Ravi's efforts had produced no results. Others saw it as a forerunner to several initiatives in the social sector. But that perhaps is missing the point. We should let Ravi have the last word. 'The inspiration of a vision motivates great effort however short we may fall of our goal. Every major responsibility requires it. A house without a vision is so many walls and a roof. It is a bare physical structure without a soul.'[27]

* * *

In December 1983, Ravi went to London with his wife, Sylloo, for a bypass operation. The operation appeared to be successful, but then he developed a clot again and had to be hospitalized. An emergency operation was performed in which most of his intestine was also removed. Ravi fought on gamely but ultimately succumbed on 13 February 1984. He was cremated at Golden Green cemetery in London. Syloo and the children Radha, Vivek, Nitya and Ashok, immersed his ashes in the Sabarmati River in Ahmedabad. But Ravi lives on at IIMA: in its culture, its conventions and in the things and the people he built. There are two memorials to his name: the Ravi Matthai Auditorium and the Centre for Educational Innovation. Sarabhai, the founder, has a library named in his memory.

Duleep

Ravi's elder brother, Duleep, was a pioneer in his field too. Born on 18 October 1924, he was a highly influential and pioneering figure in India's nascent environmental movement in the 1970s. He was among the first to raise awareness of the long-term environmental risks arising from the loss of forest cover that comes with unchecked agricultural and industrial development. Duleep's love of nature and wildlife developed from his early childhood growing up in his uncle Cherian Matthai's forested estate in Kerala. He understood the ecological role played by forests long before it became widely accepted realizing that the loss of large expanses of forests through human activity, especially in the tropical regions and uplands of India, posed a serious threat to human welfare and even survival. The current water scarcity in many parts of the country today can be attributed to both loss of forest cover and excessive water extraction with ever deeper bore wells. Securing the country's water-catchment areas—the forests—was a key campaign for Duleep.[28]

Duleep was a founding trustee of the World Wildlife Fund (WWF) in India and played an active role in promoting the organization within the country. He was largely instrumental in getting land allotted for setting up the WWF head office in New Delhi. Prime Minister Indira Gandhi discussed environmental issues with him from time to time and also invited him to join as a member of important advisory bodies set up by the government, such as the National Committee of Environment Planning and Coordination and the Indian Board of Wildlife chaired by the prime minister. Duleep was also consulted when the Department of Environment was established in 1980.

In the 1980s, Duleep was appointed to the governing bodies of the newly established Indian Institute of Forest Management at Bhopal and the Wildlife Institute of India at Dehradun. He was also a member of the steering committee of Project Tiger. Later, as vice chairman of the National Wastelands Development Board set up by Prime Minister Rajiv Gandhi, Duleep toured the country extensively to understand the challenges of restoring biodiversity, including the native species of flora, to degraded barren tracts. His solutions included aerial seeding wherever feasible. Professor M.S. Swaminathan, the eminent scientist and father of India's 'Green Revolution', regarded Duleep as the father of the ecological movement in India and described his commitment to the conservation of nature and the development of WWF India as 'truly monumental'.[29]

Duleep started his career as a management trainee in the tea industry in Assam with Jardine Henderson in 1944. In 1960, he moved to Bombay initially as J.R.D. Tata's executive assistant, before taking on senior roles in other Tata companies. Despite his busy schedule, he still found time to assist, Salim Ali, the renowned ornithologist, in extending the conservation work of the Bombay Natural History Society. The two became lifelong friends.

When he was in his mid-50s, Duleep gave up his corporate career to focus all his energies on nature conservation and environmental protection. In 2001, he became a founding trustee of the Foundation for Ecological Security, an NGO that is actively involved in the task of ecological restoration in the country. In 2007, he set up the Duleep Matthai Nature Conservation Trust, to which he donated the major part of his personal assets.[30]

The man who had played a pioneering role in trying to make people understand that the destruction of forests would end up exhausting the water supplies passed away on 5 March 2017 at the age of ninety-two, in Vallabh Vidyanagar, Gujarat. He was fond of saying: 'Nature does not need us. We need Nature.'[31] If there is a lot more environmental awareness today, we have Duleep's pioneering efforts to thank for it.

Acknowledgements

This biography of John Matthai has been many years in the making and owes much to the terrier-like tenacity of Vivek Matthai, who felt (and quite justifiably so) that his grandfather deserved a full-fledged biography. The plans for this book were laid more than eight years ago, just after my biography of Zubin Mehta was published, when I promised him that I would one day write his grandfather's biography. That it has become a reality only now is largely due to the fact that it was written in the interstices of my other work; I have not been able to follow the discipline of a professional writer. That two other books and Covid-19 intervened, only added to the delay.

My biggest debt of gratitude, therefore, is to Vivek, who while waiting patiently, gently nudged me in the direction of finally starting work on the promised biography. He provided books, letters, documents, photographs and any other material he thought relevant, over the years. As I dug for material in archives and libraries, Vivek tried his best to unearth material in the possession of the family and which had remained untouched for more than six decades. This included one serendipitous find of great value just as I was about to send the manuscript to the publisher. My grateful thanks are also due to Syloo Matthai, a spry and alert nonagenarian, Vivek's mother, and John Matthai's daughter-in-law, for sharing her memories with me and for agreeing to write the foreword.

I have accumulated many debts along the way. My greatest debt is to the Prime Minister's Memorial Library (formerly the Nehru Memorial Museum and Library), New Delhi, where I accessed the John Matthai papers. This is also the repository of the C.D. Deshmukh and Sir Purshotamdas Thakurdas papers, which have also proved to be useful in the writing of this biography. In particular, I would like to thank Vikas Kumar, library and information officer, who eased my way at every step. The Tata Central Archives provided photos and whatever material they had on John Matthai with great dispatch. Grateful thanks are owed to Rajendra Narla for his prompt response and assistance.

Inevitably, a book such as this with its emphasis on research must owe a heavy debt to libraries and archives. I would like to thank the staff at the following institutions: National Archives of India; Railway Board Library at Rail Bhavan; Central Secretariat Library, New Delhi; Parliament Library, New Delhi; Delhi Public Library, India Habitat Centre Library, New Delhi; India International Centre Library, New Delhi; A.A. Jasdenvala Library of the Cricket Club of India, Mumbai; Mumbai University Library, and the F.E. Dinshaw Commercial and Financial Reference Library, Mumbai.

A book is made possible by many institutions and people. This biography of John Matthai is based on the work of a large number of scholars and authors apart from a plethora of letters, documents and other archival records. My bibliography illustrates the full scale of my debt, but I owe an especially heavy debt to certain books and articles, and it is only appropriate that I acknowledge these with a special mention. The book owes much to *Dr John Matthai, 1886–1959: A Biography*, by V. Haridasan, which has been one of the foundations for this work. I am also beholden to Rakesh Ankit's *India in the Interregnum: Interim Government, September 1946–August 1947*, B.K. Nehru's *Nice Guys Finish Second*, Mircea Raianu's *Tata: The Global Corporation That Built Indian Capitalism*, T.T. Ram Mohan's *Brick by Red Brick: Ravi Matthai and the Making of IIM Ahmedabad*, Medha Kudaisya's *Tryst with Prosperity: Indian Business and the Bombay Plan of 1944* and all of R.M. Lala's books on the Tatas, including *Beyond the Last Blue Mountain*, his biography of J.R.D. Tata. Last but not least, John Matthai's long manuscript on his experiences in the collection at the PMML has proved to be invaluable.

Grateful thanks are due to all those who helped along the way. Milee Ashwarya, who commissioned the book, was enthusiastic about it from the start and brought her usual energy to the venture. This is our fourth book together and her support has been unstinting and encouragement, unvarying. Thanks are also due to Hitha Haridas and Manali Das, the editors of this book. An editor is often an author's best friend, and their diligent editing has brought the book to its final, publishable shape. While all efforts have been made to ensure that the facts are accurate and that no citation has been inadvertently missed out, I will be happy if errors, which I hope are not too numerous, are brought to my notice.

I would be remiss if I did not mention the contributions of B.M. Deepak and Bhavna Malhotra in assisting my research. Deepak cheerfully downloaded many megabytes of data from the Internet that included reports on parliamentary debates, numerous volumes of the correspondence of Nehru and Patel, respectively, apart from many articles. He also printed and bound some of the more important research material. Deepak also helped in many other ways, being my go-to person for all things concerning computers and information technology. I owe him my grateful thanks.

Bhavna not only typed my research notes but was also a vital link between me and the PMML, the repository of the Matthai papers. As my principal private secretary, she helped in a myriad other ways, making life easier as I struggled to strike a balance between my day job and the growing demands of the book. My thanks also go out to Ashish Mahajan, my former technical assistant in Mumbai, who was instrumental in sending me material from Mumbai as and when required. J. Sukesh Deepak was of great assistance in many ways and has my grateful thanks. I would also like to thank my friend Devendra Singh for the author photo.

My mother, Rati, my sister, Tushna, brother-in-law, Phiroze, and my nephew, Navroze, have been most supportive. As always, their encouragement and enthusiasm have proved to be crucial.

Notes

Introduction

1 V. Haridasan, *Dr John Matthai, 1886–1959: A Biography*, Publication Division, University of Calicut, 2000, p. 159.
2 Ibid., p. 40.
3 Ibid., p. 99.
4 Ibid., p. 102.
5 Ibid., pp. 101–02.
6 R.M. Lala, *Beyond the Last Blue Mountain: A Life of J.R.D. Tata (1904–1993)*, Penguin Viking, New Delhi, 1993, p. 207.

PART I

Chapter 1: The Matthais of Kottayam

1 V. Haridasan, *Dr John Matthai, 1886–1959: A Biography*, Publication Division, University of Calicut, 1985, pp. 2–3.
2 'Asan' is the Malayalam word for teacher.
3 The high ranges rise from the lower plateau of the Cardamom Hills and form a complete range of their own.
4 Haridasan, *Dr John Matthai, 1886–1959*, p. 6.
5 Ibid., p. 6.
6 Ibid., p. 10.
7 Ibid., p. 159.
8 M.O. Mathai, *My Days with Nehru*, Vikas Publishing House Pvt Ltd, New Delhi, 1979, p. 249.
9 G.P. Sharma, George Matthai (1887–1947), Foundation Fellow, Indian National Science Academy, Biographical Memoirs, p. 198 at https://www.insaindia.res.in/BM/BM14_8915.pdf.
10 I am grateful to Vivek Matthai, John Matthai's grandson, for sharing the family tree.
11 Matthai Manuscript, PMML, New Delhi.

12 Ibid.
13 Ibid.
14 Matthai Manuscript, PMML, New Delhi.
15 Ibid.
16 Ibid.

Chapter 2: Clever John

1   Jayaprakash Raghaviah, 'Conversion, Industrial Development and Social
    Engineering: Basel Mission in Malabar During the Nineteenth Century',
    Salesian Journal of Humanities & Social Sciences, Vol. VIII, No. 1 (May 2017).
2   Ibid.
3   V. Haridasan, *John Matthai: A Biography*, Publication Division, University of
    Calicut, 1986, p. 12.
4   John Matthai, 'As I Look Back', *Times of India*, 13 August 1956.
5   Ibid.
6   Quoted in V. Haridasan, *John Matthai*, p. 189.
7   Muscular Christianity is a philosophical movement that originated in
    England in the mid-nineteenth century. It is characterized by a belief in
    patriotic duty, discipline, self-sacrifice, masculinity and the moral and
    physical beauty of athleticism.
8   Quoted in Haridasan, *John Matthai*, p. 161.
9   Matthai, 'As I Look Back', *Times of India*, 13 August 1956.
10 Michaelmas Term is the first term of the academic year at many universities
    in the UK and Ireland. It is also known as the Autumn Term.
11 In the United Kingdom and some other countries, the Doctor of Science
    is a 'higher doctorate' awarded after submission of a portfolio of published
    work—typically around 80–120 journal articles. It signifies a much higher
    level of accomplishment than the PhD and is usually awarded to researchers
    relatively late in their careers. There are equivalent higher doctorates in other
    fields of study: Doctor of Letters, Doctor of Laws, Doctor of Divinity etc.
    In some other countries, the DSc and PhD are equivalent. Both get the
    honorific title doctor.
12 The Fabian Society, a British socialist organization, had as its purpose the
    advancement of the principles of social democracy and democratic socialism
    via gradual reforms rather than by revolutionary overthrow. It was also
    historically related to radicalism, a left-wing liberal tradition.
13 John Matthai, *Village Government in British India*, T. Fisher Unwin Ltd,
    London, 1915, p. 2.
14 Ibid., p. x.
15 Ibid., p. 3.

16 Ibid., p. 4.
17 Ibid., pp. 54–55.
18 Ibid., p. 64.
19 Ibid., p. 88.
20 Ibid., p. 113.
21 Ibid., p. 132.
22 Ibid., p. 162.
23 Haridasan, *John Matthai*, p. 171.
24 R.M. Lala, *The Creation of Wealth: The Tatas from the 19th to the 21st Century*, Penguin Viking, New Delhi, 2004, p. 132.
25 Ibid., p. 127.
26 Ibid., p. 132.
27 Matthai, 'As I Look Back', *Times of India*, 13 August 1956.
28 Peter Sager, *Oxford & Cambridge: An Uncommon History*, Thames & Hudson Ltd, London, 2005, p. 138.
29 Ibid., p. 138.
30 Ibid., pp. 138–39.
31 Ibid., p. 139.
32 Haridasan, *John Matthai*, p. 15.
33 C.D. Deshmukh, *The Course of My Life*, Orient Longman Limited, Hyderabad, 1974, p. 42.
34 John Matthai, 'India and the War', Papers for War Time No. 30, Humphrey Milford, Oxford University Press, p. 3.
35 Ibid., pp. 8–9.
36 Ibid., p.19.
37 Ibid., p. 20.
38 Ibid.

Chapter 3: Back Home

1 John Matthai, 'As I Look Back', *Times of India*, 13 August 1956.
2 Ibid.
3 G. Sreekumar, 'Cooperation Awaits Its "Finding Raiffeisen" Moment', *The Hindu*, 6 December 2021.
4 Ibid.
5 Published under the subject 'Books for the Times', it was a series edited by A.J. Appasamy.
6 John Matthai, *Agricultural Co-Operation in India: A Handbook for Students and Social Workers*, Christian Literature Society for India, Madras, 1925, p. i.
7 Ibid., p. ii.
8 Ibid., p. xxi.

9   Ibid., p. xxx.

10   Ibid., p. xxxix.

11   Ibid., pp. xxxix–xl.

12   Ibid., pp. 24–26.

13   Ibid., pp. 151–52.

14   V. Haridasan, *Dr John Matthai*, p. 17.

15   K. Jothi Sivagnanam, 'A History of the Department of Economics, University of Madras', Working paper No. 1, January 2016. At https://www.academia.edu/24793503/History_of_the_Department_of_Economics_University_of_Madras)

16   Ibid.

17   Sreekumar, 'Cooperation Awaits Its "Finding Raiffeisen" Moment'.

18   Sivagnanam, 'History of the Department of Economics, University of Madras'.

19   Matthai, 'As I Look Back'.

20   V. Subramaniam, 'Picture of John Matthai', *Bharat Jyoti*, 23 October 1949.

21   V. Haridasan, *Dr John Matthai 1886–1959: A Biography*, University of Calicut, 2000, p. 19.

22   Ibid., p. 181.

23   'Travancore: A Syrian Marriage', *Madras Mail*, 3 September 1921.

24   Interview with Syloo Matthai on 9 February 2024.

25   Ibid., p. 19.

26   Ibid.

27   Proceedings of the Madras Legislative Council, 7 March 1924, p. 325.

28   Ibid., p. 325.

29   Ibid., p. 1218.

30   Ibid., p. 1219.

31   Matthai, 'As I Look Back'.

32   John Matthai Papers, Vivek Matthai Private Papers.

33   Proceedings of the Madras Legislative Council, 8 August 1924, p. 699.

34   Proceedings of the Madras Legislative Council, 5 March 1925, p. 818.

35   Ibid.

36   John Matthai, *Excise and Liquor Control*, The Author's Press and Publishing House, Madras, 1924, p. 5.

37   Ibid., p. 62.

38   Ibid., p. 65.

Chapter 4: From the Tariff Board to the Tatas

1 Jaimini Bhagwati, *The Promise of India: How Prime Ministers Nehru to Modi Shaped the Nation (1947–2019),* Penguin Viking, Gurugram, 2019, p. 9.

2 John Matthai, *Tariffs and Industry* (Oxford Pamphlets on Indian Affairs), Oxford University Press, 1944.

3 Ibid., p. 4.

4 Ibid., p. 5.

5 John Matthai, 'As I Look Back', *Times of India*, 13 August 1956.

6 *Ardeshir Dalal: A Memoir*, privately published, p. 63.

7 Ibid.

8 Ibid., p. 64.

9 Ibid.

10 Ibid., p. 65.

11 Report of the Indian Tariff Board on the Iron and Steel Industry, Vol. I, Manager of Publications, Delhi, 1934, pp. 153–54.

12 V. Haridasan, *Dr John Matthai, 1886–1959: A Biography*, University of Calicut, Calicut, 2000, p. 31.

13 Ibid.

14 Ibid., p. 33.

15 Ibid., p. 34.

16 Matthai, *Tariffs and Industry*, p. 10.

17 H.L. Dey, 'Policy of Protection in India: A Retrospect', Gokhale Institute of Politics and Economics, Pune, 1950, p. 4.

18 Ibid., p. 5.

19 Matthai, *Tariffs and Industry*, p. 13.

20 Ibid., p. 20.

21 Ibid., p. 21.

22 Ibid., p. 22.

23 Ibid., p. 23.

24 Ibid., pp. 30–31.

25 The Doon School, at https://www.doonschool.com.

26 Sarvepalli Gopal, *Radhakrishnan: A Biography*, Oxford University Press, New Delhi, 1989, p. 125.

27 Matthai, 'As I Look Back', *Times of India*, 13 August 1956.

28 R.M. Lala, *The Creation of Wealth: The Tatas from the 19th to the 21st Century*, Penguin Viking, Penguin Books India (P) Ltd, New Delhi, 2004, p. 107.

29 Ibid., pp. 87–88.

30 Ibid., p. 87.

31 Ibid., p. 252.

32 Matthai, 'As I Look Back', *Times of India*.

33 R.M. Lala, *The Joy of Achievement: Conversations with J.R.D. Tata*, Penguin Viking, Penguin Books India (P) Ltd, New Delhi, 1995, p. 48.

34 R.M. Lala, *Beyond the Last Blue Mountain: A Life of J.R.D. Tata*, Penguin Viking, Penguin Books India (P) Ltd, New Delhi, 1993, p. 252; Lala, *The Creation of Wealth*, p. 85.

35 John Matthai to J.R.D. Tata, 10 April 1944, Tata Central Archives, Pune.

36 Lala, *Beyond the Last Blue Mountain*, pp. 291–92.

37 Verghese Kurien (as told to Gouri Salvi), *I Too Had a Dream*, Roli Books, New Delhi, 2005, p. 4.

38 Ibid., p. 5.

39 Ibid.

40 Ibid., p. 10.

41 Ibid., p. 11.

Chapter 5: The Bombay Plan and After

1 Raghabendra Chattopadhyay, 'The Idea of Planning in India, 1930–1951,' unpublished PhD Thesis submitted to the Australian National University, Canberra, April 1985, pp. 29–30.

2 Nikhil Menon, *Planning Democracy: How a Professor, an Institute and an Idea Shaped India*, Penguin Viking, Gurugram, 2022, p. xiv.

3 Chattopadhyay, 'The Idea of Planning in India, 1930–1951', pp. 68–69.

4 Menon, Nikhil, *Planning Democracy: How a Professor, an Institute, and an Idea Shaped India*, Penguin Random House India, Gurgaon, 2022, p. xv.

5 Ibid. pp. xvi–xvii.

6 Chattopadhyay, 'The Idea of Planning in India, 1930–1951', p. 113.

7 Menon, *Planning Democracy: How a Professor, an Institute, And an Idea Shaped India*, p. xvii.

8 Medha Kudaisya, *Tryst with Prosperity: Indian Business and the Bombay Plan of 1944*, Penguin Random House India, Gurgaon, 2018, p. xxviii.

9 Chattopadhyay, 'The Idea of Planning in India, 1930–1951', p. 152.

10 Ibid., pp. 155–56.

11 Sanjaya Baru and Meghnad Desai (Ed.), *The Bombay Plan: Blueprint for Economic Resurgence*, Rupa Publications Pvt Ltd., New Delhi, 2018, p. 2.

12 Ibid., pp. xxix–xxx.

13 Ibid., p. 81.

14 Ibid., pp. 82–83.

15 R.M. Lala, *Beyond the Last Blue Mountain*, Penguin Viking, p. 221.

16 Sanjaya Baru and Meghnad Desai (Ed.), The Bombay Plan, *Blueprint for Economic Resurgence*, p. 240.

17 Ibid., p. 283.

18 Purshotamdas Thakurdas to John Matthai, Purshotamdas Thakurdas Papers, File No 291 (Part I), PMML, New Delhi.

19 Mircea Raianu, *Tata: The Global Corporation that Built Indian Capitalism*, Harvard University Press, pp. 122–23.

20 Medha Kudaisya, *Tryst with Prosperity: Indian Business and the Bombay Plan of 1944*, p. 131.

21 Ibid., p. 132.

22 Medha Kudaisya, *Tryst with Prosperity: Indian Business and the Bombay Plan of 1944*, p. 135.

23 Ibid., p. 136.

24 Ibid., p. 134.

25 Chattopadhyay, 'The Idea of Planning in India, 1930–1951', p. 188.

26 Ibid., pp. 188–89.

27 Medha Kudaisya, *The Life and Times of G.D. Birla*, Oxford University Press, New Delhi, 2003, p. 252n.

28 Ibid., pp. 236–37.

29 Ibid., p. 237.

30 Ibid., p. 252n.

31 Lala, *Beyond the Last Blue Mountain*, pp. 222–23.

32 Ibid., p. 224.

33 John Matthai, Speech at the Rotary Club, Bombay, June 1956, published by Forum of Free Enterprise, Bombay, p. 1.

34 Ibid., p. 11.

35 Ibid., p. 13.

36 Ibid.

37 Chattopadhyay, 'The Idea of Planning in India, 1930–1951', p. 256.

38 Ibid.

39 'The Invisible Girl', *Time*, 24 April 1944.

40 Ibid.

41 J.R.D. Tata to Achamma Matthai, 18 May 1944, Private Collection of Vivek Matthai.

42 J.R.D. Tata to John Matthai, 30 December 1943, Private Collection of Vivek Matthai.

43 Ibid.

44 Interview with Syloo Matthai on 9 February 2024.

45 J.R.D. Tata to Achamma Matthai, 18 May 1944, Private Collection of Vivek Matthai.

46 Thelma Tata to Achamma and John Matthai, 18 May 1944, Private Collection of Vivek Matthai.

47 Jamshed Bhabha to Achamma Matthai, 21 May 1944, Vivek Matthai family collection.

PART II

Chapter 6: The Interim Government

1 Patrick French, *Liberty or Death: India's Journey to Independence and Division*, Penguin Books Ltd, London, 2011, p. 17.

2 'An Independent Sovereign Republic', Speech by J.L. Nehru at the committee meeting of the Meerut Congress on 21 November 1946, *Selected Works of Jawaharlal Nehru*, series 2, vol. 1, p. 17.

3 Ibid.

4 Ibid., p. 18.

5 John Matthai Manuscript, John Matthai Papers, PMML, New Delhi.

6 Ibid.

7 Ibid.

8 J.R.D. Tata to John Matthai, 3 September 1946, Vivek Matthai collection.

9 Ibid.

10 Maulana Azad to John Matthai, 4 February 1947, John Matthai Papers, PMML, New Delhi.

11 John Matthai Manuscript, John Matthai Papers, PMML, New Delhi.

12 Ibid.

13 Ibid.

14 The Constituent Assembly of India (Legislative) Debates, Vol. III, 22 March 1949, p. 1744.

15 C.D. Deshmukh, *The Course of My Life*, Orient Longman Limited, Hyderabad, 1974, p. 142.

16 Ibid., p. 143.

17 Maulana Azad to John Matthai, 4 February 1947, Matthai Papers, PMML, New Delhi.

18 John Matthai Manuscript, John Matthai Papers, PMML, New Delhi.

19 Ibid.

20 Rakesh Ankit, *India in the Interregnum: Interim Government, September 1946–August 1947*, Oxford University Press, New Delhi, 2019, p. 27.

21 John Matthai Manuscript, John Matthai Papers, PMML, New Delhi.

22 Abul Kalam Azad, *India Wins Freedom*, Orient BlackSwan, Hyderabad, 1988, p, 176.

23 Ankit, *India in the Interregnum*, p. 26.

24 Ibid., pp. 28–29.

25 Ibid., p. 31.

26 Hector Bolitho, *Jinnah: Creator of Pakistan*, John Murray, London, 1954, p. 168.

27 Ibid., p. 168.
28 John Matthai Manuscript, John Matthai Papers, PMML, New Delhi.
29 Ibid.
30 Ibid.
31 Ibid.
32 R.M. Lala, *Beyond the Last Blue Mountain: A Life of J.R.D. Tata*, Penguin Viking, Penguin Books India (P) Ltd, New Delhi, 1993, p. 217.
33 Ibid., p. 217.
34 Ibid., pp. 217–18.
35 Quoted in Arun Bhatnagar, *India: Shedding the Past Embracing the Future, 1906–2017*, Konark Piblishers Pvt Ltd, New Delhi, 2018, p. 50.
36 12 November 1946, Penderel Moon, ed., *Wavell: The Viceroy's Journal*, Oxford University Press, Oxford, 1973, p. 376.
37 13 November 1946, Moon, ed., *Wavell: The Viceroy's Journal*, p. 376.
38 Ibid., 27 November 1946, p. 383.
39 Ankit, *India in the Interregnum*, p. 35.
40 John Matthai Manuscript, John Matthai Papers, PMML, New Delhi.
41 Ibid.
42 Ibid.
43 Ibid.
44 Raghabendra Chattopadhyay, 'The Idea of Planning, 1930–1951', Unpublished PhD thesis submitted to the University of Canberra, Australia, April 1985, pp. 277–78.
45 Ankit, *India in the Interregnum*, p. 44.
46 John Matthai Manuscript, John Matthai Papers, PMML, New Delhi.
47 Ibid.
48 Kalam Azad, *India Wins Freedom*, pp. 188–90.
49 Sarvepalli Gopal, *Jawaharlal Nehru: A Biography*, Vol. 1: 1889–1947, Cambridge, Harvard University Press, 1976, p. 341.
50 Rati Bhabha Forbes, *Remembering My Father: Cooverji H. Bhabha*, Rati Forbes, 2010, p. 60.
51 Ibid.
52 Ibid., p. 62.
53 Oral History Transcript, H.M. Patel, PMML, New Delhi.
54 Wavell to Bhabha, 14 March 1947, quoted in Forbes, *Remembering My Father*, p. 61.
55 Chattopadhyay, 'The Idea of Planning in India, 1930–1951', pp. 281-282.
56 John Matthai Manuscript, John Matthai Papers, PMML, New Delhi.
57 Ibid.

58 Ibid.

59 Ibid.

60 Chattopadhyay, 'The Idea of Planning, 1930–1951', p. 281.

61 John Matthai Manuscript, John Matthai Papers, PMML, New Delhi.

62 Chattopadhyay, 'The Idea of Planning, 1930–1951', p. 282.

63 Ankit, *India in the Interregnum*, pp. 48–49.

64 John Matthai Manuscript, John Matthai Papers, PMML, New Delhi.

65 Ibid.

66 Ankit, *India in the Interregnum*, pp. 7–8.

67 Sarvepalli Gopal, *Jawaharlal Nehru: A Biography*, pp. 335–37.

68 Ankit, *India in the Interregnum*, pp. 8–9.

69 Ibid., p. 11.

70 John Matthai Manuscript, John Matthai Papers, PMML, New Delhi.

71 Record of interview between Lord Mountbatten and C.H. Bhabha on 23 April 1947, in Nicholas Mansergh (Ed.) *The Transfer of Power*, Vol. X., Her Majesty's Stationary Office, London, 1981, pp. 375–76.

72 Ibid., p. 376.

Chapter 7: Minister for Railways and Transport

1   Mahatma Gandhi, 'Third Class in Indian Railways', printed in *Third Class in Indian Railways*, Xpress Publishing, Notion Press, Chennai, 2020, p. 1.

2   Ibid.

3   Ibid., pp. 2–3.

4   Swagato Ganguly, 'The God that Failed', *Times of India*, 30 September 2005.

5   Patrick French, *Liberty or Death: India's Journey to Independence and Division*, Penguin Books Ltd, London, 2011, p. 20.

6   Railway Budget Speech, 27 February 1947, Railway Ministers Budget Speeches 1947–48 to 2006–07, Ministry of Railways, p. 1.

7   Ibid.

8   Ibid., p. 2.

9   Ibid.

10 Ibid., p. 3.

11 Ibid.

12 Ibid., p. 4.

13 Ibid.

14 Ibid.

15 Ibid.

16 Ibid., p. 5.

17 Ibid.

18 Ibid., pp. 5–6.

19 Ibid., p. 6.
20 The Betterment Fund was inaugurated with an initial transfer of Rs 12 crore from the railway reserve. This Fund was used to fund the cost of amenities for passengers, staff welfare works, and operational improvements designed to improve safety and efficiency.
21 Railway Budget Speech, 27 February 1947, Railway Ministers Budget Speeches 1947–48 to 2006–07, Ministry of Railways, pp. 8–10.
22 Ibid., p. 12.
23 Rakesh Ankit, *India in the Interregnum: Interim Government, September 1946–August 1947*, Oxford University Press, New Delhi, 2019, p. 80.
24 Ibid.
25 John Matthai to Pandit Nehru, 27 June 1947, Matthai Papers, PMML, New Delhi.
26 Ibid.
27 J. Nehru to John Matthai, 27 June 1947, Matthai Papers, PMML, New Delhi.
28 Rakesh Ankit, *India in the Interregnum*, p. 95.
29 Ibid., p. 352.
30 Ibid., pp. 353–54.

Chapter 8: The Horrors of Partition

1 Nehru to Matthai, 1 August 1947, PMML.
2 Ibid.
3 Extracts from Mountbatten's personal report dated 1 August 1947, *The Transfer of Power* 1942–7, Vol. 12, pp. 451–52.
4 Matthai Manuscript, PMML, New Delhi.
5 Aniruddha Bose, *Shunting the Nation: India's Railway Workers and the Most Tumultuous Decade in Modern Indian History (1939–1949)*, Speaking Tiger Books LLP, New Delhi, 2023, p. 96.
6 Haimanti Roy, *The Partition of India*, Oxford University Press, New Delhi, 2018, p. 75.
7 Ibid., p. 81.
8 The Boundary Award was the result of the deliberations of the Boundary Commissions of Punjab and Bengal, which were established to divide British-ruled India into India and Pakistan. It was announced on 17 August 1947 and established the Radcliffe Line that demarcated the new border between the two nations. It was named for Cir Cyril Radcliffe who chaired the Boundary Commissions.
9 Roy, *The Partition of India*, pp. 84–85.
10 Ibid., p. 76.

11 Ibid., pp. 88–89.

12 Bose, *Shunting the Nation*, p. 101.

13 Ibid., pp. 101–02.

14 Ibid., pp. 102–04.

15 Ibid., p. 108.

16 D.F. Karaka, 'From One Living Hell to Another', *Bombay Chronicle*, 29 September 1947.

17 Interview with Syloo Matthai on 9 February 2024.

18 Budget Speech, 20 November 1947, Ministry of Railways.

19 Bose, *Shunting the Nation*, p. 113.

20 Ibid., p. 122.

21 Chamanlal's Note to Sardar Patel, 18 July 1947, Selected Correspondence of Sardar Patel, Vol. 4, p. 195.

22 Nehru to Matthai, 23 July 1947, *Selected Works*, series 2, vol. 1, p. 172.

23 Ibid.

24 Ibid.

25 Ibid.

26 Nehru to Matthai, 9 June 1947, *Selected Works*, series 2, vol. 1, p. 203.

27 Sardar Patel to John Matthai, 3 August 1947, *Sardar Patel's Correspondence*, vol. 4, pp. 195–96.

28 Sardar Patel to John Matthai, 1 September 1947, *Sardar Patel's Correspondence*, vol. 4, p. 321.

29 Ibid., p. 321.

30 Matthai to Patel, 2 September 1947, *Sardar Patel's Correspondence*, vol. 4 p. 321–22.

31 Ibid.

32 Ibid.

33 V. Shankar, ed., *Selected Correspondence of Sardar Patel 1945–1950*, Vol. I, Navajivan Publishing House, Ahmedabad, 1977, p. vii.

34 V. Shankar, *My Reminiscences of Sardar*, Vol.1, Macmillan Company of India Ltd, New Delhi, 1974, p. 107.

35 Ibid., p. 107.

36 Ibid.

37 J. Nehru to John Matthai, 13 September 1947, *Selected Works*, Series 2, vol. 4, p. 67.

38 J. Nehru to John Matthai, 17 October 1947, *Selected Works of Jawaharlal Nehru*, Series 2, vol. 4, p. 165.

39 Sardar Patel to J. Nehru, 3 October 1947, *Sardar Patel's Correspondence*, Vol. 4, Navjivan Publishing House, 1974, p. 307.

40 Matthai to Baldev Singh, 15 October 1947, in *Sardar Patel's Correspondence*, Vol. 4, p. 521.
41 V. Shankar to H.M. Patel, 16 October 1947, *Sardar Patel's Correspondence*, Vol, 5 p. 90.
42 Ibid., pp. 90–91.
43 Bose, *Shunting the Nation*, p. 129.
44 Ibid.
45 Matthai to Patel, 2 September 1947, *Sardar Patel's Correspondence*, Vol. 4, pp. 448–49.
46 Bose, *Shunting the Nation*, p. 131.
47 Budget Speech, 16 February 1948, Ministry of Railways.
48 Ibid., pp. 135–36.
49 Ibid., p. 137.
50 Bose, *Shunting the Nation*, p. 139.
51 Ibid., p. 140.
52 Matthai Manuscript, PMML, New Delhi.
53 Ibid.
54 Ibid.
55 Ibid.
56 John Matthai, 'As I Look Back', *Times of India*, 13 August 1956.

Chapter 9: The Interim Railway Budget, 20 November 1947

1 Matthai Manuscript, PMML, New Delhi.
2 The Constituent Assembly of India (Legislative) Debates, Vol. I, 20 November 1947, pp. 296–97.
3 Ibid., p. 306.
4 Ibid., p. 308.
5 Ibid., p. 317.
6 Ibid., p. 329.
7 Ibid., p. 319.
8 Ibid., p. 392.
9 Ibid., pp. 393–94.
10 Ibid., p. 395.
11 Ibid.
12 Ibid., p. 396.
13 The term refers to the interval of time between two successive loadings of a wagon.
14 The Constituent Assembly of India (Legislative) Debates, Vol. I, 20 November 1947, p. 396.
15 Ibid.

16 Ibid., p. 397.

17 Ibid.

18 Ibid., p. 398.

19 Ibid.

20 Ibid., p. 399.

21 Ibid., pp. 399–400.

22 Ibid., p. 403.

23 An anna was a currency unit formerly used in British India, equal to 1/16 of a rupee. It was subdivided into four pices or twelve pies. Thus, there were 192 pies in a rupee.

24 The Constituent Assembly of India (Legislative) Debates, Vol. I, 20 November 1947, p. 402.

25 Ibid.

26 Ibid., p. 403.

27 Ibid., p. 404.

28 The Constituent Assembly of India (Legislative) Debates, Vol. I, 25 November 1947, pp. 611–12.

29 Ibid., p. 621.

30 Ibid., pp. 611–21.

31 Ibid., pp. 616–17.

32 Ibid., p. 621.

33 Ibid., pp. 623–24.

34 Ibid., p. 624.

35 Ibid., p. 629.

36 Ibid., p. 632.

37 Ibid., pp. 631–33.

38 Ibid., p. 640.

39 Ibid., pp. 641–42.

40 Ibid., p. 642.

41 Ibid., p. 645.

42 Ibid., p. 646.

43 Ibid., p. 647.

44 Ibid., pp. 647–48.

45 Ibid., pp. 648–49.

46 Ibid., p. 649.

47 Ibid., p. 651.

48 Ibid., p. 653.

49 The Constituent Assembly of India (Legislative) Debates, Vol. I, 26 November 1947, p. 707.

50 Ibid., p. 708.

51 Ibid., p. 709.
52 Ibid., p. 710.
53 Ibid., p. 711.
54 Ibid.
55 Ibid., p. 718.
56 Ibid.
57 Ibid., p. 719.
58 Ibid., pp. 729–30.
59 Ibid., p. 727.
60 Ibid., p. 731.
61 Ibid., p. 733.
62 Ibid., p. 735.
63 Ibid.
64 Ibid., p. 737.
65 Ibid., p. 738.
66 The Constituent Assembly of India (Legislative) Debates, Vol. II, 4 December 1947, pp. 1212–13.
67 The Constituent Assembly of India (Legislative) Debates, Vol. III, 11 December 1947, p. 1683.
68 The Constituent Assembly of India (Legislative) Debates, Vol. I, 20 November 1947, p. 404.

Chapter 10: The Railway Budget, 1948–49

1 The Constituent Assembly of India (Legislative) Debates, Vol. I, 30 January 1948, pp. 33–34.
2 Ibid., p. 35.
3 The Constituent Assembly of India (Legislative) Debates, Vol. I, 16 February 1948, p. 784.
4 Ibid.
5 Ibid., p. 785.
6 Ibid., p. 786.
7 Ibid.
8 Ibid.
9 Ibid., p. 787.
10 Yards where wagons are distributed with reference to their ultimate destination.
11 The Constituent Assembly of India (Legislative) Debates, Vol. I, 16 February 1948, p. 788.
12 Matthai was confusing wagon turnround with the time taken to repair a wagon. This was pointed out later by Pandit Kunzru in the course of the debate that followed.

13 The Constituent Assembly of India (Legislative) Debates, Vol. I, 16 February 1948, p. 788.
14 Ibid., p. 789.
15 Ibid., p. 790.
16 Ibid., p. 791.
17 Ibid.
18 Ibid., p. 793.
19 Ibid.
20 Ibid.
21 Ibid., p. 794.
22 The Constituent Assembly of India (Legislative) Debates, Vol. II, 23 February 1948, pp. 1086–88.
23 Ibid., p. 1089.
24 Ibid., p. 1095.
25 Ibid., p. 1096.
26 Ibid.
27 The Constituent Assembly of India (Legislative) Debates, Vol. VI, 28 August 1948, pp. 591–92.
28 John Matthai, 'As I Look Back', *Times of India*, 13 August 1956.
29 The Constituent Assembly of India (Legislative) Debates, Vol. II, 19 February 1948, p. 933.
30 Ibid., p. 937.
31 Ibid., p. 939.
32 Ibid., p. 973.
33 Ibid., p. 975.
34 Ibid., p. 977.
35 Ibid., p. 979.
36 Ibid., p. 981.
37 The Constituent Assembly of India (Legislative) Debates, Vol. II, 20 February 1948, p. 1008.
38 Ibid., p. 1012.
39 Ibid., pp. 1016–17.
40 Ibid., p. 1018.
41 The Constituent Assembly of India (Legislative) Debates, Vol. IV, 19 March 1948, pp. 2441–42.
42 This became the Road Transport Corporations Act, 1950.
43 The Constituent Assembly of India (Legislative) Debates, Vol. V, 8 April 1948, p. 3507.
44 The Constituent Assembly of India (Legislative) Debates, Vol. V, 9 April 1948, p. 3620.

45 The Constituent Assembly of India (Legislative) Debates, Vol. VI, 17 August 1948, p. 369.

46 The Constituent Assembly of India (Legislative) Debates, Vol. VI, 18 August 1948, pp. 403–04.

47 Ibid., p. 405.

48 Ibid.

49 Ibid., p. 411.

50 Ibid.

51 Muhammed Saleh Akbar Hydari to John Matthai, 6 April 1948, *Sardar Patel's Correspondence*, Vol. 6, p. 109.

52 J. Nehru to John Matthai, 6 June 1948, *Selected Works*, Series 2, Vol. 5, p. 229.

53 Ibid., p. 231.

54 Ibid., pp. 231–32.

55 John Matthai to Sardar Patel, 9 July 1948, *Sardar Patel's Correspondence*, Vol. 6, p. 395.

56 Ibid.

57 Sardar Patel to John Matthai, 10 July 1948, *Sardar Patel's Correspondence*, Vol. 6, p. 396.

58 Matthai Manuscript, PMML, New Delhi.

59 Ibid.

60 Ibid.

61 Ibid.

62 Ibid.

PART III

Chapter 11: Finance Minister

1 At the Imperial Conference in 1930, India's attitude was that, though she was prepared to consider favourably all schemes designed to encourage development of trade with all other countries of the British Commonwealth, it was not prepared to commit to a general tariff scheme within the Empire, wanting to reserve complete freedom to deal with each case as it arose. But on the 20 August 1932 the Indian delegation signed a trade agreement that accepted the principle of preference as a legitimate means of developing inter-Empire trade.

2 A.K. Bhattacharya, *Finance Ministers of India: From Independence to Emergency (1947–1977)*, Penguin Random House Pvt. Ltd, Gurugram, 2023, p. 4.

3 M.O. Mathai, *Reminiscences of the Nehru Age*, Vikas Publishing House Pvt. Ltd, New Dehi, 1978, p. 242.

4   Vikram Doctor, 'Lessons FM Can Learn from Budget History', *Economic Times*, 27 February 2008.

5   Ibid.

6   Mathai, *Reminiscences of the Nehru Age*, p. 242.

7   V. Shankar, *My Reminiscences of Sardar Patel*, Vol.1, Macmillan Company of India Ltd, New Delhi, 1974, p. 195.

8   Bhattacharya, *Finance Ministers of India*, pp. 14–15.

9   Ibid., pp. 16–17.

10 Matthai Manuscript, PMML, New Delhi.

11 Ibid.

12 Ibid.

13 Ibid.

14 Ibid.

15 Ibid.

16 Ibid.

17 Ibid.

18 Ibid.

19 The Constituent Assembly of India (Legislative) Debates, Vol. I, 28 February 1949, p. 970.

20 Ibid.

21 Ibid.

22 Matthai Manuscript, PMML, New Delhi.

23 The Constituent Assembly of India (Legislative) Debates, Vol. I, 28 February 1949, p. 971.

24 Medha M. Kudaisya, *Tryst with Prosperity: Indian Business and the Bombay Plan of 1944*, Penguin Portfolio, Gurugram, 2018, p. 23.

25 Bakhtiar K. Dadabhoy, *Barons of Banking: Glimpses of Indian Banking History*, Random House India, Noida, 2013, pp. 234–35.

26 Ibid., p. 235.

27 Ibid., p. 236.

28 Ibid., pp. 236–37.

29 Ibid., p. 237.

30 B.K. Nehru, *Nice Guys Finish Second: Memoirs*, Viking, Penguin India, New Delhi, 1997, p. 198.

31 J. Nehru to Liaquat Ali Khan, 21 April 1947, *Selected Works of JN*, Series 2, Vol. 1, p. 29.

32 Dadabhoy, *Barons of Banking*, pp. 238–39.

33 Ibid., p. 239.

34 Ibid.

35 Ibid.

36 Ibid., p. 240.
37 Ibid.
38 Nehru, *Nice Guys Finish Second*, pp. 229–30.

Chapter 12: Matthai's First General Budget, 1949–50

1 The Constituent Assembly of India (Legislative) Debates, Vol. I, 28 February 1949, p. 972.
2 Ibid.
3 Ibid., p. 973.
4 Ibid., p. 974.
5 Ibid., p. 975.
6 Ibid., p. 979.
7 Ibid., p. 980.
8 Ibid., p. 980.
9 Ibid.
10 Ibid., pp. 981–82.
11 Ibid., pp. 983–85.
12 Ibid., p. 985.
13 The Constituent Assembly of India (Legislative) Debates, Vol. I, 3 March 1949, p. 1039.
14 Ibid., p. 1041.
15 Ibid., p. 1045.
16 Ibid., p. 1047.
17 Ibid., p. 1049.
18 Ibid., p. 1050.
19 Ibid.
20 Ibid., p. 1061.
21 The Constituent Assembly of India (Legislative) Debates, Vol. I, 4 March 1949, pp. 1069–72.
22 Ibid., pp. 1084–85.
23 Ibid., p. 1105.
24 Ibid., p. 1117.
25 The Constituent Assembly of India (Legislative) Debates, Vol. I, 5 March 1949, pp. 1109–10.
26 Ibid., p. 1112.
27 Ibid., p. 1113.
28 Ibid.
29 Ibid., p. 1112.
30 Ibid., p. 1114.

31 Ibid., p. 1156.

32 Ibid., p. 1159.

33 Ibid., p. 1160.

34 Ibid., p. 1161.

35 The Constituent Assembly of India (Legislative) Debates, Vol. I, 16 March 1949, p. 1405.

36 John Matthai to G.D. Birla, 1 April 1949, Sardar Patel Correspondence, Vol. 10, pp.175–76.

37 Sardar Patel to John Matthai, 3 April 1949, Patel correspondence, Vol. 10, p. 176.

38 Bakhtiar K. Dadabhoy, *Barons of Banking: Glimpses of Indian Banking History*, Random House India, Noida, 2013, pp. 240–41.

39 Matthai Manuscript, PMML, New Delhi.

40 B.K. Nehru, *Nice Guys Finish Second*, Viking, Penguin India, New Delhi, 1997, p. 242.

41 Ibid., p. 243.

42 Ibid., p. 244.

43 Ibid.

44 Dadabhoy, *Barons of Banking*, p. 241.

45 M.O. Mathai, *Reminiscences of the Nehru Age*, Vikas Publishing House, New Delhi , 1978, pp. 242–43.

46 Ibid., pp. 242–43.

47 Ibid.

48 Prof. Dwijendra Tripathi narrated this incident to T.T. Ram Mohan, who wrote about it in his account of Ravi Matthai's role in the making of IIMA. Presumably, Prof. Tripathi had been told this by Ravi Matthai himself.

49 T.T. Ram Mohan, *Brick by Red Brick: Ravi Matthai and the Making of IIM Ahmedabad*, Rupa & Co, New Delhi, 2011, p. 65.

50 Ibid.

Chapter 13: Devaluation of the Rupee

1 The Constituent Assembly of India (Legislative), Debates, Vol. V, 5 October 1949, p. 9.

2 J. Nehru to Krishna Menon, 29 June 1949, *Selected Works of Jawaharlal Nehru*, Series 2, Vol. 12, p. 328.

3 Ibid.

4 The Constituent Assembly of India (Legislative), Debates, Vol. V, 5 October 1949, p. 9.

5   C.D. Deshmukh, *The Course of My Life*, Orient Longman, Hyderabad, 1974, p. 160.

6   The Constituent Assembly of India (Legislative), Debates, Vol. V, 5 October 1949, p. 10.

7   Deshmukh, *The Course of My Life*, pp. 160–61.

8   Matthai Manuscript, PMML, New Delhi.

9   Ibid.

10 Ibid.

11 Ibid.

12 Ibid.

13 B.K. Nehru, *Nice Guys Finish Second: Memoirs*, Viking, Penguin India, New Delhi, 1997, p. 237.

14 Ibid., p. 238.

15 Ibid., p. 239.

16 The Constituent Assembly of India (Legislative), Debates, Vol. V, 5 October 1949, p. 12.

17 Ibid., p. 13.

18 Ibid., p. 14.

19 Ibid., pp. 13–14.

20 Ibid., pp. 14–15.

21 Ibid.

22 Nehru, *Nice Guys Finish Second*, p. 239.

23 Ibid.

24 Official Report, The Constituent Assembly of India (Legislative), Debates (Part II – Proceedings other than Questions and Answers), Vol. V, 5 October 1949, p. 17.

25 Ibid., p. 18.

26 A soft currency is one with a value that fluctuates predominantly lower relative to other countries because there is less demand for that currency in the forex markets.

27 The Constituent Assembly of India (Legislative), Vol. V, 5 October 1949, p. 18.

28 Ibid., p. 19.

29 Ibid.

30 Ibid.

31 Ibid., p. 28.

32 Ibid.

33 Ibid., p. 31.

34 Ibid., p. 41.

35 Ibid., p. 49.

36 Ibid.
37 Ibid., p. 52.
38 Ibid., p. 53.
39 The Constituent Assembly of India (Legislative), Debates, Vol. V, 6 October 1949, p. 57.
40 Ibid., p. 62.
41 Ibid., p. 99.
42 Ibid.
43 Ibid., p. 100.
44 Nehru, *Nice Guys Finish Second*, pp. 498–99.

Chapter 14: Matthai's Second General Budget, 1950–51

1   V. Haridasan, *Dr. John Matthai, 1886–1959: A Biography*, Publication Division University of Calicut, 1985, p. 64.
2   Translation of a Malayalam article in *Mathrubhumi*, 1 March 1950.
3   Parliamentary Debates, Vol. I, 28 February 1950, p. 1017.
4   Ibid., pp. 1002–03.
5   Ibid., p. 1004.
6   Ibid., p. 1005.
7   Ibid., p. 1006.
8   Ibid., p. 1007.
9   Ibid.
10 Ibid., p. 1008.
11 Ibid.
12 Ibid.
13 Ibid., p. 1009.
14 Ibid., p. 1010.
15 Ibid., p. 1011.
16 Ibid., pp. 1015–16.
17 Ibid., p. 1010.
18 Ibid., pp. 1011–12.
19 Ibid., p. 1013.
20 Ibid.
21 Ibid., p. 1016.
22 Parliamentary Debates, Vol. I, 6 March 1950, p. 1118.
23 Ibid., p. 1121.
24 Ibid., p. 1134.
25 Ibid., p. 1151.
26 Parliamentary Debates, Vol. II, 22 March 1950, p. 2008.

27 Parliamentary Debates, Vol. I, 6 March 1950, p. 1193.

28 Parliamentary Debates, Vol. I, 7 March 1950, p. 1270.

29 Parliamentary Debates, Vol. I, 9 March 1950, pp. 1291–92.

30 Ibid., p. 1292.

31 Ibid.

32 Ibid.

33 She was married when she was only eight to a certain Subba Rao. She refused to stay with him on attaining maturity and the marriage was never consummated.

34 C.D. Deshmukh, *The Course of My Life*, Orient Longman Limited, Hyderabad, 1974, p. 194.

35 Ibid., p. 195.

36 Durgabai Deshmukh, *Chintaman and I*, Allied Publishers Private Limited, New Delhi, 1980, p. 29.

37 Ibid., p. 29.

38 Deshmukh, *The Course of My Life*, p. 198.

39 Parliamentary Debates, Vol. I, 9 March 1950, p. 1293.

40 Ibid., p. 1293.

41 Ibid., p. 1294.

42 Ibid., p. 1293.

43 Parliamentary Debates, Vol. II, 20 March 1950, p. 1870.

44 Parliamentary Debates, Vol. I, 9 March 1950, p. 1297.

Chapter 15: An Unhappy Interlude

1 Rakesh Ankit, Dr John Matthai (1886–1959): Between 'Bombay Plan' and 'Planning Commission', Loughborough University. https://doi.org/1080/09584935.2019.1700217.

2 Ibid.

3 Ibid.

4 Ibid.

5 Ibid.

6 Quoted in *Selected Works of Jawaharlal Nehru*, Second Series, Vol. 12, Jawaharlal Nehru Memorial Fund, Teen Murti House, 1993, p. 29.

7 Rakesh Ankit, Dr John Matthai (1886–1959): Between 'Bombay Plan' and 'Planning Commission', Loughborough University. https://doi.org/1080/09584935.2019.1700217.

8 Ibid.

9 Ibid.

10 Ibid.

11 Ibid.

12 Nehru to Matthai, 29 September 1949, *Selected Works of Jawaharlal Nehru*, Second Series, Vol. 12, Jawaharlal Nehru Memorial Fund, Teen Murti House, 1993, p. 35.

13 First John Matthai Memorial Lecture, in C.D. Deshmukh, *Reflections on Finance, Education and Society*, Motilal Banarsidass, New Delhi, 1972, p. 115.

14 Ibid.

15 Quoted in V. Haridasan, *John Matthai: A Biography*, University of Calicut, 2000, p. 102.

16 Sardar Patel to John Matthai, 31 May 1950, Vivek Matthai Collection.

17 Ibid.

18 Nehru to Matthai, 3 May 1950, *Selected Works of Jawaharlal Nehru*, Second Series, Vol. 14, Part 2 (8 April–31 July 1950), Jawaharlal Nehru Memorial Fund, Teen Murti House, 1993. p. 227.

19 Ibid.

20 Ibid., p. 228.

21 Ibid.

22 Ibid.

23 Nehru to Matthai, 4 May 1950, *Selected Works of Jawaharlal Nehru*, Second Series, Vol. 14, Part 2 (8 April– 31 July 1950), p. 229.

24 Ibid.

25 Ibid., p. 229.

26 Ibid., p. 230.

27 Ibid.

28 Ibid.

29 Ibid., p. 231.

30 Ibid.

31 Ibid., p. 232.

32 Ibid.

33 Nehru to Krishna Menon, 8 May 1950, *Selected Works of Jawaharlal Nehru*, Second Series, Vol. 14, Part 2 (8 April–31 July 1950), Jawaharlal Nehru Memorial Fund, Teen Murti House, 1993, pp. 232–33.

34 Ibid., p. 233.

35 Nehru to Pant, 2 May 1950, Quoted in Rakesh Ankit, Dr John Matthai (1886–1959): Between 'Bombay Plan' and 'Planning Commission'.

36 *Statesman*, New Delhi, 22 May 1950.

37 'Matthai's Custody of India's Finances: Nehru's Tribute to Outgoing Minister', *Indian News Chronicle*, 22 May 1950.

38 Ibid.

39 'People's Duty to Support Government', *Statesman*, New Delhi, 22 May 1950.

40 Ibid.

41 *Mrs Matthai's Work for Refugee Women Praised, Indian News Chronicle*, 22 May 1950.

42 'People's Duty to Support Government', *Statesman*, New Delhi, 22 May 1950.

43 *Mrs Matthai's Work for Refugee Women Praised, Indian News Chronicle*, 22 May 1950.

44 Nehru to Matthai, 28 May 1950, *Selected Works of Jawaharlal Nehru*, Second Series, Vol. 14, Part 2 (8 April–31 July 1950), Jawaharlal Nehru Memorial Fund, Teen Murti House, 1993, p. 234.

45 Ibid.

Chapter 16: The Matter Escalates

1 *Selected Works of Jawaharlal Nehru*, Second Series, Vol. 14, Part 2 (8 April–31 July 1950), Jawaharlal Nehru Memorial Fund, Teen Murti House, 1993, pp. 201–02.

2 *The Evening News*, (*Hindustan Times*), New Delhi, 2 June 1950.

3 Ibid.

4 Ibid.

5 Ibid.

6 Ibid.

7 Quoted in *Sardar Patel's Correspondence*, Vol. 10, p. 230.

8 Quoted in *Selected Works of Jawaharlal Nehru*, Second Series, Vol. 14 Part 2 (8 April–31 July 1950), Jawaharlal Nehru Memorial Fund, Teen Murti House, 1993, p. 243.

9 Sardar Patel to Maulana Azad, 3 June 1950, *Sardar Patel's Correspondence*, Vol. 10, pp. 244–45.

10 Ibid.

11 Ibid., pp. 245–46.

12 V. Haridasan, *John Matthai: A Biography*, p. 79.

13 John Matthai to V. Shankar, 10 May 1950, Tata Central Archives.

14 J. Nehru to J. Matthai, 4 June 1950, *Selected Works of Jawaharlal Nehru*, Second Series, Vol. 14 Part 2 (8 April–31 July 1950), Jawaharlal Nehru Memorial Fund, Teen Murti House, 1993, p. 235.

15 Ibid., p. 234.

16 Ibid., p. 236.

17 Ibid., p. 234.

18 Ibid.

19 J. Nehru to Krishna Menon, 4 June 1950, *Selected Works of Jawaharlal Nehru*, Second Series, Vol. 14 Part 2 (8 April–31 July 1950), Jawaharlal Nehru Memorial Fund, Teen Murti House, 1993, p. 241.

20 Ibid., p. 235.

21 Ibid., p. 237.

22 Ibid., p. 238.

23 Ibid., p. 238.

24 Nehru to Krishna Menon, 4 June 1950, *Selected Works of Jawaharlal Nehru*, Second Series, Vol. 14 Part 2 (8 April 1950- 31 July 1950), Jawaharlal Nehru Memorial Fund, Teen Murti House, 1993, p. 242.

25 Nehru to Patel, 5 June 1950, *Selected Works of Jawaharlal Nehru*, Second Series, Vol. 14 Part 2 (8 April–31 July 1950), Jawaharlal Nehru Memorial Fund, Teen Murti House, 1993, p. 236.

26 Sardar Patel to J. Nehru, 5 June 1950, *Sardar Patel's Correspondence*, Vol. 10, p. 232.

27 J. Nehru to Sardar Patel, 8 June 1950, *Sardar Patel's Correspondence*, Vol. 10, p. 241.

28 Nehru to Vijayalakshmi Pandit, 5 June 1950, *Selected Works of Jawaharlal Nehru*, Second Series, Vol. 14 Part 2 (8 April–31 July 1950), Jawaharlal Nehru Memorial Fund, Teen Murti House, 1993, p. 246.

29 John Matthai to J. Nehru, 17 June 1950, John Matthai Papers PMML.

30 Ibid.

31 Ibid.

32 Ibid.

33 Ibid.

34 J. Nehru to John Matthai, 27 June 1950, *Selected Works of Jawaharlal Nehru*, Second Series, Vol. 14, Part 2 (8 April–31 July 1950), Jawaharlal Nehru Memorial Fund, Teen Murti House, 1993, p. 247.

35 Ibid., p. 247.

36 Ibid., p. 248.

37 Ibid., p. 249.

38 J. Nehru to J. Matthai, 15 November 1948, *Selected Works of Jawaharlal Nehru*, Second Series, Vol. 8, pp. 206–07.

39 M.O. Mathai, *My Days with Nehru*, Vikas Publishing House Pvt Ltd., New Delhi 1979, p. 249

40 Ibid.

41 Matthai Manuscript, 1958–59, John Matthai Papers, PMML.

42 Ibid.

43 Ibid.

44 Ibid.
45 Ibid.
46 Ibid.
47 Ibid.
48 Ibid.
49 Matthai Manuscript, John Matthai Papers, PMML, New Delhi.
50 Interview with Syloo Matthai on 9 February 2024.
51 Rakesh Ankit, Dr John Matthai (1886–1959): Between 'Bombay Plan' and 'Planning Commission', Loughborough University. https://doi.org/1080/09584935.2019.1700217.
52 Matthai Manuscript, John Matthai Papers, PMML, New Delhi.
53 John Matthai, Speech at the Rotary Club, Bombay, published by Forum of Free Enterprise, Bombay, p. 9.
54 Nehru to T.T. Krishnamachari, 29 December 1953, *Selected Works*, Series 2, Vol. 21, p. 136.
55 H.V.R. Iengar, *Planning in India*, Macmillan India, New Delhi, 1974, pp. 5–6.
56 Nikhil Menon, 'Planning and democracy – Story of a unique Indian marriage', *Hindu Business Line*, 14 August 2022.
57 C.D. Deshmukh, *The Course of My Life*, Orient Longman Limited, Hyderabad, 1974, p. 100.
58 V. Haridasan, *Dr John Matthai: A Biography (1886–1959)*, University of Calicut, 2000, p. 104.
59 Ibid., p. 105.
60 Ibid.
61 Ibid.
62 Ibid., p. 107.
63 Ibid., p. 108.
64 Ibid., p. 110.
65 Ibid., p. 114.
66 Sardar Patel to J.R.D. Tata, 9 October 1945, Sardar Patel Correspondence.
67 V. Haridasan, *Dr John Matthai: A Biography (1886-1959)*, University of Calicut, 2000, p. 152.

PART IV

Chapter 17: The Taxation Enquiry Commission

1 C.D. Deshmukh, *The Course of My Life*, Orient Longman, 1974, p. 190.
2 J. Nehru to Deshmukh, 17 January 1953, *Selected Works*, Series 2, Vol. 21, p. 356.

3   Ibid.

4   *The Sunday Standard*, 12 April 1953.

5   Budget speech by C.D. Deshmukh, 1953–54, *Parliamentary Debate* (*House of the People*), Vol. I, Part-II, 27.2.1953, cc. 1137–61.

6   Ibid.

7   V. Haridasan, *Dr John Matthai: A Biography (1886–1959)*, University of Calicut, 2000, p. 117.

8   'Matthai Gospel of Taxation', *Economic Weekly*, 5 March 1955.

9   Ibid.

10 Haridasan, *Dr John Matthai*, p. 118.

11 Ibid., p. 162.

12 Ibid., p. 119.

13 Report of the Taxation Enquiry Commission, Vol. III, Government of India, p. 46.

14 Ibid., p. 519.

15 Ibid., p. 63.

16 Ibid., p. 519.

17 Ibid.

18 Ibid., p. 547.

19 Report of the Taxation Enquiry Commission, Vol. I, Government of India, p. 145.

20 Ibid.

21 'Matthai Gospel of Taxation', *Economic Weekly*, 5 March 1955.

22 Report of the Taxation Enquiry Commission, Vol. I, Government of India, p. 78.

23 Report of the Taxation Enquiry Commission, Vol. II, Government of India, p. 125.

24 Ibid., p. 88.

25 Ibid., p. 103.

26 *Commerce*, Bombay, 26 March 1955.

27 'Matthai Gospel of Taxation', *Economic Weekly*, 5 March 1955.

28 Ibid.

29 Ibid.

30 Ibid.

31 Ibid.

32 *Capital*, 10 March 1955.

33 Ibid.

34 A.K. Bhattacharya, *India's Finance Ministers: From Independence to Emergency (1947–1977)*, Penguin Random House India Pvt. Ltd, Gurugram, 2023, pp. 83–84.

Chapter 18: Rejoining the Tatas

1 Bhabha, Homi, 'Historical Note on Tata Institute of Fundamental Research', Wilson Centre Digital Archive, 1 January 1954, https://tinyurl.com/43dpnxh6. Accessed on 11 August 2022.
2 Indira Chowdhury, *Growing the Tree of Science: Homi Bhabha and the Tata Institute of Fundamental Research*, Oxford University Press, New Delhi, 2016, p. 11.
3 Ibid., p. 94.
4 Ibid., p. 21.
5 R.M. Lala, *The Heartbeat of a Trust: A Story of Sir Dorabji Tata Trust*, Tata McGraw Hill, New Delhi, 1984, p. 150.
6 Ibid.
7 Ibid., p 151.
8 Ibid., p. 152.
9 Source: https://www.tata.com/newsroom/heritage/j.r.d.-tata-for-india-initiatives
10 Lala, *The Heartbeat of a Trust*, p. 156.
11 Ibid., p. 157.
12 Mircea Raianu, *Tata: The Global Corporation that Built Indian Capitalism*, Harvard University Press, 2021, p. 156.
13 Ibid.
14 Ibid.
15 Ibid.
16 Ibid., pp. 156–57.
17 Bharat Wakhlu, Mukund Rajan, Sonu Bhasin, *Tata's Leadership Experiment*, Harper Business, New Delhi, 2022, p.16.
18 Ibid., p.17.
19 'Tata-Mistry ties started in 1928', *Times of India*, 9 January 2018.
20 Tata Staff College Inaugurals and Closings, Report on Sixth Session (1955–61), A Talk by John Matthai on the opening day of the Second Session of the Tata Staff College, 5 December 1956, Tata Central Archives, Box 998.
21 Interview with Syloo Matthai on 9 February 2024.
22 Interview with Syloo Matthai on 9 February 2024.
23 R.M. Lala, *Beyond the Last Blue Mountain*, Penguin Books India (P) Ltd, New Delhi, 1993, p. 204.
24 Ibid., p. 207.
25 Ibid.
26 D.R. Mankekar, *Homi Mody: A Many Splendoured Life*, Bombay Popular Prakashan, 1968, p.1.
27 Ibid. p. 207.

28 V. Haridasan, *Dr John Matthai, 1886–1959: A Biography*, Publication Division University of Calicut, 1985, p. 144.
29 Bakhtiar K. Dadabhoy, *'Jeh': A Life of J.R.D. Tata*, Rupa & Co., New Delhi, 2005, p. 74.
30 'As I Look Back', *Times of India*, 13 August 1956.
31 Dadabhoy, *Jeh*, p. 74.
32 Lala, *Beyond the Last Blue Mountain*, p. 208.
33 Ibid.
34 Russi Mody to Achamma Matthai, 4 November 1959, (at www. drjohnmatthai.com).
35 Dadabhoy, *'Jeh'*, p. 157.

Chapter 19: A Man for All Seasons

1   Abhik Ray, *The Evolution of the State Bank of India: The Era from 1955 to 1980*, Vol. 4 Penguin Portfolio, New Delhi 2009, pp. 626–27.
2   C.D. Deshmukh to J.R.D. Tata, 5 May 1955, Tata Central Archives, Pune.
3   Ibid.
4   J.R.D. Tata to John Matthai, 10 May 1955, Courtesy private collection of Vivek Matthai.
5   Ray, *The Evolution of the State Bank of India*, p. 586.
6   Ibid., p. 590.
7   Bakhtiar K. Dadabhoy, *Barons of Banking: Glimpses of Indian Banking History*, Random House India, Noida, 2013, p. 286.
8   Ibid., p. 287.
9   Ibid.
10 Ray, *The Evolution of the State Bank of India*, p. 605.
11 Ibid., p. 607.
12 Dadabhoy, *Barons of Banking*, p. 289.
13 Ray, *The Evolution of the State Bank of India*, p. 611.
14 Ibid., p. 613.
15 Ibid., p. 137.
16 Dadabhoy, *Barons of Banking*, p. 294.
17 Speech of John Matthai at the First Annual General Meeting of the SBI in the *Eastern Economist*, 2 March 1956.
18 Ibid.
19 The staff covered by the 'award' as defined in the Industrial Disputes (Banking Companies) Decision Act, 1955.
20 Ray, *The Evolution of the State Bank of India*, pp. 144–48.

21 John Matthai, 'Limits of Nationalisation', Speech delivered at the Rotary Club, Bombay in June 1956, Forum of Free Enterprise, Bombay.

22 C.D. Deshmukh, *The Course of My Life*, Orient Longman Limited, Hyderabad, 1974, p. 190.

23 Dadabhoy, *Barons of Banking*, p. 295.

24 John Matthai to Harekrushna Mahtab, 6 September 1955, Vivek Matthai Private Collection.

25 Ibid.

26 John Matthai to Harekrushna Mahtab, 8 September 1955, Vivek Matthai Private Collection.

27 John Matthai to Harekrushna Mahtab, 8 December 1955, Vivek Matthai Private Collection.

28 Harekrushna Mahtab to John Matthai to, 11 December 1955, Vivek Matthai Private Collection.

29 Harekrushna Mahtab to John Matthai to, 2 January 1956, Vivek Matthai Private Collection.

30 John Matthai to Harekrushna Mahtab, 3 January 1956, Vivek Matthai Private Collection.

31 John Matthai to Harekrushna Mahtab, 4 January 1956, Vivek Matthai Private Collection.

32 *Times of India*, 24 February 1957.

33 Ibid.

34 Ibid.

35 Sri Prakasa to John Matthai to, 24 February 1957, Vivek Matthai Private Collection.

36 Ibid.

37 John Matthai to Shantilal H. Shah, 11 January 1957, Vivek Matthai Private Collection.

38 John Matthai to Sri Prakasa, 25 February 1957, Vivek Matthai Private Collection.

39 Sri Prakasa to John Matthai to, 26 February 1957, Vivek Matthai Private Collection.

40 Ibid.

41 Ibid.

42 John Matthai to Sri Prakasa, 1 March 1957, Vivek Matthai Private Collection.

43 J. Nehru to Sri Prakasa, 2 March 1957, Selected works Series 2, vol 37, p. 281.

44 Ibid.

45 Ibid.

46 John Matthai, Sixth Convocation Address at The Maharaja Sayajirao University of Baroda, 13 October 1956, published by The Maharaja Sayajirao University of Baroda Press.

47 Ibid.

48 Ibid.

49 Ibid.

50 Ibid.

51 J. Nehru to John Matthai, 24 May 1956, PMML, New Delhi.

52 Ibid.

53 Morarji Desai to John Matthai, 28 May 1956 quoted in V. Haridasan, p. 135.

54 V. Haridasan, *Dr John Matthai, 1886–1959: A Biography*, p. 136.

55 John Matthai to J. Nehru, 2 June 1956.

56 Ibid.

57 Prafull Anubhai, *The IIMA Story: The DNA of an Institution*, Penguin Portfolio, 2017, p.4.

58 T.T. Ram Mohan, *Brick by Red Brick: Ravi Matthai and the Making of IIM Ahmedabad*, Rupa & Co., New Delhi, 2011, p. 4.

59 Ibid. p. 5.

60 https://www.keralauniversity.ac.in/our-history

61 Ibid.

62 Haridasan, *Dr John Matthai*, p. 137.

63 First John Matthai Memorial Lecture, in C.D Deshmukh, *Reflections on Finance, Education and Society*, Motilal Banarsidass, New Delhi, 1972, p. 116.

64 Haridasan, *Dr John Matthai*, pp. 138–39.

65 Ibid., pp. 163–64.

66 The estate was then worth Rs 20 lakh.

67 Asha Prakash, 'John Matthai Centre: A wooded campus which reverberates the name of a stalwart', 30 January 2021, (https://www.onmanorama.com/news/kerala/2021/01/29/john-matthai-centre-campus-which-reverberates-the-name-of-a-stalwart.html).

Chapter 20: Eventide

1 J.R.D. Tata to Matthai, undated, 1957, Private collection of Vivek Matthai.

2 Ibid.

3 Ibid.

4 Quoted in R.M. Lala, *Beyond the Last Blue Mountain*, Penguin Viking, Penguin Books India (P) Ltd, New Delhi, 1993, p. 208.

5 J. Nehru to John Matthai, 14 January 1959, Private collection of Vivek Matthai.

6 John Matthai to J. Nehru, 17 January 1959, Private collection of Vivek Matthai.

7 J. Nehru to John Matthai, 19 January 1959, Private collection of Vivek Matthai.

8 First John Matthai Memorial Lecture, in C.D Deshmukh, *Reflections on Finance, Education and Society*, Motilal Banarsidass, New Delhi, 1972, p. 116.

9 Ibid.

10 V. Haridasan, *Dr John Matthai, 1886–1959: A Biography*, p. 185.

11 J.R.D. Tata to Achamma Matthai, 11 November 1959, Vivek Matthai Collection.

12 Ibid.

13 V.P. Menon to Achamma Matthai, 29 November 1959, Vivek Matthai private papers.

14 Indira Gandhi to Achamma Matthai, 3 November 1959, Vivek Matthai private papers.

15 The *Times of India*, 3 November 1959.

16 J.R.D. Tata to Achamma Matthai, 21 April 1961, Vivek Matthai private papers.

17 'John Matthai', *Economic Weekly*, 7 November 1959.

18 Ibid.

19 John Matthai, 'A Socialistic Pattern of Society', *Hindustan Times*, 13 January 1956.

20 First John Matthai Memorial Lecture, in C.D Deshmukh, *Reflections on Finance, Education and Society*, Motilal Banarsidass, New Delhi, 1972, p. 114.

Epilogue: Matthai's Sons

1 T.T. Ram Mohan, *Brick by Red Brick: Ravi Matthai and the Making of IIM Ahmedabad*, Rupa & Co., New Delhi, 2011, p. 60.

2 Mrinalini Sarabhai, 'Ravi Matthai in the Eyes of Others', *IIMA Alumnus*, Vol. 16, No. 2, May 1984, p.7.

3 Ibid.

4 T.T. Ram Mohan, 'Ravi Matthai and IIMA: A Story of Institution-building' speech delivered on 2 October 2011 at IIM Indore.

5 Ibid.

6 Ibid.

7   'A Flashback', *IIMA Alumnus*, Vol. 16, No. 2. May 1984, p. 4.

8   Ibid.

9   T.T. Ram Mohan, 'Ravi Matthai and IIMA: A Story of Institution-building' speech delivered on 2 October 2011 at IIM Indore.

10 'A Flashback', *IIMA Alumnus*, Vol 16, No. 2. May 1984, p. 5.

11 Ibid.

12 Ibid.

13 Ravi Matthai, *Occasional Speeches and Writings*, Centre for Educational Innovation, Indian Institute of Management, Ahmedabad (For private circulation only), p. 12.

14 Ibid., p.13.

15 Ibid., p. 14.

16 Ibid., pp. 14–15.

17 Ibid., p. 5.

18 Ibid., p. 11.

19 Ibid., p. 25.

20 Ram Mohan, *Brick by Red Brick*, p. 215.

21 Ravi J. Matthai, *The Rural University: The Jawaja Experiment in Educational Innovation*, Sangam Books Limited, London, 1985, pp. 11–12.

22 Ibid., p. 10.

23 Inderjit Khanna, 'Modesty Personified', *IIMA Alumnus*, Vol. 16, No. 2, May 1984, p. 37.

24 Ibid., p. 12.

25 Ibid.

26 Ram Mohan, *Brick by Red Brick,* p. 233.

27 Ravi Matthai, *Occasional Speeches and Writings*, Centre for Educational Innovation, Indian Institute of Management, Ahmedabad (For private circulation only), p. 1.

28 'Duleep Matthai: 1924–2017', https://www.currentconservation.org/duleep-matthai-1924-2017/

29 Ibid.

30 Ibid.

31 Ibid.

Select Bibliography

PRIMARY SOURCES

Archives

Prime Minister's Memorial Museum and Library, New Delhi

John Matthai Private Papers
C.D. Deshmukh Private Papers
Purshotamdas Thakurdas Private Papers

Tata Central Archives, Pune

John Matthai Papers

Private Collections

Vivek Matthai Private Papers

Official Reports and Documents

Report of the Taxation Enquiry Commission, Vol. I–III, Government of India.
Report of the Indian Tariff Board on the Iron and Steel Industry, Vol. I, Manager of Publications, Delhi.
A Brief Memorandum Outlining a Plan for the Economic Development of India (The Bombay Plan), Bombay.
The Constituent Assembly of India (Legislative) Debates, 1947–50.
Railway Ministers Budget Speeches 1947–48 to 2006–07, Ministry of Railways.

Theses and Dissertations

Raghabendra Chattopadhyay, 'The Idea of Planning in India, 1930–1951', unpublished PhD Thesis submitted to the Australian National University, Canberra, April 1985.

Newspapers and Magazines

Capital
Commerce
Economic Weekly
The Hindu
The Hindu BusinessLine
Times of India
Time
Bombay Chronicle
Madras Mail
Matrubhumi
The Economist

SECONDARY SOURCES

Books

Selected Works of Jawaharlal Nehru, Jawaharlal Nehru Memorial Fund, Teen Murti House, 1993.
The Transfer of Power 1942–47, Vol. 12.
Sardar Patel's Correspondence.
Ardeshir Dalal: A Memoir, Published by the Dalal family, 1980.
Ankit, Rakesh, *India in the Interregnum: Interim Government, September 1946–August 1947*, Oxford University Press, New Delhi, 2019.
Anubhai, Prafull, *The IIMA Story: The DNA of an Institution*, Penguin Portfolio, 2017.
Baru, Sanjaya and Meghnad Desai, ed., *The Bombay Plan: Blueprint for Economic Resurgence*, Rupa Publications Pvt. Ltd, New Delhi, 2018.
Bhagwati, Jaimini, *The Promise of India: How Prime Ministers Nehru to Modi Shaped the Nation (1947–2019)*, Penguin Viking, Gurugram, 2019.
Bhatnagar, Arun, *India: Shedding the Past Embracing the Future, 1906–2017*, Konark Publishers, New Delhi, 2017.
Bhattacharya, A.K., *India's Finance Ministers: From Independence to Emergency (1947–1977)*, Penguin Random House Pvt. Ltd, Gurugram, 2023.
Bolitho, Hector, *Jinnah: Creator of Pakistan*, John Murray, London, 1954.

Bose, Aniruddha, *Shunting the Nation: India's Railway Workers and the Most Tumultuous Decade in Modern Indian History (1939–1949)*, Speaking Tiger Books LLP, New Delhi, 2023.

Chowdhury, Indira, *Growing the Tree of Science: Homi Bhabha and the Tata Institute of Fundamental Research*, Oxford University Press, New Delhi, 2016.

Dadabhoy, Bakhtiar K. *Barons of Banking: Glimpses of Indian Banking History*, Random House India, Noida, 2013.

———, *'Jeh': A Life of J.R.D. Tata*, Rupa & Co., New Delhi, 2005.

———, *Homi J. Bhabha: A Life*, Rupa Publications Pvt. Ltd, New Delhi, 2023.

Deshmukh, C.D., *Reflections on Finance, Education and Society*, Motilal Banarsidass, New Delhi, 1972.

———, *The Course of My Life*, Orient Longman Limited, Hyderabad, 1974.

Deshmukh, Durgabai, *Chintaman and I*, Allied Publishers Private Limited, New Delhi, 1980.

French, Patrick, *Liberty or Death: India's Journey to Independence and Division*, Penguin Books Ltd, London, 2011.

Gopal, Sarvepalli, *Jawaharlal Nehru: A Biography*, Vol. 1: 1889–1947, Cambridge, Harvard University Press, 1976.

Haridasan, V., *Dr John Matthai, 1886–1959: A Biography*, Publication Division University of Calicut, 2000.

Kudaisya, Medha, *Tryst with Prosperity: Indian Business and the Bombay Plan of 1944*, Penguin Random House India, Gurgaon, 2018.

Kudaisya, Medha, *The Life and Times of G.D. Birla*, Oxford University Press, New Delhi, 2003.

Kurien, Verghese, *I Too had a Dream*, Roli Books, New Delhi, 2005.

Lala, R.M., *The Creation of Wealth: The Tatas from the 19th to the 21st Century*, Penguin Viking, New Delhi, 2004.

———, *The Heartbeat of a Trust: Fifty Years of the Sir Dorabji Tata Trust*, Tata McGraw Hill, New Delhi, 1984.

———, *The Joy of Achievement: Conversations with J.R.D. Tata*, Penguin Books India (P) Ltd, New Delhi, 1995.

———, *Beyond the Last Blue Mountain*, Penguin Viking, Penguin Books India (P) Ltd, New Delhi, 1993.

Mathai, M.O., *Reminiscences of the Nehru Age*, Vikas Publishing House Pvt. Ltd, New Dehi, 1978.

Matthai, John, *Excise and Liquor Control*, The Author's Press and Publishing House, Madras, 1924.

———, *Village Government in British India*, T. Fisher Unwin Ltd., London, 1915.

———, *Agricultural Co-Operation in India*, Christian Literature Society for India, 1925.

———, *Tariffs and Industry* (Oxford Pamphlets on Indian Affairs), Oxford University Press, 1944.

Sager, Peter, *Oxford & Cambridge: An Uncommon History*, Thames and Hudson Ltd., London, 2005.

Matthai, Ravi, *Occasional Speeches and Writings*, Centre for Educational Innovation, Indian Institute of Management, Ahmedabad (For private circulation only).

Menon, Nikhil, *Planning Democracy: How a Professor, an Institute, and an Idea Shaped India*, Penguin Random House India, Gurgaon, 2022.

Moon, Penderel, ed., *Wavell: The Viceroy's Journal*, Oxford University Press, Oxford, 1973.

Nehru, B.K., *Nice Guys Finish Second*, Viking, Penguin India, New Delhi, 1997.

Nehru, Jawaharlal, *Selected Works of Jawaharlal Nehru*, First and Second Series (numerous volumes).

Raianu, Mircea, *Tata: The Global Corporation that Built Indian Capitalism*, Harvard University Press, 2021.

Ram Mohan, T.T., *Brick by Red Brick: Ravi Matthai and the Making of IIM Ahmedabad*, Rupa & Co., New Delhi, 2011.

Ray, Abhik, *The Evolution of the State Bank of India: The Era from 1955 to 1980*, Vol. 4 Penguin Portfolio, New Delhi 2009.

Roy, Haimanti, *The Partition of India*, Oxford University Press, New Delhi, 2018.

Shankar, V., *My Reminiscences of Sardar*, Vol.1, Macmillan Company of India Ltd, New Delhi, 1974.

Wakhlu, Bharat, Mukund Rajan, Sonu Bhasin, *Tata's Leadership Experiment*, Harper Business, New Delhi, 2022.

Articles

Tata Staff College Inaugurals and Closings, Report on Sixth Session (1955–1961), A Talk by John Matthai on the opening day of the Second Session of the Tata Staff College, 5 December 1956.

'The Invisible Girl', *Time* magazine, 24 April 1944.

'Travancore: A Syrian Marriage', *Madras Mail*, 3 September 1921.

Ankit, Rakesh, Dr John Matthai (1886–1959): Between 'Bombay Plan' and 'Planning Commission', Loughborough University. https://doi.org/1080/09584935.2019.1700217.

Bhabha, Homi, 'Historical Note on Tata Institute of Fundamental Research', Wilson Centre Digital Archive, 1 January 1954, https://tinyurl.com/43dpnxh6. Accessed on 11 August 2022.

Dey, H.L., 'Policy of Protection in India', Gokhale Institute of Politics and Economics, Pune, 1950.

Doctor, Vikram 'Lessons FM can learn from Budget history', *Economic Times*, 27 February 2008.

Gandhi, M.K., 'Third Class in Indian Railways' printed in *Third Class in Indian Railways*, Xpress Publishing, Notion Press, Chennai, 2020.

Karaka, D.F., 'From One Living Hell to Another', *The Bombay Chronicle*, 29 September 1947.

Matthai, John, 'India and the War', Papers for War Time No 30, Humphrey Milford, Oxford University Press.

Matthai, John, 'As I Look Back', *Times of India*, 13 August 1956.

Matthai, John Sixth Convocation Address at The Maharaja Sayajirao University of Baroda, 13 October 1956, published by The Maharaja Sayajirao University of Baroda Press.

Menon, Nikhil, 'Planning and democracy – Story of a unique Indian marriage', 14 August 2022, *Hindu BusinessLine*.

Prakash, Asha, 'John Matthai Centre: A wooded campus which reverberates the name of a stalwart', 30 January 2021, (https://www.onmanorama.com/news/kerala/2021/01/29/john-matthai-centre-campus-which-reverberates-the-name-of-a-stalwart.html)

Raghaviah, Jayaprakash, 'Conversion, Industrial Development and Social Engineering: Basel Mission in Malabar During the Nineteenth Century', *Salesian Journal of Humanities & Social Sciences*, Vol. VIII, No. 1 (May 2017).

Sharma, G.P., George Matthai (1887–1947), Foundation Fellow, Indian National Science Academy, Biographical Memoirs, p. 198 at https://www.insaindia.res.in/BM/BM14_8915.pdf.

Sivagnanam, K. Jothi, 'History of the Department of Economics, University of Madras', Working paper No 1, January 2016. (https://www.academia.edu/24793503/History_of_the_Department_of_Economics_University_of_Madras)

Sreekumar, G. 'Cooperation awaits its 'finding Raiffeisen' moment', 6 December 2021, *The Hindu*.

Subramaniam, V., 'Picture of John Matthai', *Bharat Jyoti*, 23 October 1949.

Websites

www.wikipedia.org
www.archive.org
www.drjohnmatthai.com
www.doonschool.com
www.tata.com
https://asci.org.in
www.ncaer.org

Index

Scan QR code to access the
Penguin Random House India website